D1578538

FOREIGN COUNTRY

FOREIGN COUNTRY

The Life of L.P. Hartley

ADRIAN WRIGHT

TAURIS PARKE PAPERBACKS
LONDON • NEW YORK

Published in 2001 by Tauris Parke Paperbacks
an imprint of I.B.Tauris & Co Ltd
6 Salem Road, London W2 4BU
175 Fifth Avenue, New York NY 10010
www.ibtauris.com

In the United States of America and in Canada
distributed by St Martin's Press
175 Fifth Avenue, New York NY 10010

First published in 1996 by André Deutsch Ltd

ISBN 1 86064 679 4

A full CIP record for this book is available from the British Library
A full CIP record for this book is available from the Library of Congress

Library of Congress catalog card: available

Printed and bound in Great Britain by MPG Books Ltd, Bodmin

In loving memory of
Benjamin, Nicholas and Thomas
and
Jessie Harriet Groom
who understood the 'M'

CONTENTS

ACKNOWLEDGEMENTS

This book would not have been possible without the authorisation and assistance of Norah Hartley, who gave me unlimited access to the private papers of her brother and family. I am also indebted to John Assheton and David Riddington, the executors of Miss Hartley's estate, for their helpfulness following her death.

My debts of gratitude are many. After our first meeting, Francis King (a crucial link with L. P. Hartley's last years) offered suggestions and support that did not waver throughout the writing of this biography. He also allowed me to quote from the correspondence of C. H. B. Kitchin. Clive Dunn, co-author and director of the television feature *Bare Heaven*, was the first person I approached; he offered encouragement and my first clutch of addresses. I thank him for the inspiration his work gave me. The other co-author of *Bare Heaven*, Edward Storey, gave me a tour of Hartley's Fenland that enhanced my feeling for that extraordinary landscape. Jonathan Cecil allowed me to see Hartley's letters to his father, Lord David Cecil, and to quote from the letters of his father. Lt.-Col. Christopher Sands gave me permission to consult Hartley's letters to his aunt, Ethel Sands, at the Tate Gallery Archive. At Ditchingham, Commander Mark Cheyne showed me correspondence about his family's association with Hartley. In Islington, Walter and Peggy Allen talked to me about their friendship with Hartley. At Hampstead, Nicola Beauman gave me lunch and discussed Hartley's relationship with Cynthia Asquith, the subject of her biography published in 1987. In Bath, I was made welcome by Maddie Bell, Derek Hayes and Robert Waller, all of whom added to my understanding of Hartley. At the Old Rectory, Holt, Lady Harrod gave me lunch and told me of Hartley's friendship with her and her husband Roy Harrod. In London, Derek Hill invited me to his artist's eyrie on Holly Hill to discuss his recollections of Hartley; Lady Berkeley, the widow of Lennox Berkeley, spoke of him over a plate of cream slices; at the *Daily Telegraph*'s offices at Canary Wharf, Christopher Hudson recalled his one meeting with my hero. Lt.-Col. R.C. and Mrs Allhusen gave me a bracing welcome at Bradenham Hall; Mrs Allhusen was the perfect guide for a tour of the grounds that Hartley had once known so well. Joyce Callard and Tom Gover of the Old Cliftonian Society gave me valuable information about Hartley and C. H. B. Kitchin's time at Clifton College, Bristol. Bill Abbey of the Institute of Germanic Studies at the University of London alerted me to the collection of Hartley's letters to Professor August Closs housed there, and was a sympathetic, if bewildered, presence on the day when I saw a disagreeable article in the *Evening Standard*. Kate Pool and Mark Le Fanu of the Society of Authors enlightened me about Hartley's association with the Society. Richard Hillier, Local Studies Librarian at the Central Library, Peterborough, was not only an indispensable authority on the brick industry, but went beyond the call of duty to provide me with much fascinating material, and was kind enough to read the chapter of this book that deals with the brickfields. Graham Lee and Bridgette Saunders kindly lent me their house in Brighton where some of the book was written.

I must also thank the many people who in various ways have provided assistance, suggestions and encouragement: Tom Aitken, Mark Amory, Michael Asquith, Ronald Blythe, Douglas Brooks-Davies, Peter Burton, Peter Carson, David Caute, Patricia Cleveland-Peck, Bryan Connon, the late Eric Crozier, Gina Dobbs, Jonathan Dunning, Andrew Ellis, Julian Fane, Daniel Farson, Kim Fletcher-Park, Olive Gausden, Diane Goldenberg-Hart, David Green, Priscilla Hodgson, Michael Holroyd, Elizabeth Inglis, Rachel Kemsley, William Law, Dominic Lawson, Robert McCrum, B. P. H. Orange, John Julius Norwich, Craig Orr, Derek Parker, Peter Parker, Tom Pocock, Tim Procter, Colin Radford, Ralph Ricketts, Robert Rimmer, Colin Spencer, Janet Stone, Rachel Studholme, Anne Surfling, Martin Taylor, Ann Thwaite, Anne Tidd and Howard Watson. I must also record my thanks to Penelope Fitzgerald, with whom I discussed the writing of this book. To any others whose individual contribution may not be listed here, I am very grateful.

Research for the book was made a pleasure by the helpfulness of the staffs of the various institutions I visited. I must thank Dr Anne Summers of the British Library Manuscripts Collection; Cathy Henderson and the staff of the Harry Ransom Humanities Research Center at the University of Texas at Austin; the Library of the University of East Anglia; Mr A. N. Lee of the University of Bristol Library; Maggie Parham and Elizabeth Hughes of the Royal Society of Literature; the Tate Gallery Archive; Dr Peter McNiven and the staff of the John Rylands University Library of Manchester; the Bodleian Library, Oxford; Balliol College, Oxford; Exeter College, Oxford; the British Library Newspaper Library at Colindale; the British Library Sound Archive; the London Library; Eton College Library; the Library of the University of Sussex; Mr A. D. K. Hawkyard, Librarian at the Vaughan Library, Harrow, and the English Centre of International PEN.

My thanks are owing to my publisher, Tom Rosenthal, for his belief in this book, and to my editor at Deutsch, Anthony Thwaite, whose valuable suggestions added immeasurably to the final manuscript. I must also record my gratitude to David Wilson and Joanna Walker at Deutsch, and my fastidious copy-editor Ann Douglas for the care she has taken with the manuscript. My agent, John Pawsey, has been patient and helpful throughout.

Grateful acknowledgement must be made to Hamish Hamilton for giving me permission to consult and quote from the correspondence between Hartley and Hamish Hamilton at the University of Bristol, and to quote from L. P. Hartley's published work; to the Bodley Head for permission to quote from *Eustace and Hilda*; to Hutchinson for permission to quote from *A Wiser Woman?* by Christabel Aberconway; to the Hogarth Press for permission to quote from *Mr Balcony*; to the *Spectator* for permission to quote from 'The Ugly Picture' and the tribute that accompanied it; to BBC Enterprises for permission to use extracts from the *Listener*; to Mrs Trekkie Parsons and the University of Sussex to quote from the correspondence of Leonard Woolf.

There are three people who have played a crucial part in the writing of this book. Joan Hall not only let me see the letters Leslie Hartley wrote to her, but became my ally and my friend. Our love of Leslie Hartley began our friendship, and has survived the appearance of this biography. Michael King's life has been taken over by my obsession with Hartley, and I can only hope that this book will make the three-year-long inconvenience seem worthwhile. Terry Dunning's interest and involvement, his constant suggestions, arguments and proddings, amounted to a commitment without which this book would have been much poorer. This book is theirs, as much as it is mine.

Adrian Wright
Poringland, September 1995

The irresponsive silence of the land,
The irresponsive sounding of the sea,
    Speak both one message of one sense to me:-
'Aloof, aloof, we stand aloof, so stand
Thou too aloof, bound with the flawless band
    Of inner solitude; we bind not thee;
    But who from thy self-chain shall set thee free?
What heart shall touch thy heart? What hand thy hand?'

Christina Rossetti

Introduction

THIS FIRST BIOGRAPHY of L. P. Hartley appears almost a quarter of a century after his death in 1972.[1] The extraordinary story of why it has taken so long for a life to appear – and the culmination of those efforts in the writing of this book – would make another volume, an essay in literary intrigue to match anything in *The Aspern Papers*. For the present, I have had to be content with a brief description of the book's history, which the reader will find elsewhere in these pages.

But some explanation, before setting off on the book itself, is necessary. Leslie Poles Hartley, one of the most distinguished English writers of the twentieth century, was my boyhood hero. I was in my late teens when a sympathetic librarian, Bob Illsley, steered me into the territory of *The Go-Between* and *Eustace and Hilda*; it was he, too, who set me on to C. H. B. Kitchin, who plays a significant part in this book. By the time I reached manhood (it happened, in those days, at the age of twenty-one) I had read all the Hartley I could get my hands on. Little as I could discover of the man (there seemed nothing to discover), even then I felt I knew him – sensitive, gifted with an extraordinary knowledge of the human heart, and deeply sad. Even then I think I sensed how, through his writing, he kept the world at a distance. It must have occurred to me that I would write to ask if we might meet (twenty years later I would have no hesitation about doing so) but he died a year later.

My passion for the novels never faded. I found consolation in their atmosphere of autumnal understanding, the understanding that comes from a man who knows the world too well. And my affection for the man never altered. It seemed to me that there was a link between us, a chain of communication, of spirit. Perhaps one of the reasons why I was so fascinated with him was that in his character I recognised much of my own: the eagerness to please, the deep craving for approval, the sense of isolation, the snobbishness, the feeling that the best has been long before – the list is long and largely discreditable. Without ever having met him, I felt we were known to one another, there was a contact across the ages, we shared regret. In a corner of my mind I sheltered my relationship with Leslie Hartley as something precious and known only to us two.

If that admiration and interest ever settled into complacency, it was reawakened in 1992 when, tucked away in the late night schedules of the *Radio Times*, I saw the announcement of a television documentary, *Bare Heaven*, on 'the life and fiction of L. P. Hartley'. If I had any doubt about the potency of Hartley's life in my own, it was ended now. As the programme ended, I was overcome. I would discover a few months later that reading *The Go-Between* had the same effect on Harold Pinter. I came to know that those who took the trouble to understand Hartley were often brought to tears. After seeing Clive Dunn and Edward Storey's moving tribute I knew that I wanted to write this book, and cursed myself for never having thought of it before. Was this not the natural outcome of that shared understanding between myself and my boyhood hero, the man for whom I had never felt anything but love and admiration? First it seemed to me impossible that a biography had never been written. And then it seemed impossible that someone else should not be writing it at that very moment.

Immediately, I contacted most of the few remaining figures in Hartley's life, until there was no option but to write to the person who alone could open or shut the door to me – Hartley's surviving sister, Norah. Even the most encouraging of the little army of supporters I had mustered held out little hope of penetrating her fortress. During the long birth of the biography that resulted, I made more allies of Hartley's friends than I did enemies.

I would emphasise that this book bears all the responsibility of being the first biography of its subject – it has not been possible to catch the fire of other, earlier biographies of the man. What brief accounts of Hartley's life have existed, including those that tell of Hartley's active service in France during the Great War, have inclined to the inaccurate. Nevertheless, several reasons why I should not write the book were suggested to me, in varying degrees of helpfulness. One indignant publisher demanded that I should give up the project immediately. What qualification, another asked, had I for writing it? Another thought it 'the ideal partnership of author and subject'. Doubts, it seems, had always existed. Hartley, never one to disappoint, once told the writer Kay Dick, 'The facts of my life are meagre and dull and you won't find it hard to discard them!'[2] At a party in 1976 Hartley's distinguished editor at Hamish Hamilton, Roger Machell, explained he had never commissioned a biography because his life had not been at all interesting.[3] One friend of Hartley's told me it would be almost im. ossible to write because Hartley had had no close relationships ‿ lack of qualification that would remove a great many biographies from the catalogue).[4] One of the prospective biographers – one who had been on the Hartley trail long before I sat up and took notice – told me that work on the book had only stopped when it became obvious that the result would be hurtful to Norah.[5] Another source insisted that this same writer had only halted after being fed with his stories of a happy, contented man – stories that so contrasted with the writer's understanding of Hartley that the idea had to be abandoned.[6] Clumsy attempts to waylay me in a similar way were unsuccessful.

It is only necessary to draw the reader's attention to a few points. Biographies of the great and the good often confine the activities (and even the identity) of their servants to a few lines: the lives of the hirelings are thus kept where they belong, below stairs. This is quite impossible in a life of Leslie Hartley; strip away details of his domestic background and the portrait of the man is hopelessly impoverished. Anyway, one cannot escape the suspicion that Hartley relished the lives of his staff; they are the source of much of the humour in his life, and we should be the losers by choosing to ignore them. He once, playfully, suggested he might himself write a book about 'Servants I have known'.

The reader should also know that Hartley kept diaries (his nomadic existence would have been quite impossible without them), but none have survived. We can suppose their main function was to direct him from place to place and time to time. More importantly, he committed his private thoughts to other, more seriously personal diaries, though we do not know for how many years he maintained them. These, too, have vanished. It may be that Hartley supervised their destruction. Norah denied ever having seen any such documents. However, after her brother's death, she put a great number of Hartley's papers to the fire; we can only guess at what may have been among them.[7] Anything that contained any sort of personal reference qualified for oblivion. While with one hand turning away those who came wanting access to Hartley's history – she regarded all such approaches as an attempt on his life – with the other she did her best to make sure that the curious world would never have the fullness of the truth. In this, at least, she accorded with Hartley's wishes, even if they had only been made implicitly in his novels. Thus, the present book represents the piecing-together of a man's life from original sources. It is a sad fact that a significant number of the letters and documents on which this book is based no longer exist (the reader will discover why). I must hope that the reader will take on trust material used in the book which can no longer be verified. When quoting from Hartley's correspondence I have in all cases retained his sometimes eccentric spelling and punctuation.

The responsibilities of a boyhood's hero are many and difficult; in the light of examination they cannot help but be altered by truth. Flawed heroes have a fascination of their own. During the writing of this book, I have had to resist the temptation to believe those that my younger self might have longed to believe. 'He could never have done a mean or unkind act', said one of those, even when faced with the evidence that this was not so.[8] I do not mention this to disprove the heroism of my hero, but as a reminder that the knowledge of a man should allow room enough for compassion. A flawed hero, without a doubt. At the risk of distilling the pages of words that follow into a simple statement, I will settle for the verdict of Joan Hall, a friend of Leslie Hartley's who withheld none of her caring for my hero – 'He had an empty heart.'[9] That must be tragedy enough for any man, and it may be that Norah always knew that her brother's biography, when it came to be written, would reveal him as a tragic figure.

Much has been discovered that was thought undiscoverable, but ultimately I believe this book is as Hartley would have wished it. It lacks the exact knowledge of the trauma that was to cripple his ability to lead a satisfying and happy adult life, a trauma the details of which he took to his grave. Richard Mardick, the hero of Hartley's novel *The Brickfield*, insists on his biographer never revealing the terrible truth:

> As I told you, I would like the shadow of it to be thrown on anything that might be written about me. The shadow of the fact, but not the fact itself. Never the fact![10]

In throwing the shadow of the fact across the pages of this book I have, I hope, honoured Leslie Hartley's wish.

PART I

The Pool of the Past

❧ I ❧

Little Sausages, Really

A TROPICAL HEAT beat down on England in the summer of 1900. On 11 July several thousand holidaymakers arrived at Bournemouth railway station from Blackpool to enjoy the bathing (separate huts for males and females), six special trains bearing a second contingent eager for fun by the sea. At the Queen's Bench Division, Mr Justice Mathew appeared bareheaded, explaining to the court that it was too hot for wigs. Butchers complained that people ate less meat, while at the London Hippodrome patrons were given iced lemon and fans. The troops at Aldershot were issued by the War Office with new pattern sun-hats. At Westminster Police Court a French-woman gave the heat as the reason for trying to drown herself. A Mr Godfrey Gibbs of Upper Norwood died after a game of tennis, slaking his thirst with a cold drink which was found to be the cyanide of potassium he used in his photographic studio.

In Cambridgeshire the heat was equally unrelenting. In Peterborough a Miss Hopkinson of Sutton Grange bought each of the omnibus horses a sun-bonnet (the stronger horses had been shipped to South Africa and the Boer War, leaving the less hardy to work at the cab-stands). The adventurous might find relief bathing in the river Nene, though stretches of it were choked with weeds or polluted with the carcasses of dogs. There was abundant fruit. Damsons hung so heavy on the trees that branches snapped off under the weight. On 25 July it was 93° Fahrenheit in the shade before great storms, with hailstones five inches across, broke the tension. It was the first year of the new century, and the last Victorian summer; within six months, the old Queen would be dead.

L. P. Hartley was five years old, and never forgot that summer, the memory of which inspired him to write *The Go-Between* over fifty years later. As the long, hot days went on, they seemed to him to herald a Golden Age 'almost literally, for I think of it as being the colour of gold. I didn't want to go back to it but I wanted it to come back to me, and I still do.'[1] In later years, he looked back to those days as the end of a civilisation rather than the harbinger of perfection. What he came to see as this 'hideous' century had begun.

It is doubtful that Leslie Hartley would have approved of his biography being written. Like the elderly, hypochondriac writer Richard Mardick in *The Brickfield*, he was troubled by the relationship between biography and truth. Richard warns the male companion who threatens to write a memoir of him:

> 'If they want to know about me, I'd rather they knew the truth. They mustn't know it, that's the difficulty.'
> 'They mustn't know it?'
> 'On no account. If I tell you, I won't bind you to secrecy, it isn't necessary, but nobody must ever, ever know.'
> 'Then why tell me, if I'm not to put it in the book?'
> 'For two reasons. One is that I don't like the idea of dying with a secret. And the other is that though you can't put it recognisably into the memoir, you can make its presence felt, just as you can describe the results of an accident without describing the accident itself. You can show me as the product of the experience.'[2]

Hartley's attempts at autobiography are his novels. *The Brickfield* is the most truthful and revealing because by the time he wrote it the leading figures of his story – his mother, father and Aunt Kathleen – were dead. This book, and its less satisfactory successor *The Betrayal*, is in every sense a vintage Hartley novel, in which an old man declares his obsession with his childhood. It is, like so much of Hartley's work, revealing and misleading, revealing in the way the author so often lifts a veil on our understanding of him, misleading in the signals and events he lays across what we might call the documentary nature of its truth. Because Leslie Hartley chose to make his life a sequence of novels, there could be no other outcome. In reading *The Brickfield* and other of his books, one has to remind oneself that this is fiction, so absolutely do the characters and situations match what we know, or suspect, about the author's life. The truth is that Leslie Hartley's novels are a landscape of that life, not a map.

For a time, especially after the publication of *The Shrimp and the Anemone*, Hartley was considered to be a novelist who wrote about children, but as a breed they were not an enchanted species to him. Though they are often at the centre of his fiction, he had no real fondness for them, and did not consider those he created very convincing. For one thing, they were far more concerned with moral niceties – niceties that gnawed at Hartley – than real children are.

'Children are little sausages, really', he said towards the end of his life.[3] The most well-remembered of Hartley's 'little sausages', Eustace and Hilda, and Leo Colston in *The Go-Between*, grow from childhood into an adult world where happiness is somehow withheld. In growing out of childhood, they do not leave it behind. When childhood and adulthood are weighed in the balance, there is no question which seems the most welcoming.

It is difficult to know how conscious Hartley was of this crucial fact; he seems sometimes to have had a limited understanding of the potency of his best work, or at least liked to give this impression, for he was an adept at saying the right thing, the thing that he thought most likely to be acceptable, agreeable, proper. Asked if he considered *The Go-Between* his greatest novel, he replied that 'perhaps the Eustace and Hilda books were written when my vision was clearest'.[4] Talking about *The Go-Between*, he modestly suggested that its success was simply due to the book having something for everybody in it. He once dismissed *The Brickfield* as 'about illness or suspected illness'.[5] He would shrug his shoulders when critics spoke of his brilliant use of symbolism. It did not occur to him, he said, until after the book was finished, that Eustace was the shrimp and Hilda the anemone of *The Shrimp and the Anemone*. The simple fact, so far as he was concerned, was that when a child he watched a sea-anemone devour a shrimp; in the context of a novel, its symbolism had not occurred to him. When readers detected the influence of Freud in his books, Hartley protested that he had never read him, and knew little of his theories. As a writer he professed to be, and to an extent was, an amateur. Something in Hartley always tended to the dilettante. He said, 'I always wanted to be a writer but I never particularly wanted to write.'[6] This seems a totally honest declaration, the artless enthusiast nailing his colours to the mast, but in fact may be as misleading as many other of Hartley's admissions.

What is clear is that when he wrote about childhood, it was from the viewpoint of an adult uneasy at having left it behind, or unhappy at what had come out of it. Going back, as Hartley did again and again in his writing and in his life, was a challenge and a torment. He recognised, increasingly, the foreignness of the past, but could not resist its pull. It was unfortunate that, for Hartley, that past collided with the twentieth century. He once said that he thought the rot had set in with 'jazz, and the indifference to sense, and morality, and genuine emotion that goes with jazz, which in any case has to be sung slightly out of tune. Perhaps the world has been slightly out of tune ever since.'[7] Hearing 'Hitchy-Koo', with its angular, jaunty rhythms, seemed to Hartley to augur the collapse of civilisation, a civilisation that had seemed on the brink of perpetual happiness as the old century gave way to the new.[8]

Leslie Poles Hartley's father always maintained that the Hartleys and Poles owed their middle-class status to John Bark. As an ancestor, there is no doubt that Bark set exacting standards. He was born in 1762 in Yorkshire at Wentworth, the seat of the Marquis of Rockingham. On the marquis' death in 1782 the estate passed to his nephew, the fourth Earl Fitzwilliam, of Milton Hall near Peterborough. At the age of twenty-eight John Bark arrived at Lynch Farm in Alwalton, having been sent by the earl to be bailiff of the estate centred on Milton Hall. There he remained for thirty-four years of what he called 'hard fagging'. The relationship between servant and master appears to have been exemplary. 'I never thought I could do enough for such a Master, Friend and Father as your Lordship has been to me', Bark wrote to the earl in his letter of resignation on 29 May 1824.[9] The earl replied with as much fondness:

> I must not then wonder that you are anxious to withdraw from the management of my concerns, and retire to the care of your own home. I submit, therefore, though with reluctance, to the proposal of your letter, but with respect to fixing the precise time, that must be a matter of arrangement between Milton and me, for from the day that you cease to have the care of my land I will not hold an acre. The pleasure I had in it was in the relation between you and me which it produced.[10]

This master–servant relationship was a success story that Hartley, a century later, longed to repeat. A possible difficulty was that whereas his forebear had been the servant, Hartley would always be the master.

Strength of character may have contributed to Bark's reputation. A staunch church and chapel-goer of the unbending type, mirthless and autocratic, he turned to Methodism after hearing John Wesley preach, but was equally at home as churchwarden at Alwalton church or chapel steward at Peterborough. He was devoted to his mother, remembered in her final years as 'Dame Bark', a tall figure leaning on a long ebony staff. When news reached him of her last illness, he rode off from Alwalton, changing horses at Grantham and Newark, only to hear her passing bell as he came into the village street. The line was carried on by Bark's only sister, who married a John Poles and produced seven children, all of whom Bark helped to establish in life before he died, a wealthy and mourned figure, in August 1843 at the age of eighty-one. Another John Poles, the eldest of Bark's nephews, followed his uncle into Lynch Farm, eventually handing it on to his nephew, Edwin Hartley, who stayed there until 1916. As for Bark's other nephews, William went to Wentworth, Sam was set up in a farm at Wryde, near Thorney, and Henry at a farm at Melton near Wentworth.

It was one of their sisters, Eliza Poles, born in 1816, who in marrying John Hartley, borough surveyor of Rotherham, helped consolidate the middle-class aspirations of the Poles and Hartleys. We know little of the life Eliza and John had together, beyond the fact that between 1845 and 1860 Eliza had six children, who grew to be an industrious bunch. Martha, the first born, possessed the sort of forthright personality that John Bark would have been proud of, becoming joint proprietress of a girls' school at Doncaster. She learned Spanish so that she might read *Don Quixote* in the original language, and spoke five others. A voracious reader, she owned very few books because she claimed she could remember everything she had ever read. John and Eliza's only other daughter, Lizzie, was born two years later.

The four boys, in one way or another, distinguished themselves. The strong Bark sense of good business (not passed down to Leslie Hartley) underwrote their careers. The eldest, John William, born in 1845, was a model of industry for his brothers to follow. A talented engineer, by 1870 he had taken out over 120 patents on his inventions, 80 of which materialised. Apprenticed at seventeen to a Rotherham engineering firm, he rose from junior draghtsman at the Yorkshire Engine Works to foreman of the template department, and then chief locomotive draughtsman to the North Staffordshire Railway at Stoke. In the mid 1870s he built the California Engineering Works at Stoke, making bridges and railway chairs. He designed a two-lift gas holder, a continuous water-cooler (the forerunner of the cooling tower) and a sewage distributor. Three of his four sons worked with him at the business of sewage purification (the fourth became a priest). Of John's three daughters, two remained spinsters and one became a nun.

William Henry, born in 1851, married Harriet Birks and gave her ten children, nine of which were girls. One died in childhood. Six remained spinsters throughout their lives. Two married, but had no issue. The line carried on when Cecil, the only son, married and had three children. John and Eliza's third son, Edwin, born in 1854, was twenty when he went to Lynch Farm to assist his Uncle John. An optimistic farmer and keen sportsman, he married his first cousin Annie Poles. When Uncle John retired, Edwin took over the farm until the end of the Great War when he was succeeded by his eldest son John Poles (a second boy, William, articled to Hartley's father's firm of solicitors, was killed in action in 1915).

Harry Bark, the last of John and Eliza's children, was born on 18 March 1860. Martha helped her mother nurse him but was dissatisfied with the shape of his head. When Eliza's back was turned, Martha, in an effort to correct what Nature had neglected to do, pushed the back of Harry's head forward; she often reminded him in later years that any intelligence he had was due to these exertions. Such intelligence was modestly exercised when at six years of age he attended his first school, becoming one of 'Mr Bingham's Bulldogs'; Harry never forgot the smell of the premises, above some stables. The regime was strict. Once, when he had not completed three sums by three o'clock in the afternoon, Mr Bingham took the strap to him. 'I learned something not in the curriculum', Harry recalled. 'In life, we often get punished when we never expect or deserve it or know why the punishment is inflicted. When, later in life, I read Job, I was better able to sympathise with Job and less with his comforters.'[11]

When Harry's father died in 1870, leaving Eliza with little money, it was only natural that she should look to her settled and successful brothers to help support her youngest son, now ten years old. Harry had moved to the village school at Wentworth, run by a sympathetic teacher, Alfred Murray, a Latin and Greek scholar, who was so impressed with his pupil that he wrote to Uncle John suggesting the boy would benefit from the best education his family could buy him. When the funds were forthcoming, Harry, now fourteen, went to the Wesleyan College at Taunton. Its headmaster, Thomas Sibley, had a sister who ran the adjoining finishing school for young ladies. Mary Elizabeth Thompson (known as Bessie) was one of Miss Sibley's pupils. Bessie and Harry never met at Taunton, although they almost did so. Miss Sibley was concerned that Bessie would be travelling home unchaperoned at the end of term, and recommended that she travel with her near neighbour, Harry, from over the wall at the boys' school. As this arrangement would have meant her losing a day's schooling (the boys broke up a day before the girls) Bessie politely demurred. Thus, the first meeting of Hartley's parents may have been delayed by a few years.

Murray's opinion of Harry was confirmed by his achievements at Taunton and, at nineteen, he was articled to the Peterborough solicitor Henry Cecil Gaches, and began living at Lynch Farm under the watchful eye of Uncle John. In 1883 he was admitted to the Roll of Solicitors and in February of that year entered, on trial at a salary of £80 a year, the practice of James W. Reeve at 27 High-causeway, Whittlesey. The first question Harry asked on arriving at Whittlesey was 'Is there a cricket club?' It was not only cricket he loved, but golf, billiards, football, tennis; the flight of a ball through the air fascinated him. At the end of his life he thought he must have been three or four times round the world in pursuit of a ball. When, only a few months after Harry's arrival, Reeve died, Harry took over the practice, opening a sub-office in Peterborough at 49 Priestgate.

Professional success beckoned, but left Harry with enough time and energy to pursue another interest which he followed throughout his life: politics. In 1885 he became Liberal Party election agent for the Peterborough constituency, a job he carried on for thirty-three years. He found delight in the characters he worked alongside: Arthur Brand, who won the Isle of Ely and had a wife whose renditions of 'Nellie Bligh' and 'Off to Philadelphia in the morning' earned him the reputation of having been 'sung into Parliament'; Lord Esmé Gordon, forced by his mother the Marchioness of Huntly to stand as Liberal candidate for North Huntingdonshire, who blithely went off for a week's shooting in Scotland a few days before the election (perhaps not surprisingly he did not get in). Harry's political energy was underlined by his Methodism and a passionate belief in the glory of peace: 'To any Christian, war must obviously be a satire on the New Testament teaching', he wrote.[12] As a leading figure in the Peace Society, for many years he assisted Priscilla Hannah Peckover of Wisbech in her pacifist efforts, though his anti-war stance was often in direct contrast to the feelings of the majority. In 1886 he supported Gladstone's Home Rule Bill, wanting to see Ireland resume its place as a respected nation. He was intrigued by Gladstone's policy, and by the fact that though apparently devoted to the Church of England, the Grand Old Man drew almost all his support from Nonconformists. Harry simply repudiated the need to fight wars. When, in 1938, he read press reports that the mass of people were against another conflict, he suggested that if in 1914 a meeting had been called in Peterborough for those against the First World War there would have been precious few there, 'and those that did attend would have been ducked in the Nene next day!'[13]

All who knew him recognised in Harry a man with a distinctive confidence in his own judgement. When Richard Mardick in *The*

Brickfield remembers his father, what we are given is Hartley's succinct description of Harry: 'one of the most self-reliant, self-confident and self-contained men I have ever known'.[14] Such qualities made him the ideal partner for the woman he would marry.

The Thompsons, like the Hartleys, were Wesleyan Methodists, settled in the Crowland area of the Fens. Long before Hartley became fascinated by water, the Thompsons' lives were bounded by it; water, that never seemed to move, dictated the straight lines and flatness of the landscape. Bessie's grandfather could remember open streams running down the streets of Crowland, meeting under the triangular bridge. Bessie's father, William James Thompson, was a Justice of the Peace for the Holland Division and for many years one of the Peterborough Board of Guardians. He owned and farmed Greenbank Farm, Crowland, and rented a farm at Postland. By the time Bessie, Leslie's mother, was born in 1863, her father was a demanding invalid, and her mother suffered from asthma, a common complaint of that period in what Thomas Hood described as 'the dreary, foggy, cloggy, boggy wastes of Cambridge and Lincolnshire'.

Against this background of real, threatened or imagined illness, Bessie and her sisters derived little emotional pleasure or satisfaction from their country upbringing. Money was spent on an education which was enough to reinforce the strong feelings they held about many things, but their futures were to a degree prescribed. It was one thing that the Thompson sons (there were two of them, Will and Herbert, both of whom married) might escape the confines and demands of the family circle; it was not expected that daughters should do so, their choice being basically between marriage and spinsterhood. Faced with so blatant a dilemma, it is little wonder that illness was sometimes the way of proclaiming one's importance and individuality. Evelyn, the second daughter, grew up with a reputation for enjoying faint health; as a young woman she would wave her fatigue at possible suitors like a paper sword. Bessie said of her: 'You know, if Evelyn was interested in a man she would lie on a sofa and close her eyes, and that really is not the best way to attract one.'[15] As if to prove Bessie's point, Evelyn never married. A third sister, Fanny, who genuinely had delicate health, chose not to exploit it, and made a happy marriage.

The youngest of the Thompson girls, Kathleen, was tranquil, intelligent and gentle, with the promise of so many qualities about her. Her niece Norah remembered her with affection: 'If you didn't like Kathleen, you didn't know what goodness was.'[16] Beyond

Hartley's immediate family, it was Aunt Kathleen who would enjoy a special place in his life. She became a refuge for his real feeling, a friend just outside of the tight family circle to whom Hartley could turn for consolation. Her family had ambitions for her; she grew up with the feeling that something was expected of her, and that she might disappoint their hopes. She certainly seems to have been aware of the claustrophobic nature of the Thompson milieu. Fond as she was of her sisters, she always tried to keep any rumours of her own ill health from them. The suspicion that she might have a slight chill was enough to start off a flurry of concerned letters, parcels of wholesome comestibles, entreaties that a nurse be called in.

If Kathleen was the most sensitive of the Thompson girls, Bessie (christened Mary Elizabeth) was the most intense. Henry Lamb's portrait of her in later life shows a face alive with worry and nervous energy, factors that always overshadowed her personality.[17] There is hardly a photograph of her from which she does not peer, every nerve stretched, at the world beyond. The young woman Harry saw and fell in love with was 5 feet 4 inches tall, with bluey-grey eyes and very fine hair that was difficult to manage. She never wore make-up or followed the latest fashions in clothes, though she dressed well and in good taste. She spoke softly and clearly. She delighted in poetry, Tennyson and Longfellow, loved quotations and being read to (her mother used to read Dickens aloud to her husband until he cried with laughter). Above all, her special quality, like Richard's mother in *The Brickfield*, was that 'She had the gift of living in someone else's success. She didn't think of herself in terms of success – success was not for her. The most she hoped for was to dodge failure.'[18]

And to dodge illness, one of the penalties that threatened those who lived in the Fens; in the first half of the nineteenth century, the population was especially liable to rheumatism, ague and neuralgia. Opium was at once the panacea to such ills, and the cause of others. By the middle of the 1800s, few Fenland gardens were without their bed of white poppies, from which poppy-head tea would be brewed. Even as late as the 1910s raw opium was still being sold to the elderly of Spalding to bring relief from 'fever', but it was in the more remote agricultural areas (and Whittlesey's consumption was one of the most notable) that the 'Fen tigers' depended on it so heavily. Farm animals were liberally doped with it, or its derivative laudanum, while its consumption by children contributed considerably to the high infant mortality. Perhaps the most surprising fact is that the exploitation of opium in the Fens was so open and accepted, the drug being readily available not only from druggists but from general stores, where the counters on a Saturday night would be stacked with thousands of vials containing laudanum. This, of course was the more acceptable, genteel aspect of opium, favoured by the more sophisticated or female customer, while opium pills or 'lumps', asked for as 'stuff', led the market. It seems certain that laudanum would have been known to the Thompson household, and very probably used against the ills that the Fens brought down on it. Bessie, with her frequent weakness and enjoyment of poor health, would have known its efficacy.

The lack of diversion helped to concentrate the mind wonderfully on illness. Whatever advantages living in the Fens at the end of the nineteenth century might have had, a vivid social life was not among them. Families tended to be self-contained, and even a visit to a nearby relative was considered an adventure. If there was snobbery in the farming fraternity, it was feudal, for there seemed – at least to a middle-class sensibility – to be only two classes of persons, the employers and the employed. The employers were not necessarily very wealthy, despite their servants: their superiority came from the fact that they were employers. A farmer in south Lincolnshire needed servants to keep up his farmhouse; he did not look on them as status symbols – they were necessities of life. Being a farmer was no sinecure. It carried with it a real threat of failure and the shame that this would bring. Suicides were not uncommon. And all around stretched that unyielding flatness that is the Fens, pressed down by a limitless expanse of sky.

The isolation and insularity of the life, an inevitable price for staying in this landscape, brought with it much unhappiness. People (and families) did not drop in on one another as they might now, but lived out their lives mostly within the family house. The local doctor, even more than the vicar (who could properly only deal with his own denomination), was often the only person travelling between these isolated pockets of individuals who had the intelligence and opportunity to understand the relationships within specific families. It was so when Leslie was growing up. The doctor might well know more than was strictly necessary to reach a diagnosis, and as a 'friend' of the family, privy to many secrets, could see the psychological pressures at work. For Bessie, the doctor was all too often an emotional crutch.

We do not know what part, if any, the scientific gentleman played in bringing her and Harry together. We do not know how the couple met. It may have been at a cricket match or fête; perhaps Mr

Thompson employed Harry for some legal business. Harry, now thirty-one and with every prospect of a good career ahead of him, certainly had his prospective father-in-law's blessing, and was on good enough terms with him to be staying at the Thompson's house on the night of the 1891 census. Harry and Bessie were married on 18 June 1891 at Crowland Methodist chapel where Bessie's father was a steward. The wedding was truly a family affair, conducted by Bessie's uncle, the Revd. William Squire Snow. The opening hymn, 'The voice that breathed o'er Eden', was played on the organ by Bessie's aunt. Fanny and Kathleen were maids to the bride who was, according to a local newspaper, full of an 'unassuming gentleness'. The day began what seems to have been a perfectly happy marriage. At their golden wedding, Bessie poignantly told Harry, 'I have never seen you come in without pleasure, and I have never seen you go out without regret.'[19]

The couple moved into a handsome house in the market place of Whittlesey, where Harry had his practice. A market town some six miles outside Peterborough, Whittlesey (often called Whittlesea) was hardly cosmopolitan. Its population in 1891 – embracing the surrounding Fens and the hamlets of Coates and Eastrea – was given as 6345, the bulk of which was the labouring poor. Wheat, peas and potatoes grown for the London market came out of the black loam, rich soil with an underlay of clay and gravel. There was a yard where bricks were produced by the semi-dry process.

Water prescribed the lives of the inhabitants who scratched a living from land; the Whittlesey Wash was subject to seasonal flooding. Ferryboats trundled back and forth across the water. Water marked the boundaries of Whittlesey, the river Nene on one side of the town and the Whittlesey dyke on the other. Water took up much of the parish, the Wash varying its width from half a mile to a mile and a quarter along its seven-mile way. Efforts to make the place habitable had been organised by the Whittlesey Improvement Act of 1849; by the time Harry arrived in the town its houses were lit by gas and its water supplied from private wells.

Whittlesey, unpretentious and uneventful, had its attractions. The trees alongside the dyke banks on the south side of the town created a promenade; there were pleasing views of the counties of Huntingdon and Northampton; Friday was market day, with an annual cattle and horse fair in June. There was a social club for gentlemen (only 30 members qualified) with billiard and reading rooms at the public hall, charities for the education of boys, the librarian Miss Mary Spriggs to supervise the reading habits of the population at the

Whittlesey Institution's reading and news room, and the distinction of knowing that the town was the home of one Henry Goude, the maker of the celebrated 'Genuine' Whittlesea runner skate.

Harry was a respected figure in the community, already listed in 1892 as solicitor, secretary to the Gas and Coke Company, and clerk to the second district drainage commissioners. He and Bessie worshipped at the Wesleyan chapel in Queen Street, and he was well-known as the secretary to the parish's Liberal Association. His office in High-causeway was set among thriving industry: the Misses Crisp's ladies school; William Wilkinson, chemist, druggist and photographer; Jabez Smith, butcher; Miss Susan Nicholls, straw-bonnet maker; Thomas Shelton, confectioner; Daniel Thorey, castrator.

Bessie was twenty-nine when she gave birth at Whittlesey to a daughter, Enid Mary, on Christmas Day 1892. Three years later, on 30 December 1895, a son was born, and named Leslie Poles (Leslie after Leslie Stephen, father to Virginia Woolf and editor of the *Dictionary of National Biography*). Bessie's struggle to bring up her two children can be imagined: she was never free of the fear that one of the family might fall ill. In her constant anxiety, she regarded Whittlesey as nothing more than a breeding ground for disease. As a Fenland woman, she would have been conscious of the prevalence of malaria, the fen ague. The sense of stagnation she felt was symbolised by the open-drainage dykes and drains, their surfaces covered with what locals call 'cott', a thick scum that only shifts when a strong wind curdles it and whips it up into little banks. Bessie's children had to be protected from all potential injuries. Their physical being, even more than their spiritual happiness, became an obsession to her, an obsession that never left her. Enid and Leslie, healthy as they looked, were coddled against the germs of the world. She mistook worrying for caring. Leslie, being male and the younger child, was the perfect focus for such overwhelming anxiety. In fact, as the years passed, Bessie discovered that she could serve Leslie's interests in almost precisely the way that she served Harry's, and she carried on doing so, never slackening, until her death.

The childhood illnesses that tested Leslie gave Bessie the first and perfect opportunity to exercise her worry. In later life he traced his hypochondria and neurasthenia back to the attacks of croup he suffered as a child. Croup was very alarming to witness, but not life-endangering. It began with violent spasms in the throat when the patient could not get his breath. Ipecacuanha, an emetic, would be given, leading to vomiting. Bronchitis might follow, for which linseed poultices laced with mustard and wrapped in oilskin would be applied to the chest and back. Chest-protectors (of decreasing thicknesses) had to be worn for weeks after. There was always the threat of diphtheria, and of tuberculosis, or any of the various chest complaints that Bessie feared might prove fatal. It became for Leslie a duty to keep as well as possible if he was to calm Bessie's fears. But as Harry's fortunes prospered, Bessie was better able to afford her preoccupation with the family's health, and find the surroundings of Whittlesey unwholesome. Neither she or Harry realised that at the beginning of the new century their fortunes would improve dramatically. The reason was bricks.

The Fletton brick industry (its bricks known as 'flettons') had blossomed in the late 1870s when a draper, James McCallum Craig, purchased Lot I of the Fletton Lodge Estate in the parishes of Fletton and Woodstone, at an auction in June 1877 at the Angel Hotel in Peterborough.[20] The lot consisted of 68 acres and cost Craig around £6000. It was a sound investment, 'brick earth' being noted in the sale catalogue, but Craig did not set up a works on the land until about two years later. The making of bricks, of course, was not new to the area. There had been clay pits in the Fens throughout the 1860s and 1870s, mainly in Whittlesey and Stanground, where the mass of brickyard labourers lived. For them, bricks were often a family affair, a way of life. In the spring, it was common to see the father mixing clay in a pugmill, one of his older sons making the bricks, his wife carrying them to the hacks, and her small children setting the bricks out to dry. Labour was cheap, and often provided by immigrant families who settled to a life of poverty in the Fens.

In 1880, Craig's works were taken over by two brothers, George and Nathaniel Hempsted, who subsequently leased the property out to four small partnership companies. It was one of these that probably began making bricks not in the conventional way from clay taken from the surface, but from the Lower Oxford Clay that lay beneath. It was only now that the extraordinary talent of the submerged clay was discovered; even the geologist Dean Buckland, who had first identified its presence, had not realised that the Lower Oxford would burn. It was Harry's (and his family's) good luck that his involvement in the industry happened at a time when the properties of the clay had begun to be appreciated and exploited so succesfully. Harry never forgot the debt he owed to 'great old Dame

Nature' for having deposited so rich a store of the shaley stuff in his vicinity.[21] The quality of the Lower Oxford was far superior to the superficial clays that had been excavated before. No water was needed to break it down, only grinding; the clay's inherent moisture meant that unfired bricks could be placed in a kiln without first being dried off. The Lower Oxford contained so much carbon that the bricks had only to be heated, and would then more or less fire themselves, giving a tremendous saving in coal consumption.

Prominent in the history of brickmaking were two brothers, Arthur James and George Keeble, sometime farmers and land and property speculators who rather unsuccessfully specialised in buying up large estates, carving them up into smaller parcels of land and reselling them. Harry was their solicitor, and owed much of his good fortune to them. Not content with their dealing in land, the Keebles invested in cement manufacture, iron-ore extraction and, inevitably, brickmaking. Harry, ever the astute businessman, saw the potential in the brick industry, and thought he could make a better go of it than his clients. In March 1898 he became one of three directors for the new Whittlesea [sic] Central Brick Co. Ltd. His two fellow directors were another Peterborough solicitor, W. J. Jeeves, later to be Town Clerk of St Helens, and a wealthy local barrister, Henry Wadlow. The company took over the running of a small brickworks owned by John W. Andrews of Whittlesey, this site becoming its No. I works. In 1908, another site was added, doubling the size of the Central's empire.

The family, underrating Harry's business acumen, regarded his investment as little more than a hobby, but success brought wealth. Without the bricks, without the efficacy of the clay that burns, Leslie Hartley's life would have been very different. How much truth is there in Richard Mardick's assertion in *The Betrayal* that 'He owed his material prosperity to it, as much as he owed his spiritual poverty to the Brickfield. The clay of the Brickfield had been an age-old synonym for mortality; the clay our bodies are made of, and to which they must return. But the clay of the brickworks was life-enhancing'?[22]

The Keebles were responsible for another dramatic change in Harry and Bessie's lives: the move to Fletton Tower, a Gothic hall on the very edge of Peterborough. The house had been built for William Lawrence, Clerk of the Peace for the Liberty of Peterborough, in the early 1840s. Sometime before 1865 it was sold to a Bradford merchant, Thomas Mills, who had his initials carved and painted all over the house (Bradford, too, has a Fletton Terrace, possibly named by Mills). When he died in Algeria in January 1881 'the house called Fletton Tower with the cottage, coach house, stables, out houses, conservatory, parks, garden, etc.', the whole comprising 13¼ acres, was bought for £4700 by James Bristow, a local auctioneer, speculator and wine merchant who was soon also to jump on the brickmaking wagon. In 1898 Bristow emigrated to New Barnet and sold 8¾ acres, including the house and the northern carriage drive, to the Keebles. At some later time the brothers purchased other parts of the estate, some of which they (and subsequently the Hartleys) sold off for a school, a corset factory, and housing. Finding themselves in financial difficulties, in 1900 the Keebles offered Fletton Tower to Harry, who agreed to purchase the equity of the redemption of the Keebles' mortgages on the house and land in 1908. Harry was dubious about moving his wife and their two young children into so large a house, which was clearly beyond them financially. But Bessie, perhaps for the only time in her life, had made up her own mind. Without ever having seen the house, she insisted they should go. Whittlesey's primitive sanitation, the refuse rotting in its gutters, the spectre of diphtheria that haunted her daily, had to be escaped. The fact that Fletton Tower had drains made the move inevitable. The Hartleys left Whittlesey.

Now only a few minutes from Peterborough's shopping centre and football ground, Fletton Tower is the most unexpected property in Queen's Walk. A miniature castle, a folly, the house is not far from the road, protected only by a high wall and trees that in summer hide the building from the casual passer-by. In winter, it is more obvious from the road, and the terraced houses opposite are clearly visible from the Tower. The surrounding streets were developed during the 1850s and 1860s to answer the housing needs of local railwaymen. The railway laid close to the rear of the property was the GNR London–Scotland line, and it was one of Leslie's delights to wave at the fireman on the Flying Scotsman on the 10 a.m. from London. In such surroundings, the great old house stands withdrawn but not forbidding. Bessie and Harry used to say that in the summer they lived in the country, and in the winter in town. It was two years before they could afford stair-carpets.

The challenge of Fletton Tower was a formidable one for a woman with two young children, but Bessie rose to it. Although not domesticated, she was a capable manager, and had a nimble way with the housekeeping. Comfort was essential, luxury discouraged. Proper behaviour and economy were balanced. Good table-napkins were provided for visitors, and after the meal she would pin to each napkin the name of the guest who had used it, against his return.

It would, of course, have been unthinkable not to have servants, that race of helping hands that was to play so devastating a part in Leslie Hartley's life. His first memorable experience of a servant was Nurse Woolley – Leslie could get no nearer than calling her 'Bubby' – the prototype of Minney in *The Shrimp and the Anemone*. Gentle and fond of her charges (after nursing the infant Leslie she went on to look after his cousin Maurice Riddington), Bubby came from Fleet near Spalding, and, from a class safely beyond his own, was soon Leslie's confidante and ally, who might be depended on to take his part when disputes arose between him and the naturally assertive Enid. To Bubby, the carrier of the bronchitis kettle, the spittoon, the thermometer that must be exercised four times a day, he entrusted the intimacies of the nursery sick-room. He found solace in her easy simplicity, her personality apparently free from any complex or worries of her own. She offered a sense of comfort that Hartley would seek for the rest of his life, the sort of comfort ('really', Elizabeth Bowen once told him, 'a sense of comforted-ness')[23] that throughout life he offered to his friends, and looked to them to provide for him. The friendship with Bubby showed Hartley that a relationship with a servant had a sort of perfection, free of the strictures imposed by the family circle, and by a mother whose interest never weakened. Bubby did not bring the furniture of moral criteria. She watched and understood, and sympathised, and provided, a provision that could always be trusted. Alas, very few of the servants Hartley was to meet in later life inherited her talent.

Plump-faced, with flowing hair, and, if we can trust the photographs of the nursery, dressed as a rather unconvincing tribute to Little Lord Fauntleroy, Hartley spent his childhood in the claustrophobic atmosphere of Fletton, under the never ceasing anxiety of his mother. As he grew older, he had the feeling that other families, less morally correct than his own, were socially smarter, more expansive. Social progress seemed not to be Harry or Bessie's ambition. It was almost as though they worked hard at being middle class, though Norah insisted her mother was a snob. As an adult Hartley was happy to admit his middle-class origins, but seemed always to be making every effort to break free of them. He longed, like Mr Salteena, to rise up the social ladder, and longed for it with a zest that might have appalled his parents. They discouraged excitement and delight, distrusting pleasure and ostentation. Richard Mardick in *The Betrayal* remembers, 'The puritanical streak that in my father took the form of a stoical rationalism ("You must grin and bear it" he used to say when anything went wrong) was in her case a half-emotional, half-religious conviction that in furthering the right course, no pain whatever must be spared by her or anyone else.'[24] Alcohol was frowned on, though Bessie would take a small bottle of brandy with her to chapel, in case of emergency. It was wrong to play at cards, a pastime that Bessie denounced as having been invented to amuse 'a mad king'.[25] Aesthetic indulgence was unwelcome. If Leslie was asked what he would like to do, he felt guilty because so often his desires had nothing useful about them; enjoyment for its own sake did not seem enough. Fortunately, there were grandparents and aunts and uncles to ease the load; musical evenings at which the Thompsons delighted in singing 'In the gloaming' and 'Oh my darling, think not bitterly of me', but family life was constricting. When it came to the larger emotions, it was a battlefield. 'We didn't give flesh its due', Hartley wrote in The Betrayal. 'Or perhaps we did – I've never known what my relations really thought – the Holy Family, you know. I know how they behaved, but their thoughts may have been less rigid than their practice.'[26]

Leslie and Enid were not even able to enjoy the widening experience that school might have offered, for they were taught at home by a teacher from one of the local schools who came in after his day's work. It was a sound if basic education, where it mattered very much if the children did not form their letters correctly. Leslie, in this a godsend to a biographer, quickly developed a thoroughly legible and well-formed hand; Enid's was readable but effortful. Leslie was bookish from his earliest days, delighted at finding word 'incomprehensibilities' in the dictionary he pored over sitting on the steps of Fletton Tower. If the weather was warm, Bessie would enjoin him to run about the garden rather than read, but Harry had set the example: he was a voracious reader, seeking 'the wisdom not only of the living but of the dead, the larger company who have gone before'. As a young boy, Harry learned much of books from conversations with his father, and from those he read to his father, even on his death-bed. Before he was twenty-four he had read most of the fashionable books on science, art and philosophy, Ruskin, Huxley, Spencer, Carlyle and Darwin, evolution being one of the burning issues of the day. Lightness broke in, too: he was equally happy with Edward Lear. He could not resist limericks. He recited long passages of The Pickwick Papers. It was said that Harry knew Hamlet and Macbeth by heart, passing the words and atmosphere of them on to the children, who came to know them without knowing what they meant. Never a modernist, Harry said that the Bible and the works of Shakespeare had influenced him above all else. When Leslie, who sometimes insisted he had not been a great reader as a child, came to read for himself, he frightened himself with the stories of Edgar Allan Poe.

Had he been an only child, he might have relished books more, needed the company and consolation they brought, but at home there was Enid, and always the possibility of play and conversation. Together, too, they could cope the better with Bessie's overweening anxieties. There is no evidence that Enid was other than a loving sister, expressing only the sort of disapproval that older siblings have for their young. Her opportunities to display such disapproval were probably made easier by Leslie's willingness to please, to take the line of least resistance, to do nothing that might run the risk of inviting her withering look. In having to adjust to Bessie's personality, he laid himself more open to manipulation and ascendancy from other quarters, an opening that so intelligent a girl as Enid could only explore. In the garden she probably turned up her nose as Leslie hunted for spiders – he usually had five or six of them in his apron pocket. The receipt of caterpillars (often dead) through the post, no doubt meant more upturned noses. But Enid's presence made fun possible for Leslie, who would otherwise have come into contact with very few other children. If there was an isolation in his childhood, it was shared with his sister.

One of the earliest memories Leslie had of Fletton was the night of the relief of Ladysmith, 28 February 1901. The British population, reeling from the catastrophes of the Boer War, greeted the news with an hysteria repeated at the relief of Mafeking three months later. Leslie always remembered the Peterborough crowds mad with excitement, the noise of jubilation and drums lingering in his mind 'like a great red blur'.[27] He complained to Bessie that he did not like 'the jum-jums'. The pleasurable recollections of that war were provided by the popular songs that beguiled the innocent. War, to the young Hartley, was the provider of such martial and irresistible concoctions as 'Good bye, Dolly Gray' and 'The Soldiers of the Queen', nothing more. For a child, the complexities of the conflict were reduced to a riddle that might lead to a fit of the giggles: '"Why does Kruger wear thick boots?"' '"To keep De Wett from defeat."'[28] Harry (like Lloyd George) of course championed the Boer cause, an unpopular position to have taken up in a country fuelled with imperialistic zeal. He realised the cost that would have to be paid. By the time a treaty was signed in 1902, the British had lost 6000 men in the field, and a further 16,000 had died from disease, while Kitchener's relentless rounding-up of the scattered Boer communities into concentration camps alone led to the deaths of 20,000. With so efficient a dress rehearsal for the conflagration that would break out in Europe in 1914, the arrival of Hartley's 'hideous century' was announced. But for Leslie, as for the mass of people, 'South Africa was so far away and what happened there was only, for me, a stimulus for emotion and romantic excitement, with heroism, not death, as its leading motif.'[29]

Holidays at the Norfolk seaside town of Hunstanton, looking out west to the Wash, were opportunities for adventure. Today, the little watering-place retains much of its grandeur, inevitably faded, its lordly architecture rising up above the promenade, a Victorian development to meet the needs of travellers who suddenly could reach the resort by railway. Below the town, the brightly coloured, rusting fun-fair strung out along the beach is a later addition. The little pools left behind among the rocks by the retreating tide, among which Leslie and Enid and Eustace and Hilda played on the beach, are still a source of wonder to children. Leslie and Enid delighted in using jumping-poles to project themselves from one rock to the next. It was the stillness of the pools that so attracted Leslie, who never much cared for the sea; it was the *placidity* of water that thrilled him, the river Nene, the calmness of Fen water – and, when he became a man, the Venetian lagoon, and the gently flowing Avon.

He never forgot the wonder of Hunstanton or, as the locals call it, 'Hunston' (the Anchorstone or 'Anxton' of *The Shrimp and the Anemone*), its red sandstone cliffs, the best shop to buy bucket or spade, the 'Try-Your-Grip' machine standing ready to dispense amusement, offering that rare thing, amusement only. And the images of the place were so powerful: the water-tower, under which Eustace could not pass without thrilling at the possibility that it might explode at any moment; the lighthouse, raised up against the dangers of the sea. Turned into fiction, Leslie realised the lighthouse might seem to appear 'a symbol of frustration, but it wasn't exactly that: it was actually a little further afield than my sister and I generally went for a walk: we had to turn back before we got to it.'[30]

In later life, Leslie discounted the natural theory that Hilda was in effect a portrait of Enid: how could he do otherwise when Hilda was greeted with almost vituperative scorn? But shortly before he died he was interviewed for radio by Derek Parker, who suggested that Hartley must have been a fairly extrovert child. 'I don't think I was, really', he answered. 'I could have been more so. I was very much dominated by a sister: I thought that what she told me to do was right. She was a very firm character: she was the ruling character of *The Shrimp and the Anemone*.'[31] It is more than likely that Enid recognised, or at least remembered, herself as Hilda. The fact remains that throughout his life, until its last few weeks, he denied that Enid had been his inspiration. After his death, Norah persisted in thinking Hilda had been a portrait of Bessie, the person from whom Hartley undoubtedly inherited his prejudices and his imagination.

Whatever magic Hunstanton might offer, Fletton had to be returned to. And Leslie was never happy there; a dislike of the house developed that lasted until the end of his days. Its atmosphere, somehow, was anathema to him, but, in seventy-seven years, he never offered a convincing explanation of why that should be so. Of course, Bessie's demanding presence must have made it difficult for him. But there was something, too, in his relationship with Harry, that left him uncomfortable at Fletton. Meanwhile, Leslie was confined to the closed, dark splendour of William Lawrence's Gothic tower, where the love of his mother ruled. Here, on 17 September 1903, her third and last child, Annie Norah (known as Norah) was born, another reason for Bessie's concern.

'I took after her', Richard Mardick says of his mother in *The Brickfield*. 'Home was one cocoon, school was another. The perfect insect, the imago, that I dreamed of becoming, would not be moulded, licked into shape by the outside world. It would emerge suddenly, with no intermediate evolutionary process, and in that I was right: it did.'[32]

🌿 2 🌿

To be the Hero

AMONG THE EARLIEST of Hartley's papers, on a single piece of paper on which has been drawn carefully pencilled lines, is what was probably his first essay. Perhaps it was written by order of his visiting schoolmaster, who must have been impressed not only by the appreciation of classicism, which was to prove a lifelong fascination for Hartley, but by the arrangement of the prose.

> 'Crowland Abbey' was founded BC 716 by Ethelbald: most of it is now in ruins but part of it still serves as a parish church – and a very fine – one it is too. some part of the nave is left the Arches are rather lofty and well proportioned . . . hiegth of the battlement is 90 feet and to the top of the spire is about 120 feet but the chief beauty of the Abbey is a Norman Arch this magnificent Arch is very high underneath it is a beautiful zig-zag from one side of the Arch to the other the whole Abbey must have been lovey. The End[1]

His first story was written when he was eleven and in bed with caterpillar rash. This fairy-tale sets the style for those that followed in later life – the directness, simplicity and naïvety have their beginning here.

> There was once a king who had three sons. The two eldest were proud, and scorned the younger brother, who was a poor little hunch-backed dwarf. After a time the eldest determined to go into the world to seek his fortune. His aged father implored him not to 'Lest,' said he, 'some harm may befall thee.' However, at last his father consented and gave him two splendid horses, one to carry his provisions, and one for him to ride on. In due time the prince set forth. On his way he had to get through a dark wood, and when night came on he could find no way to get out. So he sat on the ground, and proceeded to eat some of the provisions. He had no sooner begun than a hideous little dwarf with a very sad face and a very long lower lip appeared. 'Oh!' exclaimed the dwarf, 'I'm so hungry do give me some of your food.'

'What, you hideous little atom of humanity,' said the prince, 'if I were to waste this good food on thee, I should not have half enough for myself.' While the prince was saying this he gave the dwarf a vigorous kick, and he vanished with a loud laugh. Having finished his meal the prince lay down to rest. He had nearly gone to sleep when he saw a light glimmering in the distance. 'It would be much nicer to sleep under a roof than out in the open air when there is every sign of a coming storm,' thought the prince, and he got on his horse, and accompanied by the other rode towards the light. It turned out as the prince had hoped to be a cottage, and it was from one of the windows that the light preceded. He knocked. There was no answer. He knocked again. Still no answer. He knocked a third time, and the door opened and a little wizened-up old woman stood before him. 'What do you want?' she said. 'I wanted you to put me up for a night as I fear there's a storm brewing,' answered the prince.[2]

The potency of fairy-tale was clearly one of Hartley's earliest influences, even if we cannot ever know, from the fragment of the first example that has survived, if the ugly little dwarf that appears to the prince is his dwarf brother in disguise. One inspiration for such enchantment may in part have been his grandfather's fruit garden at St James' Lodge, which was

> an enchanted place, especially in the summer. Passing through the gate, flanked by a coal-shed on one side and a wispy, but rather forbidding yew-hedge on the other, was like being transported into another world – such a symphony of smells and sounds greeted one.[3]

It was here, in late August 1906, that Grandfather Thompson commissioned Leslie to eradicate the plague of wasps that was terrifying Bessie and her sisters. The agreed payment was one penny a wasp. Although timid in most respects, Leslie was brave when it came to wasps, and set his target at 1000 corpses. After successfully catching the mass of them with his butterfly net and plunging them into boiling water (and only suffering one sting on the finger) he was awarded the prize of four and twopence.

Less dangerously, he wrote a play, 'The Tower of Fletton', acting it out with Enid and wearing a black beard as the villain.[4] Although he was naturally closer to Enid, he was equally fond of Norah and, as soon as she was able, she would accompany him on various expeditions. Watching for the trains to pass qualified them almost as another set of 'railway children'. Leslie took Norah cycling to the Staunch, crossing a footbridge where there was a large bush behind which they changed into their bathing costumes. They were fascinated by a great pool, 'the forty-foot', the depth of which they tried to measure with string and stone; it was said any one venturing in would be wrapped around by the weeds and drowned. Otherwise, there were dancing classes to be got through with Enid – they find their way into *The Shrimp and the Anemone* – and lessons with his music teacher, Dr Haydn Keeton,[5] in which Leslie struggled at the piano under photogravures of Handel, Mozart and Beethoven. When he made one blunder too many, the exasperated doctor would throw open the window and take deep breaths of air.

As the children grew up, Bessie's daily routine settled into a pattern. In the early morning she would be bright and active, bustling about the house, making sure that Leslie had an egg for his breakfast, that he did not forget the dancing class which Enid sometimes seemed less eager than he to attend, but her energy would flag and by lunchtime a decline set in. Pale and listless, and incapable of keeping her mind on any one thing, Bessie would take to her bed. The doctor would be called. She then fell into a deep sleep, waking late in the afternoon. Now full of vigour, interested in everything around her, her energy lasted until late at night. Harry, whose day finished around ten o'clock, would say, 'Bess, dear, when you're passing the bed sometime you might just pop in to see me.'[6]

It must have been Harry who decided that if Leslie was to come to anything, his education must continue away from Fletton. Enid had already departed for St Felix School at Southwold, beginning an education that was cut short by Bessie's need for her as a liaison between herself and the staff at home; the inheritance of being Bessie's elder daughter came to her early. In the autumn of 1908, Leslie became a boarder at Northdown Hill preparatory school in Cliftonville, Thanet: headmaster, Mr John Deacon Holt. That Leslie should be taken so far away from home, where he had lived for almost thirteen years, filled Bessie with intense misgivings. The unfortunate Mrs Holt had the charge of Leslie's health at Northdown, but if she ever felt exasperation at Mrs Hartley's constant agitation there is no evidence of her having done so. He had barely settled in when Bessie wrote:

> I should be very glad to have just a *few* lines tomorrow and Sunday if you can, *just* to say how you are dearie – Be *very* careful when you go out for the *1st* and the *2nd* time too – You had better not

run and get a cold had you – can you put on your old blue jersey
when you first come down in case you feel a bit chill – Besure tell
Mrs Holt if you feel poorly at all when you are up – and be very
careful darling. I wish I could have you just one 1/2 hour, or even
5 minutes would be very sweet, wouldn't it?[7]

But by the end of October Leslie was able to tell his mother he was
not in the least homesick. The horrors endured by so many boys in
the name of education eluded him at Northdown and in his
subsequent schools, if we are to believe his letters home; if we accept
the details of his school life in *The Go-Between*, a very different
picture emerges, of humiliation and torture. He got on well with Mr
Holt, with Miss Shilcock who taught music, Mr Lion ('Leo') and
Mr Thomas ('old Tommy', whose grandfather was Frederick William Farrar, the author of *Eric, or Little by Little*). The other pupils
were friendly enough. When some of his schoolfellows lost his
treasured penknife (three blades) on the sands, Leslie forgave them.
Though their mostly Tory sensibilities were outraged on discovering
he was a Liberal, Leslie survived their disapproval. Now and again,
an air of freedom almost threatened to overcome him. 'I have not
washed my neck for three or four days', he recklessly told Bessie
'and the sensation of growing dirt is too delightful to mention.'[8]
Woodward, the head boy, was 'always so nice'. In fact, 'Everyone is
very kind to me, they give me everything I want, even I have a little
dish to cough and put grape-skins into, like I had at home.'[9] Perhaps
surprisingly, Leslie seemed a sporty boy. He enjoyed gym, cricket,
tennis, and shooting with an airgun, though he loathed 'drill',
inescapably part of the curriculum at this period. Less frivolously,
he told Bessie of a 'splendid lecture about Montenegro and the
Bulgarian peninsula.'[10]

She was, of course, as interested in his health as in his lessons.
Mrs Holt was given instructions that Leslie should go to bed at the
same time as the 'small boys'. He kept Bessie supplied with details
and queries: his phlegm was now loose; how long did she want him
to stay in bed?; he would put on his Thermogen wool if she wished;
he would make sure to take rhubarb and then perhaps a mustard-
plaster. Gifts of potted-meat, grapes, flowers, were despatched from
Fletton. And letters.

One of the Northdown boys, Moxey, a little younger than Leslie,
wrote to his mother to ask if Leslie might stay with them in the
school holidays. Leslie did not much care for Moxey, whose people
were prosperous coal merchants, and asked Bessie to think of a

reason why he might not go. Perhaps she resisted Leslie's plea, for in August 1909 he went to stay at Bradenham Hall, which the Moxeys had rented from the Rider Haggards, near Swaffham in Norfolk. It was here that Leslie wrote to Bessie on 16 August:

Dear Mother

I hope you were not very troubled at not getting a letter from me. I had a comfortable journey, and was met by Moxey in a motor-car, along with a chauffeur and a dog. I sleep with Moxey, (it was arranged so before I came) and also with a dog, which at first reposed on the bed ... I am coming on *Wednesday*, and will come by the train you told me of.

On Saturday we had a ball, very grand indeed, at least, not very. We always have late dinner here. There is going to be a cricket match to day, the Hall against the village. I am going to score. Good-bye, dear Mother.

Ever your loving little
  Leslie[11]

Life meets imagination at least in the mention of the cricket match, one of the great set pieces of *The Go-Between*, by which we see not only the fusion between gentry and the lower orders but the divisions that separate them. More generally, this letter is Hartley's first substantial recognition of the upper-class life that was to so fascinate him, and would mean so much to him for the rest of his life. It presents the basic predicament that Leslie would always face: he was an outsider. He was never ashamed of his middle-class upbringing, even when it seemed quite implausible, but he longed to move out into greater waters. His acceptance by the landed or literary gentry had to be worked at, for he never had a natural place among the titled people he loved to mix with or the literary cliques that he stood on the edges of. There is clear evidence that he put himself about to gain an entrée to these special companies; Virginia Woolf, Ottoline Morrell and Georgia Sitwell all had their reservations about his place in the social scheme of things; he was identified as an interloper. Leslie realised he was on the outside looking in; he wanted a place, as it were, at the fireside. Driving up to Bradenham Hall with Moxey and the dog was a bewitching experience, and then there was the ball ('very grand indeed, at least, not very' sounds like an apology to his mother's social expectations) and the unquestion-able superiority of 'late dinner' over the arrangements that were usually in place at Fletton. At once, Leslie became what he would remain – a minnow swimming with whales.

But it is the possibility that at Bradenham the seeds were sown in Leslie's mind for *The Go-Between* that provides the real fascination of the visit. Brandham Hall, the house that Leo – the book's narrator – visits in the summer of 1900, is the slightest of disguises for Bradenham; 'Moxey' is too similar to 'Maudsley', the fictional family at Brandham, to be accidental. Forty years later when he came to write of it, all that Leslie could remember of the house was its double-staircase, the outhouses overgrown with belladonna, and the cedar tree in the garden; today, there is no sign of the double-staircase, though architectural historians agree it may have existed at the time of his visit. Frank Delaney, writing in 1985 of the Norfolk church housing Rider Haggard's tomb, regrets the fact that the stained-glass window to his memory contains 'no portrait of his daughter upon whom L. P. Hartley based the girl in love for his novel, *The Go-Between*'.[12] This statement may have had its origin in an account related by Norah, of how Leslie had been confined to the house while staying at Bradenham, had gone upstairs and, wandering into the bedrooms, had discovered a diary belonging to the young lady (or perhaps *one* of the young ladies) of the house. Reading it, he had become fascinated by the story it told, a story of love across the classes; in essence, he recreated it in fiction over forty years later. While there is the possibility that it was Lilias Rider Haggard's diary that began the long genesis of *The Go-Between*, the diary may have belonged to another – one of the Moxeys, even. There is certainly no written evidence that can now give us the facts. It seems unlike Norah to have admitted that as a young man Leslie invaded the rooms of his hosts to turn over their most private papers; it seems as unlikely that Leslie would ever have admitted as much to Norah. The most tantalising fact is that, many years later, David Horner wrote of the adult Leslie's fondness for invading his host's rooms, and reading whatever private papers he found there.

After her brother's death, Norah insisted that *The Go-Between* was a work of absolute fiction, a fact that he gave no hint of contradicting throughout his life, until its last months. Only then, with Joseph Losey's filming of the novel, did Hartley begin to give himself away. In October 1971, he saw the completed film for the first time. Behind him sat Patricia Losey, the director's wife, and Harold Pinter, author of the screenplay. Hartley cried. Losey, perhaps taking it for granted that the events of the novel had been factual, asked him if the 'real-life' Mrs Maudsley had dragged the boy to the outhouse. Hartley replied that he had been made to follow her, rather than dragged. Even given his readiness to always say the most agreeable thing, this sounds convincingly like an admission of truth. And so we are back with Richard Mardick's belief in *The Brickfield* – 'I'd rather they knew the truth. They mustn't know it, that's the difficulty.'[13] The landscape that begins to turn itself into a map is obscured again. Whatever Hartley may have committed to paper about the happenings at Bradenham Hall in the summer of 1909 has not survived. Perhaps the truth was entrusted to his private journals – reason enough, in some eyes, to destroy them.

Imagination and fact conflict at Bradenham Hall. It is easy enough to imagine Leslie, like Leo, exploring the outhouses, and the present owners can confirm that the buildings were indeed overrun with deadly nightshade when they first came to the house. The Hall saw many changes after the Haggards sold it at the end of the First World War; for a time, pigs were kept on the first floor. Over fifty years later, Moxey returned to the Hall once more before his death, to look over the house and to see once more the grave of his dog, the dog who had shared Leslie's bed. The stone that reads 'Bobby a gentleman 1910' is a strangely touching reminder of Leslie's adventure, and it is at least one positive piece of evidence – the death of a much-loved dog – that links up with Moxey's, and Leslie's, past. If the old Moxey, returning, like the elderly Leo, to the scene of the foreign country, knew the links between fact and fiction, he did not speak of them.

In early 1910 Northdown had to be left behind for a public school education. Leslie had become reconciled to such a progress despite earlier misgivings. He told Bessie on 24 October 1909 that 'For some things I should like to leave [Northdown] this term, and for some things I should like to stay. I can't say I like the idea of going to a Public School at all. I myself would rather go to Charterhouse than any other Public School.' Mr Holt wrote to Harry on 13 May 'You know my opinion of Leslie: I have great hopes that his honesty, good sense and capacity for work will carry him high.'[14] If the steady Holt had noticed brilliance in his well-behaved pupil, he did not betray it to Harry; Holt clearly imagined that Leslie's industriousness and decency would mark him out for some distinguished if undefined future. The Holts had made Leslie's time with them happy; even their baby '(they call her the Babe) wanted to know if Norah was coming down here'.[15] The most delightful evidence of Leslie's Northdown life is his poem, 'Aviation', perhaps inspired by Blériot's flight from Baraques to Dover in July 1909. It begins:

> One great desire of all mankind
> From many years ago,
> Has been the conquest of the air,
> As you perhaps may know.
>
> For Daedalus in ancient times,
> Who, wise in many things,
> From Minos, lord of land and sea,
> Escap'd by using wings.
>
> But Icarus, when o'er the sea
> Too near the sun did fly;
> The wax, with which the wings were stuck
> Did melt, and he did die.[16]

Despite a master's (perhaps Mr Holt's) pencilled plea beside the second stanza – 'Where's the main verb?' – Leslie ploughs on through eleven verses, including:

> But men in present times, who are
> In all respects quite sane
> Have wonderful results obtained
> Using an aeroplane.
>
> This wonderful affair is made
> With planes both light and strong,
> While a petrol motor, strongly made,
> Sends the machine along.
>
> The chief success was gained at first
> (I do hope this line scans)
> By Wilbur (also Orville) Wright
> By nation 'mericans.

Charterhouse was denied the young poet; for some reason, Bessie and Harry chose Clifton College, on the edge of Bristol, as the public school that would continue to bring out Leslie's potential. He arrived at Clifton in April 1910 as a boarder in Oakley's house, but did not stay long. According to Leslie, he developed a chesty cough and Bessie declared the place unhealthy; he would have to be moved elsewhere. It is, of course, possible that Leslie's removal from Clifton may have been brought about by some romantic or sexual involvement with another, perhaps older, boy at the school, but we can hardly expect any evidence that this was so to have survived. Beyond the fact that he played golf and tennis, no details of his life at the school were recorded. If Clifton taught him anything, it was that he was unobservant. He was walking down a street in the town when his headmaster, Dr John King, turned to him and said, 'Do you see that?'

> I looked up, and there was an elephant walking down the middle of the street. 'It is getting used to the traffic', he said – no mean feat, even for an elephant – but I should never have noticed it unless he had pointed it out to me.[17]

The other positive contribution Clifton made to Leslie's life was that it almost certainly introduced him to Clifford Henry Benn Kitchin, a day boy in South Town house until he enlisted in 1914. Only two months younger than Leslie, Kitchin had entered Clifton Prep School in the summer of 1908 as a pupil in 3 alpha (Leslie, in 1910, was in 4 beta), and it is likely that the boys were in the same form for the term Leslie was in residence (Kitchin's younger brother, John, was also at Clifton). The boys had much in common besides their age. Kitchin, like Hartley, always insisted on his middle-class origins, claiming that he had been born in a house that was little more than a cottage, at 11 Granby Road, Harrogate. His father, like Hartley's was 'legal' – a barrister, C. K. Kitchin. The boys also shared a love of literature and, already, the knowledge that money was no problem to them. In this, Kitchin was undoubtedly in the ascendant, for whereas most of the Hartley money came from trade – indeed, Hartley may always have felt there was something almost *nouveau riche* about the family money – the Kitchin fortune was handed down through redundant relations, of whom Clifford Kitchin had a good many. In later life he was to write of them living on in various states of decrepitude in a house aptly named 'Shady Bower', where 'they seem to spend most of their days in bed, poor things, and Aunt Laura says they sometimes do not meet for days on end!'[18] If there was little time for a friendship between the two boys to grow during Leslie's three-month stay at Clifton, it was an oversight that Oxford would remedy nine years later.

If Leslie coped with his visit to the Moxeys, he seems to have been slightly less happy to stay with a Mrs Wallis (possibly the mother of a friend) at 72 St Leonard's Road in Hastings in August 1910. An appeal was sent off to Bessie when Mrs Wallis asked him to stay an extra day

> as she wants me to go to a party . . . You know I am not very fond of parties and I *do* want to come home on Tuesday. However,

they have asked me to write to you and ask if you would mind my staying. I am enjoying myself here but I am sure we should both prefer me to be at home.

Of course, if you think it would be better for me to stay, write to me and say so; it is only for a day. But still, I do want to be home again.[19]

Coming at a time when his confidence may have been shaken by his premature removal from Clifton, the uncertainty of this letter is perhaps not surprising; it lodged itself in Leslie's mind enough for it to inspire a similar letter in *The Go-Between*.

Bessie's second try at a public school for Leslie, Harrow, proved much more successful, though the distance between them remained a source of anguish. She sent tulips, irises, lilies of the valley, York and Lancaster roses, walnuts and fruit, but now Leslie occasionally displayed an air of self-sufficiency by which some of Bessie's attentions might be deflected. When she told him she wanted to stay in lodgings to be near him, he could reply, 'I am afraid we should both want to see each other oftener than would be wise.'[20] Quite naturally, the school environment and his new life in his 'house' at Harrow, West Acre, were claiming more of him, and there seems to have been little to dread from the potential horrors of his new surroundings. ' I used to think that I was very unpopular at school', Leslie wrote years later 'but it wasn't true. I don't think anybody liked me very much, but they didn't dislike me. I was perfectly happy at Harrow.'[21] He quickly learned the language spoken there, the addition of 'er' to so many of the school's institutions: the blue-coat became the bluer, the duck-pond the ducker, the speech-room the speecher, the Saturday night exercise the exerciser.

But his beginning at Harrow was not auspicious. Put in a low form, he was placed 17th out of a class of 23. When his housemaster informed him that better was expected of him, Leslie's performance improved dramatically: ultimately, he became head of the school. Even as a 'Torpid' (a pupil who had not been at the school for two years or was under sixteen), expected to go on 'Torpid runs', which Leslie managed to get out of, and denied boyish comforts, like buying sweets, he quickly settled into the new regime: up at 6.45 a.m., cocoa, lessons from 7.30 to 8.30, breakfast, lessons till 1.30, resuming at 4 till 6.45, supper, prayers at 9, lights out at 10.

Such apparent rigidity was lightened by many diversions. The elderly Ellen Terry gave a lecture on Shakespeare, acting out

Desdemona, Portia, Juliet and Rosalind, losing herself here and there and begging of her audience to 'Have patience, sweet people!'[22] Hilaire Belloc ('a funny looking fellow ... inclined to corpulence with a red face'),[23] with whose sister Leslie would later begin a long friendship, spoke on 'The Growth of London'. At concerts, Leslie, considered one of the two best pianists in the school, played solos, accompanied the violin, and sang, first alto and subsequently bass, in the choral class. The playing-fields beckoned. Despite his being told by his drill captain that he had curvature of the spine, flat feet, knock-knees and a crooked body, Leslie almost distinguished himself at sport. He became captain of the football house team, sometimes delighting in conquering the nearby Dumpton House, though he never really enjoyed the game, preferring to kick around a 'fug' (a smaller football). He won the long-jump in the house sports, became a good marksman at the rifle-range, played cricket and squash rackets. There was the ducker to skate on or swim in.

Fenlanders, too, were given evidence of the boy's sturdiness when a testament to Leslie's physical prowess appeared in the Peterborough press in 1910. Bessie, who had, according to the report, 'just recovered from an illness',[24] was on her way to Crowland in a wagonette when a squall struck the vehicle, giving the horse the staggers, and throwing her off the road into the adjoining dyke. She struggled to get on top of the wagonette out of five feet of water, and 'with the help of her son, who had gone off with the driver, but had returned, got safely to land'. What miseries of worry Bessie must have suffered after this we may well imagine. In March 1911 she was recuperating in Harrogate from (presumably another) affliction, and on her return to Fletton full-time nurses were brought in. Once back at Harrow, of course, it was essential that Leslie should take every precaution against illness. He was almost sixteen when he told Bessie, 'You will be relieved to hear that I have changed into my thickest vest, but have not changed my "never-minds" at present, as I do not think it is quite cold enough.'[25] Even Bessie's fretting, spread over several letters, about so mundane a catastrophe as a corn, necessitated replies to Fletton in which Leslie protested as loudly as he could. 'Do you very much want me to see Dr Sayer in London?' he wrote on 24 March 1912. 'I think that if I wore a corn plaster at home for some time (one of those things with a hole in the middle) for the holidays, and then if it did not get better I could see Dr Sayer when I go back to Harrow ... *by wearing bed-room Slippers as much as possible* I think we could cure it without the aid of Dr Sayer, or any other Chiropodist.' Holidays at home were more enjoyably spent by visits to Lincoln cathedral (where Leslie counted 388 steps up to the 'Central Tower'), to Boston, and to an amateur performance of Edward German's *The Emerald Isle*, accompanied by Harry and Enid. Bessie was too ill to go with them, but hoped soon to get out and about in a wheelchair.

It was not Leslie's allegedly dismal health prospects that stood him apart from his fellows at Harrow. If he in any way felt an outsider, it was the fault of politics and religion. He was the only Liberal in his house, and there were not more than twenty in the entire school. His background of Wesleyan Methodism also struck a jarring note, in as much as it did not conform to the religious tenor of the place. By the end of 1911 he was going to his form-master, the Revd Owen, for confirmation classes, and was subsequently received into the Church of England. Harry and Bessie accepted the change (though strong Methodists, they were never bigoted or overbearing), but this breakaway from family tradition was a significant step in Leslie's development; it distanced him from what they might have expected – it was, indeed, one of the few decisive steps he ever took. Religious zeal had little to do with it, and in later life his enthusiasm for religion was aesthetic rather than theological; the conversion of itself – as Richard Mardick admits in *The Brickfield* – may have been as much an act of snobbery as any other, a repudiation of the homespun respectability of provincial Methodism. His personal involvement with the organised Church was as much a social as a fundamental commitment, a view shared by Timothy Casson in *The Boat*. When Timothy communes with his god it is in his boat-house, not his church; it is his *social* horizons that are broadened by the vicar and his wife, Mrs Purbright. Eustace, like Leslie, is moved by the trappings of religion, by a nave, a transept, a stained-glass window; he epitomises the man transported by the sung Evensong without being touched by its religious intention. Interestingly, the one novel in which Leslie uses religion as a central theme, *My Fellow Devils*, is one of his dullest and least heartfelt. Even here, it is the spire of St Saviour's church that Margaret Pennefather runs to at the close, not the arms of the comforter. In *Facial Justice* the only hint of centuries of religious fervour left behind by the holocaust is a remnant of Ely cathedral; once again, architecture inspires Jael's affirmation of belief, not the teachings of the body that created it. As an adult, Leslie said that he enjoyed attending church because he enjoyed being admonished from the pulpit. He would sometimes fall asleep during the sermon, on one occasion waking just in time to hear the vicar say, 'Take marmalade, for instance.'[26]

Leslie's diversion into Anglicanism – he was confirmed at Harrow on 25 March 1912, in the presence of Aunt Kathleen – would hardly have bothered old John Bark. And Aunt Kathleen understood the conversion, and probably approved of it; if it was what Leslie wanted then it was the right decision. Kathleen's especial closeness to Leslie meant that an easy understanding grew up between them, and with George Lund, Kathleen's husband. The Thompsons, with their high expectations of Kathleen, made no pretence of being delighted at her choice of husband. Lund was a mild, unspectacular man who worked as a bank clerk and seemed to have no ambition to better that position. He had the knack, almost, of walking into a room without people being aware he had come in. But George and Kathleen adored one another, and were to live out that devotion until George's death. Many of the happiest times of Leslie's childhood were spent with George and Kathleen, joyful holidays by the sea, golfing and bathing with Uncle George, and visits to their home at Squires Lane in Finchley, where always in the background was the maid, Jane, a sort of perpetual bridesmaid to Kathleen. Having no children of their own, the Lunds found compensation and fulfilment in Leslie. More than this, Kathleen recognised in her nephew qualities that she hoped would one day bloom; what gave an extra edge to her understanding was the fact that she was herself a writer. In 1909, Dean published her first book, *Mrs Dusty-Fusser: How she swept into Society*; three novels followed, the last published in 1919. There is a distinct possibility that Leslie's journey from Methodism to Anglicanism may have inspired passages in her 1914 *Oliver in Willowmere*,[27] in which parochial uproar ensues when a new minister of the 'Methody' becomes a more attractive proposition than his Church of England counterpart:

> '*My* notion of church and chapel folk,' Uncle Anthony volunteered, 'is that one lot swears and the other lies.'
>
> 'Sho-sho!' remonstrated Clement, laughing uneasily.
>
> 'It isn't their doctrine I object to,' observed Peter with a drawl, 'so much as their architecture.'
>
> 'There I agree,' cried Timothy Golden, who had been waiting his opportunity. 'The worst thing about them is their want of – of what we call the aesthetic sense – the aesthetic sense,' he added lest someone should have missed his trite expression. 'Perhaps I ought not to say it – especially before a clergyman – but as for doctrine – excepting their lax ideas over baptism and that sort of

thing – I don't see myself where the great – the great disparity lies. I don't indeed.'

Aunt Kathleen may try to pass off Timothy Golden's explanation (which clearly endorses Leslie's views) as trite, but it is a sympathetic and reasonably broadminded attitude, at least as reasonable as the reaction of one of Willowmere's elders to the force of Methodism:

> 'I'm sure I've no objection to chapel-going for the servants,' put in Mrs Stillingfleet sadly. 'It's convenient beginning at half-past ten of a morning instead of eleven like us. The housemaid can get back in easy time to set the dinner-table; but as for prayer-meetings, there I draw the line. I call that going a little too far.'

A little too far. There is always, in *Oliver in Willowmere*, the feeling that organised religion cannot answer the needs of its followers, that something much stronger, personal, less discernible, is more reliable. In her great outpouring to the Methodist minister, Oliver Trood, whom she has loved, Maura insists on her own, hybrid, philosophy, reinforced by her Fen homeland:

> 'I stretch out my arms to the sun: it warms and fills me. What else should I ask of it? It is the same with religion. I could only feel: I could never explain. A man's soul is his own and God's: who am I to dictate? I was born, I think, without any sensation for dogmas or creeds. I have tried them, you know. The church seemed to fail me and I went gladly to you, and what you taught me I hope I may never lose. But I had to come back to my untold thoughts ... This great, rich land of ours, that touches Heaven at all points, is very quiet, Oliver. Nothing has spoken to me plainly; yet everything speaks. What you talk of in chapel, what they tell us in church is never, somehow, enough. Always the great distance draws ... the things we dream about there in the mist.'

At Harrow, Hartley accumulated most of the literary influences that were to stay with him for the rest of his life. In November 1913 he was preparing a paper on the Brontës (he read it to the Literary Society in February of the next year) but, of all that family, it was Emily who most intrigued him. Hartley developed so deep an understanding of her work that it was as if a love-affair had begun; it is no coincidence that her lines

> I've known a hundred kinds of love,
> *All* made the loved one rue

should precede *The Shrimp and the Anemone*, for they encapsulate what Hartley believes of the human condition. Possibly, Hartley admired Emily because she used her writing to rebel against the life that had been imposed on her; she had found an aesthetic escape. He thought that part of Emily's tragedy was that she did not want friendship, but love – and this tussle was one crucial to Hartley's later life. But, as a boy, it was the titles of *Wuthering Heights* and *The Scarlet Letter*, waiting on his grandfather's bookshelves, that first attracted Hartley. Of the latter, he wondered if the paper on which the letter was written was scarlet, or if the words were written in scarlet ink. When he sat down to read, the feelings these books inspired struck chords that remained with him for the rest of his life. Searching for the thread that linked the two novels in his mind, Hartley recognised that both were by writers discarding their innate Puritanism in order to get at a deeper understanding of life. And he warmed to their pessimism.

Comparing Emily Brontë and Hawthorne, he wrote:

Perhaps the parallel between these writers is not very rewarding except in so far as it illustrates the means whereby two lonely, misanthropic novelists, unwilling or unable for one reason or another to receive sustenance from the community, were still able to produce great works of art. In composing these works they found compensation, and consolation, for whatever it was in their natures that made for solitude, unhappiness, frustration, guilt. Though their circumstances differed, and their aims differed, they were kindred souls who 'desired a better country – that is, a heavenly one'.[28]

Of course, Hartley here identifies so clearly with his literary idols that when he describes them he is, in effect, describing himself. Their appeal, to a great extent, is that they reflect what he experiences and desires. How very important it was that Hartley's work would compensate and console him for the personal happiness that eluded him.

The influence of Henry James on Hartley's writing has always been emphasised, and exists (*Simonetta Perkins* is a model of Jamesian clarity and understatement), but Hartley's more passionate response to what he read had already been used up by the time he turned to James (who, by the way, described Hawthorne as a rogue who had unexpectedly found himself in a company of detectives). Hawthorne's effect on Hartley cannot be overestimated. In the summer of 1914 Hartley wrote an essay on him (as well as essays on 'A Rainy

Day', 'Ill words break no bones' and 'International and individual morality'), borrowing here and there from Leslie Stephen's *Hours in a Library*. When he gave the Clark Lectures at Cambridge fifty years later, he chose Hawthorne as his subject; for him, Hawthorne never lost the magic that began to work at Harrow. In Hartley's boyhood, many a child woke on Christmas morning to find a copy of *Tanglewood Tales* in his stocking. 'Ah, yes, that golden pen!' said Percy Buck when Hartley asked his music master for his opinion of Hawthorne's worth.[29] Years later, when Hartley was extolling Hawthorne's virtues to Edith Wharton, she answered, 'I don't like his books. He started all that nonsense about style.'[30] Undiscouraged, Hartley saw Hawthorne as 'the biggest influence on my mind and general attitude towards reality'.[31]

There was so much about him that Hartley admired: he thought no writer had ever written better prose. He was enthralled by the way in which Hawthorne (like Poe) saw reality as different from our daily experience of it; he was captivated by Hawthorne's thought that human nature must be good, when Hawthorne was convinced in his heart that it was evil. He recognised Hawthorne's preoccupation with 'the magnetic chain of humanity' and the consequences of trying to break away from it. In such pieces as 'Endicott and the Red Cross' Hawthorne delineated the guilt, or guilty secret, that leads to separation from the mainstream of life, a breaking of that chain of humanity. Hartley looked to Hawthorne for an understanding of sin, coming to terms with the theory that sin is regenerative of the power of life. How concerned Hartley was, all his days, with the question that Hawthorne posed in his novel *The Marble Faun*:

Is sin, then, which we deem such a dreadful blackness in the universe, is it like sorrow, merely an element of human education through which we struggle to a higher and purer state than we could have otherwise attained? Did Adam fall that we might ultimately rise to a far loftier paradise than his?[32]

As for James, how tempting it is for us to imagine Hartley mirror-gazing as he writes:

James was not the only novelist whose life was given to his art and who seems to have had no important emotional experience outside it ... There is no doubt that he regarded art as a substitute for life.[33]

And isn't Hartley again writing of himself, as much as of James, here?

He was a slave to standards, and not only to artistic but to moral and even to conventional standards ... He accepted conventions, and conventional opinion, as an index and criterion of morality. This is most important, because if he was an artist first, he was a moralist second – indeed it would not be fanciful to say that his art was an aspect of his moral sense – so closely was it bound up with his feeling of obligation. In all his stories there is, if not a moral theme, a continual reference to moral judgement.[34]

It may have been the solid foundation of unhappiness that lies at the soul of Hawthorne, James and Brontë that Hartley found irresistible; they set him the example that showed he could channel his own feelings into fiction. They presented a painful vision, and, complex as this vision was, it was in childhood that Hartley first glimpsed it. So many of his ideas, the philosophy and standards that were to influence him throughout life, were formed now. As time went by, nothing arrived to upset or challenge these influences.

If Harrow gave Hartley the opportunity to explore and consolidate his literary preferences, it was also effecting other changes in his life; one wonders to what extent Bessie was aware of them. What did she make of his essay, written in the early thirties, in which he recalled a very positive shift away from the protectiveness of Fletton?

Insomnia: I had suffered from it before I went to Harrow, and after; but during my time there I could not recollect one sleepless night. Then as to nervous apprehension, it was certain that of late years I had grown increasingly timid: I was afraid of thunderstorms, of meeting cows in the road, of driving a motor car. When I scratched myself I envisaged the possibility of lockjaw, and I never had a cold that I did not think would turn to pneumonia. The idea of saying a few words in public disturbed me for days. But when I was at Harrow, I remembered, these things afflicted me much less. I played football in the rain without ever expecting trouble to come of it. Once when I was knocked down (the Harrow game can be fairly rough, as anyone who has played it will testify) I bit the end of my tongue and had two stitches put in it: but I was not at all dismayed; I felt a hero and even got one or two friends to treat me as such.[35]

To be the hero seemed to Hartley the romantic ideal, something to which he perhaps should not, but longed to, aspire. Success, or even a reasonable stab, at sport offered a passport of sorts. And always, the need to please, to do the right thing, to take the attitude that would be socially and morally acceptable. Eustace Cherrington shares Hartley's need to be the acceptable social figure, the observer of the social nicety, the pleasant and pliable friend waiting in the wings of other people's lives. With Hartley, this need became an almost crippling disease. It is, of course, Hartley's experience that becomes Eustace's philosophy, recognised by Minney in *The Shrimp and the Anemone*:

> 'I always tell people you'll get on in the world, Eustace. You say such nice things to people.'
> 'Dear Minney!'
> It was delicious to be praised. A sense of luxury invaded Eustace's heart. Get on in the world . . . say nice things to people . . . he would remember that.[36]

As the years passed, that sense of luxury that followed from Hartley's ability to please others paled. He increasingly must have felt unable to turn his true face to the world, to step into that 'secret river' that his lifelong friend Clifford Kitchin once wrote of. If there was to be a place for him, Hartley felt it was as this paragon of propriety and conventionality, willing to change his 'never-minds' if that was considered the right thing to do, if it would avoid bringing pain to Bessie.

His closeness to Harry and Bessie would never be in doubt. He enjoyed his father's visits to Harrow, sometimes meeting him for tea at the Hill Tea-House near the Vaughan Library, but attempts at independence kept breaking through. In an undated letter of 1912, Hartley protested against the idea of Harry coming down to fetch him home because 'I think I am almost old enough to travel by myself, and I don't think Daddy would particularly want to come in the capacity of a hot-water bottle.'[37] For Bessie, still in frail health by the summer of the next year, the separation of Leslie's life from her own was something she could not cope with. She was away from home, probably convalescing yet again, when she wrote to Harry in August 1912:

> My darling Daddie –
> It is so cold here this morning that I have been feeling very troubled remembering Enid and Leslie are wearing their *thinnest undergarments* – and oh darling the weather is *much* too cold for them. *Please* tell them to put on their medium ones at once – I am afraid they should get serious colds and be really ill – and it

worries me very much – I have been bothering over it ever since I woke at 5.30!!

I am sure they are too obedient and good children not to do it – when they know it is troubling me so. You just look for *yourself* at what they are now wearing I am sure you will say it isn't suitable – even if it *is* August. I am hurrying to get this off by the 8. post – so that you may get it soon, and I shall be *so* thankful when I know they have changed. It would be so nice if Leslie had lost his cold when I return – wouldn't it? And *be sure* have [*sic*] a fire dear in one of the rooms – it is too cold to sit without one.

I have had a fair night and feel better this morning – I may not write again as I want to save my strength – I can't tell you how I am longing for Saturday –

I have just got your card – I am sorry Leslie doesn't lose his cold – perhaps it would be wiser to postpone going to Postland till he does. I would rather lose some of the time with him and have him *well* I think dear they had *really* better stay where they are if his cold is at *all* on his chest. It is colder in Postland – and they run more risks of cold. Father and Annie [Norah] would understand – they must go later – It is serious sometimes when you get cold after measles –

Give them my fond love and tell them I am sure they will put on their warmer things – I cannot rest till I know they have –

Much love – to you all

Bessie

Shortly after this was written, Hartley began addressing Bessie in his letters as 'Dear Mazikin' and, later, as 'Dear Muz'. How many times must Bessie's heart have glowed to read, once more, her son's letter to his 'Dearest Muz'? How expectantly, every day, did she await the post? Until her death, they would correspond with one another at least three times a week.[38]

1914 began innocently enough for Hartley. There was the possibility that he might be accepted for Magdalen College at Oxford. He sometimes bicycled over to Finchley to see Aunt Kathleen. She came to visit him, discussed the reception of her novel *Oliver in Willowmere* (which had had good notices), took Hartley to the National Gallery and gave him a life of Jane Austen. In March, he was in the sanatorium with German measles, reading *Emma*, De Quincey's *Confessions of an English Opium Eater*, Anthony Hope's *Count Antonio*, Fanny Burney's *Diary* (another present from Kathleen), Hawthorne's

A Blithedale Romance, a novel by Justin McCarthy, and *Tess of the D'Urbevilles* – he thought Hardy 'extremely pessimistic'. A week later, chicken-pox was diagnosed, and Hartley was confined to bed for three weeks, no doubt leaving Bessie wondering if whooping cough, scarlet fever and mumps might follow. His ally of the sanatorium was a Nurse Tyrrell, who seems to have shared many of the qualities of Bubby, even playing piquet with him when her professional duties allowed. Hartley gave her a photograph of himself and wrote a sonnet for her (does it, one wonders, still exist somewhere, in some relative's attic?). Another recipient of Hartley's 'photo of my blushing, beautiful self'[39] was a Mr Lee, to whom he wrote a 'billet-doux'. Mr Lee replied at length, asking Hartley to stay with him and 'his friend Mr Mainwaring'. Bessie was consulted as to whether the visit, which 'does not fill me with great terror', should take place. No evidence exists as to whether Bessie approved or disapproved, or whether the visit ever went ahead. It may have been prevented by Hartley contracting mumps that summer.

On 3 August he pinned a notice to the door of his bedroom at Fletton: 'No Admittance, Mumps in Here!' The next day, Asquith's government declared war on Germany alongside Russia and France. A few weeks later, 1100 old Harrovians had enlisted. Almost everyone on leaving Harrow was commissioned and side-stepped into the mêlée. For the moment, Hartley signed up to the school corps, attached to a rifle regiment, where he learned to 'Carry Arms' and 'Trail Arms' and even enjoyed the compulsory rifle-range practice. Clumsy as his efforts were, they were not derided too harshly by his superiors, though Hartley's schooling had inured him to a certain amount of physical and verbal unpleasantness. He didn't enlist, 'because I didn't want to. I was utterly unbelligerent, and hated the idea of fighting, in however good a cause.'[40]

His family, alarmed that his health would not withstand the test, insisted that he was unfit for active service. All around him, young men joined up, carried away by the fag-end of patriotism left over by the Boer War. In his first debate at Harrow, Hartley's proposal that 'It is to England's advantage to employ colonial troops in the War, but that Germany is justified in using Dum Dum bullets against them' was lost by 17 votes to 16. Hilaire Belloc (whose 'Cautionary Tales' Hartley had taken to reciting) visited the school to give a morale-boosting talk. Preparing a paper on Nathaniel Hawthorne, playing the piano or football, planning a visit to Oxford to sit for a place, the war sometimes obtruded. Reading the lesson in chapel, he felt that if a handful of soldiers turned up for worship he would have to join the army out of shame. His perception of war was shifting. He had expected a recrudescence of the Boer War spirit, the happy knowledge that the soldiers were a sort of football team fighting on behalf of the people at home, and for a time such a feeling did prevail. The promise of war thrilled a country still ready to believe in the romanticism that had so often surrounded it. Lord Kitchener's appeal for 100,000 new recruits, promising that no physically fit male between nineteen and thirty would be turned away, had an eager response. The army published its intention that those enlisting would be discharged immediately after the cessation of hostilities, which, it blithely hinted, might last as little as three weeks.

The autumn of 1914 was made more tolerable when he was elected one of seven editors of the *Harrovian*, but the reality of the demands of war were never far away. In October he was at the Savoy Hotel in London where a friend was saying his farewell to his two enlisted brothers. That same month Lord Curzon visited Harrow to give his views of the war, though there is no record of Hartley having heard him speak. As the conflict gathered momentum across Europe, and the number of fatalities and wounded grew alarmingly, Hartley's academic success continued, culminating in December in his winning an exhibition to Balliol College, Oxford. In April 1915 the headmaster commented before the whole school on his achievements, and he was named Leaf Scholar. His Classics form report of that time, under 'English', describes him as 'Fond of literature: has read widely: writes excellent essays, humorous and tasteful'. A month later, the ocean liner *Lusitania* was sunk by German submarines; the fact that Americans were among the 1200 lost was one of the reasons the United States joined the war. On the Western Front, the Germans introduced poison-gas and chlorine as weapons of warfare. In February, Winston Churchill's hope that Allied forces would force their way through the Dardanelles and link with Russia became reality, even if a year later the effort had claimed 26,000 of the Commonwealth troops. Lord Kitchener, who had become war minister at the outbreak of the conflict, was in the last year of his life. His efforts to send as many men as possible to the heart of the terror had not let up.

Popular songwriters, the breed that had provided Hartley with his fond musical impressions of the Boer War, now obliged with ditties that encouraged the taking of the King's shilling; the first months of the conflict were littered with them. R. P. Weston's rhetorical lyric 'Where Are the Lads of the Village To-Night?' found its answer in singer George Lashwood's explanation that they were 'Gone to teach the Vulture, murder is not culture, That's where they are to-night!' Marie Lloyd's coarser contribution held out a promise of sexual favours that would follow signing-up, as, to a swinging tune, she sang the brilliantly vulgar 'Now you've got yer khaki on', while Paul Rubens paused from churning out his pretty musical comedies to pen the dreadful 'Your King and your Country', with its black-mailing refrain that incited young men to join the ranks. Glorifica-tion of the battlefield had long been a lucrative business for songwriters and performers. In an earlier age, Leo Dryden, 'The Kipling of the Halls', found popularity with such numbers as 'The Gallant Gordon Highlanders' and 'Bravo, Dublin Fusiliers'; Bessie Bonehill, one in a long line of male impersonators, had delivered a rousing salute to 'The old Tattered Flag'. Now, another lady *en travesti*, Vesta Tilley, earned a reputation on the halls as 'England's Greatest Recruiting Sergeant', with such offerings as 'The Army of Today's All Right'; Florrie Forde made a colossal hit of 'Pack up your Troubles in your old Kit-Bag', with its persistent advice to smile, smile, smile. Arthur Wimperis' lyric for 'I'll make a Man of You' emphasised the manliness of enlisting. Even the bottom-of-the-bill soubrette Belle Elmore, remembered today as the doomed wife of Dr Hawley Harvey Crippen, squeezed into trousers and tunic and strutted about, as coquettishly as she could manage, as a soldier. War recognised the potency of cheap music long before Noël Coward did so. The resonance of such feminine entreaties, no matter how crass, proved irresistible to thousands of young men, before the public mood turned from the pastoral gentleness of Rupert Brooke to the harsher observations of Siegfried Sassoon and Wilfred Owen. As the months progressed, the flag-waving and exhortations of the women and mothers of Britain to say 'Go!' dimmed. The smell of khaki gave way to the stench of the Somme, of Ypres, of Passchendaele.

Against this background of jingoism and despair Hartley arrived at Balliol in October 1915, but it was a false start. He thought it 'really a very strange place, and the people are even stranger ... a number of black men of various nationalities, all very clever, I believe, but still, black'.[41] There were some forty undergraduates at Balliol, almost all of them suffering from some sort of physical disability that prevented their being called up or enlisting. Aldous Huxley, disabled by a disease of the eye which made him almost blind, had rooms just across the staircase from Hartley, and often asked him to his room for cocoa. Hartley was enormously struck by his new friend 'for I had never seen anyone at all like him – nor have I since. His height, his beautiful clothes, his noble white brow crowned with a thatch of unruly black hair, his mysterious, rather glamorous eyes ... It was as though culture had found a mortal envelope worthy of itself.'[42] It was not only Huxley's intelligence that so impressed Hartley, but his individuality; Hartley knew he was among swans. When they were down, Huxley wasted no time in taking him to Soho, introducing him to zabaglione (which he liked), snails (which he disliked) and a first taste of *vin rosé*.

There was no pleasure to be had from attempted profligacy, however; the climate that young men not at the war had to live in made sure of that. There were always those ready to pour scorn on Hartley's protestations of ill-health. Was it good enough that while others marched off to who knew what he could scull and catch crabs, attend concerts, sit through four lectures a week and read novels? Aunt Kathleen tactfully suggested it might be better if he kept away from dances, in case soldiers in uniform were present. The question as to what he should do needed answering. There was the possibility of volunteering for munitions work, and the threat of conscription. Hartley feared that his career was on the verge of ruin, and that others would think him a shirker.

Rumours circulated that the whole of the university might be closed down after Christmas 1915. Hartley was inclined to take a commission at the end of term rather than stay on in a depleted Oxford, an Oxford that was not itself, until June. This option was made even more attractive by the fact that if he left at Easter he would automatically be deemed to have passed his Divvers and Previous examinations. He was behind with his work for both, and by no means certain that he would be successful if he sat them. Meanwhile, he had not joined the corps attached to the college, as his doing so would have put him in line for the army; later, he was relieved to discover that nobody over twenty was eligible for the corps.

If the army beckoned, there was still the difficulty that a new rule had made it impossible for anyone to gain a commission without working their way through the ranks. There was a possibility that he might apply for one of the Home Defence battalions, but these were mostly cavalry, and 'I should not care to be let in for prancing about on a great horse.'[43] Behind these doubts, of course, was always the feeling that his destiny had been altered, his future snatched from him. 'The government seems to be laying hands on everyone it can see ... as Coxe was saying last night, "Why need it be so interfering?"

It all comes of people like Hobbes and A. L. Smith with their preposterous theories of obedience and sovereignty.'[44]

Letters discussing his plight flew back and forth across the family. One of the most forceful must have been one written to Kathleen on 10 october 1915, though by which of the family we cannot be sure, as only a lengthy and unsigned fragment has survived. What comes across most strongly is the passionate belief in Hartley's qualities that the family felt, and this passion is brought to bear in no uncertain way on Kathleen herself:

> We are very much concerned about Leslie, and would all urge that he does *not* sacrifice his education and his future to enlist or to make munitions of war. I can understand how he feels. No boy or man likes to hold back or be thought a coward. But it takes far more courage to be misjudged than to enlist. And Leslie can serve his country far, *far* better by going on to Oxford than by enlisting or doing those other things. England is going to need just such men as Leslie presently – men with gifts such as his. It is not the duty of *all* men to die for their country; certainly not until the last extremity. Which God grant may not come. No; let him do the bravest thing, conquer himself and his fear of being misjudged – even his fear of misjudging *himself*. Let him not under-value his gifts, which are God-given, and which he can only bestow by *living* for his country and by their fullest development ... To sacrifice his education would be to throw himself away; whereas he might remain to help and comfort and bind up his countries [*sic*] mental wounds when the time comes. He will be needed by his country far more later than now. We all feel this way about it. *Do your best to persuade him.*[45]

There was never a question that Kathleen would fail Hartley, inspired as she was by her 'anxiety for the fine edge of you, my dear. I couldn't bear it to be ever so little blunted. But it won't be, whatever happens.'[46] She could not recommend munitions, fearful that he might 'do something dreadful' to himself, but begged him to consider voluntary war-work before conscription made it seem that he was unwilling to offer himself for anything. She tried to persuade him to write home that he was prepared to undertake some sort of duties:

> This war can't last *very* much longer, but I do still think, when it is over, your satisfaction with life altogether will be more settled if you have turned aside and put your hand to the wheel in some

form or other. I think that you will then go back to your own work invigorated probably, whereas, under present conditions there is fear of your mind drifting in spite of you and perhaps never afterwards doing quite the best it could have done.[47]

Oxford offered no balm to Hartley, but how could it at such a time? His blood boiled when his tutor, A. L. Smith, whom Hartley found insufferably rude, gave a series of lectures 'From Hobbes to Maine', in which he argued that the state, as an embodiment of the community, could make the individual dance to any tune, however unjust its demands. Had not the doctrines of Hobbes, Maine, Rousseau, Bosanquet, Locke, created a belief in the omnipotence of the state that had made the conditions for war possible? Hartley clung to the beliefs of John Stuart Mill, of Herbert Spencer. Many years later he wrote:

> The laws of God depend upon faith; the laws of the State depend on fact: in the material and to some extent in the moral sphere, the State can make you do what it likes, whereas God cannot; the State has usurped the Kingdom, the power and the glory. The individual has been devalued.[48]

It is a cry he would send up until his death. The frustration that Hartley felt was exacerbated by the demands made of him by the fact of war, and the fact that he had been unable to answer them adequately. By February 1916, he was asking if Harry would come to Oxford to talk things over with him, but it seemed inevitable now that he would have to offer himself up for service, despite any remaining doubts. 'If you and Daddy think it much wiser that I should stay on', he wrote to Bessie, 'my inclination to join the army is not very strong, though it, the Army that is, does not appear quite so formidable as it did.'[49] Between leaving Balliol and enlisting, Hartley took for a few weeks an unlikely job in the office of Perfect and Co., suppliers of meat to the Army. He was amused by the staff answering telephone calls and announcing themselves as 'Perfect', a sport he could not join because he had a horror of speaking on the telephone that took him many years to overcome.

In April, Hartley enlisted 'as a gunner in a regiment called the Royal Garrison Artillery';[50] a great friend of the Hartleys, the artist Harry Clifford Pilsbury, painted a portrait of him in his khaki.[51] Bessie's intervention may have been responsible for the medical certificates Hartley waved at the authorities. At Cooden Camp, Bexhill, he waited to see if doctors would press him into active service, but hoped to persuade them to let him spend the war doing farm-work at Alwalton. He became expert at making 'puffs', little piles of gunpowder built on molehills and crowned with cordite which, when lit, sent up beautiful flares. In August he was moved to a camp at Shoreham, before being transferred to an infantry regiment at Catterick Bridge in north Yorkshire where a talent for ballistics (Hartley had none) was not required. On the way there, he saw a headline from the then popular journal *John Bull* that asked, 'Why so many suicides at Catterick?' The camp seemed enormous, with its own railway, 'The Catterick Bridge Express'. The weather that winter was bitterly cold. Each hut (housing thirty men) was heated by one central stove, but beyond it the temperature was almost freezing; it was the nearest to privation Hartley ever came.

But he was not unhappy here. He found fulfilment as the camp's postman, delivering letters and parcels at Christmas. He, who longed for the act of hospitality, had never felt so popular or wanted as he did now. He was looked for with eagerness as he approached the lighted huts on those winter days. Outside, it seemed to him to be always dark, until the door of the hut opened and the men cheered and laughed to see him, the postman, the bringer of messages, the go-between. What they offered him was an unqualified welcome, wholehearted approval; a meeting without censure. It was a short-lived enchantment. When he received a summons to attend an officers' training corps at Sidney Sussex College, Cambridge, the corporal in charge of his hut at Catterick touched him by saying, 'We always thought you were a gentleman.'[52] The conditions at Cambridge were tolerable; only four men to a room, and the tuition of a kind-hearted sergeant-major who pointed out what Hartley well knew, that he could not keep in step. Luckily, he was never called on to drill any men (nerves made him feel incapable of doing so) but studied the infantry regulations and learned, to some extent, how to *behave* like an officer. Then, 'having passed, or avoided, various tests I became Second-Lieut. Hartley, only fit for Home Service, which, in my case, meant defending the coast of East Anglia against possible German invasion.'[53]

Along with other officers, he was given VIP treatment at the Meeanee Barracks at Colchester with the 30th (City of London) Battalion London Regiment. There was practically nothing to do all day; he read, played billiards, snooker, Russian pool. Identified as having been in contact with an infectious disease, he was sent in March 1917 to an isolation hospital at Middlewich where the cold was so severe that his chilblained hands blew up to twice their normal size. At the Subraon Barracks in April he impressed his commanding officers with soldierly knowledge which he had picked up, or swotted up on, from others. He was given charge of a Roman Catholic priest who had outstayed his leave and was awaiting a court-martial. Hartley must have made the most sympathetic of gaolers; more than once the priest tried to persuade him to convert to the Roman church. Eventually, Hartley was moved out of the Colchester barracks and billeted in the town at 55 Crouch Street. That Christmas he wrote to Harry:

It isn't opinions or even beliefs that take harm from the war's interference, as long as it merely changes and does not destroy them: there is as much satisfaction in holding one opinion as another and there is even a pleasure in convincing yourself that you hold a new belief. But in the dimmer regions of small desires and aspirations, of unconscious expectations and personal points of view, there the war does make havoc, for it changes you and everything so that when they rise up you can't realise them properly, and when you can realise them, a 'tertium quid' steps in to deny them satisfaction, with the result you are constantly worried by a lack of something, and naturally can't put your finger on it, for it has become part of life.[54]

In February, he was at Walton-on-the-Naze, which offered a change of scenery but little more in the way of military employment. Walton was scarcely a bustling community – he even had to go into Colchester to find a barber's shop. Dame Clara Butt and Lady Beerbohm Tree arrived, alleviating the boredom by giving a concert. But Hartley found a new role in his new home, several roles, and not too likely sounding – as battalion education officer and battalion sports officer. It was turning out a peaceful war, and continued peacefully until an attack of bronchopneumonia put him in the Third London General Hospital for two months, where the doctors considered his lungs and heart to be in a poor way. He went before a Medical Board which recommended a month's special leave, during which he would have medical attendance, and after which he must return to face another Board. With Bessie, he decamped to the Glebe Hotel at Hunstanton, making the most of the glorious summer weather and, as he recovered, playing tennis and bathing.

At his next Board examination, a friendly orderly in the waiting-room advised him to drink some black coffee to 'play his heart up', but there was no time before he was called to face his inquisitors, presided over by the benign, elderly Sir Frederick Treves,[55] who had once removed Edward VII's appendix. The very kindliness of the Board made Hartley feel an object of pity. Eventually, having struggled through the duration of most of the war, he heard Treves' welcome verdict: 'My poor boy, you have done your utmost for King and Country.' What did it matter that Hartley knew this was not true? It was enough that the unhappiness he had endured was over. He was invalided out of the army in September 1918, a month after Haig launched the battle of Amiens, a campaign that was to mark the turning point of the war, and the sureness of the Allied conquest. Bessie's sense of relief at her son's emancipation must have spilled over into joy. She wasted no time in responding to the Board's recommendation that he should spend a year recuperating at some healthy resort. She arranged rooms in lodgings at Mundesley on the north Norfolk coast. They had hardly settled in when all around them the villagers began dying from the Spanish influenza that was ravaging the country: worldwide, the pandemic caused the death of some 20 million. Bessie's apprehensions must have been fearful as the coffins piled up and visitors stayed away, but the danger diminished, and a revival of normality began.

Hartley always blamed the war for lifting a curtain on his 'hideous century'. In the years that followed, the effect on the *status quo*, as the growth of material prosperity filtered into the lives of the middle and working classes, alarmed him. He considered that such new-found delight in wealth and ownership had turned the English from one of the most honest races into one of the most dishonest. His belief in his fellow man was corroded in the aftermath of war. There was a loss of confidence in human nature, the knowledge that another man would do him down if he could. And always, Hartley traced such changes back to 1914, when the State had asserted its powers so irresistibly, and made way for a moral deterioration, denying that belief in the essential goodness of humanity that had underpinned the Edwardian summers. His simplistic adieu to the war was that a terrible lesson had been learned, that war could never again wear the same face. It occurred to him that, before 1914, pessimists such as Hardy and Schopenhauer, in taking so gloomy a view of humanity, had put the blame on Fate. With one blow, Man and the State had made sure that Fate need no longer bear so heavy a responsibility. The Great War had claimed some 10 million lives, and some 20 million wounded.

But Hartley's involvement with the world's horror was never passionate. Of course he felt the pity of it, the senseless lost argument, but the terrors of the war had for him been only a distant threat, an interruption of style and purpose, after which he seemed to pick up the old life much as he had left it four years before. Once he was out of the army, the war, never close, receded even further from him; he and Bessie barely noticed the signing of the Armistice. It was not that his own role in the war left him with a consciousness that he had somehow stood to one side; he seemed to accept the inevitability of what had happened to him. And yet it must have left him with feelings that were difficult and confusing. The loss of young men, boys almost, seemed beyond reckoning. Clifford Kitchin, serving in France as a lieutenant with the 8th Royal Warwickshire Regiment, had been wounded in January 1917. His brother, John, aged nineteen, was killed in action in 1918. Perhaps it was inevitable that, caught in the web of conflicting emotion Hartley must have felt, and faced by the deaths of so many young men, many as gifted as he was and all of them gifted at least with hope for a future, he should become even more obsessed with his own place in the world the war had left behind. At the end of 1917 he had written to Harry:

> ... in normal times the Past stands by you, a kind of harmonising bckground that justifies what you are; but when the majority of the people have lost the 'Sense of the Past' how is one to rediscover oneself both to oneself and other people? ... The difficulty is that one cannot gaze into the pool of the past and see one's reflection tranquil there: the spirit of the Present sweeps across and troubles the waters.[56]

This need to 'rediscover oneself both to oneself and to other people' was something that Hartley saw as central to a successful existence. Its achievement was to prove elusive, the more so because he had allowed the pressures of Bessie and the family to work on him. Fighting shy of the pacifism that was central to his father's conviction, he wriggled free of any decision. Bessie's influence made the most of his pliability. Kathleen's had been the voice of reason, resisting the family's demands that she keep Hartley out of the war. She knew that the lack of any action on his part could only lead to that 'fear of your mind drifting in spite of you and perhaps never afterwards doing quite the best it could have done'.[57] She knew him as a writer, understood the process of writing that must be faced (in 1916 her novel *The Pupil of a Little Monk* appeared and, her final book, *In and Out of the Wood*, in 1919).[58] But Kathleen could not work her magic with him. In turning away from her advice, Hartley set an alarming precedent for never being his own person; it marked out his place in life, on the edge of it. And though in later life he would often speak of the Great War, and the State having laid claim to young lives, he perhaps lacked the resource of anything approaching outrage or pity at the death of men. Turning the pages of Kathleen's letters, feeling again her urgent best wish that his action, or lack of it, should not wear away the 'fine edge' of him, we know that we are in the presence of an accurate prophet.[59]

A Place at the Fireside

THE TWELVE MONTHS following Hartley's retirement from army life were his lost year. Although we do not have exact dates, it seems that the exile to Mundesley was protracted; in November 1918 Enid was sending off from Fletton a consignment of eggs, jam and a hamper, as well as a batch of Leslie's vests and socks. In the New Year Hartley, Kathleen, Bessie and probably other members of the family stayed in rooms at West Hill Road in Bournemouth. It was with Aunt Kathleen that he went to see George Robey perform, presumably at a music hall, both of them laughing at Robey's vulgar jokes, which Hartley made a point of remembering so that he might relate them to his uncles. The West Hill Road household included two sisters who delighted at having a twenty-two year old and an ex-soldier at their mercy. They tried out all kinds of practical jokes on him, sending him forged letters, as if from the proprietress, complaining about his piano-playing late at night; wrapping up an artichoke to look as if it had been sent through the post to him; sewing up his pyjamas. Escaping their pranks, Hartley's Grand Tour of recuperation continued. The following summer he was holidaying with Kathleen and Uncle George in Shropshire, rowing on the river Severn, visiting Ludlow, climbing in the Malverns. On the night of the Peace celebrations, they formed part of a triumphal procession through the streets in their dress clothes; 'The people are much impressed', Hartley wrote.[1] Kathleen reassuringly told Bessie, 'The food is excellent – [Leslie] has milk for lunch and dinner every day and there is thick cream on it always.'[2]

But Bessie must have been beside herself with worry when Hartley returned to Oxford in October: he had hardly arrived before she was making arrangements to visit him. Emerging from the tight family circle that had surrounded him in convalescence into a second phase of university life cannot have been easy; it was a violent change of environment, even if there was a sense that his life at Oxford had only endured an interruption. Ostensibly, Hartley was there to read Modern History under his supervising or 'moral' tutor, H. W. C.

Davis (called 'Fluffy' because of his hair, not his character, which was rigid and uncompromising). Hartley, while fascinated by the characters of the Balliol dons, mostly found them unfriendly and unsympathetic; that immediate sense of approval so necessary to him was not always forthcoming. His other tutor, K. N. Bell, whom Hartley celebrated in verse, was no more of a favourite:

> The reason why I cannot tell
> But this I know, I know full well
> I do not like thee, Mr Bell[3]

It was not that Bell was an exacting taskmaster, and there were attempts on his part to make friendly overtures to Hartley, inviting him to an evening with his family at which he had to endure dumb charades, 'a great strain on my dignity'.[4]

Much more to Hartley's taste was the hospitality of Francis Fortescue Urquhart, a Balliol Fellow fondly known as 'Sligger'. Sligger was an easygoing, benevolent bachelor, strengthened by a devout Roman Catholicism and an interest in the emotional and intellectual development of undergraduates; in his hands, tutorship developed into paternal friendship. Around half-past ten in the evening his rooms at Balliol, overlooking the Protestant Martyrs' Memorial, would fill up with students ready to discuss or gossip. Hartley was ready to luxuriate in such a haven, which remained open until the early hours of the morning. Friendship, the pleasure of company, of good talk, all were made possible by Sligger, presiding over 'an atmosphere of natural and easy enjoyment'[5] – that ideal atmosphere of comfort that was to provide Hartley with a model for life.

Beyond Sligger, the opinions of Hartley's Balliol masters were to a great extent irrelevant to him, for almost as soon as he returned to Oxford one thing became clear: he was going to be a writer. With a sense of wonder, he began to meet other writers, to call them his friends. Aldous Huxley had rooms very close to Hartley and 'to my great amazement he stalked in, peering to left and right in a most sinister fashion'.[6] It may have been Huxley who suggested he should contribute something to the *Oxford Outlook*, the university's literary periodical financed by the Independent Liberals. Another friend thought a piece Hartley had written, 'Conscription in Heaven', might do, but Hartley had his doubts, worried that 'the pacifist views therein maintained (though I still hold them) would probably fall rather flat. Nor should I particularly wish to subscribe my name to them and I think all contributions must be signed.'

Now, of course, Oxford offered a sense of freedom and opportunity that Hartley had never known before. He luxuriated in the brilliance of his fellow students, moving from one intercollege society to another, relishing in the talk, the rush of ideas. Like those that Eustace Cherrington thrilled to at Oxford, these groups of young men had 'a Ninety-ish air, unashamedly aesthetic. Mushroom growths for the most part, they had their moment of glory. Their members sported striped silk ties, impossible to mistake for an old school tie, so friendly were the colours to each other.'[7] And, like Eustace, Hartley found that the friends he made at Oxford 'tended to be well off'.[8] At a meeting of the Brackenbury Society (a college society founded in 1877 and made up of 'a most select circle')[9] he sipped mulled claret and ate bananas, throwing their skins into the fireplace as the debate that 'we are heavy and stupid and dull and growing heavier and stupider and worse' raged on.[10] Compared to Fletton, his life at Balliol was turning out to be a modest Saturnalia. As a member of another society, the Pagans, he took part in dramatic productions and contributed quotations from Sir Thomas Browne and the Elizabethans. At one of their meetings he read his paper 'Some Aspects of Gregariousness', revived forty-seven years later for *The Novelist's Responsibility*, in which the stored hatred of the system that had so altered the fate of his generation poured from him:

> Those who believe in the essential gregariousness of the human race, or those again who put forward the view, so useful to the apologists of government, that man is inconceivable apart from his fellows, that he reaches his highest development through association with them, seem to ignore or to deny the fundamental separateness of individuals ... We are most truly ourselves when caught in the eddy of some common emotion, when identifying ourselves with that beautiful mirage, the General Will – that prophet, in whose infallibility, provided he is dumb, we are bound to believe, though every word he speaks is admittedly a lie, discrediting him and betraying us. Even Mill and the champions of individual liberty take up a defensive position, contending that except in cases where a man's action is likely to injure the liberty of others, he 'ought' to be allowed to enjoy his freedom and rule his life on lines prescribed by himself. Such an attitude regards the fundamental irreconcilability of men as an end to be attained, rather than a fact to be faced.[11]

As President of the Pagans Hartley also had the 'dreadful' task of introducing and thanking Siegfried Sassoon, an affair that 'went off fairly well – though Sassoon himself gave a rather incoherent address. He is a poet, of sorts.'[12]

It was in the Hilary Term, one day in 1919, that Hartley first met Lord David Cecil walking along the High:

> Probably we had met before, but, although I did not know him, or he me, we recognised in each other what I like to think was a kindred spirit and a friendship began ... There were many others who had just come to Oxford as ardent as he was. There were his relations and friends on whom the war had left its mark of horror and sadness, but not the indelible bruise of actual experience from which (for instance) Siegfried Sassoon, Osbert Sitwell, and Edmund Blunden suffered. The new-comers – Eddy Sackville-West, Anthony Asquith, and how many others – only knew the war as a disappearing shadow. They helped to form a circle into which I, though much their senior, found a place.[13]

The fourth child and younger son of the fourth Marquis of Salisbury, Lord Edward Christian David Gascoyne Cecil was lean, tall, willowy, with a long face, long fingers and long mouth. A studio portrait of him at this time shows a Byronesque figure, the collar of his greatcoat turned up, the attractive face half in shadow under a large hat, the eyes intelligent, an almost finished cigarette resting between fingers that seem to go on for ever. It is an image that must have appealed to Hartley, for whom the photographer's art could not work such miracles; his portraits of the same period are unimaginative and dull, they stare directly at his stolid frame, the eyes restful and acquiescent behind pince-nez, their subject clearly unhappy at being in the photographer's grasp.

But Cecil had much in common with Hartley. He had been a delicate child, very attached to his mother, and had suffered from tuberculosis. In later years, he always travelled with a thermometer. At Eton, he had felt himself too gentle and aesthetic to be fully accepted, and had only survived its rigours by spending one day of every week in bed. By the time he arrived at Christ Church, he had already developed a talent for brilliant talk, talk that was altogether more sympathetic than the often acerbic brand in fashion there. He spoke in a high voice, his words rattling out, falling over themselves in their eagerness to argue some fine point. He almost literally devoured books. Left alone in a room he would fall on them with such energy that they often fell apart in his hands, so passionate was his need and love of them. For Hartley 'David held a torch – not for war heroes, or anti-war heroes, but for people who led quiet lives, studious and sociable, into which the idea of violence never entered.'[14]

Hartley, left dissatisfied by his own part in the war, could find a ready comfort in Cecil's presence. He admired all that youthful urgency harnessed to intellectual argument, the passion for life that took its inspiration from literature. And what did Cecil find appealing in Hartley? If great bursts of verbal enthusiasm were expected of Cecil, Hartley was more likely to respond with a murmur. It may be that Hartley's sheer receptiveness, his ability to watch and listen and absorb, was precious to the younger man, a plateau on which his ideas could land and work themselves out. As precious was the sense of humour they shared. They laughed together, intense discussions erupting into jokey interruptions. We can imagine their meetings during those first months at Oxford, when word would go round that the two men were lunching together at the Gridiron Club and must on no account be disturbed, for they were perceived by their fellow students as a pair, a meeting of minds and attitudes and fun. Food was secondary (Cecil was never interested in it, and Hartley to the end of his days preferred rather nursery fare) to the talk by which they carried one another long. Cecil was refreshed by exercising his ideas on this older man who had gone through the war. For Hartley, Cecil was a creature from beyond the social divide he longed to cross, a creature in whom every element seemed to coalesce. Fifty years later Hartley recalled

> his appearance, slightly dandified, with a tie or a waistcoat that one doesn't quite expect; his hair which seems to move as rapidly and take on as many aspects as his mind, and his gestures, which are so much his own, fidgety but not irritable. His feet, rocking to and fro from his knees, might be thought to be kicking an imaginary football; the sudden outflung movement of his arms and hands, might be dismissive of something he has just said, or a spontaneous recognition of a truth that someone else has just said. His whole being, physical and mental, seems to act together, and represent the same thing.[15]

How could Hartley not help but be fascinated by a personality that seemed so successfully to have brought together its disparate qualities, a feat he knew to be quite beyond himself? He derived satisfaction from Cecil's reflected glory, and felt pride when Cecil's brilliance claimed the attention of some literary lion. In Cecil's company he could put behind him at least some of the feelings of inadequacy that pursued him, reminding him that, whatever he had been told, he had not done his utmost for King and Country. In Cecil's company he had found approval, and a bond of friendship was begun. It must have occurred to Hartley that all this might be the foundation of a life that could be shared, that one of Emily Brontë's 'hundred kinds of love' was flowering.

In September 1922 he was invited to stay with the Cecils at the Manor House, Cranborne, sleeping in King John's Room, taking irregular baths because his hosts were said to disapprove of them, and tied to the house because the woods roundabout were full of adders. Cecil and he played tennis every day in a court by the churchyard. He told Bessie, 'He is very nice and we discuss endlessly on matters of great moment.'[16] Hartley was twenty-six and Cecil nineteen, and for Hartley there was the possibility of enchantment in the air. Although transplanted into the heady atmosphere of the Cecil household (where Lord Salisbury, Cecil's father, surprised him by being so gentle and considerate), Hartley's upbringing did not easily allow of any emotional release. He may have imagined a relationship with Cecil of almost mythological proportions. The possessiveness of Bessie's love alarmed him, but others (including another Oxford student, Ralph Ricketts) detected a possessiveness about Hartley's fondness for Cecil – Bessie's inheritance, of course. That one example of its overpowering strength made Hartley hold back from participating in a fullness of life, in natural expression. Perhaps the most dangerous thing about love was to declare it.

By February 1920 Hartley was settled in rooms at 40 Beaumont Street, looked after by a forgetful landlady who had survived a delicate childhood by taking quantities of two-year-old beer and cod-liver oil. He was writing stories. Louis Golding, collecting an anthology of Oxford and Cambridge prose, expressed interest in one of them, 'Talent', though he found fault with what he called its 'psychological development'.[17] This piece, eventually included in Hartley's Night Fears, has the storyteller informing a writer friend that his work is of no value, that 'there were no seeds of development in it. Even if you had pursued it ... it wouldn't have lived, it wouldn't have lived.'[18] Grateful to learn the truth, the disappointed writer walks off into the darkness, but the narrator confesses that 'some lines from a poem of his (lines – the whole poem, perhaps! lying lifeless under the interdict of his red pencil) kept ringing in my head.'[19] How clearly here we can see a reflection of Hartley's doubts about the value, the quality, of his own work, the dubious potency of criticism, and how easily true talent may be snuffed out.

The following month Hartley was made a co-editor of the *Oxford Outlook* alongside Gerald Howard and A. B. B. Valentine, and began to commission work from such writers as Charles Morgan, L. A. G. Strong, Edmund Blunden, Louis Golding, John Strachey and C. M. Bowra. His own work started appearing in its pages: an essay on 'The Cat' and 'Night Fears' (which would give his first published collection its title), a moody piece about a night-watchman visited by some otherworldly figure who brings murder. It had its *frisson* though Hartley (and Harry, often asked for his opinion) regretted it did not have a better ending. 'Truly journalism is an unpleasant business', he complained.[20] Other stories followed, including 'A Portrait', 'A Summons' and 'A Condition of Release', and a brief dramatic pastiche, 'The Duke's Tragedy'. Soon, Hartley was also contributing reviews – of Clifford Kitchin's collection of poetry *Winged Victory*, of Aldous Huxley's *Crome Yellow*.

Bessie's pride in such achievement must have been tempered by concern at some of her son's antics, which he unblushingly reported to her. After a meeting of the Annandale Society,[21] an undergraduate dining club, the members (including Hartley) rioted for two hours in the Balliol quad, dancing in a ring and singing 'loud but not musical', 'Here we go round the Mulberry Bush'; a similar shindig by the Annandale in 1912 had resulted in several people being sent down. 'Afterwards', Hartley told Bessie, 'like a good boy I took my temperature: it was nearly a degree sub-normal, so I think that kind of thing must do one good by stealth.'[22] In fact his involvement with the Annandale was less taxing than he had expected: 'the members quarrel so bitterly among themselves that anything like concerted action – such as would be necessary to uproot a lamp-post – is quite out of the question.'

It was through Aldous Huxley that Hartley opened another door into the wonderland of that other class that had always intrigued him, for which the visit to the Moxeys, resplendent with that 'late dinner', had given him a taste. Huxley went to his rooms for tea on 6 June 1920, made complimentary noises about one of Hartley's stories, 'A Portrait', and told him that Ottoline Morrell had expressed an interest in meeting him. It was from Huxley that Hartley first heard her name, Huxley stressing the sound of it by insisting she was '*Ott*oline'. It was well-known that many undergraduates beat a path to her door, but Hartley was dismayed to be asked. He borrowed a push-bike (his own had a puncture) and, with Huxley, pedalled straight off to Garsington Manor, arriving late that afternoon. At this, the first of so many meetings with her, they talked together of Plotinus and Dean Inge, subjects close to Otto-line's heart, for she, like Plotinus, might be said to have given her life over to converting her disciples to the highest intellectual and spiritual plains (and Inge's Gifford Lectures of 1918 had revived interest in Plotinus' theories).

Ottoline appeared almost as a vision to Hartley; he was dumb-struck by her eccentricity, her graciousness, her receptiveness and knowledge. 'She was stupendous', he told Bessie.[23] She had on a flowered black satin upper garment over a skirt of peacock blue, white stockings and red morocco shoes, cross-gartered. Hartley thought her reddish hair a wig, and noted that her face was free from the inch of powder he had heard described. He thought the face designed to show the ravages of time and her voice indescriba-ble, something between whining and singing. There was also her husband, 'The unfortunate Mr [Philip] Morrell, alliance with whom she is said publicly to deplore on the ground that he was beneath her, was quite affable and I thought intelligent – she tolerated his remarks, if not with enthusiasm, yet without disdain. Before leaving I wrote my name in a book provided for that purpose and murmured how glad I should be to come again. Though only there for a short time I outstayed my welcome and detained the party from dinner or at any rate from dressing for it.'[24]

Hartley had begun what he called his 'Social Offensive'. The insecurity he felt at being welcomed in such privileged circles is obvious in the pushy suggestion that he would like to be asked again, the feeling that his time with Ottoline had run dry. She, too, felt this nervous eagerness, perhaps mystifying to one who had never had to earn a place at the fireside. She noted that this young man always put himself forward when there was the opportunity to meet anybody influential at Garsington. Hartley knew himself to be the outsider, knew that his place, elusive and alluring, would have to be won as it could not be inherited. Ottoline, twenty-two years his senior, assumed such importance in his life not only because she was the first literary chatelaine who opened her arms to him but because she almost certainly became a mother-figure to him, lacking both the control exercised through adoration and the precaution of Bessie. Ottoline brought into Hartley's life an exoticism, otherworldliness and grandeur that was irresistible to him; the pricelessness of it was accentuated by the fact that such friendship could be dipped into, picked up and set aside, without the loss of feeling on either side. The commitment was understood but hardly ever challenged.

Events were now moving with a rapidity that must have startled

Bessie. A month after his first meeting with Ottoline, Hartley was invited by Sligger to travel with a 'reading party' of undergraduates to his chalet – the Chalet des Mélèzes – at St Gervais les Bains, close to Mont Blanc in the Haute Savoie. Sligger had begun the annual expeditions to his summer home in the French Alps in 1891, establishing a tradition that continues to this day, when parties of undergraduates still visit the chalet. Here, Hartley climbed mountains and walked up to 12 miles a day, telling Bessie that 'this place seems to do my chest and catarrh a great deal of good'.[25] The expedition probably qualifies as Hartley's greatest physical adventure, though his natural caution sometimes held him back. When the party discovered a fine waterfall at a gorge crossed by a bridge, constructed from fir stems, 80 feet above the chasm, Hartley waited and watched as his bolder colleagues strode across. Sligger and company played golf on a mountain-top while Hartley and Gerald Howard stayed behind to entertain the Eton master 'Tuppy' Headlam, and 'a super-Etonian guardsman, one Victor Cunard – connected with the liners, I suppose'.[26]

The weather was stormy, by turn hot and bitterly cold, making Hartley grateful for Bessie's insistence that he pack a great many warm clothes. Her own love of dramatic landscape may explain her apparent willingness to let him embark on so potentially dangerous an escapade, only a matter of months after he had been cosseted against all ills for the best part of a year. There was more than a hint of an outward-bound sense of fun about it all. Although he complained of missing his bathing, Hartley explained that Sligger had fixed up a shower with a length of pipe and the nozzle of a watering-can. On 24 July he was scrambling about with the others on top of a glacier, remarking that '*never* have I seen anything to compare in ugliness with the lower portions of a glacier'.[27] Gerald Howard's enthusiasm for scaling Mont Blanc was successfully deflated, for 'the snow blinds you, the sun scorches your face so that, though you grease it never so thickly and often, the skin comes off and a yellowish-pus exudes, mountain sickness attacks you and you bleed profusely at nose, mouth and ears.'[28]

The adventure was not ended, however. Two days later, Hartley told Bessie he had 'made a nearer acquaintance with mountains and can confidently declare they are a delusion and a snare'.[29] Howard and he had started off before lunch, calling into the village where Hartley had his shoes nailed, to join the rest of the party at les Contamines, five miles up the valley. From here, they climbed to the Hôtel de Tré-la-Tête and ate an enormous supper before going to bed. They woke at 3.30 the following morning and half an hour later, accompanied by a guide and porter, began the ascent of the Tré-la-Tête glacier to the last point of the Mont Blanc range, Mont Tondu, standing at over 10,000 feet. Hartley was understandably unhappy hopping over the slippery, deep crevasses; once these were left behind, the party was roped together and eventually reached the Col de Tondu. Here, the guide informed them it would take another three hours to reach the summit, still some 500 feet above them. Visibility was so poor, and the cold so biting, that after a hearty meal the attempt to climb the pinnacle was abandoned. In fact, the downward journey proved as tricky as the climb. At one point one of the roped party slipped, bringing down Sligger, who 'shot off like a comet', and the man ahead of Hartley, who somehow managed to keep his footing and looked on amused at his friends spread-eagled in the snow.[30] The guide made footsteps for them to follow in, and for a time things improved (they even tobogganed on their bottoms for a considerable distance) until the guide lost his way and they had to negotiate great crevasses at high speed before reaching the sanctuary of the Hôtel de Tré-la-Tête at midnight, where their clothes were taken from them and dried. There were, he assured Bessie, no evil results from this misadventure:

> I paint it somewhat black as a set-off against your faith in mountains and all that pertains thereto. I was a beautiful sight in my shoes, white tennis socks lent by Gerald (my thick ones being in the wash). I acknowledge that you were quite right about the boots, and they must certainly be taken to the Lakes.[31]

In England, the doors to society were opening wider. In July 1921 Clifford Kitchin, whose career at Exeter College, Oxford, had, like Hartley's, been interrupted by the war, took him to weekend with the Asquiths at the Wharf, Sutton Courtney, in Berkshire. The one-time Liberal Prime Minister, Herbert Henry Asquith, was some-times a guest at Kitchin's house at Boar's Hill, Oxford, and it was here that Kitchin first invited Hartley to meet and play cards with him. Concerned that Kitchin's bridge was so good, that Asquith's would almost certainly be better than his own, and that the stakes might be too high, Hartley asked that the invitation might not involve any games. It is possible that Asquith and Hartley had already met by the time of the first visit to the Wharf through Hartley's friendship with another of his Oxford colleagues, Anthony 'Puffin' Asquith, but acceptance at the Wharf was to confirm his position as a member of a society far beyond the dreams of anyone at Fletton.

The personalities that Hartley encountered at the Wharf presented a formidable challenge to any undergraduate. For his first game of tennis at the house his partner was Lady Cynthia Asquith, daughter of Lord Elcho, later the eleventh Earl of Wemyss; it was the inauspicious beginning of a lifelong friendship. She terrified him and was so disgusted with his playing (being nervous he could only serve underhand) that she complained of a pain in her big toe and marched off the court. But Cynthia and Hartley immediately warmed to one another. Of his very many female friends, she was certainly one of the most important.

It was not only her vitality and intellectual qualities that fascinated Hartley, but the feeling of sadness that surrounded her. She had married, in 1910, 'Beb' (Herbert) Asquith, the second son of the great man, but it was not a completely happy marriage, and much sadness lay ahead. The First World War had claimed two of her brothers, for whom she had an intense affection. The war over, she had to supplement Beb's income, when he returned from active service with his health impaired, by becoming private secretary to her friend, J. M. Barrie; in fact, she was Barrie's staff and support, running every aspect of his life, a task she fulfilled until his death. Writing brought in needed funds, but it was not as an author that she distinguished herself, rather it was as a loyal and trustworthy friend of many, D. H. Lawrence, Rex Whistler and Desmond MacCarthy among them; in friendship, the beauty of her personality flourished. There was, as well, a sharp sense of humour – not always evident in her writing – that sometimes lapsed into a fondness for severe practical joking. There was nothing grand about Cynthia's beneficence towards the men who made up her entourage, no suspicion of possessiveness, which alone must have made her an ideal ally for Hartley. Her outstanding qualification, and one that Hartley looked for as the essential, was the skill she applied to friendship, elevating it almost to an art.

But much of this first visit to the Wharf was a trial. Hartley loathed the supercilious manservants, and was alarmed at having to help himself to breakfast and lunch (never the middle-class way). Asquith was a rather uncommunicative host. Margot, his second wife, lived apart in a barn but made occasional appearances in the house. Agnes Murray, who, with her father Gilbert (Regius Professor of Greek at Oxford University), was another of the guests, persuaded Hartley and Beb to take her out in a boat one evening, and encouraged them to bathe in the nude (they did not). And there were discomforts at the Wharf. Hartley thought the whole place higgledy-piggledy, made up as it was of three cottages joined together, with its passages and tiny bedrooms – he had to do with a sloping couch – plagued with mosquitoes. None of this, of course, deterred him from returning again and again, for dinner and bridge or piquet; it was not only the social splendour, but the eccentricity, the bookish liveliness of the circle that drew him back.

Other friendships, besides that with Cynthia Asquith, blossomed during his first visits to the Wharf, notably with the voluble Elizabeth Bibesco, Asquith's daughter and, by marriage, a princess. Hartley found he was having conversations 'of extreme intimacy' with her when he spent the Easter of 1922 at the Wharf.[32] Two years younger than Hartley, Elizabeth wasted no time in fastening him to her, an aide to her energetic social life lived out under the shadow of her mother's powerful reputation. Elizabeth could be witty and pleasing, and had already published a collection of stories – *I Have Only Myself to Blame* – in 1921, but hers was a flawed personality despite her wealth of literary knowledge. Marie Belloc Lowndes, not renowned for viciousness, did not think her 'so very brilliant. She is not a patch on her mother ... She longs, one can see, to be married, and so start her own life.'[33] Another friend, Desmond MacCarthy, noted her almost total lack of social intelligence, fortified by liberal quantities of drink which made her garrulous and embarrassing, though there was never any maliciousness in her.

Descended from the Kings of Moldavia, Elizabeth's husband, Prince Antoine Bibesco, was a Romanian diplomat with literary leanings, a friend of Proust and a womaniser. Enid Bagnold, an earlier lover of Bibesco's, described him as 'gay (but dipped in melancholy)'. The melancholic strain in him was heightened when his beloved brother Emmanuel, who had long threatened suicide, poisoned and hanged himself in 1917. By this time Antoine and Elizabeth were lovers, and in 1919 married, consolidating a relationship that was not to be altogether happy, and to which Hartley became attached. By July 1922 he was enough part of the family circle to be asked to accompany Margot Asquith and Puffin to their home in Paris, where he acted as Lady Asquith's escort to the play, to the home of a countess, and of the Baron Pichon, who on being introduced to Hartley bowed three times. Hartley found Margot talkative, impatient and outspoken, qualities he might not have tolerated in someone of less social splendour.

If it was clear that he was being accepted in some of the leading families of the land, his professional future still seemed uncertain. What would happen after Oxford? There was the possibility that he might win a fellowship to All Souls, where Sir John Simon was looking for an applicant with a cultivated mind and sound general knowledge; Hartley felt that in being so long at Oxford he had lost both. The fellowship went elsewhere. Louis Golding showed some of Hartley's stories to Austin Harrison, the editor of the *English Review*. Bessie did her bit by speaking about her son's work to the Canadian humorist Stephen Leacock (Hartley hoped she had made a note of any jokes he made). Charles Morgan, now working for the publishing house of Black, remembered Hartley's stories from the *Oxford Outlook* and hoped he might soon have a completed manuscript that the firm might consider. Clifford Kitchin had already finished a novel (probably *Streamers Waving*, eventually published in 1925) but, like Hartley, was full of doubt about his own abilities. It was a doubt that neither Hartley or Kitchin, particularly in his later years, ever shook off. He might have been speaking for Hartley when he wrote: 'I feel convinced that nothing I write can ever appeal either to the gross but lucrative public, or to the select and jealous circles of literary critics. I shall always be a little out of touch . . . out of tune. When I pipe, they dance not. When I weep, they laugh.'[34]

Hartley found magnificent and unselfish understanding in Aunt Kathleen. In an undated letter of 1921 she wrote:

> Your father knows so much more than I do, and my inclinations, based on my own likes and dislikes, are so strongly towards literature if it could be combined with a good living, that I have felt I had better keep quiet. Whatever you may feel the best thing to do you will always realise, won't you? that I take the kindest, proudest delight in all your achievements. Nothing I ever could have done myself would have interested me so much, for the simple reason that I neither admire nor love myself (happily) as much as I do you. I could never tell you, my dear (what a sudden burst!) all you have meant to me these many years, the unspeakable something of immense worth that you have added to my life: and to your dear Uncle's, I know. Blest be you!! There. Your writing is not only immensely attractive to me, but I am certain *is* good, apart from my prejudice, and it *will* come out more or less (I mean according to the time you can give it) I haven't much doubt.[35]

This was unswerving encouragement. There is a sense, too, that this may have been the first time that Kathleen described her love of

Hartley to him (we cannot be sure as only a few of her letters were preserved). Her advice is warm and sensible; it shows a perfect understanding of the particular potential Hartley had. Later, she told him that though his writing might never be exactly popular, he would make money from it. She offered suggestions that clearly worked themselves into Hartley's future:

> ... if you start on literature, don't be tempted to rush at it – I can't think you would – as so many of these clever young men and women seem to do – as if they were afraid they might forget what they want to say or were very eager the world should acknowledge them – the intellectuals of the world! Give us something really fine, my dear – I long to see it, for I feel you can – But I would gladly *wait* to have it excellent.[36]

In fact, Hartley's ability to resolve the direction of his life was facing severe difficulties and now demanded solution. About this time he proposed marriage to a Joan Mews of Upper Portslade in Sussex. The fact itself is all we can know of what happened, anything that once held the evidence of that relationship being long lost. If his proposal was accepted, it seems to have been on the understanding that marriage would follow almost immediately. Hartley drew back. He felt constrained by a lack of confidence, the fact that he had no proper career, but possibly too in taking so drastic a step. Whether this was what brought on Hartley's nervous crisis in early 1922 is unknown – it clearly contributed to it – but he certainly suffered from some sort of breakdown during this period, for which he sought a medical diagnosis (the incident reappears in *Night Fears* as 'A Tonic'), and was still plagued with it three years later. On 11 April 1922 Kathleen wrote:

> About the other affair I don't know enough to say; only I do feel it would have been terrible if you had made a mistake the other way about, and as things were, I don't see how you could have acted differently. Therefore you have nothing to blame yourself for. If she did not care enough to wait till you were in some sort of position, it wouldn't have been of any use ... one feels if she very sensitively understood your case she would know better how things were with you – certainly would know that you were worth waiting for. For you are, my dear – This is what I want you to feel sure of. Keep faith in yourself.

Just before leaving Oxford for a trip to Paris in July Hartley saw the announcement of Joan's engagement in *The Times*. It gave him a shock 'though not so much as when I heard the false report of it in March. It seemed to be inevitable. I keep feeling sad about it at odd times; but two or three years ago I should have felt it more acutely – somehow. I suppose it is the passing of time.'[37] Hartley almost certainly questioned his ability to achieve a satisfactory hetero-sexual relationship, or indeed to maintain any sexual relationship whatever its nature, with all the demands it would make on him. Perhaps his attempt to settle on Joan Mews was yet another way in which he might do what Bessie, and society, required. Of course, his feelings for David Cecil contradicted that attempt; it was Cecil without whom Hartley was desolate. What Kitchin made of Hartley's effort to deform his personality by marriage we do not know (beyond the fact that he would make a novel out of it), but he would have known it to be an error. Kitchin was a well-adjusted, practising, unrepentant homosexual; but this was hardly an example Hartley could be expected to follow. At least the decision not to marry seems not to have put an end to the friendship between Hartley and the woman he may have loved. In the late August of 1922, he was once again staying at Upper Portslade and playing piano duets with her.

While Joan enjoyed the congratulations that flooded in on her engagement, Hartley left for Paris with Kitchin, after which the couple spent a few days with Harry in Cumberland. Responding to Bessie's worries over Hartley's health, Harry told her that 'very much must be left to men of his age'.[38] And Bessie was informed of Kitchin 'of whom [Leslie] is clearly very fond – and there was something nice about Kitchin, in spite of his little airs. I should imagine also that he is not a bit of a harum-scarum but a man who knows his way about the world – perhaps a little too much.' Harry's observation was at once accurate and naïve. In the early 1930s Kitchin, with Ken Ritchie, subsequently Chairman of the Stock Exchange, and the bibliophile Richard Jennings, dedicatee of *Mr Balcony*, shared a flat in Great Ormond Street to which all three would bring back 'trade'; T. S. Eliot also lived at the flat for a time. More enduringly, Kitchin went on to two successful long-term relationships, only ended by the death of his partners. If Harry or Bessie had known Kitchin's true nature, their approval of him might have been more muted, but Hartley was now moving through a society of which they had only a limited understanding.

Kitchin, whose somewhat acerbic façade disguised a kindly and sympathetic nature, certainly understood Hartley's crucial dilemma; the fact that he did so may be one of the reasons that their friendship, though lifelong, was often prickly. And there was something critical about Kitchin's attitude that disconcerted Hartley, even now when their friendship was at its strongest, when Kitchin's sexual frankness may have encouraged Hartley to confide any doubts he might have about his own sexuality.

Decades later, Hartley insisted that Kitchin had portrayed him as the hero of his second novel, *Mr Balcony*, published by the Woolfs at the Hogarth Press in 1927. There is a playful, Firbankian texture to Kitchin's prose (a technique he abandoned for his later work) that makes the book seem frigid, and its characters insubstantial, but in the portrait of Mr Balcony Kitchin certainly created a man whose beliefs and sufferings reflect Hartley's. Mr Balcony's list of the 'Evils of Life' starts off with 'The fear of death. Disease. The fear of disease. Unrequited love. Our unkindness to those we love. Unwelcome attentions. Faithlessness of friends. Misfortunes of friends'.[39] Mr Balcony meets a friend who tells him of 'our enemy, the crowd, life's mass production, the spawn of that monstrous fish, humanity. They shout with one voice, act with one purpose, see with one vision. And they will have none who differ from them.'[40] This perception of society is one that Mr Balcony will be obliged to adopt – Mr Balcony with his morbid fears of ill-health, his awareness that marriage will lead to 'inevitable catastrophe', his apprehension of 'a horrible celibacy'.[41] He sails for Africa, taking a party of inconsequential social hangers-on, but also the fascinating Gloria Swing. It is she who is exhilarated when the ship arrives at Gahta, feeling within herself 'the opening of a door'.[42] Mr Balcony's fate has already been prescribed, for he had long before 'conceived the idea of altering my character, of doing violence to myself, and being all that nature had not intended me to be, and nothing that she had'.[43] The novel's denouement is deliberately obscured, though we are told of the knife that makes Mr Balcony's sacrifice, perhaps castration followed by death, possible.

It seems to have been Kitchin who pointed a way forward to Hartley, who first persuaded Hartley to visit the city that would come to mean more to him than anywhere else, the city that released his imagination and offered a perfect sanctuary. 'Clifford is probably relying on me to go, but I don't want to very much', he told Bessie in August,[44] but two weeks later he was in north Italy, skirting Lake Maggiore, 'exquisite with the acacia hedges and soft bright sunlight ... I am feeling very well and anxious to board my gondola.'[45] By mid September, having managed to smuggle his tobacco and cigarettes through three custom houses (a regular trick of his) Hartley had his first view of Venice as he arrived at the Grand Hotel, where Kitchin was already installed. He was enthralled:

> It is most delightful here ... It has been sunny all the time and I bathed on what must be the safest shore in the world, the Lido. Beautiful trapezes emerge from the water so that you can fall in from all possible angles ... It is the least arduous town in the world – the gondolas are so soothing and the journey, though long, is as easy as falling off a log.[46]

There is little hint here of the tremendous effect the city had on him when first he saw it; like so many others before and since, Venice offered Hartley too much, defied the organisation of words to describe it at a first meeting. He explored a few of the many churches, peering at their paintings in the often impenetrable darkness, saw 'acres' of Tintoretto and Titian, visited the Doge's Palace and the dungeons at the Bridge of Sighs. Time had to be set aside for the 'Social Offensive'. Elizabeth Bibesco had given him an introduction to the Princess de Polignac, said to be of Bohemian tastes 'but I hope, good social standing'.[47] Venetian society seemed even more difficult to break into than its English counterpart. Many years later, in his story 'Mrs Carteret Receives', Hartley described the period between 1890 and 1940 when

> English people, emigrants or semi-emigrants, had established a hold, based on affinity, in many cities of Italy, chiefly Rome, Florence and Venice. Others went further afield; but the lure of Italy, for many English people, especially those with aesthetic tastes, was irresistible ...There was a genuine feeling of affection, based on more than mutual advantage, between the two nations. I remember my gondolier saying to me when the troublous relationships between our two countries began over Sanctions, 'There was a time when an Englishman was a king in Venice.'[48]

It was, in its upper reaches, a snobbish society, at its core an Anglo-American colony of residents living in Venetian splendour. It looked down on what it called the Settembrini, the wealthy visitors who paraded the Lido and retired to highly populated hotels. The Italians of Venice seemed to live apart from this select band of moneyed invaders, often pleased to accept their hospitality but slow to return it. It was the colonial circle, presided over by Mr and Mrs Humphrey Johnstone, who had inherited the mantle once worn by Lady Radnor and Mrs Curtis, the friend of Henry James, that Hartley needed to break into. By this time the colony was not as distinguished as it once had been, but the Johnstones ruled over it with a strong sense of moral disapproval from the Palazzo Contarini dal Zaffo overlooking the island of San Michele. Mrs Johnstone (on whom Hartley models Mrs Carteret) was a formidable hostess with a rigid expectation of behaviour, a mission to keep out the profane and vulgar: an unmarried couple living together would not be given an entrée to this Venetian aristocracy. Dinner-parties at the Johnstones can hardly have been easy going occasions. Venetian evenings, according to Mrs Johnstone, were 'meant to reconcile us to the grave'.

But that first visit to Venice may have held the promise of other adventures. There can be little doubt that it was as much its sexual as its aesthetic dimension that so attracted Kitchin to the place, its rugged gondoliers, its muscular stevedores. Once in Venice, an Englishman's wings might be spread in a way that was altogether more difficult in England. Gondoliers, as a character in Hartley's first novel would not hesitate to point out, were no more than male prostitutes. Only a few years before, Frederick William Rolfe, the self-styled 'Baron Corvo' and author of *Hadrian VII*, had died in Venice, having given himself over to homosexual excess. Rolfe's scandalous reputation was well-known to Kitchin and to Hartley. Kitchin, too, was always on the look out for 'gay', and must have longed for Rolfe's Venice – the Great Good Place – where he might stumble across 'half a dozen ribald venal dishonest licentious young gondolieri, quiet and alone on their wicked knees round the grave of a comrade'. The opportunities for homosexual enjoyment were very different from those offered by England, and it may have been Kitchin's hope that Hartley's natural sexuality would flourish in so paradisiacal a setting, where lust and love, in the easy familiarity of the water-borne city with its dimly lit streets and passages, might claim Hartley for their own.

Back in England a giddy social round awaited Hartley. At the Wharf he began a lifelong friendship with Marie Belloc Lowndes, the novelist sister of Hilaire, whom Mr Asquith had taken a liking to 'whenever there was nothing more attractive in the vicinity' on her visits to 10 Downing Street.[49] She gave Hartley an introduction to her brother Hilaire. Sir Maurice Bonham Carter promised an introduction to the editor of the *Times Literary Supplement*. There were more meetings with Ottoline at Garsington and visits to the Wharf. He met the composer Gerald Berners (who played duets with Puffin) and Siegfried Sassoon, whom he expected 'to maintain his usual absolute silence' at Sutton Courtney. Hartley spent the

New Year there – 'I always pray in the New Year with Puffin.'[50]
Returning from a trip to Paris with Leslie, Elizabeth Bibesco assured
Bessie that 'it is always delightful to be with [Leslie] anywhere ...
what a rare and precious blessing his friendship is to me!'[51]

Virginia Woolf was less impressed, at least at their first meeting
at Garsington in the early summer of 1923, one afternoon when
there were 'thirty seven people to tea; a bunch of young men no
bigger than asparagus'.[52] Her description of four of those young
men is irresistible:

> Lord David is a pretty boy. Puffin Asquith an ugly one – wizened,
> unimpressive, sharp, like a street boy. Sackville West reminded
> me of a peevish shop girl. They all have the same clipped quick
> speech and politeness, and total insignificance. Yet we asked Lord
> David and Puff to write for the Nation, and also a dull fat man
> called Hartley.[53]

For his part, Hartley thought Mrs Woolf 'a cruel teaze'.[54] True to
form, he was frightened of her, but it was not a barrier he particularly
wanted to break down; the couple did not meet often, and Hartley
was never inclined to be part of the Bloomsbury set. In later years,
with his back, as it were, against the critical wall, he would be
unreservedly savage about Mrs Woolf. Edward Sackville-West,
despite the rarefied appearance that made him the object of specu-
lation in the street, would be a constant friend of Hartley's as would
Puffin Asquith. As natural inheritors of wealth and position and
good family, they were prize examples.

But Hartley's greatest allegiance, if he had one, was to Ottoline
Morrell, to whom he appeared almost anxious to open his heart. By
now he was a regular visitor at Garsington, delighting in staying for
the weekend and being accepted as part of the literary coterie that
surrounded his hostess. He showered her with compliments. After a
visit in March 1923 he confessed that if their discussion about
mysticism had lasted any longer he would have had 'an ecstasy'.[55]
He placed himself at her feet, and, often, at the feet of her circle.
On one occasion he travelled from Garsington to Oxford with one
of its most distinguished members, E. M. Forster, who, in Hartley's
presence, had made a great point about a novelist's need to observe
people. Terrified that he would be the great man's study, Hartley
leaned as far back in his corner as possible. He admitted to Ottoline
that he might write more poems, though it seemed to him as if they
occurred after some misfortune, and might therefore be unwelcome.
He was confident enough about 'Disparity in Despair' to send her a

copy of it, suggesting that the emotions it represented were still especially meaningful to him. The poem's clumsy title is perhaps the weakest thing about it:

> If the despair that you and I have known
> Were accurately apportioned, each to each,
> Not every pebble on a shingly beach
> Not every grain of wheat for harvest sown
> Mustered and piled, would bear comparison
> With your despair; for your despair would reach
> The stars: the volume of your griefs would teach
> Astronomers a new dimension.
>
> But mine, I think, would be a small despair
> That I would carry with me, portable;
> A caked cold cinder from the fires of hell
> A souvenir, a trophy. I would wear
> It carelessly, and sometimes I would tell
> Its story, all save this: who found it there.[56]

The very admission of that 'small despair' is subject to the restriction Hartley puts upon it – his refusal to disclose the identity of the person who recognises it. If there was a hidden message in the poem it was one he wanted to lay before Ottoline, for he felt that he was able to offer up to her at least some of the longings that threatened him. To her, he spoke of Cecil's temperament being 'far less mercurial than his mind and he knows his emotions well and hasn't a moment's doubt about them: though that wouldn't prevent his changing them, alas! But he isn't hasty or wayward, do you think?'[57] These are curious words; there is some sort of danger in them, but Hartley felt safe to confide them to Ottoline.

The interest she took in Hartley extended beyond him to Bessie and, certainly, to Norah; 'tell Norah', he wrote to Bessie from Kitchin's Boar's Hill home, 'that Lady Ottoline spoke of her with affection and means to answer her letter'.[58] Norah had grown from being the baby of the family, naturally subordinate to Enid, to a strongly intelligent young woman. Her education was very different from that given to her brother and sister. She had gone in the early months of the Great War to a day school in Peterborough run by an Irishwoman called Miss Gibson, the first Freewoman to be elected by Peterborough City Council. Miss Gibson was over eighty years of age, almost completely blind and full of very strong opinions, a trait that Norah may have inherited from her. She lived in the cathedral precincts, 'and had her finger in every ecclesiastical pie that there was'.[59]

Bessie's plan was that Norah would follow Enid to St Felix School at Southwold, but its exposed coastal situation had necessitated its removal to Scotland. Instead, Norah went to Cheltenham Ladies' College, from where she won a place at St Hilda's Hall, Oxford; Hartley visited her there, noting that she now wore her hair in a fashionable bob. Unlike him, Norah saw her future clearly, at least in terms of what she did not want from it – she did not want to marry. After gaining a Third Class Honours degree in English Literature in 1925, she announced her intention to Harry. She wanted, she said, to breed dogs, and so it was that, in her early twenties, she mapped out the life that was to consume her until the end of her days. Although she and Enid were devoted to one another, Norah did not show either the capacity or willingness to follow Enid's example at Fletton. Norah was to remain resolutely undomesticated all her life; it was Enid who knew where the provisions were kept, what the servants were paid, where blankets were aired. And, even if her entire life was lived out at Fletton, Norah had a spirit of independence about her that did not always make home life easy. 'My mother and I didn't really get on', she would say.[60] They would argue, Norah flying into a temper at Bessie, resisting her attempts to smother and direct her. She was, she thought, the least favourite child in Bessie's eyes. On one occasion, an exasperated Norah asked Bessie, 'Why do you want everyone to do everything your way?' 'But I don't, my dear', Bessie answered, 'I only want people to do things the *best* way.'[61]

Hartley was disappointed to leave Oxford with a Second Class in Modern History. He felt aggrieved that he had not done better, that in the awarding of it he had been let down by those who should have been unreservedly approving of him. The sense that he had somehow been 'done down' by his fellow man asserted itself early in life. Six months after leaving Oxford he became a reviewer for the *Spectator* at the invitation of its editor, John Strachey,[62] beginning an association with that journal that lasted until his death. By 1923 he was contributing to the *Nation and Athenaeum*, and though his contributions to the *Nation* finished in April 1924, he was already in consistent demand as a reviewer of contemporary fiction. The following November he joined the *Saturday Review*, for which he wrote weekly reviews of three or more novels until March 1930, the year his notices began to appear in the *Week-End Review*. There was also regular work for the *Calendar of Modern Letters*, but his greatest allegiance in the inter-war years was to the *Sketch*, a glossy magazine which Hartley joined in October 1929, finally signing off as the book page's 'Literary Lounger' at the end of 1943. Concurrently, he was reviewing for the *Observer* from 1935 to 1942, for *Life and Letters Today* from 1943 to 1946, *Time and Tide* and the *Illustrated London News*. Almost without his being aware of it, journalism, by the mid twenties, had become his profession. By the time he joined the *Sketch* in 1929, the newspaper could introduce him to its readers as 'a very well-known literary critic; indeed, he has been described by Mr J. B. Priestly as the best reviewer of fiction in the country now.'[63]

Hartley brought a steadiness, perception and integrity to reviewing that he maintained throughout the twenty-odd years that he practised it, and they were qualities he managed in the teeth of an almost numbing schedule. His work for the *Sketch* alone he later described as 'slavery'; certainly, his by-line of 'Literary Lounger' was a euphemism for a man who had to read, on average, five books a week. The pressure of absorbing and responding to such a mass of material was an obvious impediment to his wish to write a novel; it took away from the spirit of his own imagination. 'I feel', he told Cecil in 1931, 'that with every fresh "Literary Lounger" my personality shrinks – with every new Book of the Week I become duller.'[64] During the years of reviewing, Hartley later reckoned he must have read well over 6000 books, years of intensive reading that eventually wore away his enjoyment of books; at the end of his life he would read little.

But Hartley denied to reviewing none of his careful use of words, intelligence or understanding. For the reader, there was the confidence that the review was the work of a man of taste and sympathy with an ability to illuminate his subject. For the writer, there was the confidence that his or her work had been judged considerately, and even – when Hartley was writing at his best – brought to new life by his words. Hartley did not hesitate to criticise, although a particularly unappealing new work by a friend or acquaintance might make life difficult – and being averse to any form of criticism of his own work helped give his criticism of others an acceptable voice. His judgement was seldom questioned; its wisdom was often acknowledged. L. A. G. Strong told Hartley how his review of Strong's latest book 'got the book's weakness in a way that will help me in the future ... I've always respected your judgement, as I do few other men's, however it falls.'[65] Priestley noted how 'every time you put your finger on something that most people seem to miss ...

you always say something that makes me see my own work more clearly';[66] Hugh Walpole welcomed him as 'the only critic I know who is wise and kind too'.[67] Four years later Walpole assured Hartley:

> You are more of a help to me than you can possibly realise. It isn't praise that an author needs (although he likes it) nor blame that he minds (for more than a moment) but Understanding is balm to his soul ... you have really made writing a less lonely business for me.[68]

It cannot only have been their friendship that made Kitchin tell Hartley that his review of *Streamers Waving* had 'transmuted my lead into gold'.[69] Even into the forties and fifties (by which time Hartley's reviewing was more occasional) writers were paying tribute to his contribution not only to the literary scene but to their creative work. Pamela Hansford Johnson recognised his notices as 'the most helpful kind of reviewing – the kind that makes the novelist think an effort worthwhile, and determine to do better next time',[70] while Louis Golding praised 'a critic whose honesty and exactness in criticism I won't permit myself to doubt, though he has long been a friend'.[71]

Hartley's first review for the *Spectator*, written when he had influenza, was of Elizabeth Bowen's collection of stories, *Encounters*. He was so impressed by her work that he arranged to meet her with Cecil at the Ivy Restaurant, a meeting that began a close friendship between the three of them. Once, when Hartley and Elizabeth attended a literary function together, they were mistakenly introduced as man and wife; Hartley politely explained that they were not, but if he had ever married she would have been his choice.

Work began flooding in after the Bowen review, fitted in between arrangements to spend a week in Paris with Ottoline, Puffin and Elizabeth Bibesco. By September 1923 Hartley was working on two reviews for the *Spectator*, and five books arrived from the *Nation*, 'which fills me with delight', though he was conscious of writing as though under Mrs Woolf's eye.[72] The social calendar was hectic. That summer he stayed with Kitchin at Boar's Hill in Oxford, at Puffin's house in Bedford Square, at the Wharf, at the Bower House at Ightham in Kent, at Grasmere, at Penzance with Eddy Sackville-West, who was nervous of going about the harbour because of the fishermen who stood about staring at him. There was a weekend at the John Stracheys which Hartley hoped 'would consolidate my position – it may of course have the opposite effect', and he and Mrs

Strachey discussed 'the application of psychology to the Servant Question and the relations of parents and children'.[73]

It was not only as a journalist that Hartley was making strides. In December he had his first meeting with 'a charming American, who had heard of me from Lady Gooford', the publisher Constant Huntington.[74] A year younger than Hartley, Huntington had enough sympathy and patience to make him the ideal person to oversee Hartley's developing talent. Born in Boston, he studied architecture after leaving Harvard, and joined the publishing firm of G. N. Putnam in 1902, coming to England as head of their London office three years later. Huntington was just as charming as Hartley described. In appearance he was rather martial, with striking good looks. As a publisher, he was highly individual, adopting authors in whom he took a passionate interest and nursing their careers with integrity and almost startling enthusiasm. His clients included Florence Barclay (author of *The Rosary*), Leo (L. H.) Myers and Marie Stopes, before her views were considered respectable. His meeting with Huntington was one of the most important of Hartley's life, beginning an association that would test the two men and only really take flower over twenty years later. Now, Huntington expressed an interest in bringing out a volume of Hartley's short stories. Though not exactly enthusiastic about them, advising that it would be better to begin with a novel, he gave Hartley the vague impression that he might take them.

Five months later, in May 1924, Huntington published the stories as *Night Fears*. The *Times Literary Supplement* noted that the author wrote 'with such elegance and conscious care that one regrets that lack of body which is the dominant characteristic of his volume'. Not unexpectedly, the book did not sell well; it was at once an encouraging and disappointing start, bringing in no money. But it was an impressive collection, with the personality of the many other collections that would follow – some inhabiting or bordering the supernatural world, others that are a positive reflection of the author's obsessions, the need for friendship, the need of approval, the disease of hypochondria. 'The Island' is about a young man awaiting the arrival of his hostess, Mrs Santander, in a great soundless house in the middle of the sea. The innocent visitor has to make do with Mrs Santander's husband. Below the house, the sea sucks and spouts as he shows his guest the finger nail he has broken while strangling her:

> He pushed his hand towards me over the polished table. I watched it, fascinated, thinking it would stop; but still it came on, his body

following, until, if I hadn't drawn back, it would have touched me, while his chin dropped to within an inch of the table, and one side of his face was pillowed against his upper arm.[75]

Mr Santander may be happy with the convolutions of his body, but it is the author's nervousness of the working of the human frame that is most striking. Uneasiness, in fact, breaks out everywhere in *Night Fears*, mostly through heroes with whom the author clearly identifies. Philip in 'The Telephone Call' is not an uncomplicated young man – 'a hint of discomfort was always necessary to Philip's peace of mind.'[76] He is invited to the house of the wealthy bachelor Marigold brothers, where Stephen Marigold, with his 'a little cultured, a little critical, gracefully appreciative of, but never rapturous' attitude to the great paintings he owns, is probably a sketch of Clifford Kitchin, whose taste was fastidious but detached.[77] He is obliged to ask at the house of an old friend if he may use the telephone, thus unwillingly opening up the possibility of the renewal of friendship. Coming away (for there is no telephone in the house) he realises he has left his hat there, and returns once more. Thus friendship again becomes triumphant. The young man in 'A Sentimental Journey' returns to a church where he was once recognised as highly individual, a face that stood out in a crowd, but, in returning, he is found to be indistinguishable from his fellows. The need to return is also at the heart of 'The Last Time' where the hero, in the final days of his life, visits the places of his past, including

> the scenes of his 'home service', not on account of their beauty but because, in the inflamed emotionalism of those days, they had bitten deeply into his consciousness. The milieu of incidents where his mediocre military talents had exposed him to ridicule, especially attracted him.[78]

More dangerously, he askes to see a woman from his past, 'reopening an affair that had always been mysterious, whose precise meaning for both parties had never been understood ... Smoke there had been for all to see; no one could find a flame.'[79] The relationship here is hung about with 'tentative emotions', out of which the man is unable to 'realise the emotions, the reconciliation, the passionate re-assurance, the sense of parting overpowered by the sense of fulfilment which he had counted upon.' We can hardly avoid wondering if the problems of this story are those that Hartley associated with Joan Mews. In this fiction, the return to a meaningful heterosexual relationship cannot be happy, because the nature of the bond is beyond his understanding; the feelings necessary to it will not come. If this is a mere lack of confidence, it is shared by the hypochondriac hero of 'A Tonic', who confesses to a medical specialist:

> I am an uninteresting specimen; they told me so when I was passed for a sedentary occupation into the Army. They said I was a miserable specimen, too. They said I wasn't the sort of man you would want to look at twice.[80]

Pessimism is at the heart of *Night Fears*, as is the danger of love. Love, presumably, has been responsible for the murder of Mrs Santander by her contorting husband; women, like Helen in 'The Last Time', are unable to offer the comfort so necessary to the hero. Miss Ada Quilt, the schoolteacher in 'St George and the Dragon', is in her modest way the forerunner of many Hartley heroines, strong, manipulative. It is Miss Quilt who sets up one of the men at her school to attack another, less muscular, colleague, who walks her through the woods. It is a venomous deed, for which she is paid by being left alone while the attacker tends his victim. Her reward is terrible, ironic and deserved:

> In her the lines of two men's fates had met: majestic confluence! But with the collapse of that colossal distention she had lost her magnitude, even the puny magnitude of dreary commonplace days.[81]

We are left with the conviction that new friendship between the two men – 'the lines of two men's fates' – will come of this. It is perhaps one of the few happy endings in *Night Fears*.

Cecil asked Hartley to visit Venice with him that April. The love-affair with the city was strengthening, and blossomed with the novel that Hartley was embarking on, but the mental worries that had afflicted him through the past years were still with him. In March 1925 Aunt Kathleen wrote:

> My darling
> I feel disturbed about you. I wish I could have seen you more. All this time I have been picturing you having on the whole a good time, enjoying your work and at intervals your friends, and I fear I have been too optimistic. But don't be alarmed my dear. People do have these queer sensations and entirely grow out of them. I

think we as a family are inclined to become sturdier in mind and body as we get older. At your age I was horribly nervy. I remember once feeling myself to such an extent outside myself that in a second or two I believed I was dead. It gave me a great fright; but afterwards an extraordinary calm. Those sensations in the head, or similar ones, I have had too. They are not as alarming as they seem – they will all pass. I believe if you get sufficiently interested in your novel to feel that the characters live and you know them, that your nerves will improve. Of course it *isn't* well to dwell on these things – I mean symptoms that are depressing to us. I have not much faith in excitement as a lasting good – in fact none; but *interest* in other matters is of the greatest value. There is nothing really amiss with you dear. All those tiresome feelings mean nerves ... Your writing is a joy, and I am convinced that with your exceedingly sympathetic nature, you are bound to give something that will appeal, even generally – as those short sketches [the stories in *Night Fears*] had no chance of doing. It was not to be expected that they would sell; they were not the style, but your writing may be just as good and your matter a bit more unusual, and then you will see.

The 'unusual' matter was achieved through the inspiration of Venice in a novella, 'Lavinia', intended to be read to the '63 Club, a literary society whose meeting place was at 63 St James's. Kathleen told him that 'some people seem to consider me in some strange way responsible' for the book. Hartley sent it to Huntington, before staying with Kathleen and George at the Victoria Hotel, Lyme Regis (where they often holidayed together), nephew and uncle making the most of the sunny weather with bathing, golf and rowing. Elizabeth Bibesco had volunteered to check the Italian of 'Lavinia'. In August, Hartley saw a good deal of Cecil in London; they went to Pirandello's *Henry IV* and on to supper at the Savoy where they had 'a very severe argument about Russian novelists lasting till nearly two' with the Bibescos.[82]

It was around this time at Garsington that Hartley met the painter Ethel Sands. He never forgot his first sight of her tall, slender figure, descending Ottoline's staircase in a pearl-coloured dress. Whatever gifts Ethel had, handsomeness was not among them; those meeting her for the first time would ask if she was any relation to the famed beauty Mrs Mahlon Sands, the friend of the Prince of Wales? Mrs Sands' daughter had inherited none of her mother's loveliness: she was bony, had protruding teeth and sharp features, deficiencies she made up for with a natural charm and accomplishment and that flair for friendship that allured Hartley. Armed with such talents, Ethel was a natural hostess to a great circle, embracing both artists and writers who included Henry James (whose novels Hartley always felt she had just stepped· out of), Virginia Woolf, Walter Sickert and Clive and Vanessa Bell. The Sands were Americans, but had come to England, where they hoped the reticent Ethel might make a social success. Shyness did not overcome Ethel's independent spirit; she wanted to be a painter, and at the age of twenty-three went to Paris in 1893, where she met another American painter, Anna Hope Hudson. Ethel and 'Nan' fell in love, beginning a relationship that would only end with Nan's death. Hartley came to know them both, though it was Ethel rather than Nan, whose much more outspoken and formidable character made her a less easy ally, that Hartley befriended.

Ethel was the strongest link between Bloomsbury and Chelsea, and it was at her house at 15 The Vale that the two might come together in harmony. Virginia Woolf, the Bells, Desmond Mac-Carthy and Raymond Mortimer (whom Hartley identified as the high priest of the Virginian cult. 'What are the Wild Waves saying?' he cheekily asked Mortimer after the publication of *The Waves* in 1931; Mortimer neither smiled nor enlightened him) were frequent visitors, as were Boris Anrep – who decorated Ethel's hall with mosaics – George Moore, Logan Pearsall Smith, Percy Lubbock and Arnold Bennett. Ethel, of course, was the inspiration of such gatherings; Nan was happier in a more restricted milieu, especially when painting in Normandy, where they eventually acquired the Château d'Auppegard. But they were more than moneyed Bohemi-ans. During the 1914–18 war their country house at Newington near Oxford had become an army hospital, Ethel had become the forewoman of an overall factory, and she and Nan had gone to work as nurses in France. The two women never lost their interest in the welfare or happiness of others, a quality that was reflected in their own deeply felt love of one another. For Hartley, Ethel was the gentlest, most undemanding and caring of friends, but even so he was in awe of the social glitter that surrounded her, and perhaps of her blissful homosexual happiness. ·

Putnam published *Simonetta Perkins* (the renamed 'Lavinia') in October 1925, 'full of terrible mis-prints, indeed the Italian is like Czech'.[83] Four weeks later, Huntington sent a cheque for £5.5s. for sales, telling Hartley that if the book carried on selling as well the sales would probably run into thousands. Huntington's prophecy was misguided, for the book brought Hartley a total of £12. Some criticism came from devastating quarters. Lady Millicent Hawes (the Duchess of Sutherland) bought several copies and wrote from Paris to ask who L. P. Hartley was. Virginia Woolf so surprised him by asking 'Have you written any more shabby books, Mr Hartley?' that he dropped the parcels he was carrying. He asked which of his books she meant. 'The one that might have been written by a man with one foot in England and the other in Venice', she said, adding in a more kindly tone, 'If only you could break up your crystal sentences.' In the *Saturday Review* the young novelist was welcomed as 'one of the most hopeful talents that the last few years have revealed to the reading public';[84] the *Calendar of Modern Letters* found the style 'unerring' in 'a distinguished first novel'.[85]

Thirty years later, when he was in Paris for the launch of the French translation of *The Go-Between*, a reporter told Hartley that his latest book was nothing like as accomplished as *Simonetta Perkins*. Hartley 'knew it was true, and that after thirty years practice [it] was still, technically at least, the most accomplished of my books. I hadn't studied technique when I wrote it . . . it only took me about a fortnight to write, but I knew just what I wanted to say and the technique for saying it came automatically.'[86] In both books, Hartley felt he had for the only times in his career departed from a straightforward storytelling, though only in *Simonetta Perkins* is the spirit of Henry James so strongly felt. That spirit is so strong through some of the book's pages that it is almost possible to think of the novel as a Jamesian pastiche, even if Hartley later acknowledged that he might have been slightly influenced by Forster, notably in *A Passage to India* and *A Room with a View*. *Simonetta Perkins*, apparently so fragile and sometimes overworked a piece, takes on a life of its own through the passion that runs beneath it; like so much of Hartley's work, its surface, like that of the Venetian waters over which Lavinia glides, is deceptive. The craft of suggestion, of understatement, of things half said, half understood, arrives on its pages fully-formed. The novels that began to appear over twenty years later can justifiably be seen as variations on this first theme; the skill adapts, flourishes, but retains (in the best of his later work) the originality of voice.

Today, we cannot read *Simonetta Perkins* without the feeling that Hartley's innermost feelings – 'I knew just what I wanted to say'[87] – are transmuted into those of Lavinia Johnstone, the carefully cultivated girl from Boston, USA (Huntington furnished Hartley with descriptions of Boston high society) holidaying in Venice with her mother, who expects her to make a suitable marriage. Lavinia is attracted to the gondolier, Emilio, and becomes infatuated with his physicality, asking advice of a friend about an imaginary girl called Simonetta Perkins who has fallen in love with a gondolier. At the end of the book, Lavinia leaves Venice without ever having let him know. Against a carefully painted background of the city's social life, one of the characters describes her as 'an unlighted candle ... a candle by a corpse'.[88] Poor Lavinia 'could face the reproaches of her friends, the intimate disapproval of her conscience; they were part of her ordinary life. But the enmity of convention was outside her experience, for she had always been its ally, marched in its van. She could not placate it because it was implacable; its function was to disapprove.' That disapproval makes impossible any real response to Emilio's sexuality, his accessibility to pleasure and his instinct to 'render pleasure back'.[89] The worldly Mrs Kolynopulo informs Lavinia that gondoliers are no less than male prostitutes. Fascinated as she is, and knowing that she will never see Emilio again, Lavinia

> was afraid to look back, but in her mind's eye she could see, repeated again and again, the arrested rocking movement of the gondolier. The alternation of stroke and recovery became dreadful to her, suggesting no more what was useful or romantic, but proclaiming a crude physical sufficiency, at once relentless and unwilling. It came to her overwhelmingly that physical energy was dangerous and cruel, just in so far as it was free.[90]

That 'alternation of stroke and recovery' would reappear almost thirty years later at the crux on which the story of *The Go-Between* turns – the horror of Ted Burgess and Marian Maudsley's sexual congress, his penetration of her body, the making of the shadow that opens and closes 'like an umbrella'. *Simonetta Perkins* is probably Hartley's most dangerous novel, and certainly (until the writing of *The Harness Room* at the end of his life) the least reticent, the least prudish, the least respectable. It at once fixes his fascination with the sexual act, and his inability to accept it. He was to say that Kitchin had influenced its writing (was the idea sprung during that first visit of 1922?) and there is something of the jewel-like delicacy of Kitchin's *Streamers Waving* that Hartley never quite recaptures in later books. In the summer of 1925 they again went to Venice together, though Kitchin felt diffident about the visit. On reading Hartley's novel he wrote assuring him that 'no one can fail to appreciate the formal perception, the splendid style, and the graceful but austere logic of its crescendo and accelerando. I cannot, of course, help regretting the volte-face at the end.'[91]

In deploring the volte-face, Kitchin was letting Hartley know that he was fully aware of his predicament, that Lavinia's sexual longing cannot be resolved by sexual activity; the only resolve comes from running away from it. It is Hartley's emotional dishonesty that Kitchin recognised, a dishonesty that Lavinia shares. Just as she invents Simonetta Perkins to protect and distance herself from the criticism of the world, so Hartley has invented Lavinia for the same purpose. In *Simonetta Perkins* Hartley for the first time reveals himself as a novelist specialising in disguise of the truth.

The shift of responsibility on to Lavinia's shoulders is not altogether convincing. It is the fascination with masculinity that invades her mind and irradiates the most passionate sequences of the book – Emilio's eyes that 'annihilated time', his sun-tanned body, the unbearable closeness of his hands and ringed fingers, his smile, his every moment that is

> accessible to pleasure; at every moment, unconsciously, he could render pleasure back; it lived in his face, his movements, his whole air, where all the charms of childhood, youth and maturity mingled without losing their identity.

Yet there is a masculinity in Lavinia's appreciation of the gondolier's body that threatens to expose itself as the author's, not his character's, thoughts. Whatever infatuation, lust or love she may feel, it must be subdued for fear of the degradation that a fall would bring. Just as with Hartley, Venice had taken Lavinia to the brink of sexual fulfilment, and she had turned her back on it.

There may or may not be autobiography in *Simonetta Perkins*, but it is certainly at the heart of a short story Hartley had finished by the end of 1925. 'I've been reading your "Back to Cambo". I am enchanted with it', Bessie wrote on 8 November. In later years Hartley remembered he had submitted it for a competition which it did not win. The story is of a brother and sister, playing in the rock pools on a seashore, and of the rescue of a shrimp from the lips of an anemone.

PART II

White Wands, Waving

❧ 4 ❦

The Venetian Years

IT WAS INEVITABLE that when Venice became a necessity to Hartley it would determine the pattern of his life. Fletton was made impossible not only by Bessie's emotional demands, the dominant closeness of Harry, and the atmosphere polluted by Peterborough's chimneys, but by the sheer dullness of his days there; if he crossed the road at a different place it qualified as an event. Already, there was the constant possibility of escape to the many boltholes where he had established himself as a welcome guest. Friendship bred friendship. In the late August of 1927 he paid his first visit to Ethel and Nan's home at the Château d'Auppegard, *en route* to the Asquiths' house at Quai Bourbon in Paris, where he met up with the Bibescos. With Leo Myers, Hartley travelled on to Il Castello in Portofino Marc, where he stayed in a room of the gardener's cottage, reviewing Kitchin's *Mr Balcony* and coping with a visit from Ottoline and Philip Morrell. When he was not 'droning away at my reviews' he spent much of the day bathing.[1] By 28 September he was in Milan, accompanied by Elizabeth Bibesco and Myers, *en route* for Venice and the house that would be his home for most of his Venetian life: San Sebastiano 2542.

Today, the *fondamente* of San Sebastiano and the bridge that, a little way to the left of the house, crosses the rio, is busy with the traffic of university students, the more adventurous tourists, and the young and old of Dorsodura. Pink-washed and dilapidated, shown up by the modernised façade and trim balcony of its neighbour, San Sebastiano 2542 remains resolutely Venetian. This part of the city belongs to its inhabitants, the locals who stand gossiping outside a tiny café, blocking out its window, opposite the great church. The present-day pilgrim must leave behind the familiarity of St Mark's or the Rialto, with its ribbon streets of market stalls and souvenir shops, to cross the bridge of the Accademia and make for Dorsodura. There is a way to be found through the thin alleys, or along the Rio Terra Antonio Foscarini until the church of the Gesuati. Here lies the Zattere, that often deserted but most grand of *fondamente* that stretches alongside the Giudecca canal, with its palaces that have seen more glorious days – days of which Hartley was a part, for he was a frequent visitor to the Palazzo Clary. The spot where the Zattere leaves Venice behind is marked by a small, friendly bar and a water-bus stop, and offers a view that Hartley not only knew but understood. It is a view across the Giudecca that seems at first sight to have little to do with the wonder of Venice – the monstrosity of Stucky's Flour Mill. A late nineteenth-century intrusion, this great building was one that Hartley assimilated into his love of Venice; its presence, just where he turned to reach his house, not only brooded but gave up its beauty to him, for he saw it in the context of everything around him:

> . . . in the thick, white sirocco sunlight the colours of the houses on the Giudecca – grey, yellow, terracotta, pink – seemed to merge and lose their proper qualities in a uniform lack of tone; and what stood out was the fenestration, the whitish oblongs and truncated ovals of the windows, monotonously repeated. Except for a dreadful travesty of Gothic, three enormous eyelets beyond the Redentore, scarcely a single pointed arch could I see. I suddenly felt a respect for the five factory chimneys, and I looked with indulgence, almost with affection, on the great bulk of Stucky's flour mill, battlemented, pinnacled, turreted, machico-lated, a monument to the taste of 1870, that might have been built out of a child's box of bricks. A romantic intention had reared it, and left behind something that was solid and substantial and a benefit to mankind.[2]

Turning from the view of Stucky's ornament (which has more than a hint of an exaggerated, nightmare version of Fletton Tower about it), the brief walk along the *fondamente* San Basilio leads directly to San Sebastiano itself, watched over by its church. From the window of his room, Hartley could see the figure of Sebastian, that most handsome of saints, apparently oblivious of the arrows that pierced his body, standing guard over the marble façade of his church. It never occurred to Hartley, during his happy association with Venice, that the long-suffering saint had any significance to the throng of Venetians who daily filed beneath him; only many years later, when he was distanced not only from the city but the emotions that had led him there, did Hartley come to see Sebastian as 'a symbol of mankind'.[3]

The church is at once imposing and reticent, almost tucked away in the corner of the triangular *campo*; in Hartley's day visitors had to peer at its treasures through a dim gloom. Now, artificial lighting reveals the comfortable splendour of Sebastian's church – though it is as much Paolo Veronese's, for the body of the artist, as well as exquisite examples of his work, rests here. Sebastian is everywhere: the letter S, shot through with a single arrow, is carved on the arches that open out to the altar; he is among the group of saints who attend in Veronese's 'La Madonna In Gloria'; he reigns again in Veronese's version of his martyrdom.

Here, Hartley had constant access to overwhelming beauty. His home may have been in a poor quarter of Venice, but it was a poverty that he easily overcame. He had not only his own gondola but his own gondolier, Pietro Busetti (who, for a while, had been whisked away into the employment of some friends of the Cole Porters), and it was the Venetian water that dictated the routine of his foreign life. If the weather was good, the best of the day would be spent on the lagoon, lunching in the gondola, perhaps making for one of the islands, or for the landing-stage of a Venetian friend's home. 'Just like a coffin clapt in a canoe', wrote Byron of the gondola, acknowledging, as others before and since, its association with death, but the gondola was Hartley's greatest expression of happiness. Despite the vagaries of the Venetian weather, the challenge of the *sirocco* and *bora* (north wind), the temperament of the gondolieri and the difficulties of navigating the canals of the city – passers-by often leant a hand to get Hartley's gondola under the flattened arch of the Ponte del Carmine – it was Venice's water that lured him, kept him. There was a feeling, too, that he wanted to be part of the city's everyday life, to be absorbed into the crowds that walked through its streets, avoiding the little armies of hungry cats that everywhere looked for food.

I liked to walk, though the air in the *calli* is stagnant, the pavement monotonous and dead under one's feet, and one sometimes comes back feeling more tired than exercised. But tired only in body. To the eye and the mind the streets of Venice are a perpetual refreshment. Ruskin was right to call his book *The Stones of Venice*. In some moods, though not in all (for the Venetian climate conduces to nervous irritability and a critical outlook), every stone seems to have been laid with love. And not only in places where the builders' handiwork may have been supposed to catch the eye, but in half-hidden spots where you have to peer and crane your neck to see it. To palace and hovel alike the Venetian builders gave of their best, achieving an effect of harmony out of the most incongruous jumble of styles and sizes.[4]

No. 2542 was owned by the Baroness van der Hoeven, an elderly Russian dowager who had been left widowed by a Dutchman. Formidable, idiosyncratic and argumentative, it seemed that the baroness – who was often in residence at the house – was always trying to force some nostrum on Hartley. She made an art of contradiction. 'Pleurisy is a serious thing', Hartley once said to her, 'one can die of it.' 'One can die of anything', the baroness replied. 'I have known two men who died from pimples on their chins.'[5] In a more conciliatory mood, she would ask him to play the piano for her or try to interest him in a new device for relieving flat feet. When she was at home, Hartley made a point of visiting her every day in her inner sanctum but he always felt 'fidgety and fretful' with her.[6] Having escaped the overbearing attentions of Bessie, he could hardly be expected to welcome those of another.

What Hartley expected of Venice was not only its hospitality, and its ability to foster his imagination and consequently his writing, but that it would serve as the perfect backdrop for his many friendships. The comings and goings of the October and November of 1927, when friends were willing, eager and able to visit, are typical of Hartley's happiest times in Venice. It was Cecil, of course, who stood out among this crowd, Cecil who brought contentment as well as excitement, Cecil who made Venice whole. Here, away from the strictures of England, their friendship might take on that special quality that elevated and transformed it, at least in Hartley's mind, to something deeply meaningful, even if there were often other figures in the landscape. Cecil was with Hartley for the first part of October; 'I think he is the most adorable young man', announced Mrs Johnstone, 'I don't think you ought to bring such people to Venice if they have to go away again.'[7] Leo Myers and the exhausting, talkative Elizabeth Bibesco were other October guests. The 11th was the most wonderful night Hartley had ever known in the city; they patrolled the Grand Canal until one o'clock in the morning but, he told Bessie, 'I am lonely without David.'[8] Always there was the distraction of the books that poured in for reviewing, most of which, especially the many American novels, Hartley thought boring, passing them on to Anne Johnstone who 'demolishes each one with the utmost violence'.[9] She once returned a book by Lady Longford with 'four pages of abuse, and a play upon words to the effect that such a Countess should be discountenanced'.[10]

It was not only the never ending demand of his reviews – 'servile and non-committal'[11] – that depressed him but, even at so early a stage in his love-affair with Venice, that his new lover had let him down. Anne Johnstone had assured him that Venetians were the most hospitable of people. He was always welcome at the Johnstone's grand but remote palazzo with its garden designed by Jacapo Sansovino that bordered the lagoon, but it proved harder to penetrate the genuine Venetian society. He was sent visiting cards as large as a sheet of notepaper, but very few invitations or calls followed; the truth was that the Johnstones' influence did not much extend beyond the colony of English–American expatriates. It was with them that Hartley's Venetian life was involved, with the Hultons, the Berwicks, the Bakers,[12] the Berkeleys. What did it matter if the Countess Marosini did not invite him to her ball, even if Pietro had called on her with Hartley's card? The resident cast of Mrs Johnstone's set, bolstered by visitors from England, offered continuous entertainment, but he was unable to achieve anything substantial in the way of writing. The *sirocco* might be blamed for his short temper – 'The Venetian miasma has as usual a little befogged my brain', he told Ethel.[13] He seemed a part of his surroundings and apart from them, willing to be a part of the city and its culture but denied total acceptance. On 11 November, bands of children celebrated the feast of St Martin by going through the streets, standing beneath his window and banging tambourines and saucepans until he was almost distracted. He went to the Anglican church, St George's, where the Johnstones were regular worshippers, and then lunched under the lee of the island of Santa Rosa, until the wind forced him to return to the mainland, and dinner with the Johnstones. He longed, just as he had in England, for the place at the fireside.

With every return to Venice, arriving to spend three months or so both in early spring and autumn, Hartley picked up the threads of his foreign life. Friendships grew in the long gondola days. In April 1928 he rowed Lord and Lady Berwick and the Hultons out on a picnic. Teresa Berwick, whom Hartley visited at Attingham Park that summer (commenting on her long-haired dachshunds, 'a strange, unnatural breed'),[14] was to become a lifelong friend. She had grown up in Venice; her father, the painter William S. Hulton, had known Walter Sickert and Henry James. But it was with another visitor to Venice that spring that Hartley began a much closer friendship: Molly, Countess of Berkeley. The Berkeley's home in Venice was the Palazzo Balbi-Valier on the Grand Canal, with its view towards San Stefano, across the way from where Molly Berkeley had lived before her marriage, in a house that had belonged to D'Annunzio, whose bed she had slept in. Leslie and Molly Berkeley's sympathies agreed. One of her greatest pleasures in life was to ride in a gondola, a pleasure Hartley was only too ready to offer, and on 18 of May he rowed her and a guest to San Francesco del Deserto, an island near Torcello, where they met several friendly Franciscan monks.

Another eminent addition to his circle was Millicent, Duchess of Sutherland (then Lady Millicent Hawes) who had been staying with the Cole Porters when Hartley met her in 1926. He was immediately fascinated by her 'melting, adorable, irresistible quality that no one who knew her will forget'. Of course he was a little blinded by the sheer extravagance of her existence – her Pekinese, the yacht always held in readiness to take her out to sea, the special trains that would be laid on for her – but she had made her life a creative force, her world revolved around others. Although nicknamed 'Meddlesome Milly' (caricatured by Arnold Bennett in *The Card* as Interfering Iris), her character was basically serious; her beauty, which might have been gift enough, was transformed by what Hartley called her 'special radiance, an affluence of personality'. In the Great War she blossomed, working as a nurse at Namur until cut off by the German advance. She wrote an account of her adventures, *Six Weeks of War*, using the proceeds to finance an ambulance unit with which she travelled to France. Here, she did her nightly rounds dressed in nightdress and tin hat. But her 'meddling' was not confined to times of war. As well as being an indefatigable worker for the Red Cross, she campaigned for the improvement of workhouses, the Cripples' Aid Society, women suffering from lead poisoning in the Potteries, and the cottage industries of Scotland. She might truly be said to have been 'in revolt against grandeur'.

But it was always Cecil who was at the core of Hartley's Venetian days. In April 1929 Elizabeth Bowen invited Hartley to lunch with her at Padua, but he declined, explaining that Cecil was with him, trying to complete his life of William Cowper, eventually published as *The Stricken Deer*. 'I feel he ought to have every inducement to bring it to an end', he told her.[15] Attempts to finish the manuscript were hampered when part of it was destroyed after Cecil left it on top of the terracotta stove in the San Sebastiano sitting-room. Hartley wondered at Cecil's calm acceptance of the charred remains, but the damage was less extensive than they at first thought. In March of the following year, both Cecil and Leo Myers were with

Hartley, dining with the Johnstones and entertaining them and the Hultons. His relationship with Anne Johnstone had relaxed, he enjoyed her company, and did not see her as often as he would have liked, though he thought it unjust of her to accuse him of leading a double life (presumably between England and Venice) – 'I haven't the art to lead even a single one properly.'[16]

Cecil's visit was marred by his digestive problems, and by the middle of May he had returned to England, from where news reached Hartley that he had decided to leave Oxford, a decision that came as a complete surprise. We can only guess at Hartley's frustration at the pressures that affected his fondness for Cecil. Hartley's temper was unpredictable, and he was making conscious efforts to control it, aggravated as it was by the books for review that continually arrived and the lack of progress with his own fiction. Hutchinson offered to publish a volume of short stories if he would write another 20,000 words, a task he felt beyond him. The baroness did not help matters, moving in and forcing him to retire into 'those holes and corners that open out of the passage'.[17] He had, in her absence, been sleeping in her bed, *'una persona e mezza'*, and insisted that he could sleep in no other. She submitted, but at dinner – an occasion she often used to expound her theory that the earth had shifted on its pivot – she announced, 'It is a strange thing, that the people I want to die usually die in about twelve months.'[18] By the next spring, the baroness had retired to the left wing, leaving Hartley to occupy her bedroom and salon.

Cecil spent the Easter of 1932 at San Sebastiano, as did Jimmie Smith, Cecil's cousin and second son of the second Viscount Hambleden. A director of W. H. Smith, he had an easygoing personality and a pleasant singing-voice that made him an especially welcome guest in any gathering, and was to remain one of Hartley's most appealing male friends, one for whom he never had a bad word; Jimmie Smith, it seems, understood Hartley's definition of friendship.

Another welcome visitor was the writer Marie Belloc Lowndes, whose friendship with Hartley would last until her death in 1947. Her birdlike appearance and small stature gave little hint of her industry, which outdid anything Hartley would ever manage: almost fifty novels, five volumes of short stories, five plays, five books of memoirs and five biographies. Her crime novels alone, precursors of the 'psychological' thriller, mark her as a distinguished writer. One in particular, *The Lodger*, based on the Jack the Ripper murders, was hugely successful. Marie's outlook on life, fortified by her strong

Catholic faith, is captured in the title of one of her memoirs, *I, Too, Have Lived in Arcadia*. There was a happy marriage to F. S. A. (Freddie) Lowndes, who for twenty years was in charge of the obituary column of *The Times*: Marie's knowledge of society, her friendship with Henry James, her encouragement of young writers (among them Hugh Walpole, Frank Swinnerton, Margaret Kennedy, James Hilton, Graham Greene and, of course, Hartley), and her cosmopolitan way of life, with her love of France where she had been brought up and of America, her second home, made her his ideal partner. Hartley may have had reservations about her qualities as a writer (he was once put out when someone said his work was similar to hers), but none about her qualities as a friend – for Hartley, she had 'that glowing nature where love and friendship dwelt'.[19]

Teresa Berwick was another visitor, followed by Leo Myers in early June. Leopold Hamilton Myers, though not an exacting friend, was a far more complex figure than Jimmie Smith. Fourteen years older than Hartley, he seemed to have all the qualification for being part of Leslie's circle: he was enormously wealthy, and, like Leslie, a novelist who bloomed in his forties. He was a hypochondriac, highly strung and given to periods of great depression. As a writer, he was much concerned with the conflict between the material world and the spiritual. Both men knew they were of the Elect, but Myers longed to descend to the everyday level. It was a tormented wish. He once said that the idea of one of his characters walking down Piccadilly oppressed and frustrated him. By 1932 he had already embarked on his great tetralogy set in sixteenth-century India (though the nearest he ever came to it was Ceylon), eventually published as *The Near and the Far*.[20] Leo Myers had that capacity for friendship that Hartley recognised and cherished, even if his consuming interest in communism, an interest that was eventually to take over and destroy his life, sometimes troubled the waters. What distinguished Myers from the rest of Hartley's circle was his distaste for the privileged classes of which fate had made him a part. It could make him an uncomfortable companion, liable to attack his friends (as on occasion he attacked Hartley) about their way of life.

These friendships, clamouring for Hartley's attention, filled out his life in Venice. By 1932, the pattern of his days here was well established. It was an unexceptional Venetian spring, days in the gondola, the welcome of another consignment of friendship, evenings at Casa Baker, dinners with the Johnstones, until a letter from Cecil brought the most startling change to Hartley's life. It read:

Dear Leslie,
I am engaged to be married to Rachel McCarthy [*sic*]. You will know how – outside my own family I would tell you first of anyone. My dear Leslie – if I had the pen of Milton and the glow of Proust I could never tell you what happiness and wisdom you have brought me in my life – My dear Leslie
　　David[21]

Besides the original, there was a copy of this letter found at Fletton, in Hartley's hand, as if in writing out Cecil's words he was tracing the emotions that brought it into being. Perhaps Cecil entrusted to a letter what he felt unable to communicate face-to-face; the letter distanced him from Hartley's reaction, the depth of which he can have been in no doubt of. Perhaps most painful is the finality of the letter, for it is a parting. It has the residue of love about it. The totally unexpected news swept Hartley off his feet, but by the time he wrote to Ethel on 25 August he had tidied his personal sorrow into something more socially acceptable – the engagement, he confessed, had come as 'somewhat unwelcome tidings':

> They give unmitigated delight to everyone else! And I suppose one ought to feel pleased, for Rachel is so nice, and eminently suitable to be the wife of a friend. Still, I wish one's friends could continue to remain unmarried. I had no idea that David was contemplating this desperate step. He went abroad at the end of July, was very unwell, and immediately he got back he became engaged. I haven't seen him, but letters, somewhat valedictory in tone, have passed between us.[22]

The complete truth of Hartley's disappointment would surely have been safe with Ethel, who well understood the depth of homosexual love – was not her passion for Nan the perfect example of it? It may be that in later years he confessed his feelings for Cecil to her; Ethel, and certainly Ottoline, who had a good understanding of Leslie, must at least have suspected the profound effect the news of Cecil's departure from his life would have on him. The evidence suggests that Cecil had been moving away from Hartley immediately leading up to his engagement. But it is the voice of Cecil's letter that is so striking, the testament to all that Hartley had meant to him and, implicitly, all that Cecil had meant to Hartley. Above all, it was a repudiation of their intimacy. Had Hartley ever told Cecil what he felt for him? Could he have brought himself to the point, or was the possibility of a descent into chaos too repulsive for Hartley to contemplate? What is obvious is that Cecil was aware of Hartley's passion for him; even if it had never been spoken, Cecil's letter takes it as understood, and, having understood it, puts an end to the matter. It was Cecil who had decided to curtail the possibility of their life together. Hartley was powerless to do anything, and must have felt the want of having stood back from any proclamation of love. Nothing would be the same between them again. In announcing that he was walking out of Hartley's life, Cecil had committed the greatest act of betrayal.

If Hartley regretted the loss of all they had had together, it was not in his gift to turn away from Cecil. Far from shielding himself from the pain that Cecil and Rachel's relationship brought him, he transformed himself into a sort of consort to the happy couple, accompanying them on expeditions to find a suitable house within reach of Cranborne and London, and agreeing to be best man at their wedding at St Bartholomew's, Smithfield, a favourite scene, Hartley recalled, of martyrdoms. The trust he invested in friendship had been destroyed by the most precious companion of his life, but he could not look beyond to the hope of some new emotional force. The links would never be broken; in later years Cecil himself appeared to want to sustain at least the vestige of intimacy, even if his wife was now part of the equation. The friendship turned into adherence, shared Christmases, shared houses, promises to visit, long telephone conversations, remnants of what had been. Best man, and godfather to Cecil's first son, he might be, but Hartley would never forgive him. In many of his letters of later years, whenever he mentioned Cecil, it was with a sense of bitterness.

The fading of the one great friendship could only be compensated by the great line of other friendships that stretched through Hartley's life. The loss was terrible. 'How many lives you must lead!' he told L. A. G. Strong that October, 'I hardly lead one.'[23] He complained to Ethel that summer that he was 'a little tired of communal life and gregarious pleasures – as you know they are contrary to my individualistic principles and solitary temperament',[24] but the social round continued in England, including visits to the Berwicks at Attingham, and to the Elchos' home, Stanway House, where a harassed Cynthia was coping with an often bedridden J. M. Barrie. At the end of October, Hartley returned to Venice where he stayed (his usual procedure) until the beginning of December, but, he admitted to Ottoline, 'I feel a little out of love with it, the weather was so horrible and my Venetian personality irked me.'[25] He sent her 'the usual bottle of "Colomia del Re"', one of the perfumes he regularly bought her from Venetian perfumeries, whose wares would be sprayed over him in the shop for his approval; bottles of 'the same mixture as before' were often sent off to Ottoline.

At least the publication of *The Killing Bottle*, a collection of ghost stories, some commissioned by Cynthia for inclusion in her anthologies, reintroduced him to the public as a writer of fiction. A marked advance on *Night Fears*, its stories are at once more substantial and determinedly Gothic, revealing Hartley as the natural successor to M. R. James and E. F. Benson; it might be said that Hartley does for the English house party milieu what James had already done for the ecclesiastical. The conviction that the human body is capable of physical deviousness is no less strong than in the first collection, becoming even more terrible when placed against the slightly fustian social background of the country house, the constant 'weekending'. There is a sense of control of the material that is impressive, the ability to introduce the fright at the most effective, often understated, moment. When horror arrives, it is not only unexpected but a repudiation of the smooth lives of the smart set that peoples the pages. The ghastliness of the unexpected visitor is often distinguished by the flexibility of its limbs. In 'Mr Blandfoot's Picture', set amongst a group of Benson-like English ladies presided over by the fading hostess Mrs Marling, the newcomer Mr Blandfoot is 'put together so loosely that one or other of his limbs always seemed on the verge of dislocation',[26] hardly surprising in a man whose dictum that 'the flesh, for example, is the circumstances of the soul' unnerves the genteel society of Settlemarsh.[27] And it is the flesh that makes up Mr Blandfoot's most unusual (but never described) picture, flesh that is horrific to the ladies of Settlemarsh, who had so longed to see Mr Blandfoot's work of art. Blasphemous or repulsive Blandfoot's picture may be – it is a mark of the story's skill that we can only guess – but it is certainly an obscenity.

Fog and wetness pervade 'A Visitor from Down Under', in which Mr Rumbold is made aware of his nemesis in a wireless broadcast of a children's party, the insistent voices of the 'Here We Come Gathering Nuts and May' telling him that he will be 'fetched away' by Jimmy Hagberd, a man Rumbold has murdered. Murder must have its retribution, and when there is no relative or friend to act on the victim's behalf, the victim himself is stirred to revenge. The dead Hagberd arrives at Rumbold's hotel, asking the porter to deliver his message – 'Would he rather that I went up to him, or that he came down to me?'[28] Rumbold sends a message wishing the visitor to

Hell, where he belongs. Later, a shot is heard, and the porter enters his room, sickened by 'the sight of an icicle on the window-sill, a thin claw of ice curved like a Chinaman's nail, with a bit of flesh sticking to it'.[29] *The Killing Bottle* is full of death stepping over the threshold of polite social gatherings; it enlivens the pointlessness of it all. Death is the gatecrasher that gets into the carefully regulated household for 'The Cotillon'; it is the monstrous duty of 'The Killing Bottle', through which the beauty of the butterfly is at once made still and everlasting; it is in every aspect of the great old house in 'A Change of Ownership', with its threatening garden and

> that odd flat tract in the long grass. It always looked as if something large had trampled upon it, lain upon it, really: it was like the form of an enormous hare, and each blade of grass was broken-backed and sallow, as though the juice had been squeezed out of it.[30]

It is man's identity that is treated here, the unsureness of one's own being, exaggerated when the hero is faced with getting into the house he has always loved, and longed for, even if (just as in Hartley's attitude to Fletton Tower) it frightens him. Limbs, again, play their part. The housekeeper eventually discovers four sets of curious marks, 'the prints of hands. The fingers, pointing into the room, were splayed out and unnaturally elongated; where the hand joined the wrist there was a long shapeless smear.'[31] Despite the evidence of two pairs of hands, we know that the hero dies when he at last faces the evil presence within the house: it is his 'own face, a hateful face, and the face of a murderer'.[32] Thus does death deal with the usurper, the social outsider.

Only 'Conrad and the Dragon', the final story, breaks away from those that precede it. This is no ghost story, but a classically shaped fairy-tale within its framwork of 'Once upon a time' and 'lived happily ever after'. This is the world of woodcutters, pretty princesses, bold knights in armour and unvanquishable beasts, that Grimm would have recognised, though here the fairy-tale form is exploited to present material, so personal to Hartley, that would have been almost impossible to convey within the confines of a less disciplined genre. When, as a writer, he wanted to commit some deep truth, he often turned to the fairy-tale: he would do it later in 'The Crossways', in 'Roman Charity', in 'The Ugly Picture', and in the novel *Facial Justice*. The use of fable forces his writing to the bareness of truth; in the simplicity of the form, his strongest feelings about the human condition break through uncluttered, undisguised, perhaps even unknowingly.

So it is in 'Conrad and the Dragon'. Conrad, a seventeen-year-old peasant, follows in the footsteps of the many brave young men who have tried for the hand of the elusive and lovely princess; all have been killed by the dragon whose 'hate, rage, and lust of blood were clearly reserved for those who really loved the Princess'.[33] As elsewhere, limbs play funny tricks: the princess has a shadow that has a life of its own 'which, like a dog that dreads reproof but cannot bear its banishment, had stolen back to the wall',[34] and, when Conrad at last manages to deliver a terrible wound to the dragon, the princess's attendant hurries through the palace to her room, 'though how he could go like that, his face looking backwards all the time, Conrad did not understand'.[35] In fact, the beauty of the princess bears the price of malevolence, and it is Conrad's skill in forming words before the dragon that sound like praise of her loveliness 'but to him, the speaker, would mean something very different' that prepares the way for Conrad's slaying of the beast.[36] Fatally injured, the creature slinks out of sight, and Conrad enters the palace, where he finds the dying princess, with the same gash in her neck as the dragon. There are no answers to Conrad's question: 'Why should I kill her? I love her. It was the Dragon I killed.'[37] Thus is the link between love and death established, in the baldest of narratives. Like Lavinia Johnstone, the princess turns away from the possibility of love and sexual fulfilment, and the price she pays is higher than Lavinia's. The price, of course, is that paid by many other of the characters that would come down the years of Hartley's fiction. In 'Conrad and the Dragon' the lesson has already been learned: love is killing.

It was in the Venetian spring of 1933 that Hartley first met another of his lifelong friends, Osbert Sitwell, who, with the composer Gerald Berners, was a guest of Victor Cunard's. Hartley dined there on 2 April, nervous that the writer should present him in one of his books as one of 'the idle and idiot well-to-do'.[38] Five days later, Berners and Sitwell dined at San Sebastiano, an event that Hartley dreaded – 'I feel sure my false teeth will fall out.'[39] 'I like Osbert Sitwell very much and enjoy his stories', he told Marie Belloc Lowndes, 'but they're not very kind, are they? He keeps giving me searching looks, as though committing some defect to memory, for subsequent use.'[40]

It was now, too, that Hartley met Sitwell's lover, David Horner.

Hartley enjoyed years of correspondence with both men, but David Horner supplied the liveliest of the two friendships. Horner loved gossip, and loved to spread it, and the directness of his letters sometimes spills over into mischievousness. Slender, with a delicate face and a head of blond curls, and beautifully dressed – Sitwell described him as 'orchidaceous' – Horner (who said he was descended from the Little Jack Horner of the nursery rhyme) had a flamboyance, and certainly an ease about his homosexuality, that seemed light years away from Hartley. But they took to each other, beginning a friendship that survived most of the years when Horner was caught in the crosscurrent of hostility between the Sitwells, who grew to revile him. Only age, illness and misunderstanding finally wore away their relationship. As a regular visitor to Renishaw Hall, the Derbyshire home of the Sitwells, and to their Italian seat at Montegufoni, Hartley was warmly welcomed as a constant friend to Osbert, David Horner, and Edith.

Biographers of the Sitwells have sometimes suggested there was little more to Horner than his machinations among the Sitwells and his sex-seeking escapades, but he was a man of taste (perhaps encouraged by his mentor, the Vicomte Bernard d'Hendecourt, with whom he had lived in Paris) and literary ability. The fact that he understood the quality of his friendship with Hartley made him especially important. 'I can't tell you how I value yours', Hartley told him seven years later. 'I feel it is a contract – not a cruel contract – and as I should like it to be in duplicate, may I say how much I treasure your friendship and the times we have had together?'[41] Their relationship was strengthened with 'the assurance of pleasure that comes from sympathy and affinity and mutual confidence'.[42]

Jimmie Smith was the perfect companion for ten days in April – 'He is so nice, I am very fond of him'[43] – and sang at a concert Hartley arranged at San Sebastiano. The performers probably included Hartley's other guests, the poet and Chinese scholar Arthur Waley and his mistress (whom the Johnstones, naturally, refused to receive) Beryl de Zoëte; a proficient dancer, nicknamed 'Baby Beryl' by Edith Sitwell, she was no doubt persuaded to dance to Waley's flute-playing. Victor Gollancz called, turning Hartley's revolving bookcase in search of any yellow covers, impressing Hartley as bluff, hearty and inhospitable. Rosalind Lyell, a friend who had somehow fallen foul of Anne Johnstone, arrived in Venice hopeful of a reconciliation with the great lady: 'I flutter about', Hartley explained, 'a rather heavy dove burdened with olive branches.'[44] At the Johnstones he met Princess Marthe Bibesco (Antoine Bibesco's cousin)

who was passing through Venice with her cat. Evenings spent at
Casa Baker could be difficult when Hartley was asked to chatter to
his hostess, a feat made difficult by having to shout every word into
'a forbidding-looking instrument, which hums like a top'.[45]

'A lot of people have passed through', he wrote to Ottoline at the
end of April, '. . . one meets and talks, but nothing seems to come
out of it all.'[46] He felt this never ceasing round of people he did not
really wish to see was part of the penalty of living in a foreign
country. Anne Johnstone observed that Venice was the only place in
the world where 'if you don't see people, you are compelled to say
you don't like them – which complicates life very much.'[47] All this
had to be coped with in what Hartley confessed to Ottoline was a
neurotic state. His reviewing he saw as nothing less than a substitute
for life itself, a device to keep him at arm's length from experiences.
Duckworth offered him £35 for writing a brief life of John Bunyan,
but he turned it down – 'I am a dilatory and unrejoicing worker.'[48]

Bessie Hartley and Harry Clifford Pilsbury arrived in Venice in
May, leaving him at the end of the month feeling 'very lonely and
forlorn'. 'The house seems very silent', he wrote, 'and not itself at
all. I hoped you might have left some little thing in your bedroom,
but you haven't – only a faint perfume which will soon disappear
when I begin with my cigarettes . . . You were so sweet – Everyone
misses you – I the most.'[49] Is it too harsh to suspect a disingenuous
quality in Hartley's regret that 'Dearest Muz' had returned to
Fletton? She, after all, was one of the main reasons for his Venetian
life. She had helped to make exile attractive, necessary. Hartley
needed the geographical gap between himself and Bessie; the
countless letters dispatched to Fletton were, Norah always insisted,
his way of keeping Bessie at arm's length. From the evidence
available, it seems that Bessie made only two or three visits to
Venice, on one occasion accompanied by Enid (Norah never made
the journey).

Three weeks later, after a visit from an Oxford friend Rex
Littleboy, who brought 'an American youth he is looking after',[50]
Hartley left Venice en route for Paris and so on to England where
by mid July he was complaining of being worn out by London life.
Returning to Venice in the autumn, he worked at extending 'Back
to Cambo', which he had laid aside seven years before, but by the
middle of November was once again at a standstill. It was not only
the stream of people that passed by, but the enforced switching of
his mind to other people's writing, that so distracted him from any
creative work of his own. More guests provided another reason for

setting the book aside. Ian Campbell-Gray stayed long enough to paint a portrait of Pietro in the gondola, followed by Leo Myers with whom Hartley spent long days in the gondola, rowing to the port at Marghera and to the island of Podolo.

A continuous stream of visitors made the pilgrimage to San Sebastiano in the spring of 1933. Hartley had arrived in Venice in late March after six days in Rome. It was his first time in the city 'and I found it rather bewildering. I felt I never wanted to see another statue. How untrue it is to speak of the forgotten, or the vanished, past!'[51] The people he thought 'so full of curiosity and (apparently) of malice',[52] though he returned for three days in November as the guest of Philip and Phyllis Nichols, visiting Tivoli to see Hadrian's villa in the fading light of day. His first days in Venice were more solitary: he rowed out towards the men's lunatic asylum at San Servilio, and made another expedition to the desolate Podolo where he rescued a starving cat, stalking it with pigeon bones, an incident used for the story 'Podolo' in *The Travelling Grave*. Jimmie Smith came, and the Morrells in early May. Ottoline 'couldn't have been nicer and Philip too was most amiable';[53] they took tea with the Johnstones and Hultons and met the Princess Aspasia. Ethel Sands, whose material wealth (along with Nan Hudson's) had declined sharply – they were planning to live at Auppegard with just one maid – came in mid-May, and brought Kenneth Clark to dinner. Gabriel Herbert arrived on the 23rd, then Cecil and Rachel and, again, the Morrells; the presence of so many 'altered the rhythm of my life'.[54] Ottoline was offered 'that big room with the Marat bath' and the rather poky eyrie at the top of the house.[55] 'You are the perfect guest', Hartley assured her,[56] a view perhaps shared by Anne Johnstone who almost commanded Hartley to bring Ottoline to lunch. When he refused, she wrote to Ottoline describing Hartley as 'intransigent'. It seemed to him as if very few people were coming to Venice, and those that did come were not always welcome. Mrs Keppel, a guest of Sir Hubert Miller's, was one such: 'I don't take to her very much, do you?' he asked Ottoline. 'She fills up the room so, somehow.'[57]

England, as usual, gave him no cause for rejoicing: 'I think I have a sterilising effect on my surroundings: nothing ever happens where I am.'[58] There was the obligatory time to be spent at Fletton, as well as a holiday with Bessie and Harry at the Le Strange Arms Hotel in Hunstanton, visits to Gower Street to see Ottoline and to deliver the latest smuggled bottle of perfume, and the usual hectic round of house-parties and weekends. His frustration at not being able to finish his 'Eustace' story grew stronger, perhaps fuelled by the theory that its publication might mean he could give up reviewing. 'I long to!' he informed Ottoline,' – and yet shrink from facing the world, and my relations, without an earned income (however small). It shields one from disapproval, I feel.'[59] He was working at the book in Venice in the winter of 1934 but felt little sense of progress and 'It is difficult in any case to write about children without condescending to them or being funny at their expense or seeing more depth and continuity in their emotions than there really is.'[60] At Fletton the following April the book was about a third completed, and already Hartley was seeking its approval. Cynthia read it, and made encouraging noises, urging him to 'get on with it as quickly as possible'.[61] Elizabeth Bowen especially pleased Hartley by her delight in Hilda. He replied:

> I was afraid her rigid outlook and repressive behaviour might alienate any respect, liking, sympathy or patience the reader might have felt for her. I always seem to put her in a situation where she displays her passion for moral censorship. Later on, I trust her character will appear more *noble* – she is meant to be a bigger gun than poor Eustace.[62]

But what hope was there of his ever being able to finish it? By the middle of April 1935 he had picked up his Venetian life once again, welcoming Jimmie Smith, Leo Myers, Bessie and Enid (who came in May), and the redoubtable Sibyl Colefax with whom he 'whirled about the town and countryside, despoiling china factories'.[63] Lady Colefax departed in late June – 'another day and I might have had nervous prostration'[64] – but the difficulties of the Venetian set would not go away. Hartley's relationship with Anne Johnstone was strained by her continual pinpricks at him; he seriously considered severing the connection, but weathered the storm. Mrs Baker, on a visit to San Sebastiano, announced that 'the discovery of your sense of humour, Mr Hartley, is not the less welcome because it comes after many years.'[65] There was the opportunity to renew his acquaintance with the talkative and still dancing Beryl de Zoëte and the taciturn Arthur Waley, she 'wonderfully accomplished and agreeable specially after six months ... with native dancers at Bali'[66] before his summer return to England (via Ethel Sands and Auppegard). The summers of these Venetian years must have been eagerly awaited by Bessie. For many years she and Hartley would rent Cynthia's house at 8 Sussex Place for several weeks, but her hours with Hartley were subject to constant disruption. 'I wish we didn't have to be separated', he wrote to her on 1 August, 'but it won't be for long.'[67] His tour continued: from Frome to Pixton, from Henley on Thames to David and Margaret Davies (alias Margaret Kennedy) at Hendre Hall in Wales, from Renishaw to Clovelly Court in Derbyshire, and so on to Lady Violet Bonham Carter at Tilshead Lodge in Wiltshire.

The worsening political situation between England and Italy did not prevent him from returning to Venice in November, when a *rapprochement* was reached with Anne Johnstone, who now insisted that she hated Anthony Eden as much as Italians did, especially his eyelashes; in Venice, a restaurant called the Eden had changed its name to the Aloisi. In fact, Hartley had hesitated to make his second visit of the year. His friend Ernest Saltmarshe had written from the Grand Hotel in late September that 'Outwardly everything is just as usual here, and, save for the Piazza and other buildings being plastered with portraits of the "Duce" and patriotic sentiments, there is nothing to show that anything is going on.'[68] Pietro had made enquiries about Hartley's intentions, but Saltmarshe could only advise against Hartley making the journey at a time when the Italian press was becoming ever more bitter about England, and Saltmarshe himself left Venice, it was said for good, the following year.

Paris may have held more obvious charm, when Hartley stayed with Edith Wharton for three days in October 1936 at her house, the Pavillon Colombe, in St Brice-sous-Forêt. His introduction to the novelist may have been through Ethel, whose circle intersected with Edith's. At this meeting – not their first – Edith was 'very nice ... [she] grows less formal on nearer acquaintance', he told Marie.[69] Of course, he was in awe of her, remembering that somebody had once said of her that 'She despised the rich for not being writers, and writers for not being rich.'[70] She must, indeed, have been one of the biggest fish Hartley ever landed – she carried heavy guns, both social and literary, and proclaimed her standards of art and behaviour. The visit must have been a trial. Hartley was almost afraid to breathe, let alone sit down, the house was so well ordered; being in her company, he said, was like 'entering for a race'.[71] Within ten months, Edith Wharton was dead.

Whatever hospitality Venice had offered (never as much as the Johnstones had promised) was fading away, but Hartley required it to go on giving what he had always expected of it, that it should be a haven of sympathy, of understanding, of escape. With the death of Anne Johnstone in January 1937 it seemed that the days of such reassurance were, if not over, at least threatened; her passing coincided with an awareness of the decline of the Venice that Hartley had known. He felt her death more strongly than might have been supposed, but he had never underestimated resilient personalities even if 'fond as I was of her I should have found her personality too emphatic for daily use.'[72] The dwindling colony over which she had reigned was left without a leader; Venice, as well as Mr Johnstone, had been widowed.

Hartley was already aware that his life would have to change. Reading his letters to Ottoline there is a feeling that it was to her alone that he could unburden the doubt and unhappiness he felt. She, after all, had been his first model (beyond Aunt Kathleen) of sympathetic friendliness, free of the moral strictures that kept Anne Johnstone on a different level. When he arrived in England for the summer of 1937, he was seriously considering buying a house, perhaps in Wiltshire, but was uneasy that having his own property would mean that he would spend even less time at Fletton. There had been no lessening of the guilt he felt about Bessie's needs. There was never a doubt that he would have settled for Venice, the one place where he was happy for any length of time; 'it is where my thoughts turn and my roots go deepest – though supported on piles!'[73] But San Sebastiano had lost many of its amenities; the *rio* was being turned into a canal exclusively for motorboats, making it impossible for him to ride up to the house in his gondola, or leave it below his window. Where to settle was problem enough, but Ottoline identified two other areas of major concern. Hartley agreed:

> As you say, writing a book that interested one would be a great help and having fewer and more intimate friends, another: I don't despair of effecting both these reforms! As to the little personal details which life in an English village might provide I get them, I think, in Venice: they, the Venetians, take so much interest in one, it is easy, or easier, to give it back. Easier than here, I think, where class distinctions are stronger.[74]

There was no longer any hope that Venice might effect any great transformation in him. If he had looked to Venice for inspiration in his fiction, it had largely failed him. He complained of losing his temper with the staff at San Sebastiano, of his 'peevish' moods. Hypochondria was a constant threat, made worse by his feeling of guilt that any illness was brought on by his own imprudence. He described his nerves to Ethel as 'little gusts of panic that come on when I have to sit very still and only last for a few seconds, but leave one unreasonably depressed';[75] Ottoline was told of his 'more or less chronic' neurotic state.[76] Perhaps the visitors to Venice were fewer now, but still they came in 1937: Harry and Bessie in May, Eddy Sackville-West who took to gondola life and stayed for a month, the painter Henry Lamb and his wife Pansy, the painter Adrian Stokes. In England that year he was more than ever migratory, never in one place for more than a day or so, seldom able to collect his belongings, let alone his thoughts 'which are always, in any case, *very* far below the surface!'[77] Few friends now ventured out to Venice, some found the journey too long or too expensive, or were discouraged by the political uneasiness and Hitler's visit to the city in 1938. Leo Myers, who had, despite his own riches, always detested the lives of the moneyed classes, took against Italy completely.

Ottoline Morrell's death on 21 April did more than rob Hartley's Venice of one of its reasons for being; she had been the ideal medium through which so much of his early life had been conducted. Hartley's letters to her may strike the reader as obsequious (he was always in awe of her), but she never exercised any haughtiness over him and, her richest gift of all, she showed Hartley how friendship might be elevated on to a sublime plane. For Ottoline, 'social encounters were not a mere exchange of civilities on the beaten track of hospitality, they were adventures in which the prize was a shared moment of great significance and beauty'.[78] She gave of herself in a way he had never experienced before; she did more than lend enchantment to existence, she interpreted it, gave it new light, offered new perceptions. 'You re-created Venice for me', Hartley had once told her – 'while you were there I saw it with new eyes.'[79] For Hartley, her whole being had been achieved by genius. The potency of her approval, her fondness, her willingness to give him comfort, was perhaps never achieved by any other. At the end of his life Hartley told a friend that he regarded gratitude as the greatest of the emotions, and, in having known Ottoline, he displayed it now:

> We shall not forget her welcome, which stole through one's being like an elixir; still less her farewells which, prolonged like a phrase of music that cannot bring itself to die, renewed themselves on the doorstep and in the street, testifying in a hundred tones and cadences to the preciousness of friendship and the sorrow of parting. With a last fluttering wave, a final half encouraging, half despairing cry, she submitted to the encroaching distance; but the gesture and the voice, so uniquely her own, lingered in the memory and still linger.[80]

It may be that a last bottle of perfume, 'Sea Appeal', was never delivered. 'She was a very good friend to me', Hartley wrote to Marie, 'and I miss her.'[81]

Even now, with Ottoline gone, there was a quantity of friendship both in Venice and England that survived her suggestion that Hartley was somehow constricted by it. The summer of 1938 was as hectic as ever: in August he and Bessie stayed with Margaret Kennedy in Wales, and travelled on to Northumberland, to Renishaw, to Cynthia at Weymouth, to Greenlands at Henley on Thames with Jimmie Smith, to Cranborne, Fletton and London, where he attended the première of one of Marie's plays. And so to Venice, mosquito bites and the wetness of the late October. His temper was frayed, despite the efforts of Victor Cunard to calm it. Together they rowed the six miles to the Brazilian Bertie Landsberg's enchanting villa, Malcontenta, where Hartley was a frequent guest, across the lagoon, past the port of Fusina along the Brenta to the lock-gates and swing-bridge which revolved to make room for the gondola at Malcontenta's water-gate, hung over with willows. A very fat Bertie Landsberg was standing at the top of steps crowned by a great colonnade, ready to offer a welcome of Latin exuberance that included kissing Hartley's cheeks. Malcontenta was Landsberg's passion, its restoration his mission, and Hartley gloried in the Brazilian's torrential conversation, the life that poured out of him, made irresistible by such affection and sensibility, even if the good lunch was spoilt by the chilly room and vinegary wine.

What remained of Venetian society did its best to make Hartley welcome. Mr Johnstone presented him with his wife's set of Gibbon: Mr Johnstone 'grows ever more like Youth at the Prow – I only wish I were more like Pleasure at the Helm'[82] – an unlikely prospect, for Hartley was lonely and, he told Bessie, 'sulky'.[83] Even at this late stage of his Venetian life, there were new recruits. He dined with Mr Johnstone, meeting the Prince and Princess Charcharadze and understanding little of their French conversation. Lady Drogheda came to dinner at San Sebastiano, bringing her little dog which peed on the carpet. Victor Cunard introduced his new tenant, the towering, Roman-nosed Lady Juliet Duff, a welcome, if minor, addition, to Hartley's collection of *grande-dames*. Like Ottoline and Ethel, her outstanding talent was said to be for friendship that embraced writers and artists. Her charm was held in high regard by her great friend Hilaire Belloc, inspiring his lines:

First in his pride the orient sun's display
Renews the world, and changes night to day.
A little later – round about eleven –
Juliet appears, and changes earth to heaven.

A more provocative visitor was Alick Schepeler, once the mistress of Augustus John, and a combative conversationalist who, like Myers, was given to railing against the rich among whom she happily circulated. The baroness, as contradictory as ever, paused to paint a picture of Hartley 'a good deal unclothed',[84] and November wound on, bringing, on the 26th, 'the most beautiful day of my stay'.[85] He took Dorothea Watts (who would eventually marry Bertie Landsberg, despite the late Mrs Johnstone's condemnation of the Watts family, whom she claimed used brass cutlery that was poisonous to the system) 'gondoling' to the canal between the acacia trees beyond Fusina. As they came back at the end of the hot day, the Alps were clear and the water so still that they could see the mountains and their pinkish snow crests reflected in it. Two days later Hartley was in Rome as the guest of Lady Perth at the British Embassy, before returning to Venice for a few days and so, reluctantly, back to England.

Bessie's hope, of course, was that Hartley would resolve his life, and hers, by making Fletton his permanent home. She even instigated some major rebuilding work at Fletton to lure him back, a clear signal, Kitchin advised, that he should at last look for a home of his own. If not at Fletton, Bessie hoped they might live together in London, where he would be near his smart friends, and she would have access to the very best doctors. If this was impossible, she hoped he might be persuaded to take a house within easy reach of Peterborough. She sent details of a property at Godmanchester that she thought might be suitable, but Hartley replied, 'do you think 5 bedrooms would be quite enough? And I don't feel sure that the Fens really suit me.'[86] Whatever decision had to be made, he was incapable of making it; he clung to the pattern of his life that he had followed for the past twelve years, still coping with the constant stack of reviewing (even if Harry, or Norah, or Victor Cunard, sometimes wrote them for him when deadlines became impossible). This was not an infrequent arrangement: Harry especially, was always happy to offer up his judgement of a new novel, even if his review was published in disguise as the work of one of Britain's most respected critics. And Venice, to which he returned in the spring of that last year, gave him the perfect excuse for indecision.

The Bibescos were with him in June, arriving so late that he had drunk most of their cocktails and received them in 'a sadly over-heated state'.[87] He recognised the tensions between them. When Elizabeth stipulated that she and Hartley should lunch alone in the gondola the following day, he understood how Antoine somehow cramped her style. When Antoine got Hartley alone he fired off any number of questions, asking not only how Elizabeth might give her writing more popular appeal, but quizzing Hartley on other, more intimate matters. There was lunch on the lagoon with Bertie Landsberg and Lord Gerald Wellesley and bathing at St Giorgio in Alega. Pietro impressed Hartley by saving a man with two artificial legs who had fallen overboard. For a few days Hartley left Venice to stay with Molly Berkeley in England, making his return journey to Venice for the first time by air. It was the only time he travelled to Venice by plane, and proved a disastrous journey; he wore earplugs and drank champagne during the flight only with difficulty. After three days of deafness, a doctor extracted 'an immense *wad* which was travelling slowly to my brain'.[88] An air of desperateness hung about his wanting to go back. He longed for Venice to offer what it had always offered him, and Venice was powerless to do it. Yet again, he could only cling on to the last moment, could only stand and watch and wait. The beauty and comfort of Venice was fast dwindling, and was suddenly inaccessible. Within a few weeks, there was war.

✣ 5 ✣

'Why do we have to have a War?'

WHEN HARTLEY COULD no longer find sanctuary in Venice, he blamed England. Just as the promise of the long summer of 1900 had been dashed by the arrival of jazz, and the First World War, so now 1939 had to carry the blame: it was 'the Great Divide ... [cutting] the umbilical cord which joined us to the past'.[1] Three problems had to be resolved: what would he do in the war, where would he live, and who would look after him?

His enthusiasm for the new war was as slight as for the first. He offered himself as 'a blood-transfuser. I had vaguely thought of this as a rather heroic thing to do, and plaintively asked if I should take a rest after it.'[2] He thought he might be told that he would have to rest in bed for a week after giving blood, but was cheerfully told, 'Oh, you'll feel much better.' Bessie was alarmed when he considered helping to night-watch at the local post office. For her, of course, the happiest solution to his problem was that he should come home to Fletton for the duration, but he must have known this would be an impossible situation. Besides, he wanted to live near the water; if he could no longer row on the lagoon in a gondola, he could take a skiff out on the river. Hartley's communion with water, sanctified by Venice, had to continue; he needed to journey across its flat, restful surface, to ride on from the life he had on land into his gentle idyll. Like Molly Berkeley, he longed 'to float on and on in a gondola over the lagoon to the mirage, and from the mirage over the end of the world'.

By October 1939 Hartley had rented Court House, on the river at Lower Woodford in Salisbury, but had only just moved in when he discovered that the local obstructing landowners forbade boating on that stretch of the water. The events that were to inspire *The Boat*, Hartley's great novel of wartime England, published ten years later, had begun. The characters that run through the book had their origins here, too, for it was at Court House that he set off in earnest on the adventure with servants that was to last until the end of his life. It was, of course, unthinkable that he should manage without them, and not only because he was almost totally devoid of even the most rudimentary skills. He could not even turn on a wireless. He had never known a household without servants. His Grand Tour of social stops at the houses of the grand and famous would have collapsed had their hosts been unable to rely on staff. When servants became impossible to obtain or simply impossible, the only alternative seemed to Hartley to be a life in hotels. Servants made his life function. Those that he employed over the years became the people he spent most time with, outside the social circle around which he endlessly moved. To them, sometimes, was entrusted a view of Hartley denied to his admiring friends, as if he had returned from a never ending masked ball.

The world from which these servants, hirelings, paid companions, came, fascinated Hartley. In later life, he said he might have written a book about his experience of them; in fact, he wrote several. When these characters strode into his books, they often brought with them a strong whiff of *nostalgie de la boue*. Many of them have a natural, almost inherited, sensuality, a powerful sense of the vulgar, of artfulness and the urgent need to live life. They also know about sex, which makes them dangerous as well as attractive. Emilio, Lavinia's gondolier in *Simonetta Perkins*, is only the first hired man at the head of Hartley's queue, threatening to interfere with what is socially respectable and sexually admissible; behind him stand Stephen Leadbitter in *The Hireling*, Ted Burgess in *The Go-Between*, Fred Carrington in *The Harness Room*. All four are a kind of man that Hartley could never have been, they wear life easily and casually, do not turn from physical enjoyment, have strong, well-formed bodies which they know how to use. In real life, the underclass of society from which 'staff' came seldom provided such Adonises, and, anyway, Hartley always said he had no talent for picking the right person: his inability to do so would lead on to the gathering catastrophe of his last years.

That could hardly be said of the man who became Hartley's major-domo in 1939; Charlie Holt was very far from being mistaken for Emilio or any of his kin. Taller and a good deal thinner than Hartley, Charlie was a smart, erect figure, an ex-policeman who had been working as doorman at the Jermyn Street night-club L'Aperitif (by which name David Horner always referred to him) when Hartley offered him, his wife and their two young children the chance of a new life. Walter Allen, who met Charlie in later years, saw him as the embodiment of Leslie's own conscience;[3] in the car to or from the house he would pontificate on the ills of the world and his favoured solutions. Charlie looked after Hartley with extraordinary care. Of course, servants were always a class apart for Hartley, who grudgingly acknowledged the necessity of having them. Even the dullest of them brought fresh air from another sphere of life that was unknown to Hartley: their experiences, their philosophy, their values, intrigued him. But it is Charlie who stands alone at the long line of those who were to serve Hartley through his life. Charlie, despite persistent bouts of ill-health, was the steadiest of men; there was no danger in him. As soon as they were installed at Lower Woodford, he began keeping chickens and talked about buying some pigs. It was he who suggested that Hartley try to get the petrol owing to the vicar's son's car which Hartley was garaging at Court House, an idea the vicar received very coolly, pointing out that it would be against the law and that Hartley might be liable to a fine of £20, though he agreed that Hartley might occasionally use the vehicle. There was also the irritating restriction on boating, about which Hartley appealed to the vicar and his wife 'who were very amiable, especially the Vicaress ... but my secret service tells me that her temper is unreliable'.[4]

It was not only that Charlie had the running of Hartley's life, he was to be the one fixed point of his existence for the next twenty years. There can have been no corner of Hartley's domestic existence that Charlie did not know. Charlie's approval, whether of friends or new members of staff, was looked for. When he did not accompany Hartley on his social progress in England and overseas, he remained at home as the protector of his master's household, coping with unwelcome visitors looking over the house, forwarding parcels, sending off warmly friendly letters written in his bold, slanting copperplate. A bundle of them has escaped destruction; in turning their pages, Charlie's latest news is made new again. What we read here might be the life of Mr Polly after he had found happiness, with its details of his visit to his aunt and uncle at Clapham where they took tea on the little lawn at the rear of the house, his chickens, his children, House the gardener's grief at the savage frost, until Charlie signs off:

Well Sir, I haven't any fresh news to write about at present, so will close with the old saying 'Look after yourself'

Please give our regards to Mother and all at home when you write to them.

Cheerio, All the best Sir
    Charlie.

P.S. Have you got any fags, if not I will send some on to you.[5]

Comradeship, the easy exclusivity of men, the whiff of the barrack room – this relationship between master and servant has all, and both understood the friendship it created. Each knew the other's life was something beyond him, but Hartley admired what Charlie had made of himself, and he knew that secrets of life had been granted to Charlie that had been denied to him. For Hartley, it was inevitable that in his fiction Charlie would be romanticised, eulogised, that his sexuality would be explored and transmuted, its potential nurtured and fixed at a point of supreme masculinity.

Hartley thought the Lower Woodfordians, like the Venetians, were slow to offer hospitality, but he knew his stay there was only temporary. He had to put up with the damp climate and the problems of having taken the house unfurnished. The owners interrupted his days by sending prospective buyers to look over the property. 'I am more like a caretaker than a tenant', he complained. 'I don't think I should find a house I like better than this: the garden is so lovely now.'[6] The search for a more permanent home went on. The days filled themselves. The phoney war, the 'bore war', drifted on for what seemed an eternity. When the weather allowed, he bathed in the river from the landing-stage at the bottom of the garden, or went for long bicycle rides, sometimes accompanied by Charlie. It seemed almost as if he had been prised from Venice for nothing. 'Why do we have to have a war?' he asked Bessie.[7] 'The news isn't good, is it. I wish we could come to an agreement now, instead of fighting on, but I suppose one ought not to say so.'[8] Sometimes, there did seem to be a war going on. In the summer of 1940 a seven-year-old evacuee from Portsmouth called Thomas Wallis turned up on Hartley's doorstep ('infinitely self-assured, and during the introductory interview I trembled before him').[9] When an Air Force officer asked if he and his wife might move into Court House Hartley resisted.

Meanwhile, the social roundabout continued revolving with as much speed as the first months of war allowed. An unwelcome Violet Hammersley proposed herself for four days, the vicar and vicaress came for tea, Mrs Holt made a sausage toad for Cecil and Rachel (Cecil was now living in Shropshire with his sister, and told Hartley he would come to see him from time to time). Hartley stayed with Cynthia at Sullington Court, where 'it was sad to see the things from Sussex Place pushed in here and there.'[10] He visited other friends reeling from the turn of international events: at Berkeley Castle, Molly was 'in a state of nervous distraction';[11]

Osbert Sitwell asked him to come to Renishaw where, with David Horner now in the forces, 'events are driving him cuckoo.'[12] Other friends presented other problems, not least Margot Asquith with her embarrassing habit of sending begging letters, written at 3 and 5 a.m. 'One asked for £12 – a curious sum', Hartley thought ... 'In the end I sent her five pounds, but not with a good grace.'[13]

In the spring of 1940 he began making quite frequent visits to Puffin's cousin, Stephen Tennant, at nearby Wilsford Manor, the sombre Edwardian house inherited from his doting mother, Lady Grey, which he had transformed into an exquisite retreat for the bright young things he enjoyed having around him. Now, Wilsford Manor was decked out in lively pinks, fishnets in shades of pastel hung over the banisters, shells had been inlaid into the ceilings. Stephen Tennant's guests, including his lover Siegfried Sassoon, delighted in putting on make-up and the costumes that their host had designed, to act out fantastic masques on Wilsford's meadow-lawns. Rex Whistler designed a small theatre to replace the more mundane tennis-courts. When Hartley became Tennant's neighbour, Syrie Maugham was redesigning the house (her work was later largely undone by the invading Red Cross) in an attempt to keep the war at bay. Compared to the Tennant of Wilsford Manor, the tenant of Court House's attitude to the times appeared almost warlike; when the fighting was all over, Stephen Tennant sought escape from the post-war world by staying in bed.

The exoticism of Wilsford Manor – where he met, among others, E. M. Forster and Margaret Rutherford, who was taking a rest from *Blithe Spirit* – can only have accentuated the insistent domesticity of Court House, but that homely arrangement was upset when, in October 1940, the house was bought by a family who had given Hartley, in his caretaker role, 'a lot of trouble and not a penny by way of tip'.[14] It was an unsettling time for him, with the question of where he might live weighing on his mind 'which seems absurd in the middle of a war, but there it is'.[15] The attitudes of those involved in the ownership and tenancy tangle of Court House irritated him. 'I am now so used to being done down, cheated and overridden that I suppose there is no good pursuing the matter', he told Harry.[16] Even now, through all the years, we can almost feel Hartley's anger at what had happened to him, his impotent frustration at having been turned away from Venice, his enforced return to a country that seemed as foreign as any other, a country for which he now had only a grudging, flawed affection, a country that had driven a wedge between him and his favoured life by pursuing a war that might have been avoided with appeasement. England seemed to be exploiting his natural talent for being moved like a pawn across a chessboard.

More irritation was provided by Lady Janet Bailey, who offered to take the lease of Court House off his hands – 'She spoke exactly as if I had been a recalcitrant furniture depository'[17] – but he took in some of her things. He remained on poor terms with his landlady: he had been left almost no linen, only one pudding basin, the telephone was to be cut off because the previous occupant had transferred her account. 'You shouldn't buy a pig in a poke', he told Bessie,[18] though he hadn't, of course, bought it. He considered acquiring Ipsden House near Wallingford, and looked at houses in Market Harborough. Nothing satisfied; too much irked him. A proposal by a lawyer friend, Cecil Binney, that he should put Hartley's name forward for a full-time War Office job at Blenheim Palace came, as might have been expected, to nothing. Meanwhile, Hartley was getting what he could out of Court House. Cynthia and Beb came to stay, Ethel and Nan, Osbert Sitwell and David Horner, and Algernon Cecil.

Cecil, son of Lord Eustace Cecil, nephew of the third Marquess of Salisbury and the author of biographies of Metternich and Thomas More, was one of Hartley's more formidable male friends. Hartley, as so often with his smart friends, rather quailed before Cecil, and others shared his nervousness: Marie Belloc Lowndes disapproved of the way Cecil shut his mind to anything that challenged his own, fiercely held, views. But he and Hartley took to each other and, at their best moments, enjoyed an almost cosy relationship. In a letter to Marie Belloc Lowndes of 14 October 1944, Hartley describes evenings spent with Cecil at Rockbourne reading, antiphonally, stories of Sheridan Le Fanu.

Over one weekend that must have tested Mrs Holt's talent with the rations, Sibyl Colefax, Lady Juliet Duff and Thornton Wilder stayed. For their host, the greatest success of the visit was 'the abundance of towels. I felt that though the guests had nothing to wash themselves in, or with, they could most luxuriously and copiously *dry* themselves.'[19] On Sundays, willing guests might accompany Hartley to church, where he was now sidesman: 'Indeed, I am almost every official connected with the church it is possible to be.'[20] His need to conform, of course, goes some way to explaining his active participation in his local church. He delighted in the homespun, village activity of its workings, never subscribing to the greater belief that underpins the Christian attitude to religion; the fabric of the church, not the meaning, assumed the greater importance. At church meetings he was a regular, if usually silent and acquiescent, attender.

When the quiet of the early war months vanished, and bombs began to fall on England, Hartley managed to ignore it with as much vigour as he could muster. In 1941 he managed a miniature Grand Tour around England, including at least three stays at Renishaw. There, retiring for the night, he found, awaiting him on his bed, a yellow pullover that Edith Sitwell had knitted for him. 'It is really *very* beautiful, and a good fit as far as it goes, but it doesn't go quite far enough (downwards).'[21] That summer, he spent a week at Berkeley Castle with the plump Molly ('every cubic inch a Countess', according to Sitwell who had just seen her),[22] driving at fifteen miles an hour through the Gloucestershire lanes with Lord Berkeley, his Lordship's doctors having insisted that this was essential for his health. After tea, Molly and Hartley clambered on to their bicycles and rode down to a belvedere at the river's edge to have supper. When moments of such enchantment were still possible, the war seemed sometimes imperceptible.

By the summer of 1941, Cecil and Rachel had decided to move from their home, West Hayes at Rockbourne, but wanted to keep the house on. Hartley had been told it was unlikely he would be able to remain at Lower Woodford after March; the obvious, if again temporary, solution was that he should move to Rockbourne. There were the Holts to consider, Charlie with his indifferent health and his wife with her glum moods and her insistence that if they moved with Hartley she would evacuate the children back to Salisbury. Hartley soon decided that 'by going to Rockbourne I should be doing David a good turn and save about £101 in rent [that is, from October to March 1942].'[23] Most of the time Hartley would have the house to himself, for Cecil only intended to be there for three weeks around Easter. As always with Hartley, there was the difficulty of making up his mind. In August, fed up with waiting for a decision, Cecil put the house in the hands of agents. By October, Hartley had agreed to go, and arrangements moved swiftly ahead. 'I said a fond though hasty farewell to Court House', he told Bessie on 21 October. 'House [the gardener] said I was going away "with the respect of all the village".'[24] While the Holts coped with the move, and remained sweet-tempered about having to re-evacuate their brood, Hartley took himself off to Pixton Park at Dulverton and to Renishaw.

Another, more painful journey had to be made, to Taunton, where Aunt Kathleen languished, her mind tired and dull after the death of George. Her devotion to him had never wavered, through all the years of the Thompsons' faint disapproval of the match. That disapproval had been totally unjustified; he had been a kind and supporting husband to Kathleen, and had risen to a distinguished position within the Bank of England. George's decline had been long and terrible, a complete breakdown fuelled by some religious torment, the details of which will now never be recovered, though Hartley used his uncle's death in *The Brickfield*. With George gone, the centre of Kathleen's life was ripped out. Her writing had fallen away from her. The vitality and inspiration she had invested in Hartley's future could no longer exert itself; what life was left to her was a lingering malaise, during which her loving maid Jane never left her. Jane, triumphant she was no longer the servant, cared, sorrowed and tended until such time as her mistress should no longer have need of her.

The weeks that followed, the first weeks of Rockbourne, were hectic. Invitations for visits were sent off to Violet Hammersley, Marie Belloc Lowndes, to Ethel and Nan. The rector, the Revd Hibbert, proved friendlier than his Lower Woodford counterpart, persuading Hartley to attend his first jumble sale. Of the Rockbournians he was happy to be able to say, 'They have shown me more hospitality in a week than the Woodfordians did in a year!'[25] One of the villagers, Miss Dora Cowell, was soon under Hartley's spell; she was fascinated by him, and a long friendship, flowering in many hundreds of letters, began. Those of Miss Cowell's that have survived are evidence of her haste to answer her hero's pleasure; they dash themselves off across the page, seldom failing to thank him for the kindness he has bestowed on her. 'My dear Don Quixote', they begin, and there is indeed an air of heroic romance about her affection for Hartley. How thrilled Miss Cowell, who lived with her female companion, must have been to have him as a regular visitor to 'Dunbury', where she might offer hospitality with the most genteel enthusiasn. 'Would you care for a glass of *waine*?' she would ask.[26] She thrived on village life, gave parties for the local children with generous offerings of cakes and charades and, through the fluke of geography, became a fond part of Hartley's life; their knowing each other was, for her, probably the greatest achievement of her own. And Hartley, the practitioner of undying friendship, did not disappoint. What tribute could be more lasting than the fact that, almost twenty years later, he dedicated *The Go-Between* to her?

It was as if Hartley felt an almost instant sense of belonging at Rockbourne. Apart from the welcome the village gave him, the reduction of his expenses was another bonus. 'I'm quite well off now', he told Bessie in December. 'It's more than sweet of you to smooth the financial path for me and I am so very grateful, but I can get along all right now.'[27] The servant problem, however, had not been left behind at Court House. Charlie's ulcers were playing up, and a new girl, Alice, announced that she would be leaving in January. Would Lily, one of the Fletton helps, come to Rockbourne for a week or two? Prospective cooks were interviewed in Salisbury. Could the Regina Employment Bureau, through which Bessie had recently found a nurse-companion, find a new cook? Charlie was bad-tempered at the news that Violet Hammersley had now invited herself for a week. 'I feel very much tried with her', Hartley wrote, 'and shall only be able to extend a *scowl* of welcome when the ambulance rolls up.'[28] During her visit, rugs, shawls, fur coats and foot muffs had to be moved around the house with her, while the temperature had to be kept at a stifling 90°. Violet, of course, was ever a difficult guest to postpone, let alone cancel; Nan Hudson told Hartley, 'If you said there was small-pox in the house she'd say she'd been vaccinated.'[29]

Mrs Hammersley's association with disease and her fear of acquiring new varieties was a well-known fact; if anyone could have understood her disposition, it was Hartley. Her hypochondria did not stifle her talents. It was, of course, her reputation as a benevolent and sympathetic hostess, as yet another *grande dame*, that made her an essential part of Hartley's circle. In her Parisian childhood, she had made a friend of Somerset Maugham, and went on to become a patroness of the artist Philip Wilson Steer, and a great friend to Nancy Mitford, Duncan Grant, Arnold Bennett and George Moore. She had been left a widow in 1912 after ten years of marriage to Arthur Hammersley, a rich widower twice her age, who left her with three young children to bring up. The consolation of financial comfort was shattered when she lost much of her fortune in the collapse of Cox's Bank in 1923, but she never failed to live out life in a grand way. If she had beauty, it was the beauty of El Greco's daughter, with the voice and bearing of some great tragic actress; in her richest days, she loved nothing more than floating down the Thames from her house at Bourne End in a gondola, its gondolier specially imported from Venice *à la* Marie Corelli.[30] It was, to some extent, as a provider of the vestiges of yesterday's world that Violet turned so often to Hartley. He, understanding that, did not demur.

Hartley's fondness for painters matched Mrs Hammersley's own, including his friendship with Henry Lamb who lived nearby at Coombe Bissett. It was Hartley's association with Lamb and his wife Pansy that led to Hartley's curious and unexpected contribution to the history of the war. When Neville Chamberlain died in 1940 without having completed a series of sittings for Lamb's portrait of him, Hartley came to the rescue, posing in Henry's studio, a top hat in his right hand, a walking-stick (making do for an umbrella) and gloves in the other. 'My hands are smaller than the late Prime Minister's, and didn't look right, though they looked like mine.'[31] The painting hangs today in the National Portrait Gallery. There was also the possibility of visits to Augustus and Dorelia John at Fryern Court, Fordingbridge, whom Hartley had first met one afternoon in September 1934, on which occasion he had swallowed two cocktails and then began to feel in harmony with the surroundings. John had seemed to him 'rather formidable . . . but exactly like my idea of a great man'.[32] The painter once wrote of Wyndham Lewis, 'What a mistake it is to have a friend – or, having one, ever to see him', but he came to enjoy the sight of Hartley's bicycle turning in at his gate, and would often go with Dorelia or his daughters to visit Hartley. At Fryern Court, John would recite Matthew Arnold as he and Dorelia sat knitting, offering Hartley gin that tasted of methylated spirits. When Hartley entertained, the guests might be persuaded to join in some useful local activity, as when Violet, a comical figure on her hands and knees, helped Hartley collect the Revd Hibbert's cider apples from his orchard floor.

From January 1942 the new cook, Miss Romaine, reigned over Rockbourne, making a promising début despite the occasional uncooked potato, but dissension soon broke out, with Charlie warning Hartley that she was fast exhausting the food store that had been so carefully built up. Miss Romaine warned Hartley that the arrival of guests would put an unbearable strain on her. Informed that they were expected, she said, 'If they choose to come, they must take the consequences', later informing Hartley that 'It will be better when you go away.'[33] For four months Miss Romaine and the gardener did not speak to one another. Hartley's heart sank when she informed him that though she had never stayed in one position for longer than two years, she intended to stay with him forever. To complicate the domestic landscape, two Irish boy evacuees, aged five and six, were billeted in the house, springing out at Hartley from behind bushes, sweeping off their caps and bowing to the ground (did they, one wonders, ever know that this kindly but remote figure would immortalise them in *The Boat?*). How long would Hartley be able to call Rockbourne his home? Cecil announced that he and Rachel intended returning to live there for three months at the end of June 1942, but made it clear they would like Hartley to stay on with them.

Meanwhile, little progress was being made with the novel that was growing from 'Back to Cambo', *The Shrimp and the Anemone*. In April, Huntington reiterated his belief in the book while encouraging Hartley to get up half an hour earlier each day to complete it. His praise was, to put it mildly, fulsome:

> Your psychological insight is consummate, not like a psycho-analyst with invented scientific irrelevances, but like God, with perfect sympathy and understanding of each one's needs ... It would be a sin against the Holy Ghost for you not to go and finish this novel, which is just what I said in 1935.[34]

Sending the manuscript back to Hartley for the second time, Huntington insisted that 'the third time it must be in proof sheets: And you will have lots more proofs in the future, and the row of novels of L. P. H. will grow in bookcases all over the world.'[35] So extravagant were his words that friends, rather crushingly, told Hartley they thought his publisher must be mad. Perhaps thinking that the book might never be finished, Huntington wrote again, the same day, suggesting

> a new plan. Why not think of our *Shrimp and Anemone* as a study of childhood? Certainly without any difficulty you could go on long enough to make a substantial book with the same sort of scenes and experiences that you have so exquisitely described so far. And readers would be perfectly satisfied, whether an adult sequel ever came out or not. We must do something to preserve what you have already done. In the weedy wilderness of contemporary writing it is like manna from heaven.[36]

Hartley was alarmed by the idea of having to write another 20,000 words to finish the novel, complaining that [publishers] 'make a lot of fuss about quality, but quantity is what they *really* want. I told [Huntington] I had already written about 2,000,000 words in reviews! – and the effort had left me rather tired.'[37] The work needed to get the book ready for publication had, of course, to be slotted into the social calendar of 1943: cocktail parties at the Hibberts, visits to Wilsford where Stephen Tennant and Leslie discussed the Brontës, to Renishaw where Edith was in a perpetual muddle with ration books and identity cards, to London for Ethel's birthday party, to Ethel at Fyfield House, Marlborough, to Phyllis Nichols at Lawford Hall, Manningtree. At Rockbourne, the visitors continued to come. Molly Berkeley, Pansy Lamb, Victor Cunard, Alick Schepeler, Puffin Asquith, Marie Belloc Lowndes all made demands on Miss Romaine. When she was whisked off to hospital with water on the knee, the kitchen was left in an apparently filthy state. 'I wish I could find some one else instead of the poor old thing', Hartley lamented.[38] Charlie and Mrs Windsor, the gardener's wife, worked together to concoct his dinner when he returned from doing harvest work with one of the Holt children, having been 'much photographed before the proceedings began, holding a pitchfork etc.'[39] Earlier, the Revd Hibbert had declined an invitation to dinner on the grounds that he would be too tired after his labours in the fields. Though he afterwards changed his mind and came, Hartley could not help thinking this had been a hint.

As Hartley, after the gap of so many years, brought *The Shrimp* to its conclusion, the advice of family and friends was sought. It was not that he welcomed criticism; rather, he abhorred it, and in later years rigid indignation or a threat of legal proceedings might follow from it. What he needed from those entrusted with the manuscript was reassurance, the confirmation that he had pleased. Having set out his own ideas he thus opened himself up to any influence the recipient might bring to bear on him. Up until Hartley's death, David Cecil remained the arbiter of good taste to whom he turned. It was unlikely, of course, that Hartley would commit some literary or social solecism about which he might be pulled up, but he needed that approval, the knowledge that he had not offended, to bolster whatever confidence he had in his own work. Advice was offered from other quarters. Dora Cowell suggested (as did Bessie) that Hilda should be a little more amiable in the later stages of the book; Margaret Kennedy suggested appropriate ages for Eustace and Hilda, nine and twelve respectively, 'but of course, had Hilda been only 12, Dick wouldn't have noticed her'.[40] She went on to advise various resorting of the text, of chapters and pages, enough to strike terror into the heart of any author. Hartley was appalled to learn she earned £200 a week writing film scripts – 'isn't it disgusting? I could hardly conceal my annoyance!'[41]

Hartley completed the book by the middle of the summer, his

sense of relief left suspended when Huntington's welcome of it proved 'quite nice on the whole, though not so complimentary as I hoped'.[42] A revised manuscript was sent off to Putnam on 13 November, Hartley confessing that he was glad to see the back of it. Should he, he asked Huntington, continue to be known as 'L. P.' or reveal himself as Leslie? 'But of course L. P.', Huntington replied. 'The note of dignified austerity is just what is needed for a story about childhood that might sound sloppy.'[43] He couldn't 'abide' any of Hartley's suggested titles, from *The Reward of Virtue* to *Master Eustace*, suggesting instead *The Shrimp and the Anemone – A Prelude*. In fact, Huntington was full of ideas, with this as with Hartley's later novels, pleading that Hartley had left him so much to decide on.

The guest list, despite the amount of work that he was now producing, grew no shorter. In November, Ethel and Nan stayed, mercifully 'looking after themselves', and were then joined by their great friend Raymond Mortimer. A few days later Lady Jebb brought Nancy Rodd (*née* Mitford) to stay, both 'pretty and lively and I'm enjoying their company'.[44] When, fifteen years later, Nancy stayed with Hartley at Bathford, she was making a progression that included visits to Evelyn Waugh and Anthony Powell, but it was Hartley who offered 'the warmest house and warmest heart', as he must have at their first meeting.[45] Though she thought that he, like his peers, took himself rather seriously, she responded to his cosiness, that 'sense of comfortedness'. In search of such happiness, Hartley went on finding delight in the simplest experiences. After dining one evening with Stuart Wilson, he looked admiringly on when five Canadian officers arrived, 'very simple and nice and one sang extremely well, sitting on a sofa quite unconsciously – I don't think an Englishman could have done it.'[46] Hartley, of course, could not have: as always, when confronted by an apparently completely integrated personality, he could only marvel at the magic that had made it possible.

Eustace suffers as much. That need to belong and be accepted (by Hilda, by Miss Fothergill, by whoever is able to hand out praise) is at the heart of *The Shrimp and the Anemone* as it is central to Hartley's existence:

> The effort to qualify for his sister's approval was the ruling force in Eustace's interior life: he had to live up to her idea of him, to fulfil the ambitions she entertained on his behalf. And though he chafed against her domination it was necessary for him; whenever, after one of their quarrels, she temporarily withdrew her jealous

supervision saying she didn't care now, he could get his feet wet and be as silly and lazy and naughty as he liked, she would never bother about him again, he felt as though the bottom had dropped out of his life, as though the magnetic north had suddenly repudiated the needle.[47]

And so the line of imagination begun almost twenty years before in 'Back to Cambo' was ended by the publication of *The Shrimp and the Anemone*; the story of Eustace and Hilda, inspired by Hartley and Enid's childhood days on the shore at Hunstanton, was finally told. The book's reputation as an exquisite study of childhood was quickly established. It is, of course, the relationship between brother and sister, and their love for one another, that is the novel's centre. Emily Brontë's words at the head of the text are at once the warning and explanation of what follows, the proof that all love makes 'the loved one rue'.

It is Hilda, sure, proud and dominant, who decides that the shrimp must be rescued from the sea-anemone that is eating it, an allegorical beginning that gives us in a few strokes Hilda's thrusting decisiveness and Eustace's terrible doubt – what Paul Bloomfield has recognised as symbolising 'the peculiar relationship of Eustace and Hilda, born to kill each other (figuratively) by kindness',[48] that brand of kindness practised by Bessie. Just as the shrimp and anemone are separated, so does Fate seek to break the bonds that tie Eustace and Hilda together. It is Hilda's mischievousness that introduces Eustace to the crippled, frightening Miss Fothergill, propelled along Anchorstone's cliffs by her worldly companion Miss Grimshaw, who thinks she knows Eustace's game: 'He's a tactful little boy', she notes.[49] It is the very innocence of his eventual friendship with the rich Miss Fothergill that alerts Miss Grimshaw's suspiciousness, with some justification, for it is to him that the old lady leaves her fortune, transforming his life and marking the difference that will separate him from Hilda.

Perhaps it is her lack of imagination that is Hilda's real besetting sin; she cannot be accused of a lack of love for her brother, even when she infects him with her own insecurity. Her problem is in loving him too much, Eustace with his conviction that in other children 'obedience had not got into their blood, it was not a habit of mind ... they were not haunted, as he was, with the fear of not giving satisfaction to someone else.'[50] For it is Hilda who must be answered to, satisfied. Beyond her there is the unpretentious Cherrington household (father and aunt), the glamour of Nancy Steptoe (whom Hilda rightly sees as her rival for Eustace's affection) and the impossible grandeur of wealthy Dick Staveley, whose smile so enchants Eustace with its ability to be 'intimate and suddenly cooled, as though it was a gift not to be bestowed lightly'.[51] The lure of the grand life, that had proved so irresistible to Hartley, is the turning point of the book, and it is money that effects it. But, in the transition, something is lost to Eustace. It is his nurse Minney – Bubby, of course, the bearer of the bronchitis kettle, the one trusted keeper of secrets, the understanding and ever sympathetic Bubby – who, Greek chorus-like, alone has the measure of poor Eustace. It is Minney who sees brother and sister as they are, uncritical Minney who alone escapes Miss Fothergill's terrifying denunciation of the females in Eustace's life as 'designing women'. And it is Minney who pours out the book's simplest emotions as she tells Eustace of his benefactor's funeral, Minney who watches from the window of Cambo as the children, their legs tied together for a three-legged race against 'the whole world', struggle along the shore to the chalk road at the top of the cliffs; 'and to Minney, watching from a window, it looked as if they were bound to come to grief before they arrived at the white gate of Cambo.'[52]

Seldom moving out of the minor key, *The Shrimp and the Anemone* is Hartley's most understated novel; he largely stands aside to let the story tell itself. It is the perfect introduction to the reader who knows nothing of its author, revealing as it does so many crucial components of his personality – the novel as confessional. It is a book that hardly ever raises its voice, except to Heaven in Eustace's rapture on the west window of Frontisham church as the Cherring-tons take tea at the Swan Hotel. Here, that sense of otherworldliness so essential to Hartley's being (and to Eustace's) ends with Eustace's desire to become one with the ecstasy of the window; his limbs become magical:

> Disengaging himself from the tea-table he floated upwards. Out shot his left arm, caught by some force and twisted this way and that; he could feel his fingers, treble-jointed and unnaturally long, scraping against the masonry of the arch as they groped for the positions that had been assigned to them. Almost simultaneously his other limbs followed suit; even his hair, now long like Hilda's, rose from his head and, swaying like seaweed, strove up to reach the keystone. Splayed, spread-eagled, crucified (but for fear of blasphemy he must only think the shadow of that word) into a

semblance of the writhing stonework, he seemed to be experiencing the ecstasy – or was it the agony? – of petrifaction.[53]

All of Aunt Kathleen's unending belief in Hartley is here, but she was not to see its publication. By the summer of 1942 she had suffered so severe a mental collapse that she was taken from her home at Taunton into an institution. Bessie, beside herself with the horror of it, signed the papers. 'It does seem such a dreadful thing to happen, especially after that sweet, unselfish life', Hartley wrote consolingly.[54] No one in the institution, he told her, was certified. Jane, who would not be parted from her, made this last journey with her mistress, but there were no more than a few terrible months left to her. The 'unspeakable something of immense worth that you have added to my life' – her passionate trust in Hartley's future – remained. And it is the name of Kathleen Lund that should be remembered in *The Shrimp and the Anemone*, as Hartley did in his dedication. Her love for him had been beyond reproach, and needed no reply. 'And now', she had written to him in 1925, 'don't write for a long time – I understand the effort too well to wish it. I know you too well to need it.'[55]

There had never been a formal arrangement between writer and publisher; only in March 1944 did Huntington send one, with a cheque for £200. And he persisted in pushing Hartley towards being a full-time novelist, despite a new offer of regular reviewing work by the *Illustrated London News*:

> In normal times [Huntington wrote] I would guarantee that two full-length novels in three years would bring you in the £300 a year that the I. L. N. is dangling ... Can you deliver the goods if you refuse the I. L. N.? Wouldn't that leave you as you are with the same burden of reviewing that has always so interfered with the novels that you owe it to yourself and the public, not to say, posterity, to write?
>
> I believe that after the War you could make yourself one of the most highly paid writers in England, but it would mean sacrificing the bird-in-the-hand and concentrating more than you might find easy.[56]

Clearly, Huntington was aware of the social interruptions that demanded Hartley's attention, so it must have been a surprise, perhaps to both men, when the sequel grew rapidly: by September, it had reached 70,000 words. As usual, Hartley was coping with the suggestions of friends as well as ideas put forward by Huntington. There is an ominous hint of Huntington's uneasiness with Hartley when he asks, 'I wonder who your adviser is with whom I habitually disagree? Is it a Jawkins to save you from having to fall out with me?'[57]

The domestic scene continued to offer its own disagreements – Miss Romaine angry and tearful when there was nothing for lunch, Mrs Windsor complaining the atmosphere indoors was too unpleasant, Charlie physically sick after an 'ulcerous' attack, Windsor sacking the gardener's boy. A new housekeeper, an evacuee called Mrs de Silva, moved into the house with her infant daughter. For a time, both house and garden seemed almost to breathe an audible sigh of relief at her arrival. One night, the little girl, Jacqueline, left a posy of grasses, buttercups and daisies on Hartley's pillow. This pastoral idyll was not to last. Soon both Charlie and Miss Romaine were complaining bitterly about their latest colleague. The denouement came when Mrs de Silva made 'surrealist decorations in my bedroom (excuse this Maugham touch) with roses, pipes and cotton-wool, and even made an entry in the book where I keep my private pensees'.[58] The Relieving Officer was summoned to take the unfortunate mother and child back to the workhouse, but there was a last confrontation when they walked into Hartley's room and Mrs de Silva said, 'Look at him, Jacqueline, an Oxford Man and a cad. Say goodbye to the gentleman, darling, he's an Englishman – they're LOUSY.'[59] Hartley recorded the woman's misdoings on four sheets of foolscap paper for the benefit of the Relieving Officer.

It was, as ever, a relief to escape into the social pool, though the stock of London friends had diminished a good deal with the war. Ethel and Nan, constant providers of the sanctuary that Hartley craved, welcomed him to Fyfield House; they were lovely days. He told Ethel, 'Never since the war have I lived in conditions which seemed so proof against the malice of the world – Not by keeping the world at a distance, for you and Nan are so much in it, but by showing how the graces and amenities of life could survive it, undiminished and undimmed.'[60] Nearer at hand, Dora Cowell dispensed sumptuous teas. Meanwhile, the pilgrimage to Rockbourne continued almost unaffected by the war: Sibyl Colefax, Elizabeth Bowen (arriving the day that her bedroom ceiling had been bombed), Eddy Sackville-West, the ever welcome Jimmie Smith, the troublesome Mrs Hammersley. Alick Schepeler provoked her usual disagreements, not only with her constant railings against the rich, even more savage than Leo Myers, but with her definitive generalisations (Miss Schepeler: 'I don't like Italians.' Hartley: 'I don't much care for Russians, come to that').[61] The overlapping of disparate guests was avoided whenever possible, especially after Marie Belloc Lowndes complained that Algernon Cecil, although supposedly a man of the world, 'doesn't understand the infinite gradations between shaking hands with someone and jumping into bed with them'.[62]

A friend already lost to Hartley, Leo Myers, killed himself in April 1944. Contemplative, melancholic, and consumed with a fanatical urgency to alter radically the shape of society, Myers had simply turned away from even his closest friends (among whom he counted Hartley) when the passion for Communism took him over, writing to tell them that, despite his affection for them, he never wished to set eyes on them again. Now, Hartley felt the loss of that friendship for which Myers had a tremendous capacity; turning over his letters in later years, Hartley was filled with sadness, even if he knew that Myers had gone to his death in triumph. His widow accepted that fact; Constant Huntington recognised that 'the awful thing was that he was most cheerful when he referred to his suicide. If one tried to dissuade him he became bored.'[63] But what was Hartley to make of Myers' ultimate, brilliant repudiation of the society he no longer wished to be part of? In extinguishing himself, Myers had bowed to the philosophy of the guru in his novels *The Pool of Vishnu*: 'Intention must never be adulterated. A terrible purity of intention is demanded of man.'[64]

The death of those he loved, or the deaths of their lovers, never failed to bring Hartley to a pitch of deep feeling. That death could bring an end to friendship and love merely confirmed his innate pessimism. After his own death, Kay Dick presumed that Hartley was always 'prematurely fearful of death, and therefore unable to view the delights life offers without seeing the skeleton at every turn ... Not for a moment could he escape from the final catastrophe of dust and dirt.'[65] In protecting himself from the hazards of any committed emotional or sexual life, he insured himself against what death might do to him. Lacking passion, he was at least rewarded by the unbroken line of his own existence; there was no danger that his life might be suddenly cut into. If Hartley needed proof of the consequences of love, Clifford Kitchin was about to provide it.

Kitchin's second war was very different from Hartley's, as his first had been. He was now living with his lover Clive Preen at 'a very ugly house',[66] The Byletts, at Pembridge in Herefordshire, having acquired 350 acres that gave long views of wooded hills, and a sound agricultural investment. The Byletts was a school and Kitchin a teacher of small boys, loathing the life and the house which he considered had been turned into 'a tiny St Pancras station'.[67] He felt the old order of his settled, comfortable life slipping away, as throughout the thirties he had known it would; unlike Hartley, he recognised the coming of change, the inevitability of which permeates the novels he wrote in the years immediately before the war, *Olive E* (1937) and *Birthday Party* (1938), very different from his 1929 detective story, *Death of my Aunt*, which had enjoyed enormous success and given his reputation some currency.[68] They are full of the warning of what will happen when established social standards crumble, where the rare creatures like the wealthy Isabel Carlice of *Birthday Party* insist that 'life must have a drawing-room if it's to be civilised',[69] that 'the happiness of one person is just as important as the happiness of a million people.'[70] Awareness of the social revolution sharpened Kitchin's perception, even when it pained him. Of course he hoped the changes might not come. He told Hartley, 'It is strange how to be a member of a privileged class – at one time thought worthy of so much admiration – is now regarded as a criminal offence.'[71]

Yet Kitchin was a man of the world, a qualification Hartley never achieved, and he deserved Hartley's description of him as the most talented man he had ever known. Kitchin was a brilliant pianist, and could improvise wittily at the keyboard, giving musical impressions of those he knew which conveyed his feelings for them – a radiant burst of melody for a friend he loved, a few thumps or discordant chords for one he did not. He bought three new suits a year and dined in the best restaurants. He was fiercely superstitious, and would fall into an agony of unhappiness if he saw a single magpie, searching the countryside until he found its mate. He was an eager mathematician and farmer, and he loved boating, venturing forth on the Helford river in full nautical rig. He was an enthusiastic collector of *objets d'arts* (his craze for paperweights, he claimed, had been spurred on by Eva Peron) and postage stamps. In all of these he took as much a monetary as an aesthetic interest; he was a natural *habitué* of the sale-room. But the appreciation of beauty was essential to him. A fleeting glimpse of a lovely man or woman would send him into raptures. In his London years, he would often take a bus from his home to a Camden park, watching the visitors and lovers that lingered there – *A Short Walk in Williams Park* has its root in these excursions – and, after buying a bunch of flowers, catch the bus for the homeward journey.

Kitchin had his own way of dealing with the war. To speed its end, he turned to the works of Balzac, convinced that when he had read every word the conflict would be over. Unfortunately, the war was still raging when he closed the last book, but he was delighted to discover that the supposedly complete set was lacking one volume. But, conscious as he was of the reality of war in a way Hartley never would be, Kitchin was less content than Clive Preen with the humdrum life that he felt the war had imposed on him. Once, when Kitchin was lamenting the fact that they no longer had a proper home of their own, Preen turned to him and said, 'Home is where you are.'[72] One can almost feel the stillness of the moment, the kindness of the voice. Five words, the only shred of knowledge we have of what Clive Preen said to Clifford Kitchin, but in them the two men live again, if only for a moment. The value of such intimate consolation was denied Hartley. When he stayed with the two men at The Byletts in August 1941 the strength of their relationship must have been clear to him, for he always appreciated the wonder of homosexual devotion. To Hartley, the friendship of Kitchin and Preen, of Sitwell and David Horner, of Ethel and Nan, had an unsulliable classical quality.

When Clive Preen collapsed and died at a Liverpool hotel in April 1944, Kitchin's world almost literally fell apart. 'I have lost Clive', he wrote, feeling as if 'my real life began in 1930 [when he and Preen had met] and ended in 1944.'[73] Three months later, he was suffering from 'a gnawing sense of the futility or worse of my continued existence, to which a poor shadow of myself seems still to cling ... the steady purpose, which during the last thirteen and a half years had given everything, even in my nerviest moods, a reality and a justification, has gone ... For every memory (of myself) for which I am thankful, there are ten which hurt me.'[74] There was no deliverance from Kitchin's conviction that he had been 'the one who took and did not give, – in the real sense'.[75] Life dropped away from him. He read little, attended no plays or concerts, saw few friends except those of Preen's who offered a tenuous link with the past; he lost interest in beauty, putting aside the novel he was writing.

The war was four years over when *The Auction Sale* was eventually published, its extraordinarily elegiac atmosphere a testament to Kitchin's adoration of Preen. This lament for a lost England, its gentle, decent values swept away, is underwritten with a plangent understanding that comes from having loved and lost. The quiet, good Miss Elton, once employed as secretary to Mr Durrant at Ashleigh Place, Markenham, returns to the house many years later to attend the auction sale instigated by its new owners. As the lots are announced, so her memories are awakened, memories of the platonic, brief love that blossomed between Mrs Durrant and poor Dr Sorenius. There is pessimism, of course, and the knowledge that life and the old social structure is ebbing, but Miss Elton (as Kitchin must have hoped to) understands and moves forward, alone, into the future, hopeful of a path of salvation. She carries from the auction sale two trophies that give the promise of contentment, a painting called 'The Pleasures of Love and Retirement' and a bowl on which is inscribed 'He knoweth thy walking through this great wilderness', going 'on her way somehow comforted by that hope'.[76]

Hartley must have seen that the ecstasy of vision that gives *The Auction Sale* its lambent quality was a translation of Kitchin's love for Preen. The pain that gave clarity to that vision, as well as the experience that made it possible, would never happen to Hartley. His letters to Kitchin have not survived, beyond the merest scrap that Kitchin quotes back at him. 'The truth is', Kitchin wrote, 'that I simply can't envisage living an ordinary life again – alone ... You say you have "played for safety, but it doesn't pay". I have formed a sentence to follow this, but I shan't write it.'[77]

❧ 6 ❧

Endings and Beginnings

As THE LAST YEAR of war began, the need to find a home of his own, his first, pressed harder on Hartley. He was forty-nine years old. Bessie's offer to buy him a house was gently refused. Cecil was still trying to persuade him not to leave Rockbourne and 'In that he might seem to have been successful! – though my mind was made up – as far as it ever *was* made up – before he came.'[1] Hartley considered buying the haunted Lawford Hall at Manningtree, with its angelic housemaid, unstinted supply of Brussels sprouts and accessibility to Peterborough, but he shrank from the thought of beginning all over again in a new place among strangers and, anyway, the gardeners' wages of £4 a week seemed very high: he would have to ask Cecil for his opinion. Molly Berkeley had a property in the Royal Crescent at Bath, or there was a house in a village just outside the city, very ugly, with almost every room turned into a kitchenette. Ultimately, he turned down Lawford Hall, promising its owner that if no one else could be found to purchase it, he would move there. 'I am much too neurotic to weigh up pros and cons', he told David Horner. 'I really suffered *severely* while the last hours of the ultimatum were running out – David is obviously delighted that I'm staying.'[2] Cynthia told Hartley that Cecil was looking years younger.

A few weeks later, Charlie was sent to bid for a property called Court Place, though Ethel had warned him that the sound of shunting from the nearby railway would prevent sleep. Hartley had been asked to close on the sale at £6500 and had declined; when the house was auctioned, Charlie's top bid of £8300 was eclipsed by one of £11,650. 'I still mourn for it', Hartley told Ethel. 'It would have been England *and* Venice to me, I now feel, and have solved the vexed question of my whereabouts once and for all ... I long for a free opportunity to display my bad taste.'[3] As it was, he was stuck at Rockbourne where 'I am surrounded by rather dreary bits of furniture for which I have no use.'[4]

But Eustace continued to divert him: 'I keep adding new passages to Eustace's later history, but I don't feel very sure about them and wonder if it wouldn't be better to leave him undeveloped.'[5] As the words poured from him, there did not seem to be that option. A short story, 'Hilda's Letter' (published in 1945), in which Hilda tries again to intervene in her brother's future, was a brief echo of the atmosphere of *The Shrimp and the Anemone*. A first draft of the next Eustace and Hilda book, published as *The Sixth Heaven*, was completed as early as September 1944, though even at the end of the year he could tell Elizabeth Bowen it 'doesn't go very well, I'm afraid. How difficult it is to find the right circumstances for writing, and the right frame of mind.'[6] Huntington was reassured that 'Cynthia said the Oxford part was the best thing you have done yet, and now that you have got Eustace to Venice I am sure he is safe.'[7] He sent a telegram: 'Immensely Enjoyed Sequel You Are A Master Novelist', followed in a letter with more of the same:

> As I hope my telegram implied, your 'Sixth Heaven' more than confirms my high opinion of your stature as a novelist. Now and henceforth my opinion becomes not high, but exalted. The treatment of emotional and dramatic subjects is the test, and with them you scale the mountain tops, and dwell among the immortals.[8]

When Huntington met Hartley for lunch a few days later, Huntington had made a great many pencil notes on the manuscript, said there were parts of the book that he did not like at all, and further irritated Hartley by talking more about his family problems than about the novel; Hartley felt faintly unsure that he meant to publish it. There was, of course, no doubt about Huntington's commitment to the new book in particular and Hartley's work in general. It was largely thanks to Huntington that Hartley was beginning to accumulate a reputation. A second edition of *The Shrimp and the Anemone*, 5000 copies, was being planned. Doubleday was due to publish the American edition, as *The West Window*. There were discussions with the publishers Arkham House of Wisconsin about bringing out a collection of Hartley's supernatural stories, for which they were willing to advance £500 (the book eventually appeared in 1948 as *The Travelling Grave*, published in Britain three years later). As for Eustace and Hilda, Huntington asked Hartley to 'try to be good about the SIXTH HEAVEN, and take your time. It might be well to go straight ahead with it until you come to the end of what would have been the third volume. That is what I would like.'[9] Running alongside was the tiresome interruption of revision and the correcting of proofs (a job Hartley detested, having no talent for making the many often minor decisions it demanded; his critics, of course, might point out that he was equally incapable when faced with *major* decisions). 'All my life', he told David Horner, 'is so much in arrears that it presents the melancholy appearance of a whole station-full of missed trains.'[10]

Advice from Huntington sometimes conflicted not only with the author's own inclination but with the received opinions of Hartley's coterie. Huntington told him that the first chapter of *The Sixth Heaven* needed alteration; Sitwell agreed; Cecil did not; Hartley tried to alter it, but without success. Returning for a few days to Fletton in September 1945 after seeing Sibyl Colefax and staying at a hotel in Bewdley from where he investigated the possibility of buying a house in the neighbourhood, Hartley was still feeling harassed by the book, despite being so far advanced with the third volume. Another publisher, Hamish Hamilton, whom Hartley had met at one of Sibyl's gatherings, congratulated him on the American reviews for *The West Window*, though one critic had said he preferred a boy like Huckleberry Finn or Tom Sawyer to Eustace Cherrington. Huntington remained ominously silent, and made no effort to see Hartley when he was in the vicinity that summer. Hartley had been warned that 'Huntington was well known to be difficult. How troublesome all these cross-currents are. I wish people could be more *business-like* – and not make publishing a matter of the feelings.'[11] By mid autumn, the third novel was almost completed: 'If I make a great effort I might almost finish it today', Hartley wrote on 13 October.[12] A week later it was done, though he felt dissatisfied with its ending, feeling it would need a good deal of revision. Angela Hibbert of Rockbourne was given the manuscript to type, and copies were distributed to various members of Hartley's circle. He apprehensively awaited Huntington's comments, meaning to stand firm and, if Huntington demanded major alterations, to take the book elsewhere.

Whatever sense of achievement Hartley felt at having finished Eustace's biography was mixed, perhaps inevitably, with a dissatisfaction that was certainly exacerbated by the goings-on at Rockbourne. He was on edge. After a visit by Ethel and Nan ('Medusa and Hecate') he wrote apologising for the 'silly and hysterical not to say rude and offensive outburst [Miss Romaine again?] yesterday'. The looming threat of another visit from Violet, talkative and deaf, froze the smile on his face; he made her share a room with her housekeeper-companion Mrs Hook 'for warmth. Warmly I did not greet her, and she remarked that I had changed.'[13] Charlie had given notice 'in no uncertain terms',[14] but subsequently seemed to have withdrawn it; he was, anyway, occupied with the village's VJ Day celebrations, rehearsing the children's tableaux and helping to make their costumes. With Cecil, Hartley motored to Long Crichel to see Eddy Sackville-West who had settled there with three male friends. 'Les Boys' were entertaining Benjamin Britten, 'an extremely nice man, but I could not enjoy thoroughly his Serenade which was played to us on the gramophone in his presence ... it was so cerebral! *My* conception of art is not.'[15] Quite apart from the difficulty of listening to a new piece of music with the composer sitting across the room, Hartley's taste in music was never adventurous; Dr Keeton's efforts had not had the effect of galvanising his pupil's musical enthusiasm. Nevertheless, he and Cecil 'tried to behave like two Queens of Sheba'.[16]

Having patiently steered Hartley through to the end of the Eustace and Hilda books, Huntington wasted no time in getting a new agreement with his author, the main thrust of which was that Hartley should complete another novel by the end of 1947, though Hartley noticed 'there are a good many other things which might be interpreted in more than one way!'[17] Under the terms, he would get an income from Putnam of £60 a month for the next three years; but it was this contract which opened the way for the deterioration in the relationship with Huntington, who was also concerned that Hartley had entrusted his agent, David Higham, with his next book. In fact, Higham had approached Hartley about writing a life of J. M. Barrie, in about 30,000 words, for an advance of £100 and subsequent royalties. Tempted (and feeling that Cynthia would be able to offer help when it came to research), Hartley asked Ethel, 'I don't think I can, do you? For one thing, I should stir up two savage hornet's nests, the pro-Barries, who would think I'd done him too little justice, and the anti-Barries who would say I'd done him too much.'[18] Huntington was strongly of the opinion that Hartley should turn the project down; nothing came of it. Harry and Higham had to be consulted about Huntington's new contract, but by June Hartley had signed. It was now clear he would have to turn his back finally on the chore of regular reviewing that had both financially sustained him and held him back over the years following the disappointments of *Night Fears* and *Simonetta Perkins*. He knew he must resign from the *Sketch*. He of course put off doing so.

The decision as to where he should settle was one he could no longer avoid. On a visit to Bath in March 1946 he saw Avondale, a tall, handsome house in neighbouring Bathford, with a garden that sloped down to the river Avon. Standing on the busy London road along which lorries frequently thundered, it was protected from the outside world by a wall. Hartley at once recognised that here at last was the England and Venice he longed for, with no fear of his having to endure the strictures on boating that he had endured at Lower Woodford. The eighteenth-century stone mansion belonged to a market gardener called Street, in a line of distinguished owners that had included the reforming William Wilberforce and Dr Oliver, inventor of the 'Bath Oliver' biscuit. The towering grandeur of the house concealed a warren of surprisingly small rooms on different levels, many with delightful views of the river and the country beyond. Terraces went down from the house to undulating grass, to the water's edge and the boat-house. There were stables, an old forge, a coach-house. The site had once been a Quaker settlement and contained a Quaker burial ground. By June, he was deep in plans for the new home, going with a builder to inspect the almost roofless boat-house that was one of Avondale's chief delights, but even as he was in the process of buying the property, he confessed to being 'in a particularly sensitive state, feeling that everything I do brings – not pain, that would be presumptuous – but dissatisfaction and disappointment to *some*one'.[19] While Hartley struggled with the proofs of *The Sixth Heaven*, the sadness of leaving Rockbourne surrounded him as the appointed day, 23 July, approached. In church, the Revd Hibbert broke down in the pulpit and had to retire to the vestry, returning a few minutes later to preach a sermon on the sufferings of Job.

By the time of his departure from Rockbourne, Hartley's reputation as a novelist was fast establishing itself. With the publication of *The Sixth Heaven* Eustace had reached Oxford, having survived the Great War by courtesy of Hilda's determination to keep him out of it – tied, as his friend Stephen tells him, 'to the chariot-strings of this beautiful Boadicea and whirled out of harm's way'.[20] The masters of his college, St Joseph's, have the measure of Eustace, just as Miss Grimshaw had. They speak of his work as being 'palatable and nicely served', aware that his policy in life is 'to make the time pass agreeably, and not only for himself, but for a large – an increasingly large – number of people'.[21] Eustace, it is clear, has shaken off none of Hartley's characteristics. Neither can he (or his family) quite accept his access to the Fothergill fortune. It has led to privilege, and to Hilda (with whom Eustace has shared his inheritance) being able to support the children's clinic of which she is the fearsome secretary, but does not bring Eustace the knowledge of belonging to the exalted circles in which he moves.

When the doors of high society open, when he achieves the entrée to Anchorstone Hall, he knows he can never be one of its number, even though he is eager and resigned to join it. He is the Pretender, and not everyone is fooled by his striving. To Dick Staveley, Eustace is no more than a means of reaching Hilda, with whom he flies off in an aeroplane while Eustace remains, earthbound, in a 'sixth heaven', elated at having brought his sister and his boyhood hero together. Lady Staveley, a forerunner of Mrs Maudsley in *The Go-Between*, sees through him; she thinks him a little too eager to please, and 'Eustace was always pleased to please.'[22] It is Lady Nelly, the *grande dame* with the talent to nurture Eustace, who alone accepts him for what he is, inviting him to be taken up in her Venetian life. What she cannot overcome is his conviction that without Hilda he is 'something alien and inimical, a noxious little creature from outside who had crept into this ancient and guarded enclosure to do it harm.'[23]

We are left in no doubt, even after Hilda and Dick's return from the skies, that 'A kind of crust had formed around [Eustace's] relationship with Hilda, impervious to air and sunlight, banishing humour, making for stiffness.'[24] Thus has their love for one another altered by the end of *The Sixth Heaven*, its final notes suggesting, as did the final notes of *The Shrimp and the Anemone*, an impending tragedy. Now, Eustace at least knows that Hilda, unlike him, has no wish to recapture the feelings of childhood that remain essential to him.

As soon as he moved into Avondale (which was given the nickname of 'Paradise Paddock') Hartley slipped easily into that amphibian way of life that so suited him. He bought a second-hand skiff; within weeks, he became a familiar figure, patiently rowing the Avon. He had, in fact, several boats, including one from Venice that he did not know how to propel. On land, workmen invaded the house. 'One can do anything in the building line (far more indeed than one wants) if it is to house somebody, especially somebody of the *proletariat*. For *them*, lavatory basins, electric heaters, concrete roofs, portable W.C.s are simply *poured* out. You don't have to fill in anything.'[25] Charlie was building a hut for the children, turning it into something 'absolutely *Ritzy*',[26] in preparation for bringing his wife and family back from London where they had spent the last months of the war. Ominously, he warned Hartley that he did not

think Mrs Holt would like Miss Romaine's 'ways'. Charlie's 'duo-
denal' milk was being commandeered by Miss Romaine and given
to the cats, though Hartley suspected that she, not the cats, was
drinking it, noting that three pints had vanished and that 'there
remained (or Romained) I think only a cup-full.'[27] Before Christmas,
she had given notice, leaving Hartley feeling frightened, though it
soon became clear she meant to stay. When a new daily help
appeared on the doorstep at Avondale with her illegitimate baby,
Miss Romaine went through the house wailing, 'She has had the
misfortune, she has had the misfortune.'[28]

Life at Avondale, with its market garden, its fusion of land and
water, its animals, its servants, its sense of having somehow volun-
tarily withdrawn from the world beyond its wall, had all the potential
of a Utopia. Charlie became a well-known figure in the village;
William Law, a villager, remembers how he played the drums at the
Royal British Legion on Saturday nights. Hartley, inevitably,
remained a rather remote figure, despite his willingness to be
associated with village life in almost every way. He became a member
of the church council, attending services regularly, sitting in a pew
towards the rear of the congregation. He made it his duty to
negotiate the friendship of Bathford's Miss Skrine – 'the Horner or
Sitwell of the district'[29] – and invited her to lunch with Horace
Vachell, the highly conservative and somewhat terrifying author of
The Hill, who lived at nearby Widcombe Manor. As a guest, the
elderly Vachell could keep Hartley on his toes, complaining at the
suitability of a sherry, or the texture of a potted shrimp. Even the
socially confident Miss Skrine may have trembled at the occasion.
Vachell, a fearsome snob with a belief in an elected band of
privileged beings of whom he considered himself a member, was 'at
his most expansive and uncontrolled' and scarcely spoke to his fellow
guest, although Hartley had a lingering memory of Vachell turning
to Miss Skrine at one moment and saying, 'Not *epicene*, madam, not
epicene! Obscene, or anyhow not fit to be seen!'[30]

At least Bathford gave Hartley the opportunity to escape social
demands. Walking gave him happiness; he would spend many hours
climbing to the head of the village, to a seat that faced out to Bath,
overlooking the valley. But it was the river that offered the most
sacred joy. Here, as ever before, he was at once at peace. If the
achievement of isolation was the ultimate goal, it might still be
managed, even with interruptions. Just as his 'gondoling' days had
often involved ferrying guests back and forth across the Venetian
lagoon, so his new days of sculling on the Avon could tolerate the

presence of others. A Bathford teenager, Derek Hayes, found Hartley 'extremely kind to children'.[31] The middle-aged author 'kept two single scullers in his boat-house. He quite often used to have a mock race with me in my yellow Spitfire Rescue dinghy and would always speak when we met on the river.'[32] There seemed, for many years, only one impediment to the divinity of Avondale – swans, unpredictable swans that swept out at the oarsman in an effort to protect their offspring and might threaten to capsize a craft. For the moment, Hartley satisfied his annoyance at their behaviour by demolishing their nests and throwing the eggs into the river.

Home or market garden, Hartley was conscious that Avondale should pay its way; more income was supplied by tenants, the Waller family. Robert Waller had been a soldier, and subsequently worked as secretary to Desmond MacCarthy (of his daughter's marriage to David Cecil, MacCarthy once remarked to him, 'Fine couple of lovebirds they are. They know nothing of the world.')[33] Hartley had been in London to give a talk at Broadcasting House when he first met Waller, who was then a Talks Producer for the Third Programme. 'What sort of clothes do you wear when you broadcast?' Hartley asked him.[34] It was when Waller decided to move down to the West Region with the intention of doing 'rural' programmes that he took up Hartley's offer and installed himself, his wife and two young children in Avondale's top two floors, where they stayed for over a year. Waller was aware that he came from a very different world from that which Hartley inhabited. 'What's it like going on a bus?' Hartley once inquired.[35] Waller's full-pelt assault on life seemed as strange to Hartley as Hartley's reticence seemed to Waller:

> He was a terrible snob, of course, and there was something flabby about him, both physically and spiritually. He was still, in a way, in the womb. He was afraid of the world. He lived in an aura of friendship, and he put up this great aesthetic screen. I think he liked me. I remember his saying 'I do envy you your terrific passions.' I was far too shy at the time to get close to him, to break through the social veneer. I always felt Charlie resented being his servant; he was inward, monosyllabic. Appearances were so important to Leslie. Once, when Lady Cunard retired for the night at Avondale, she found a cold hot-water bottle in her bed. Leslie was in paroxysms of grief. He talked of nothing else for days.[36]

Domestic problems ruled at Avondale. When Mrs Holt returned, it was clear she was very unwell; diagnosed as having neuritis or fibrositis, she grew worse. Hartley called in doctors, and was furious at their dilatory ways. Three days later, having lost a great deal of blood, she was rushed to hospital. Then, the Holts' daughter, Jean, was killed by a lorry in an accident on the London road just outside the house. Charlie was utterly broken. It touched Hartley to see how he wore 'an immensely flamboyant Fair Isle pullover' to visit his wife in hospital, believing it might cheer her up. Miss Romaine poisoned the air by suggesting that Jean had been called away because she was proud and wore lipstick, and expressing the hope that she had been wearing clean underwear when she was taken to hospital. Charlie's detestation of Miss Romaine could only grow; Hartley felt there could be no peace until she had gone. He was amused when John Betjeman, reviewing *The Sixth Heaven* for the *Daily Herald*, praised the fact that though Hartley's characters were from the privileged classes he had made them real and lovable. Hartley told Ethel it would have been truer for Betjeman to have written that 'Most of the characters belong to the working class, but, etc. . . . Really, when I think of them and how (to use their own expression) they "play one up". Miss Romaine is too old for me to reform (as you once said of Mrs Johnstone), either as a cook or a woman.'[37] Hartley was so impressed by the staff at the Athenaeum that he wished he might persuade them to migrate *en masse* to Avondale. Whether any of them would have been adept at the market gardening that helped sustain the household is a moot point. For financial purposes, Hartley now expected to be regarded primarily as a market gardener, an argument that did not convince the authorities, who demanded 'monstrous' rates. Doing his bit, Charlie built a stall from which produce could be sold.

Whatever Avondale offered Hartley, it was not happiness. Although he had not seen Clifford Kitchin for several years, he wrote assuring him that 'I can say to you things I can say to no one else.' Hartley described Avondale to him as 'a very public dwelling':

You asked me if this house was home. I don't know that it quite is. Mother cannot reconcile herself to my living away from Fletton; every letter she writes is a sort of persuasion to me to go back there. I do go, every month or so, but I don't want to live there.[38]

Robert Waller, young, vibrant, his emotional life healthy and intact, decided to move his family out of Avondale, convinced by

Jean's death that the house was not a safe place to bring up young children. Hartley felt a sense of loss at his departure. Avondale, already, was beginning to fail him. He felt his heart still to be in Venice, longing for the kindness of his servants there. Though Avondale seemed to supply elements of the paradise that Venice offered in profusion, it was inevitable that Hartley would go back to the city that had given him refuge. When he arrived in Venice in May 1947 it was for the first time in eight years. Pietro, his face shining like a copper moon, was waiting at the railway station; like the city itself, he seemed eager not to disappoint. Hartley, so alert to the emotions that pulled him back to the past, must have been nervous of his return. Conscious of what the war had done in Britain, he was prepared to see great changes in Italy; could Venice give him the beauty and consolation it had once given with such pleasure? Hartley's willingness to fall under its special spell blunted any sense of disappointment he now felt. Some of the network of support he had known before the war was still in place. The baroness opened her doors to him – he felt himself at home once again – but he did not know if San Sebastiano welcomed him as a guest, paying guest or tenant. He was confined to two rooms, a bedroom, with no outlook, within the house, and the dining-room, the baroness having reserved the garden bedroom for her own use. Beyond these narrow spaces, Venice did not withhold its pleasure. It was all 'delightful, a little, perhaps I should say a good deal – lacking in friends, but with most welcoming faces all round, and shouts of greetings from strangers'.[39] It was as if Venice had intrinsically understood how vital it was for its returning guest to be cheered, to be greeted with smiles, with approval. If the circle of friends was grown smaller, there were Bertie and Dorothea Landsberg, and the baroness, who motored back from Nice a week after Hartley's arrival, her enthusiasm undimmed at the age of ninety-two. Molly Berkeley and the three little orphaned boys she was bringing up swelled the numbers.

The Venice waters, of course, could never disappoint Hartley. Plagued as he was by the thirstiest mosquitoes and dogged by sleeplessness and a gondolier, Sergio, 'neither amiable nor clever',[40] he still recognised the enchantment of the lagoon. There were long days spent in the gondola, and bathes in water that was hotter than the air. Whatever its mood, the Venice water provided the ideal sensation; moving across it, Hartley's senses were bound together into a contentment that no other experience, physical or spiritual, could achieve. As he returned by gondola from a night with the Landsbergs at Malcontenta, the Brenta looked lush and lovely.

Around him, the nightingales sang in full voice. 'I can't say', he told Ethel, 'that the magic has not returned.'[41]

The gondoliers, too, despite Sergio's apparently boorish manner, were ready with what seemed an almost orchestrated expression of affection, as if they wanted to revitalise Hartley's passion for Venice. When Signorina Alzati, the Italian translator of *The Shrimp and the Anemone*, visited San Sebastiano to spend three days working on the text, they invited her and Hartley to a concert they were giving. After a speech of welcome, a lady with 'a rather hard soprano voice' rose from the table and sang songs from Italian operas.[42] At the end of the evening the gondoliers gave Hartley and his guest a tremendous send-off. Venice was doing all it could to persuade its old admirer that it was as beguiling, as seductive, as beckoning, as before. Like an ageing and perhaps jaded lover, Hartley desperately wanted to believe that the passion had never faded.

When he was not 'gondoling' he wrote: bread and butter stuff had to be got over before he could return to the new book. In March, he had asked the *Sketch* to allow him a year off, but the new editor had replied that this was not possible and that he might like to consider resigning. No sooner had he arrived in Venice than he began his final *Sketch* piece, turning to an article for *Time and Tide* and, at last, to *The Boat*. He found an excuse to postpone the already slow progress on the novel after realising he had set the story in January, an unsuitable month for his hero to yearn for boating on the river. 'I shall have to go through it scratching out ice and snow and substituting daffodils and tulips.'[43]

Huntington planned to publish *Eustace and Hilda* on 23 June. Two weeks before, Doubleday published the American edition of *The Sixth Heaven*, over which Doubleday's Donald B. Elder had enthused: 'It's the best piece of writing I've seen over here since *The Shrimp and the Anemone* ... I only hope that the great dumb film-fed public won't think it too fine for them.'[44] When Hartley returned to England, via Molly Berkeley and Assisi, it was to the critical reception of *Eustace and Hilda*. It was not altogether complimentary, and Hartley had feared that, as Cecil had warned, reviewers would find fault with its liberal splashes of Italian dialogue; he had simply felt too lazy and tired to thin it out. Besides Elizabeth Bowen's glowing notice for the *Tatler*, most of the reviews left him with a feeling of anticlimax. After the vast amount of time and energy that had been expended on it for over twenty years, this was to be expected, but the achievement (of the trilogy as much as of its last great volume) was recognised. Walter Allen in the *New Statesman* thought the books 'one of the few masterpieces in contemporary fiction'. Many years later, he recalled them as 'the most satisfactory and most satisfying of [Hartley's] works, at once the most humanistic and the most human'.[45] Writing in 1951, P. H. Newby classified Hartley as a 'quieter' writer than Joyce Cary or Graham Greene, 'and his work is more consciously literary in flavour, yet no situation or character in these three linked books has been accepted at second hand from another book. Every page is authentic and the vision, charmingly melancholy like a sunny day in late autumn, is shared by none of his contemporaries.'[46] John Betjeman thought *Eustace and Hilda* a social novel in the class of George Meredith.

The greatest consolation for having persevered was the appreciation of friends and writers whom he respected. Edith Sitwell told him that the book was 'really hardly bearable. And there isn't one touch that is wasted – not one. I think it is the most amazing study of a selfish woman – one of those dreadful good women – that I know. How I hate her ... Nobody could appreciate or – I think – understand that book better than I do.'[47] Inevitably, those who knew Hartley well (or thought they did) were able to see the work more directly than those who merely suspected that the author had plundered his own psyche. It was as if the work was instantly decoded. Kitchin expressed this perfectly when, after reading *The Sixth Heaven*, he admitted, 'I can't treat your books in the detached fashion of a critic appraising a work of art. I spoil them (from that angle) by reading into them too much of what I know, or think I know, of you. Thus every page has its excitements which produce a cross-rhythm with the real beat of the book.'[48] Now, putting down *Eustace and Hilda*, Kitchin, 'throbbing with excitement', wrote, 'I can only say that you have moved me very deeply – you have diverted me (when you meant to), you have entranced me, you have frightened me. Full as I am at this moment, of the ending, I think it is fear that I feel most.'[49]

In *Eustace and Hilda* the trilogy reaches its apocalyptic conclusion. Eustace is Lady Nelly's guest in Venice, adjusting to the reputation of being in the process of writing a book, and never free of the knowledge that he is in fact an outsider, beyond the social grandeur of Nelly's circle. Indeed, it is noted how Eustace always speaks of his upper-class friends in a low, respectful voice. A chance meeting with a world-weary, divorced Nancy Steptoe offers Eustace the chance of a sexual liaison, but he turns away from it, anyway, he feels he has had love 'scolded' out of him by his upbringing. Venice is left behind when news reaches him of Hilda's illness, of the breakdown and paralysis brought on by reading a newspaper announcement of Dick Staveley's engagement. In returning to Anchorstone, where Hilda lingers, Eustace hopes to expiate whatever sins he has visited on her. Consumed with doubt about his 'improper' book – it is for him 'the unconscious self-betrayal of a wish-fed mind'[50] – and isolated from the calming affection of Lady Nelly and Venice, Eustace is once more inextricably linked with Hilda. In the book's final pages, the other characters leave the stage; the focus on brother and sister, the life-altering relationship that bestrides the novels, is gradually sharpened. Only Minney, the true begotten understander of Eustace, remains, and he becomes once again her little boy, little Eustace for whom it is essential to be 'on special terms with somebody or something'.[51]

It may well be that Hilda has blackmailed Dick with her unhappiness (did not Bessie use her unhappiness against Leslie in this way?), but it is left to Eustace to engineer the shock to her system that alone may bring her back into the living world. He elects to do it, to stage-manage a near death experience on the cliffs. At the very moment of truth, he collapses, but in doing so manages to stop Hilda's bathchair from hurtling over the precipice. By default, he has delivered the jolt to her senses and saved her. Minney watches from the window of Cambo as the restored Hilda wheels back the broken Eustace in her bathchair, fulfilling the prophecy in the final lines of *The Shrimp and the Anemone* in which Minney, seeing the two children limping home together in their three-legged race, knows they will eventually come to grief. At last, Hilda declares her unstinting love for Eustace, even if she asks him to shave off his new moustache, tells him that writing novels 'isn't a life's work', and demands much more of him if she is ever to feel proud. The time comes to say good night:

> Eustace kissed her on the cheek.
> 'That's not the way to do it,' said Hilda. 'He's a lot to learn, hasn't he, Minney? *This* is the way.' And she gave him a long embrace on the lips.
> Eustace, though a little breathless, was grateful to her. The gesture crowned the evening with a panache he couldn't have given it – nor could Hilda, a few months ago.[52]

There is the slight repugnance of the wrong, the misjudged, physical act here, that uneasiness with the body's capability that would always plague Hartley: that 'long embrace on the lips', a little glancing blow among the 700 pages of the novels, at once sanctifying and corrupting. And, for Eustace, a crowning. He drifts off into dreams, a world of possibilities and contradiction in which he is a well-known visitor, until the great climax of the books, that extreme moment of reality and fantasy, of life and art, of fact and invention, when once more he stands on the childhood sands of Anchorstone's shore at the edge of a pool. Hilda has gone home. Within the pool a rock, and the white plumose anemone stroking the water with its feelers. The shrimps elude it, and it will surely die. Stepping into the icy water, Eustace slips his fingers into the lips of the breathing flower, knowing that the moment has come for him to awake from his dream. 'But the cold crept onwards and he did not wake.'[53]

Eustace's death, his sacrifice, his martyrdom, is one of the quietest in English literature, and one of the most affecting. Having brought about the miracle of Hilda's restoration – her recovery from the dangers of sexual attraction and love – Eustace's death is natural, needed. Like many of Hartley's heroes that would follow, he dies at a moment of supreme acceptance, aware that there can be no life of value or meaning beyond the point of ecstasy that has been reached. So will die Ted Burgess in *The Go-Between*, Stephen Leadbitter in *The Hireling*, Lucy Soames in *The Brickfield*, Fergus Macready in *The Harness Room*. It was Hartley's intention that Timothy Casson in *The Boat* should die too. And when death does not come to rescue the victim of love, the survivors, like Leo Colston in *The Go-Between* and Richard Mardick in *The Brickfield* and *The Betrayal*, are left emotionally disfigured; the experience of ecstasy has left them fatally flawed.

To other families, a love-affair might be 'the sweetest of stolen waters', but, as Eustace knows, love-affairs do not suit the temperament of the Cherringtons, or the Hartleys. It was an inescapable by-product of Bessie's understanding of love that any sexual expression of it should be kept out of her children's lives. In the end, no matter how strong the resistance or the realisation that 'school stretched the elastic; the war, Oxford, Venice, they all stretched it', the harm is done.[54] And this is unmitigated autobiography. If love has been passed down, it has been a poor, fractured thing, misunderstood into something else. Thus is Eustace handicapped by his conviction (Bessie's conviction) that 'not to worry was the same as not to care'.[55] And thus everywhere in these pages is the collision of fact and fancy, the putting-on of thin disguises, the balancing of truth and deception.

At the heart of the story of Eustace and Hilda is a sense of innocence – Eustace's, Hartley's innocence – corrupted only by the knowledge of self. It is, of course, our knowledge of Hartley that throws up the books into such startling relief. All very well that, a decade later, Hartley should have Isabel Eastwood in *A Perfect Woman* insisting that 'Looking for an author's life in his books is vulgar anyhow, and can be most misleading.'[56] The truth is that without the fabric of Hartley's life, Eustace's story would have no substance in fiction. The two men share one tragedy; the mist, the disguise, the accessories of truth and deceit, can only surround it.

Let us leave *Eustace and Hilda* with two observations. First, Hilda's breakdown is induced by seeing the announcement of Dick's marriage in a newspaper, just as Hartley had discovered, in the matter-of-factness of print, the engagement of Joan Mews, the woman to whom he had proposed, in the columns of *The Times*. Second, there is the fact of Hilda having fallen in love. We can never doubt the strength of her attraction to Dick. Love, when it comes to Hilda, is overwhelming, bringing with it the power to throw her, the supremely self-possessed Hilda, out of control. And so to Enid, the Enid of almost arrogant beauty in photographs that leave us in no doubt that she was once lovely. There was once a romance in Enid's life, we know, but that is the sum of all we know.[57] Norah said that Bessie did not encourage it, probably disfigured it, possibly destroyed it. Love-affairs, after all, 'did not suit the temperament of the Cherringtons',[58] or, for that matter, the Hartleys. For the moment, of course, Hartley resisted any hint that Enid and Hilda might live one in the other. He, and Enid, must have known otherwise, but Hartley, incapable of the emotional honesty that would have allowed another course, could not bring himself to own up to Hilda's inspiration, even to Enid. At the last, he confessed it to the world, if not to Enid. Hilda, Enid, the anemone to Eustace's, to Hartley's shrimp. It is in the pages of his great trilogy, written when Hartley imagined his sense of vision to be more radiant than at any other time, that Enid lives still, somewhere between dream and waking.

🍃 7 🍃

The Dissatisfaction with Truth

THERE WAS LITTLE time to linger on the aftermath of *Eustace and Hilda*: there was the new novel for Putnam, and the continual social demands, despite the various austerities left behind by the war. Cynthia came to stay in late July, enchanted when Hartley took her out on the river, but this happiness – as he knew it must be – was only temporary. After lying in a coma for a few days, Beb died in early August. 'Poor Cynthia', Hartley told Bessie, 'how unlucky she is, and always has been.'[1] From Hartley, who must have felt himself to be emotionally luckless, there was no lack of sympathy; being so fond of Cynthia, how could there be? In what way, if any, Beb's death shifted Hartley's friendship with Cynthia, we can only wonder. Beb's death did not mark the beginning of a closer relationship; it may, on the other hand, have driven a subtle wedge between them. Devoid of any sexual dimension, the friendship may have prospered or faltered or stayed exactly as it was; we cannot know. There is always the possibility that, without Beb, Hartley felt his friendship with Cynthia to be less defined, less safe. If she fully understood Hartley's character, as perhaps she did, she would not have allowed him to feel intimidated by Beb's passing. The safety of Hartley's fascination with her was left intact, an arrangement supremely suited to both parties.

At Avondale, the wall that separated Hartley from the London road could not keep the world at bay; only on the river, and in his writing, could it be distanced. Miss Romaine made cakes (*'uneatable'*) when Dora Cowell came for tea. Miss Romaine quarrelled with the daily help, who left. Miss Romaine, according to Charlie, let his dog, Bruce, out in the street without lead or collar in revenge for Charlie telling her that Snowball's (Avondale's cat) next litter would be drowned at birth. Hartley was now vice-president of the Bathford branch of the British Legion (a post he no doubt regretted accepting as soon as he had done so) and was also in demand as a broadcaster; this summer there was an invitation to give a talk on Emily Brontë for the Third Programme. Hartley, of course, dreaded such occasions, never said no when invited to deliver them, and, as the date drew nearer, wished he had declined. Huntington was also pointing at the calendar, annoying Hartley by telling him that unless he completed his novel by the end of the year his monthly payments from Putnam would cease. It was Hartley's original intention to publish *The Boat* in two parts. In February 1948 this seemed an ideal arrangement, for he had almost finished the first. Huntington, understandably, wanted a completed novel that could be brought out in one volume, and soon. The tensions between writer and publisher were mounting. Hartley was also urging Huntington to reprint *Simonetta Perkins*, a request met with a silence that 'seems hardly sane';[2] Hartley considered sending off a solicitor's letter.

Though Huntington had criticisms, he assured Hartley of his 'firm foundation of sympathy and admiration for the work as a whole'.[3] He was full of praise for the first instalment of *The Boat*. 'To my mind you have caught the 'bus. In other words, there is a pre-occupation with servants in the present affairs of men which you have taken at the flood, and I hope it will lead on where Shakespeare says it will.'[4] By June, Hartley had completed a first draft of the whole book, which Huntington declared had far too many loose ends and was impossible to publish. He liked the scenes with Desirée, finding them by far the most realistic and convincing, and reminiscent of the quality Hartley had shown in *The Shrimp and the Anemone*. He was less happy with Hartley's intention to drown his hero, feeling that Eustace's death had undermined such a denouement. (In the final version of the novel, Timothy merely falls asleep from exhaustion in the back of a car, a depressingly ineffective ending, and one devoid of any deeper interpretation, unlike the last line of *Eustace and Hilda*.) Huntington suggested that Timothy might return to Venice. Perhaps, in Venice, Hartley would find the inspiration to bring Timothy to a happy conclusion? But by the end of the year the now frail Huntington was still waiting for a publishable manuscript.

The painful birth of *The Boat* dragged on. Rex Littleboy was horrified when Hartley asked if he thought he could use the word 'bugger' in the book. What, Littleboy asked, would his mother say? '"I do not write for my parents", I replied haughtily.'[5] And Hartley could not keep track of the names in the book: 'I kept on forgetting them.'[6] A copy was sent off to Fletton, only to be received with 'an alarming silence ... I fear it has shocked them, as Littleboy thought it might.'[7]

It was a time marked by the fatigues of friendship, needing all

Hartley's considerable skills. He met Kitchin for the first time in several years. After Clive Preen's death Kitchin had kept Hartley, like so many other friends, at arm's length, fearing any meeting with him. Any gap that had existed between them before had widened. It was not only that Kitchin's aestheticism seemed to have been eclipsed by dog-racing (he kept greyhounds at Potter's Bar and was becoming well-known 'to half the toughs at Stamford Bridge').[8] Kitchin felt he had lost a place in the world through which he had once moved with such promise and assuredness. When he and Hartley met for dinner at the Athenaeum, the event was a sad failure, Kitchin so irritated at the late arrival of unpalatable food that he wanted to go elsewhere. The Athenaeum may have been having a bad day, but there is little doubt that Kitchin's fastidiousness was aggravated by a low tolerance level, a characteristic shared by another homosexual friend of Hartley's, Sir Roderick Meiklejohn, at one time Asquith's private secretary. Henry Lamb was proving 'rather touchy' about arrangements to visit Avondale, but persuaded Hartley to visit him at a château he had taken near the Loire in July. Staying at Wilsford, Hartley's friendship was exercised when he had to endure four-hour long sessions with Princess Marthe Bibesco and Stephen Tennant who, like 'wood-pigeons, cooed French poetry' (little of which Hartley could understand) at each other.[9] Charlie, who accompanied Hartley, was spared these ordeals, but demolished the preciousness of Wilsford by declaring it was 'All for show, nothing for comfort.'[10] To Hartley, Tennant's extravagances were 'so tremendous that one feels quite economical by comparison. He has draped the house with silk and damask, but I had no toothglass in my bedroom!'[11] What Tennant thought of Avondale, where he was an unpunctual and (with the staff) unwelcome guest, we can only imagine.

It was Miss Romaine's future at Avondale that most troubled Hartley at the beginning of the year. A new cook, Mrs Turner, seemed willing to move in; she could be with him in March. 'Now, what to say to Miss Romaine?' Hartley asked Bessie, unable (unlike Leo Myers) to relish the dismissal of servants. 'How to put it? Some time perhaps you will be able to think of a formula and tell me?'[12] Miss Romaine discovered her fate when she read a letter to Enid that Hartley had left on view. She became anxious to please, feigning surprise when Hartley eventually plucked up courage to tell her she must leave. Triumphantly, after explaining to him that her last twelve months had been a purgatory and having provided him with enough copy to fill pages of *The Boat*, she departed, leaving behind one pot of jam, half empty. Ominously, Mrs Turner's March arrival was deferred until April. In the interregnum, Hartley had time to reflect on his long association with his awkward but characterful old cook. He went into her room, realising for the first time how very poorly it was furnished. Her passing left him feeling 'a little sad, for she has been with me for over six years, which is quite a large slice'.[13] (In fact, Miss Romaine's tenure was by no means over. It appears from Hartley's correspondence that she returned for at least one further period of employment.) Mrs Turner had barely arrived when a small war broke out about the tenants leaving their baby's pram outside the kitchen window. Charlie scowled at the new cook or treated her to one of his silences; Hartley recognised 'a woman of iron resolve under a melting manner'.[14] When, after a few months, he offered her a holiday, 'she said sadly that if she once went away, she didn't think she'd ever come back! I seem to have to spend all my time cosseting their egos!'[15]

It was now that a new friendship blossomed from an old acquaintance. Hartley had known Christabel Aberconway slightly for many years. A great friend of the Asquiths and of Osbert Sitwell, she began a relationship with Hartley that would last until his death. She was one of those ideal personalities who might have been made for him to luxuriate in. Five years his elder, Christabel Macnaghten had, as a baby, smiled at Oscar Wilde from her pram. When she was four, her family moved first to Ovingdean, then to Rottingdean, where as a little girl a tramp had once assaulted her, shouting 'I want a woman, I want a woman, and I'm going to have you. I'm full of fuck and I'm going to fuck you.'[16] Her mother consoled her by describing the assailant as 'a lonely and I fear a dirty and sad old man'.[17] He had, she said, merely wanted to take Christabel for a stroll. The relish with which Christabel would relate this story, and others as coloured and unlikely, give a clue to her irreverent, sprightly wit, which must enormously have appealed to Hartley. She was not the type of woman whom it would have been safe to invite for tea at Fletton. There was no possibility that she would become a mother-figure to him.

At eighteen, she married Henry McLaren, who in 1934 became the second Baron Aberconway. She developed a taste and talent for being a hostess on that grand scale that attracted artists, those who had achieved and those who hoped. Moths to her flame, they respected a woman who, asked whether she would prefer Renoirs in the dining-room or a good cook, plumped unhesitatingly for the cook. All sorts of people, from taxi-drivers and porters bewitched by a fleeting exchange to many of the intelligentsia, opened their hearts to her and felt they were in safe hands. Having sublimated many of her own artistic yearnings she was left, as it were, ready to receive the outpourings of others – receptivity was her great talent. Although not spectacularly gifted, she could slip on the mantle that made her seem so. She felt, and many friends agreed, that she had magic powers. 'I knew', she wrote, 'that when people were sad I could make them feel happy. When people felt tired, I could make them feel well. When I wanted something to occur, it *did* occur.'[18] Useful gifts, no doubt, to any friend of Hartley's.

Osbert Sitwell rejoiced in her; Sacheverell Sitwell came to detest her machinations and distrust her allegiances. It was certainly the mischievous, if not malevolent, side of her that appealed so strongly to David Horner, who thrived on gossip and startling confidences. But there was kindness too. After Munich, the Aberconways' home at Bodnant in North Wales was invaded by nannies and their charges when Christabel suggested that Bodnant was the perfect haven. What, one wonders, did they make of this proud creature with her high-pitched, plummy voice, this woman who in the Great War had not blushed when a soldier informed her, 'It isn't the fucking fighting that fucks us, it's the fucking fucking about'?[19] How could Hartley, so guarded, so careful to please and conform, not be attracted by this brilliance? And, like him, she loved drinking. As a supplier of that comfort that was nectar to him, she was a steadfast friend.

She could not, of course, give him love, love that was Bessie's prerogative. That had never weakened, it endured while her body perished. When the Second World War began, Bessie was struck down with what was diagnosed as rheumatic fever. Whatever the cause of this new illness, it had kept her in bed for a year, undermining what little resistance she had. Her last visits to London, when with Hartley she visited Ethel and Nan, were her social swansong. Throughout the war, she did not leave Fletton for a single night. Harry, as steadfast and dependable as ever, and still serving the Brick Company as a director, stayed with her, doing his best to ease her troubled mind. There is very little tangible in Hartley's correspondence from which we may build up a picture of the relationship he had with Bessie and Harry in their late years. The emotional repulsion Hartley felt for Fletton Tower was always a barrier to closeness between them; the distance from them that he had created could never be bridged. The discomfort of Bessie's love, the strength of Harry's moral conviction, left Hartley defenceless to the end.

At the beginning of 1948 she was so unwell that there was talk of moving her into a nursing-home, but it was arranged that Nurse Alexander, or Nurse Guest, or some other paid being, would come to look after her. By the summer, there was no improvement. Towards the end of September, Hartley travelled to Peterborough for what would be his last meeting with her. Her great fear, now that her mind was muddled and her memory fading, was that when she held out her hand there would be no other to take it. In her lucid moments, there was no doubt whose hand would most have comforted her. When her son left her bedside to return to Avondale she said, as she often did, 'Come back soon'. He knew she was coming to her end, but did not stay by her side. Two days later, when he telephoned, she seemed almost happy, a little like her old self. The following day, 27 September, she was washing herself in bed, stretched out her hand for a sponge and fell back dead into the pillows. One of her last acts was to telephone a London specialist whom she hoped would help her. Her mind cannoned from worry to worry; even as death waited she could not give up the struggle, could not give herself up to dying. Hartley knew she had, finally, lacked the resource to face death with contentment. 'I feel I have lost her', he told Ethel, 'not someone who had ceased to resemble her, and the wrench is great ... She loved flowers and trees and mountains, but her real life was in the affections – she lived for them.'[20] Suddenly, the anxiety that had been directed at Hartley for over fifty years, that passionate need for his happiness, was cut off.

The Boat was 'finished' by the end of January 1949, but Hartley thought it much too long and 'it was written in too many moods and has at least one supernumerary character, whose whole nature changes on every page.'[21] Huntington seemed to have no reservations: – 'At times I felt the awe that the heights of art always evoke', he wrote in April;[22] the following day, it was 'high among the very few literary masterpieces of our time'.[23] But Hartley was soon resisting Huntington's insistence that there should be cuts. He didn't see why, if he had written a masterpiece, it needed to be revised.

He made regular escapes from Avondale, worried as to what the Inland Revenue would say about the losses incurred by its market garden, and left cookless after Cynthia seduced Mrs Turner into her own employment. In retreat, he stayed with Violet Hammersley at Totland Bay on the Isle of Wight, where matters were very much under the thumb of Mrs Hook, who did not warm to visitors. There were days with Ethel at Chelsea Square, and in Paris with Millicent, Duchess of Sutherland, at her apartment in the Rue St Louis-en-Lille, where she lived in a perpetual twilight, the 'modern comforts' protected from the outside world only by a flimsy domestic curtain, 'so I had to announce my times of occupation by volleys of coughs and throat-clearings'.[24] The almost deaf duchess was ready to understand his exasperation with the Avondale ménage. 'Servants', she suggested, 'seem to belong to long ago and to be really efficient should be like the Polish ones of that period who were never less than sixty to a room and kissed the hem of your garment as you passed – even the turn-up on your trousers.'[25]

In May he arrived in a wet, windy, cold Venice, taking a flat at the Palazzo Bonlini in San Trovaso, having forsaken San Sebastiano because of its 'mutilated' state. 'How very disagreeable!' announced the baroness, but then became 'most gracious. I suddenly realised how nice she was.'[26] She offered to sell him San Sebastiano for £1250, but Hartley was too concerned about the obstacles that would be put in his way. The ideal would have been for him to have both Avondale *and* San Sebastiano; otherwise, he considered selling Avondale and then living in Venice and at Fletton. As for Venice, he informed Enid, 'I can't *tell* you what a relief it is to have servants who seem to want to please you, and never make a fuss.'[27] At the Bonlini he had a long gallery to himself and 'three and a half other rooms as well, with commanding views of rain and rooftops'.[28] He was supposedly revising the typescript of *The Boat*, spending most of the day gazing from his window at the canal beneath.

Sibyl Colefax, indomitable and so ill that Hartley feared she might die on him, arrived in June for what she said would be her last visit to Venice. At the beginning of July (his permit would not allow him to stay longer) he was back at Avondale to a sweeter domestic atmosphere; he imagined Charlie had probably gathered he was thinking of selling up. A visit from Violet Hammersley coincided with the arrival of Signorina Alzati, much to Mrs Hammersley's disgust. There were visits to the Aberconways at Bodnant and (between struggling with proofs) to Teresa Berwick at Attingham Park. Cecil and Rachel brought their son Jonathan to Avondale for the day, and the four of them went into Bath to see the Roman baths. Sibyl Colefax came in early autumn, so bent that she could not be seen over the back of a chair; most of her friends had fled the district on hearing of her arrival. So were the days spent, time given over to friends whom Leslie often had little interest or pleasure in seeing. In less than three months he changed his abode and position on the map twenty-eight times – 'really too unrestful'.[29]

Hartley was complaining of what the printers had done to *The Boat* in late September, but Huntington was still championing it as 'an illuminating X-ray picture of life'.[30] Two months later, Putnam sent Hartley details of sales for the Eustace and Hilda novels. *The Shrimp and the Anemone*, which had been out of print since May 1948, had sold 9520, *The Sixth Heaven* 7935, and *Eustace and Hilda* 5930 (of a 9184 print run). *The Boat's* publication, planned for November, was put off until January 1950 – more time for Hartley to be plagued with doubt about its appearance. What would Bessie think? 'Shall I ever dare to venture into "the valley" [of Bathford] again?' he asked David Horner. What would the vicar and his wife from Lower Woodford, invited to lunch in March, make of it? The wider critical reception, at least, recognised the achievement, even if it corroborated Huntington's theory that a masterpiece might well have its flaws. What all reviewers seemed agreed on was that Hartley had attempted greatness. *The Boat*, said the *Spectator*, was 'an achievement outstanding even for Mr Hartley'; the *Manchester Guardian* saluted 'a work of the greatest brilliance and of a memorable humanistic cast', even if there were pages where there was 'too wide an assortment of aims'. It was not, according to the *New Statesman*, 'a wholly satisfying or convincing novel'. Writing to its author, Edith Sitwell praised the 'brilliant, wise, subtle, brave and truth-telling book ... It is layers and layers deep ... And it is full of beauty, as well as of a terrifying insight and understanding ... No book could make most of the work of our time look more shoddy, more cheap, more jerry-built.'[31] Thirty years later, Walter Allen held to his opinion that it was 'the most riddling of Hartley's novels and perhaps the most disturbing', the 'representation of a recurring pattern in his life ... the slightly Kafka-esque world he seemed to live in'.[32]

Hartley can hardly have warmed to Huntington's reaction to David Cecil's review of *The Boat* in the *Observer*. 'I have always thought him more of a scholar than an artist', Huntington wrote, 'and I was disappointed when I saw his name.'[33] One can feel Hartley's pique rising at the implication, but Huntington, despite his flights of exaggerated rapture, was a wily and acute literary lion. He had a point. There is a very real sense in which Cecil's cerebral appreciation of Hartley's work obscured it; by accentuating its intellectual and spiritual efforts, he succeeded in throwing yet more disguise over what was already heavily disguised fiction. Somehow,

Cecil took his friend's work a little more into the distance, sanctioned its rarity. He imbued Hartley's words with what was almost an exclusivity of sensitiveness. He did not cut through to the reality, the terrible truths, of them. But how could he? As the guardian of good taste, Hartley canonised Cecil's approval, but the unspoken pact between them, with Cecil offering the books to the public as something exquisite, indefinable, full of the mysteries of the soul, held them back from a just appreciation. When, at the end of his life, Hartley finally bared one crucial aspect of his soul in *The Harness Room*, Cecil was left with no defence, he could no longer respond by singing the old song over again. For years, he covered Hartley's work in a mist, and it is this that Huntington detected, feeling that Cecil's approbation did Hartley no good. Hartley, of course, would never have agreed with him, for he saw Cecil as the ultimate seal of approval, the person who sanctioned his polite progress, his propriety, his ability to write the proper thing.

It is in *The Boat* that Hartley first plunges headlong into autobiography. All his life at Lower Woodford is here; the distancing of the novel from reality is almost minimal. Timothy Casson, a bachelor writer who had found contentment in Venice, is obliged to return to England in 1940. He takes a house by the river, where he may pursue the rowing that is central to his existence. His is a life lived on distinct levels that seem never to overlap. There is his life among the household's servants: Effie and Beattie, and Windsor (modelled, surely, on Charlie), whom Hartley paints in bold, Dickensian strokes, with heavily conscious attempts at below-stairs humour. Beyond the staff is the society of Upton-on-Swirrel, whose approval and welcome Timothy craves – the vicar and his wife (the Purbrights), their fighting son Edgell, the alluring but treacherously communistic Vera Cross with whom Timothy enjoys a milk-and-water romance, the elusive landowner Mrs Lampard and the whole gallery of Upton-on-Swirrelians. Beyond this exists another level where Timothy's smart friends can be found, friends who exist for him mainly through letters. Letters interrupt and disfigure the book to such an extent that we can be in no doubt about their importance to Timothy – and to Hartley (though those in *The Boat* run on at far greater length than any he ever wrote in life).

Timothy's world crumbles when he realises the locals are preventing him from taking his boat out on the river, thereby reinforcing his feelings of being an outsider, of never being a complete person. Only when he communes with his boat, the reason for his being, does pure happiness make itself known, and even exceeds itself, for the boat-house is Timothy's cathedral. Its spiritual dimension has an overpowering strength.

> The magic of the place, its numinous exhalation, came out to meet him, like a breath of sanctity from a shrine. The door had a key which he always carried with him; not that anyone was likely to steal the boat, but Timothy enjoyed the formal, ceremonial entry. There, in the dim religious light, the prostrate god was lying, its outriggers, extended like arms, reaching almost from one side of the narrow dock to the other. Steps went down to it, disappearing into the water ... It had the air of waiting for something. For what? For sacrifice, perhaps. Yes, yes, the beckoning fair one seemed to say; come with me, cast off, lower away, forget whatever it is that holds you back. The lure of the invitation grew stronger and Timothy could feel it tugging at his will.[34]

In order to effect his triumph over the river and the reigning locals, Timothy, 'so certain of being in the right', declares his own war against his enemies. Death is the price that must be paid, but it is not demanded of Timothy, who might seem the book's natural sacrifice. Instead, it is Vera Cross and the resourceful, all-understanding Mrs Purbright who die – a death of both Evil and Good. And it is Mrs Purbright's loss that we feel, Mrs Purbright who somehow stands in for Timothy on the sacrificial altar. Timothy, like Eustace, left exhausted by life, can only fall into a sleep as the novel ends; unlike Eustace, we know he is only having forty winks.

The Boat is a great, rambling, muddling monster of a novel; to Paul Bloomfield it is 'this deep, sometimes baffling, book'.[35] Part novel, part confessional, every page is alive with the author trying to make sense of his own life; it seems as if every irritation, every conviction that England had somehow done him down, is poured into its pages. It is Hartley turning his old trick, as Huntington suspected, an X-ray illumination, if not of life itself, then of its author. Whatever complex truths emerge or are disguised in *The Boat* were, it seemed to Hartley, greeted with disapproving silence at Fletton. Perhaps what he feared from them was the dissatisfaction with truth. Osbert Sitwell, recognising with what fidelity Hartley had caricatured his staff and the supporting cast of Lower Woodford, suggested he might do well to sack his servants before they lynched him.

❧ 8 ☙

The Go-Between

AT THE BEGINNING of 1950 Hartley went from Renishaw, where he was welcomed like the Prodigal Son, to Rockbourne, and from a week staying with Algernon Cecil to Avondale, all the time feeling at a loose end, with nothing suggesting itself for him to write about. In March, he went to stay with Ethel Sands for a few days, and visited Sibyl Colefax, sitting at the bedside of the now slight, porcelain figure who spoke despondently of herself, and fired off a volley of letters to him after his visit. After one last call to her boudoir in April, Hartley was accused of not inviting her to stay with him. Sibyl Colefax died that September. Despite the differences that had sometimes come across their friendship, Hartley knew that her death was the passing of a landmark. 'She seemed immortal', he told Ethel. 'Never have so many owed so much to so few, might have been said of her.'[1]

The critical wash left by *The Boat* had not subsided. A visit to Millicent, Duchess of Sutherland, in her new flat overlooking the Botanical Gardens in Paris, was spoilt by her continual onslaughts on the book. Feeling unwell, Hartley grew weary of her unremitting warfare, suspecting that it was the novel's politics that had upset her, hers being rather pink. From Paris, he went on to Montegufoni, where Sitwell, David and Edith were in residence, spending a day with Sitwell in Florence, but the Vespa motorcycles whizzing around everywhere worried him. Relief was at hand at Molly Berkeley's, though he was robbed of 20,000 lire as he boarded the Assisi train. Molly, at least, was appreciative of *The Boat*. By early June he was at the Palazzo Bonlini in a fiercely hot Venice, where he was invited to the wedding of Prince and Princess Clary's daughter, but not to the reception, held in so precarious a location that the bride's parents were frightened the floor might give way under his weight. The bulkiness that set in in middle age, aggravated by the consumption of alcohol and the lack of exercise, would lead Francis King to describe him, in his last years, as 'pear-shaped'.

Between bathing and boating on a lagoon stiff with enormous

jellyfish, Hartley was now working on the book that would become *My Fellow Devils*, having at one stage threatened friends with a novel about a Roman Catholic who loses his faith after reading Evelyn Waugh and Graham Greene. He now considered turning the heroine of his story, who marries a film star, into a Roman Catholic, but realised he did not know much more about Roman Catholics than he did about film stars.

His time in Venice was marred by his getting on bad terms with his landlady. 'She *is* an unpleasant woman', he told Ethel Sands, 'and I don't think I should want to go back *there*, in spite of all the advantages her apartment has' (but go back he did).[2] Venice no longer wore so friendly a face. Apart from the mounting cost of living, the dependable Pietro was nearing seventy, suffering from astronomically high blood pressure and unable to manage the gondola as nimbly as he had. There was also an increasing sense of loneliness in the city that had once nurtured him, a loneliness that could to a certain extent be kept at bay by his work. The writing of *My Fellow Devils* proceeded. In August, at Renishaw, he was a few chapters off the end, but had been taking advice (including some from a high-up in the Vatican) about whether Catholic priests might give intending converts discouraging instruction if they thought their reasons for conversion to be the wrong ones. Hartley's solicitor, David Horner, Enid and Harry were consulted on other points. His father was less helpful when Hartley hoped for a distribution of some of the wealth from the Brick Company, fighting the move tooth and nail. One indignant director had wondered why Hartley should want any money from the company. 'You're not married, are you?' he asked. 'You don't even keep a dog.' 'I keep a cat', Hartley replied frostily.[3] By February 1951, harassed at having to pay almost £800 supertax, he was also hoping that some of Bessie's money might be made available to him.

The death of Pietro, leaving his widow inconsolable and Hartley robbed of an old friend, did not make Venice seem any more desirable when Hartley travelled out in May 1951, though he was diverted on the train journey by meeting a man who showed him the typescript of some revealing letters of Baron Corvo, letters that almost certainly contained colourful accounts of Rolfe's homosexual activity; Hartley found them an eye-opener, and after reading them found he liked Corvo better. He was soon once more installed at the Palazzo Bonlini, unheated and with no hot water. On the surface, it seemed that all the old routines of his Venetian life could continue untroubled. He rowed on the lagoon, was pleased with his new, if timid, gondolier, bathed and wrote. Angiolina, Pietro's widow, whom others had described to Hartley as grasping, was trying to sell him Pietro's gondola, which she tied up below his window, for 500,000 lire. Hartley was suspicious of the bills he was paying in Venice, discovering that while he was being charged 4700 lire a day for his rooms, the inclusive price at a good *pensione* was about 2600 lire. Gondolas were a luxury. It now cost 1000 lire for the shortest journey, though he secured a bargain in getting one for a daily rate of only 2500 lire. Even with a gondola, it was not easy to arrange meetings with such friends as were left over from the pre-war days, while a journey to Malcontenta posed almost insuperable difficulties; even if Malcontenta was reached, there was still the nervous energy needed to stand up to the personality of Bertie Landsberg's house. There was the fear that Venice might now fall to the Communists in the elections, but though Hartley's district returned a Communist, Venice as a whole resisted. Nuns had been swarming up the pillars of their church to tear down the party's posters. There was excitement when the Duke of Edinburgh arrived in Venice with a detachment of the Fleet and was seen floating down the Grand Canal in a gondola with 'a highly coloured Englishman, a centre of social discord . . . said to be buying two palaces'.[4]

Less heady occasions awaited Hartley back in England. That summer he was asked to open the Bathford fête, and could not get out of his head his possible opening words: 'Some fates are better than others. It is my happy fate to open this fête.' There was, too, no respite from publisher problems, for dealings with Huntington were now at breaking point. As for James Barrie, nephew of J. M. Barrie and Cynthia's co-publisher, Hartley had told Cynthia how disappointed he was with his terms. When she had discussed publication of *My Fellow Devils* with Hartley, she had mentioned a £400 advance and Barrie had paid only £250. On the spot, she wrote out a cheque for £150 from her own account, which Hartley took, but was loath to bank. He sent Barrie's agreement to Denys Kilham Roberts at the Society of Authors, who agreed that the proffered terms were too low. Hartley was unwilling to pester an unwell Barrie, saw that his friendship with Huntington was slipping away, and feared a breach with Cynthia. 'I begin to wish I had never let her publish my short stories!' he told Harry. 'How true the proverb is, never do business with a friend.'[5]

The dispute with Huntington, who had so assiduously nursed Hartley's potential through a crucial period, was almost desperate in its misunderstanding. Huntington maintained that their agreement of 2 June 1946, which had referred to the 'next three years', meant 1948–50, whereas Hartley claimed it meant the three years following the date of the signing; was Huntington within his rights to claim *My Fellow Devils* as his property? Cynthia's position, too, was uncomfortable. She told Huntington she had only suggested that Hartley offer his novel to Barrie because he fully intended taking it to a third publisher, and that she had thought Huntington had no intention of taking *The Travelling Grave*. She pointed out that her firm would be happy to publish Hartley's book about the Brontës, should he ever write it (he never did). Huntington eventually gave way, agreeing that the contract had terminated in June 1949, but for Hartley the victory was aggravated by the damage done to his relationship with Cynthia and Huntington, and by the fact that Huntington's final offer had been almost twice that of Barrie's. Huntington faced it squarely; he realised that 'now [Cynthia] has become a publisher you must be the author she wants most.' It was already decided that Barrie would publish the British edition of *The Travelling Grave*, published in America three years earlier, but its appearance proved a disappointment, made up as it was of two stories from *Night Fears*, the bulk of stories from *The Killing Bottle*, and a handful of new, but unexceptional ghost stories. Huntington even suggested that Cynthia might take over all the earlier works of Hartley that Putnam had published. 'All this means', he told Hartley on 16 February 1950, 'that she can have the greatest contemporary novelist for an investment of something like £700 which, knowing what she got for Sullington Court, I should think she could afford.'

Barrie's enthusiasm, or lack of it, may have disguised the fact that *My Fellow Devils* was an unsatisfactory effort, a major disappointment after the richness of *The Boat*, and certainly Hartley's weakest novel of the fifties. The style has shifted. The canvas is reduced, the concentration on the central characters strengthened. The passionate opulence that threatens to take over the best of his earlier work is banished to allow the humdrum sensibilities of his new characters to take the stage, a technique carried through into *A Perfect Woman* and *The Hireling*. Hartley's intense involvement with the heart and mind of Everyman is exhaustively explored in the novels of the fifties, most successfully, of course, in *The Go-Between* where feeling, not always the case with Hartley, seems inspired and inescapable. In *My Fellow Devils* feeling never emerges; it is as if we are reading the translation of a foreign work, a work which the translator has faithfully transcribed but never experienced.

The plot is unpromising. Margaret Pennefather's infatuation with the handsome film star Colum McInnes destroys her engagement to a one-time school-friend of Colum's, the barrister Nicholas Burden. She marries Colum, a Roman Catholic, and means to convert to his faith, but is persuaded against doing so by a priest, Father McBane. Colum's professional career as a roguish charmer (his new film is called *The Devil is so Distinguished*) runs into trouble, and Margaret discovers him to be a thief, a liar and (almost) a murderer. Unable to resolve her unhappiness through her religious beliefs, she asks Nick to intervene. Reluctantly, Nick agrees to see Colum, but the effect is catastrophic, for Margaret is left realising that Colum 'had stolen Margaret from Nick and now he had stolen Nick from Margaret'.[6] Having withstood Colum's erratic love and his need to have her at his side as his 'darling accessory' (an accessory, as it were, after the fact of sinfulness), Margaret's release comes at a banquet given to celebrate the opening of the new movie. Colum toasts the health of 'our old, dead and distinguished friend, the Devil'.[7] Shouts of 'Satan!' greet him as he begins to address 'my lords, ladies and gentlemen, and dare I say, my fellow-devils?'[8]

Margaret's emotional collapse is followed shortly after by the birth of her son, but she is consumed as to what she should do about his father. 'To her overwrought, exhausted mind it seemed that Colum not only played the Devil's part, he was the Devil, and to be avoided like the Devil. She yearned for a simplification of her affairs, and did not realise that theology, complex as it is, is simpler than life.'[9] Colum moves on to what Hartley insinuates is a ménage-à-trois with Nick ('Old Nick' as Colum takes to calling him) and Lauriol, surely an ex-lover. No longer thinking of Colum as a person, but as an evil influence, Margaret recognises the Church as her refuge from him. Another adviser, Father Grantham, warns her, 'You must beware of ecstasy, ecstasy is for the saints, and even they have sometimes mistrusted it.'[10] She smiles when he accuses her of being 'an enthusiast, a perfectionist, perhaps', but realises that he did not mean this as a compliment. With gathering steps, she turns to the Church. 'It was not true that she was returning to her old life; she was entering on a new one, about which she knew nothing.'[11] Her heart shouts and sings with recognition as she runs towards it.

Throughout, it is Father McBane who brings Margaret to the point of truth, demanding that she faces Colum's badness, and warning her that her soul is in peril if she stays with him. Surely, she pleads, love covers a multitude of sins? 'Oh what do *I* matter? Why must I be so careful about my soul? And is not love the best thing for my soul? We are all sinners; if I am not to love a sinner, whom can

I love?"[12] Who indeed? But, despite the urgency of the message, *My Fellow Devils* is never successful, never gets off the ground. The characters are shackled to the moral theme, against a backcloth of the film world about which Hartley knew nothing; even the few dabs of reality that might have saved the day are missing. That moral theme is constantly reiterated, but too often imposes itself on the story-telling. An air of suppression runs through the book. The relationship between good, evil and love is obviously eating away at the heart of the writer, but we are kept away – perhaps deliberately – from an understanding of his concern by his puppet-like characters and his placid style.

Margaret's climacteric scamper into the arms of the Church may only disappoint those who might have preferred a more secular and physical, resolution. Perhaps we should not be surprised that Hartley shuns this; it is never really an option for him, in writing as in life. Does he want us to feel that Margaret's ultimate conversion, to the organised morality of the Church away from the murkier, less definable morality of physical life, is a victory or a disappointment? Either way, it is difficult to believe in. And always there is the feeling that too much is unsaid, corroborated by a letter to Peter Bien (an American academic preparing a study of Hartley) in which Hartley admitted that Colum had had a homosexual relationship with Nick at school and that the two men eventually lived together with Lauriol. 'All this, as no doubt you know, is *in* the book but I played it down as much as I could, because I didn't want to write a specifically "homosexual" novel, and I didn't want to suggest that Colum was misled because of his homosexuality, but because he deliberately used it to break up the friendship between Margaret and Nick.' How interesting that Hartley sees Colum as 'using' his sexuality to effect the split; presumably, this is the greatest evil any devil may do. The possibility that Colum and Nick might be naturally attracted, that their coming together might be mutually beneficial and even spiritually and morally good, does not enter into Hartley's argument. No matter how destructive it proves to the novel itself, their passion must be suppressed.

Hartley was at Montegufoni in October, feeling slightly intoxicated by the pungent smell of the wine crop swirling around underneath the castle. He arrived with what David Horner thought the most disreputable baggage he had even seen outside a third-class carriage in a French train, and suffering from a heavy cold. A week later, Horner told Christabel that Hartley was up again snorting and puffing and wheezing. The puffing is worst, as he puffs so far and so determinedly I cannot say that he has been a welcome guest, as when not polluting the air he spends his time creeping into bed-rooms and writing-rooms to read all one's letters, inspect one's clothes. It is such a bore having to lock up everything, and really his behaviour is worse than Beryl's [Beryl de Zoëte] – so beware.[13]

After *My Fellow Devils* Hartley turned to a novel quite unlike any he had attempted before, a novel of the future, that might have been expected of Orwell or Huxley, but hardly the author of the intrinsically backward-looking *Eustace and Hilda* or the rustic extravagances of *The Boat*. Progress was slow, because he had no idea of what was to happen next. Much time was spent staring at blank sheets of paper. He was still plagued with publisher problems. Barrie's terms for reprinting *Simonetta Perkins*, published that year, were not good, and Hartley felt sure he could get better offers elsewhere. But almost as soon as he arrived in Venice in May, he put aside the futuristic novel and began work, despite not being in a writing mood, on the book that would become *The Go-Between*. In writing its opening line, 'The past is a foreign country: they do things differently there',[14] Hartley at last signalled the willingness to give himself up completely to his deepest feeling. His heart poured into the new book in a flood of inspiration that would be unique in his experience.

If we look for any understanding of Hartley, it is surely here, at its strongest in *The Go-Between*'s prologue and epilogue. Here, the man's thoughts as he discovers the childhood diary that will launch him on a remembrance of the terrible event that affected him for the rest of his life are too personal, too knowing of the truth, to make comfortable reading. Even as we understand, we are overtaken by pity, by our knowledge of the empty heart that beats through these words. It is as if, in these pages, Hartley exposes the terrible sadness of his dilemma to us. In the writing, he tells us what we should never be allowed to know about him, the central tragedy of his place in the human chain, and we can only find it unbearable. 'I should be sitting in another room', he writes, 'rainbow-hued, looking not into the past but into the future: and I should not be sitting alone.'[15] With such dreadful realisation, a journey is begun that must be seen through to the end. The book was writing itself with speed, until mid June when Hartley reported 'I am stopping to *think*, which perhaps I ought to have done before.'[16]

Charlie came out to join him for the last few days of his stay. He was, thought Hartley, happiest when apart from his sickly wife, even if the tensions between employer and employee sometimes erupted with force. One day Charlie told Hartley that he treated him like dirt. But Venice had proved reasonably inviting. Hartley lost four and a half pounds through rowing, as well as managing some social life, enjoying the drawn-out tea-parties that lasted until 7.30 p.m., and visits to the few friends that still survived there, such as the Clarys and the Landsbergs. Drama ensued when the baroness, now ninety-seven, was taken ill and given only two hours to live. A little later she was sitting up and chatting away in three languages with all her old spirit.

Hartley was now stuck at the description of the village cricket match that was to be one of the great set pieces of the new novel. At first, he imagined that the boy at the centre of the story, Leo Colston, who secretly carries love letters between the daughter of a wealthy family and a tenant farmer, would know nothing of the nature of the messages, but then decided the boy *should* know something of them. Hartley always had great difficulty remembering what had given him the idea for *The Go-Between*. Though some habitual train of ideas had begun it, the most obvious stimulus was that enchanted summer of 1900, the first time the weather had assumed an almost mystical importance with him, the long, hot days heralding the new, 'hideous' century. He did not choose 1900 for its period possibilities, but rather

> I wanted to evoke the feeling of that summer, the long stretch of fine weather, and also the confidence in life, the belief that all's well in the world, which everyone enjoyed or seemed to enjoy before the First World War. No doubt those with their ears to the ground detected creaks and mumblings in the structure of international relations ... But the average person didn't; to the average person the idea of a world war that would involve everyone in tragedy was unthinkable. The Boer War was a local affair, and so I was able to set my little private tragedy against a general background of security and happiness. No novelist can do that now; he has to remember that in most people's lives tragedy has been the rule, not the exception.[17]

Looking back, Hartley found it difficult to remember how the novel had developed and changed during its writing, but knew he had set out to write 'a story of innocence betrayed, and not only betrayed but corrupted ... There shall be a proper aggregation of sheep and goats and the reader shall be left in no doubt as to which of the characters I, at any rate, feel sorry for. I didn't know what was to become of Marian and Ted, but through their agency Leo was to be utterly demoralised. "Now find excuses for them if you can," I meant to ask.'[18]

It was Hartley's attitude to Marian and Ted that underwent such a sea change, for he softened towards them, realised he could not paint them in such dark colours, or make them out to be the Peter Quint and Miss Jessel to Leo's Miles; they became flesh-and-blood characters, irresistibly manipulated by savage forces over which they had little control. Hartley later regretted that he had not made the fact that Marian was under pressure from her mother to marry Lord Trimingham clearer, which to an extent excused Marian's bad behaviour towards him. Hartley the moralist thought it necessary to have an epilogue (a device for which he was much criticised) in which he could pass some sort of judgement on Marian (and on Ted, whom Hartley thought had behaved only a little less badly than she), to show how her actions had found her out. This apparent need to pass judgement on his characters was the antithesis of Clifford Kitchin's viewpoint. Kitchin confessed to Hartley that he was 'rather shocked to find in how many crimes my sympathies are instinctively with the criminal and not with so-called justice.' Justice, for Hartley, had to be served, certainly to Marian:

> She was condemned by the strength of her feelings (which in my view was her best quality) to live in a place she hated in order to be near the grandson who she must have known disliked her. I was afraid that the critics would say I had portrayed a monster but they didn't; indeed one of them said that though it was obvious I disapproved of Marian he was on her side, she represented life in its richness and complexity ... Of course any novelist would rather have it said that he had drawn an attractive woman than that he had upheld the Moral Law.[19]

But the morality of *The Go-Between*, the axis on which it turns, concerned its author perhaps far more than it concerns the reader. It was beyond Hartley to accept that all its characters, in their own ways, are victims. In an article, 'Too Much Compassion?', written about the time of the book's publication, Hartley described compassion as 'a perversion or an extreme form of humanism which would do away with the whole conception of moral worth, and substitute compassion for justice'.[20] Such public pronouncements at the moment when *The Go-Between* was appearing seem somehow contradictory to the book, and the effect it would have on its readers. But, in December, when Hartley gave a talk at Leicester, he was thrown off balance by discovering that the au ence sympathised with Marian and Ted. 'I wonder what the M. ands are coming to', he told Jamie Hamilton.[21]

How much of Hartley is in Leo, Leo the boy or Leo the man? How much truth, disclosure of long-dead secrets, or fantasy, is there? Bradenham Hall, of coure, the Moxeys, the outhouses with their great locks of belladonna. 'I would hate you to think that the book is based on fact', Norah would insist, but, like us, she did not know.[22] What can be in no doubt is that *The Go-Between* contains material essential to our understanding of Hartley; what remains questionable is whether the central trauma of the book, the emotional stopping of Leo's life through his association with the disastrous love of Ted and Marian, represents the truth. The destructiveness of love claims Ted, who shoots himself, but Leo offers up a different martyrdom, for after the discovery of the lovemaking, his life can never be fulfilled.

Hartley apparently did not know what a friend had to point out to him: that Leo is a natural go-between, that this is his function in life. It is an easy happiness, as Hartley had discovered in his days as an army postman during the Great War, and brought him approval, the sure knowledge that people would be pleased to see him. But it is also Leo's (like Hartley's) middle-class upbringing, his middle-class ethos, that isolates him from everything around him. Caught between the two worlds of Ted (a worthy example of the working class) and the social rarity of Brandham Hall, Leo spends the book travelling between two foreign countries, while his own roots atrophy. Fifty years after the events that scar him Leo is still, in the epilogue, the same person, 'his character was his destiny and it hadn't changed. His only life was in the lives of other people: cut off from them, he withered.'[23] Marian, at the last, recognises in Leo what Hartley may well have seen in himself, that 'every man should get married – you ought to have got married, Leo, you're all dried up inside, I can tell. It isn't too late; you might marry still, why don't you? Don't you feel any need of love?'[24] When she asks Leo to tell her grandson 'there's no spell or curse except an unloving heart',[25] Marian is urging the same philosophy that Aunt Carrie (Hartley's fictionalised Aunt Kathleen) uses persuasively on the boy-hero of *The Brickfield*. Like Marian, Carrie understands the importance of spells, feels that most people are under a spell of some kind, that one's spell is a kind of protection, that in breaking someone else's spell one breaks one's own. Like Marian, Carrie insists on the central mystery of life, that the most important thing that can happen is to tell of one's love, to pass it on to whoever it might concern. '"The opportunity, the *opportunity*, my dear Richard," she almost gasped, "may not come twice – and you mustn't refuse it, you mustn't refuse *love*."'[26] In *The Hireling*, the widowed Lady Franklin, having learned her own lesson, decides, 'I think that love should always be told. I didn't tell mine.'[27] She warns her chauffeur that 'If there's ever anything you want to tell anyone ... tell them. Don't wait till it's too late or it may spoil your life, as it has mine.'[28] This almost trite philosophy, reiterated so often in Hartley's work, and at the heart of *The Go-Between*, is the more potent because it seems to come directly from the writer's heart.

The *Go-Between* was written much more quickly, over about five months, than any other of Hartley's novels. It was almost an improvisation, for his original ideas were vague; he had jotted down only the briefest of notes before beginning. Its techniques grew naturally out of the story and, as with his earlier work, the symbolism (with which the critics said the book was rife) was unconsciously introduced. In a letter to Peter Bien, he also offered a tantalisingly incomplete hint of what gave the book its special quality, for 'when I was writing *The Go-Between* I made a vow, which I kept, and have sometimes thought it had something to do with the book being so much more successful than my other books. But I don't think I could do it again!'[29] We can only wonder what the vow was.

Now there was the question of who would publish. Hartley mentioned a large sum to Jamie Hamilton, who wanted the book, hoping for a substantial financial reason to leave Cynthia and Barrie. When Denys Kilham Roberts suggested that the Society of Authors (of which Hartley had become a member of the management committee in 1951) should act as Hartley's agent, Hartley thought this might at least take away some of the responsibility and shame of whatever action he eventually decided on. The difficulty that had arisen between Cynthia and Hartley was a major concern by the beginning of 1953, despite her assurance that, whatever happened, there could never be any personal upset between them. 'Jimmie [Barrie] has spent a great deal of energy, time and money on you', she told him on 30 January. Urging him to let Barrie handle the novel, 'a five times better book' than *My Fellow Devils*, she warned Hartley against a fickle approach to publishers. According to her, Huntington was letting it be thought that he had let that book go to another publisher because he thought it unworthy. Cynthia had Hartley's interest at heart, wanting to acquire all his earlier books for Barrie, as well as trying to establish his Collected Works as a standard wedding present. She hoped that, eventually, he would become the firm's literary adviser. 'I think you are chronically disappointed because none of your later books has come up to the Shrimp, but you must remember that, apart from its superlative merit, *that* book came out during the War when every novel sold whatever number of copies the publisher could spare paper for.' While she felt it would be too undignified to plead with him, she concluded, 'We most vitally need you, and I shall be in agony of suspense until we hear from you.'

By February 1953 Cynthia had bowed to the inevitable, unable to risk the heavy losses that Hartley's financial demands threatened. He told Violet Hammersley on 10 March that 'It is the friendship element that is so tormenting – whether Cynthia A. will ever speak to me again I don't know. I tried for an hour this morning to bring myself to the point of telephoning to her, and Oh the relief when she was out! ... I seem to see everything in terms of *injury*, nowadays, (and insult, too!)'

In March he signed the contract with his new publisher, Hamish (Jamie) Hamilton, that gave him a £600 advance and a 15 per cent royalty. Hartley wasted no time in suggesting a new volume of short stories, provisionally called *New Lamps for Old*, but two months later he was 'so badgered that I hardly know which way to turn'.[30] The distractions were three broadcasts for the BBC, and his contribution to a serial, 'Sequence Sinister', in the *Sketch*, to which Hartley contributed an episode, along with Dennis Wheatley, Laurence Meynell and Geoffrey Household, among others. In Hartley's hands, the hero was soon reduced to a quivering neurotic. After Hartley left for the Palazzo Bonlini towards the end of the month – Jamie Hamilton having supported his application for a Special Travel Allowance – Hamilton sent off proofs that were lost in the post. A second set was mailed to Assisi, but only when he returned to Avondale at the beginning of July were they completed. He had softened Marian's outburst against Leo in deference to a friend who pointed out she would not have been abusive to him. And, he asked Hamilton, was his description of Marian and Ted's intercourse – 'two bodies moving as one' – 'going too far? I don't want to shock anybody, at the same [time] I want to make it quite clear what is happening.'[31]

With the publication of *The Go-Between* Hartley's reputation seemed assured. The reviews were almost uniformly ecstatic. David Cecil played a great role in bringing the book to the forefront of public attention. He wrote a eulogy for the *Times Literary Supplement* and articles for the *Observer* and *Sunday Times*, in which he announced 'a book of classical distinction and authority';[32] it was 'such an accomplished piece of work, and achieves so exactly what it sets out to do, that there is little that can be written about it: it is there to be read and admired.'[33] The novel was eagerly taken up for publication in the States by Knopf. Hartley immediately warmed to Blanche Knopf, enjoying his meetings with her, but, as with all his publishers, the relationship would sour. An internal Knopf reader's report neatly identified the source of future discontent. The author was

> no novice and has only recently made a come-back, which can be counted a succes d'estime more than anything else. His work lacks vitality and unless he can maintain his present standard or improve upon it he will very easily, automatically sink back into comparative obscurity. It is not a particularly hopeful prognosis.[34]

Hartley chose Denys Kilham Roberts of the Society of Authors to handle the negotiations with Knopf, who accepted the book in September, heartened by Hamilton's assurance that 'it is the most distinguished novel we have published for many years.'[35] Knopf also had an option on publishing *The White Wand*, but wanted to withhold its publication until Hartley had finished his new novel (*A Perfect Woman*), which he described to Blanche Knopf as having a 'rather improper' plot, 'being a sort of variant of the theme of Les Liaisons Dangereuses'.[36] Dealings between Kilham Roberts and Knopf quickly deteriorated, with Knopf complaining about his endless correspondence. He appealed to Hamilton to 'tell him the time of day. I can't cope with him any more.'[37] Hartley agreed to revise the cricket sequence, taking out technical terms where he could in an effort to make it intelligible to Americans. He was willing 'to re-cast it as a kind of meditation on the game – perhaps as a sort of ballet'.[38]

The reviews that greeted the Knopf edition in the summer of 1954 looked set to establish Hartley's reputation in America. The *New York Times* welcomed 'a triumph of literary architecture',[39] noting that 'Action and meaning reinforced another to produce one of those rare books which enrich and enlarge one's experience',[40] the *New York Herald Tribune* 'an exceptional, probably memorable quality'.[41] The book was soon on the *New York Times* bestseller list, though Knopf warned Hartley that, despite the superb notices, it was not a good time for English fiction. By November 1954, only

6000 copies of the American edition had been sold. There was compensation in that the book had already been translated into Swedish, Danish, Norwegian, Finnish, Japanese, French and Italian. W. H. Auden, after reading it, told Hartley in July that he was his favourite novelist. *The Go-Between* won the 1954 Heinemann Award, shared with a book of poems by Ruth Pitter, *The Ermine*. The following July Hartley was presented with his prize of £100 by 'Rab' Butler at the Royal Society of Literature, of which he was made a Fellow. Molly Patterson, its secretary, became a friend, and would often invite him to a cold supper at her basement 'under the shop' in Hyde Park Gardens.

In fact, *The Go-Between* was a success story marred only by Cynthia's continual pinpricks that Hartley had not let her publish it. He felt persecuted by her, and on the point of saying something he would regret. Had the book been a flop, he felt he would never have heard another word about it from her. The 'special' relationship that many of his admirers maintained he had with Cynthia seems to be based on slender evidence. She had already committed the solecism of stealing his cook. There had been the tensions involved in dealing with her on a business footing, a footing of which Hartley was very far from confident. And in June 1948 she and Algernon Cecil invited him to a 'subterranean dive called the Sedan Chair'.[42] When he arrived, she presented him with a drink which he gulped down. It was neat vinegar.

❧ 9 ❧

The Sleeping Beauty of Bath

LIFE AT AVONDALE was never without its drama, drama that was heightened when the Rural District Council – 'a monster with no nerve centre'[1] – informed Hartley that a sewer was to be laid under his garden. Enraged, the individual against the state, he consulted three lawyers who all assured him it would be pointless to object. Officials (whom he christened 'sewer-rats') made appointments to call, arrived two hours late or came on the wrong day, insisting on calling him 'Mr Hart' as they pointed out where manholes would be placed and what shrubs and trees would have to be dug up. By 3 November 1953 the work (calculated to last for two to three weeks) had started, but by the end of January only 70 yards of trench had been dug. It flooded. Water pumps, a noisy distraction, were installed. To reach the boat-house Hartley had to take 'a death-defying leap' across the slippery edge of the six-foot gap.

All this was as nothing compared to the behaviour of the workmen, which infuriated him, confirming, if he had ever had any doubt, his view of the 'W.C.' (here earning, or so Hartley claimed, £10 an hour plus overtime). A guest staying with Hartley undertook to watch the men for half an hour, noting that only two of them did any work. One man spat but did nothing else. When cold, the men threw stones at whatever floated by on the river. They drank from flasks and bottles or repaired to a nearby café. To get into the garden, they climbed over the boat-house roof, in which they made a gaping hole. Hartley asked a Council representative to come and witness it all. When the invitation was declined, Hartley threatened an injunction and was celebrated in the local newspaper. Five months after work had begun, the foreman told Hartley his men had finished, but they had not. Later, the Council informed him that his sewer would have to be connected to the main sewer. The two pipes were joined, but one of the workmen had blocked the flow by leaving a wood plug *in situ*, and the sewer exploded, deluging the garden with effluent. 'Since then the sewer has slept beneath its manholes, only a long depression in the lawn marking its lonely bed. But one day – who knows? – it may wake up again.'[2]

The summer of 1953 was hectic and social. Against a background of excitement in the Holt household (where Stanley, Charlie's son, was getting married), the guests came and went (there were forty-eight separate visits by house guests this year). With a large party, including Cecil and Rachel, and Joyce Cary, there was a week at the Welcombe Hotel, Stratford-upon-Avon, accompanied by Charlie, who saw all the plays and was, according to Hartley, becoming a real Shakespearian. The onset of autumn was discouraging; as Hartley and Kitchin had once agreed, the first two weeks in September were notable for nervous crises. There was the nagging business of income tax, with Hartley shy of declaring Bessie's brick shares in his returns. The income from the market garden was disappointing, two rivals having set up shop on either side. Unhelpfully, the Rural District Council seemed loath to pay anything but a fraction of Hartley's 'sewer' claim. Neither was he pleased when John Strachey replaced Osbert Sitwell as Chairman of the Society of Authors, feeling that Strachey 'is much more a political than a literary figure – and a very Leftish one at that'.[3] Hartley saw the year out at Fletton, but 'though everyone here is kindness itself my nerves have something against the place, and I shall get back to Bathford as quickly as I can.'

Hartley's new work, *The White Wand*, was a collection of short stories, published by Hamilton, who, despite Hartley's frequent dissatisfaction, would publish all his subsequent output. The book was dedicated to Kitchin, whom Hartley had recently asked to be his literary executor, a task from which Kitchin shrank, telling Hartley, 'I should be lost without your help.'[4] Kitchin now responded to Hartley's gift in typical style. 'Can I hear your readers saying, "Oh, he's dedicated this one to C. H. B. Kitchin. It can't be one of his best!"'[5] Kitchin himself had a collection of stories, *Jumping Joan*, published in July 1954 by Secker and Warburg. 'I fear that the book is an utter flop', he told Hartley, who may have seen his own work reflected in stories that tread that hinterland between reality and the supernatural so well known to Hartley.[6] Kitchin's fiction, of course, moves more credibly into lower middle-class and working-class environs, and is always imbued with a delicacy of touch and understanding, an underlying worldliness. In *Jumping Joan*, the title story and 'The Maze' are pieces that concede nothing in style and point to anything in *The White Wand*, which appeared in August. Five of its stories had previously appeared in *Night Fears* and one, its title story, in *The Killing Bottle*, though Hartley had reservations about resurrecting some of this material; he certainly thought 'Witheling End', from *Night Fears*, too reminiscent of Henry James.

The Madame Butterfly-type story that had been written in Venice immediately following *The Go-Between* gave Hartley's new collection its title. Here, fascination and disenchantment with Venice consumes him, the end of a love-affair made even more distressing by his having fallen out of love with England. The war, that separated him from the solace Venice had offered, must be blamed: 'The war turned us into a nation of thieves';[7] 'with the war friendship had come to an end'; 'For me the war dried up the springs of liking.'[8] As if to sweeten the bitterest feelings, the storyteller relates a story told to him by the 'hero' of the piece, a man in whom Hartley obviously detected something of F. B. Pinkerton. It is a clumsy attempt to put the story at a remove from himself. The hero (Hartley, of course) is a man to whom personal relationships are almost a religion, a man who has lived through multiple personal relationships in which 'One has a different self for every friend ... That is their most precious gift to one – a new self. The boredom of always being the same person!'[9] The fabric of his existence is made up of friendship, so vital that 'It had no rivals. I did not care about money, or position, or even present or posthumous fame, so long as I could feel about me the fabric of friendship protecting me equally against the heat and cold of life ... protecting me ... against life itself.'[10] In middle age, however, it is the very quality of his relationships that seems questionable; perhaps, he thinks, it was only his youth that made him an attractive proposition to the elders of Venice, they 'being all people who might have written, but had not. They attached too much importance to the accident of literary creativeness ... their lives were a creation, for they made an act of living.'[11] Now, it is a feeling of death that pervades the city, with its churches and clamouring bells, the overwhelming vitality of its people everywhere. The hero recognises life and love as the deadliest of enemies. 'Love keeps out friendship', the hero proclaims, as if friendship is always to be preferred above adoration.[12] 'Isn't there something rather putting off ... unattractive ... in the spectacle of somebody's meaning so much to someone else? ... You can tolerate it perhaps, but you can't like it.'[13] This is a precise reminder of Leslie's reaction to the 'spectacle' of his beloved David having fallen in love with Rachel MacCarthy, proof enough to Hartley that love could do dangerous, hurtful things that could not be undone. The plot of 'The White Wand' exercises these feelings when the hero becomes fascinated by a waving white wand in a window of the palazzo that faces his house. He begins a tormented search to find the room and its occupant, at last discovering a young crippled woman, whose pale, delicate arm (the white wand) had been fluttering to attract his attention. They fall in love but, warned off by her doctor, he deserts her and returns to England, where he learns of her death. Unable to cope with the threat of love, he loses his lover, Venice and any promise of happiness in the future.

Other limbs, as well as the white wand-arm, intrigue Hartley in this collection. The bachelor writer in 'W.S.' is sent a series of postcards from a character who repeatedly promises a handshake. Slowly it dawns on the writer that W.S. (as well as being his own initials) is a character from one of his books, a man whom he has painted as totally evil, without one redeeming feature. Here, it is the malevolent gentlemanliness of limbs that Hartley persistently exploits as, with every postcard, W.S. looks forward to 'Another hard handshake';[14] 'My hand feels a bit cold to-night, but my handshake will be just as hearty.'[15] When W.S. arrives on the writer's doorstep, he gives his creator the opportunity to discover one word of compassion in his portrait. The writer can find none, and must die. It is the handshake that means death, yet another example of Hartley's obsession with the separateness of limbs, the suspicion that a body is not a satisfactory whole but many entities, never resolving or coming together; always there is the feeling that Hartley is unhappy with the human body being at ease, integrated.

Friendship can compensate even for this, or at least disguise the discontent that comes from the author. In 'A Rewarding Experience' (which had earlier appeared in *Time and Tide* as 'And the Yellow Dog Laughed'), another bachelor writer, bereft of inspiration, who realises he has kept life, and marriage, at bay, and does not care for the human race, is exhilarated when a fracas in the street between a woman and two dogs brings her into his house. The need for coping with his own life is thus momentarily, blessedly, suspended. When she ventures out once more, the marauding dog reappears, and she scuttles back, with her own meek pet, into the sanctuary of the writer's house – much to his delight. He had thought, 'If only he could tell her how much better he liked the house this way, fouled and blood-stained! But he couldn't; he couldn't pierce the shell of her shame and remorse. He felt that they were turning against him.'[16] So much of the quality of the stories in *The White Wand* comes from Hartley's ability to translate his most immediate and truthful emotions in a way that was so often suppressed when a story developed into a novel.

In June 1954 Hartley was at San Lorenzo ('Mollyville', as David Horner called it) with Molly Berkeley, where they were joined for dinner one evening by the writer and publisher John Calmann. Molly ruled the occasion 'explosive, talkative and very lively', behaving like a Queen. 'She is very straight from the shoulder, and completely terrifies Mr L. P. Hartley ... who sits like a delightful old pussy listening and purring contentedly. A pleasant man, but so obsequious that I could not believe he really wrote [The Go-Between].'[17] The trio sat beneath the full moon as Molly's liveried servants served the chicken in aspic by candlelight. Far below lay the blackness of the Duomo in the still night, all around the smell of honeysuckle. From Assisi Hartley went on to the Hotel Europa in Venice, where the elderly Bernard Berenson was staying, disgusted (as was Hartley) by the type of pictures being exhibited in the city, and telling him that 'All art now is inspired from below the waist, the genitals and the bowels.'[18] After two nights spent visiting Cynthia Jebb (wife of the British ambassador) in Paris, where The Shrimp and the Anemone and My Fellow Devils were published in the summer (dropping, according to Hartley, 'like stones into a pool'),[19] it was back to Avondale, the sewer problem, the disappointing reviews of The White Wand and news of The Go-Between.

Hamilton, insisting that most people thought it the best novel of the past decade, was nevertheless disappointed that sales were under 50,000, having hoped for twice that figure. While he felt that the hypersensitive might have been shocked by its ending – the 'two bodies moving as one' – he told Hartley that he should not pull any punches over his next novel. Alexander Korda seemed to have made his mind up about filming The Go-Between, taking up the option he held only a few days before it expired, after arrangements were in hand to offer it to another producer, Aubrey Baring. Korda assured Hartley he would get his money but could only afford to pay by instalments as one of his companies was in the hands of the Receiver. Fortified by this, and the fact that Puffin Asquith might direct the picture, Hartley lectured at a writers' summer school in August, where he was treated by the 250 students as a celebrity, though he complained that there was almost no drink available. At Renishaw, he joined Edith Sitwell, enjoying the afterglow of having been made a Dame. Advancing on the Queen to receive her award, she had noticed the band suddenly strike up a selection from Annie Get Your Gun. Meanwhile, the cats at Renishaw were in disgrace for catching mice; one mouse had been frightened so badly that it could only be revived with brandy.

(*Left*) Leslie (standing) with Enid dandling a well-behaved Norah, 1904. (*Right*) Enid Hartley, the inspiration for Hilda in 'Back to Cambo', the short story that became THE SHRIMP AND THE ANEMONE

Bessie Hartley, Leslie's mother, whose lifelong wish was to live with her son

Harry Hartley with Leslie, Enid (seated) and Norah

'You have done your
utmost for King and
Country': Hartley in army
uniform, 1916

Kathleen and George
Lund at home in Finchley

(*Top*) In the garden at Garsington
Manor with Lady Ottoline
Morrell, the first great hostess to
befriend the young Hartley.
(*Above*) Hartley and David Cecil
in the grounds at Fletton Tower

David Cecil at the door of
Fletton Tower in the 1920s

A tense family portrait at
Fletton in 1945 with Harry
and Bessie Hartley, Enid
(standing), Norah, and a
clearly uncomfortable
Leslie

Osbert Sitwell, Enid (left)
and Norah outside Fletton
Tower in the 1950s

(*Left*) The novelist Clifford Kitchin in 1954. 'I can say to you things I can say to no one else,' Hartley told him. (*Right*) Hartley 'gondoling' in Venice, with (at rear) his gondolier Pietro Busetti

San Sebastiano 2542 (with balcony). From his window Hartley could see the statue of the martyred St Sebastian

Hartley at his happiest – sculling on the River Avon

Hartley at Avondale: 'You asked me if this house was home? I don't
know that it quite is,' he told C. H. B. Kitchin

(*Left*) Joan Hall around the time she first met Hartley. He kept the photograph by his bed. (*Right*) Hartley on a rare visit to Fletton Tower in the mid-1960s

Norah at Fletton Tower with one of the Rotherwood deerhounds to which she devoted her life

Leslie Poles Hartley 1895–1972

By January 1955 Hartley was able to report to Hamilton that he had written 72,000 words of his new book, begun in October 1953, the novel 'with a Go-Between theme – I can't get away from it'.[20] In February he suggested that 'Perhaps it would be better to keep it, as Forster has done his last novel, unpublished.'[21] The never ending social demands of his life made long, concentrated periods of writing almost impossible; he wanted, he told Hamilton, to lead a more Flaubertian existence; he was 'sorely harassed' by having to 'revise that *interminable* novel'.[22] The exasperated opinion of Roger Machell, Hartley's editor, was that if Hartley did not write unnecessary letters, have endless weekend guests and gallivant around the country, he might make better progress. Patience was a prerequisite of any publisher of Hartley's. The typescript of *A Perfect Woman* was warmly received in May, and an advance of £1000 sent off.

Hartley had gone to Peterborough for Harry's ninety-fourth birthday in March 1954. The old man was as interested in business as ever, coming out strongly at a Brick Company meeting against one of the directors who had suggested the dividend might be increased, but by the autumn it was obvious that his health was failing. His final illness lasted only a few days, until when he had been quite his old self, keeping his sense of humour. Norah and Enid nursed him at Fletton. Hartley was not present at the end. On 30 November, when asked what he would like for supper he answered in a strangely loud voice, 'Brandy sauce', and died. Returning to Fletton, Hartley found 'the material happenings of death very terrible, and sometimes find to my shame that my nerves respond more violently than my emotions'.[23] He told Christabel that he now realised what an indulgent man his father had been, letting him lead a literary life when the family had very little money and Hartley seemed to have no prospect of making any. 'He was a most reasonable and affectionate and even-tempered man, and grew more so as he got older.'[24] A year before his own death, Hartley wrote to Cecil, 'Fletton, for some reason, is inimical to me. Whether my father was more severe than other Victorian parents I don't know – he certainly didn't mean to be – but I always felt at Fletton I had done something *wrong* – especially in the North wing!'[25]

With what honesty these memories were recalled we cannot know. It seems to be Bessie who bears the lion's share of the blame, if blame it is, for her son's life. But the uneasiness in Hartley's relationship with his father cannot be ignored. The guilt that hung over Hartley fed on the knowledge that he had displeased, he had not been approved of, he had been discouraged from the experience of ecstasy. Harry, of course, was responsible for the bricks, the provider of material wealth; so far as the bricks went, Hartley knew he had inherited none of his father's passion, or interest. Harry's devotion to the business distanced him from Hartley, emphasised a central predicament of his life, the fact that somehow the brickfield had brought Hartley, like Richard Mardick, material prosperity and emotional sterility. Turning the pages of *The Brickfield*, all of Hartley's feelings about and against his parents are brought into the light of day. 'Any sort of disobedience to my parents' wishes – which to me meant doing wrong – worked on me, if it was deliberate, like a poison'.[26] 'I could only be happy if I was doing what they wanted.'[27] It is Richard Mardick, too, who must bear the brunt of Hartley's ultimate denial of Harry's love. 'He began to feel that all the mistakes and wrongdoings of a lifetime were summed up in his betrayal of the Brick Company.'[28] And so to Harry must fall some of Bessie's blame, the making of Hartley's particular tragedy, the creation of a son who perfectly understood the human heart but could never participate in its wonder. The finger is pointed, accurately, in *The Betrayal*, when a friend of Mardick's tells him a terrible truth: 'Your youthful self knew something about human nature that your adult self didn't, or forgot.'[29]

After Harry's death, Hartley wrote two devastating short stories, the form he so often used for matters that concerned him intensely. One, 'The Pylon', eventually published in *Two for the River*, is the darkest of his works; as he told David Horner, it is a story about a boy in love with his father. Shrouding it in fog as he does, he cannot hide its meaning. In a later piece, 'Roman Charity', published in *Mrs Carteret Receives*, the father is once again the perpetrator of horrors, obliged to drink milk from his daughter's breast. In the first, it is the father as aggressor, in the second it is the father as victim. And, at the end of his life, at last writing the homosexual novel he had spent so many years avoiding, young Fergus's father in *The Harness Room* is made to shoulder the blame for his son's martyrdom at the hands of his lusty chauffeur. Here, the father acquiesces in the relationship that will bring death. Whatever Hartley's feelings about Harry, it is in darkness that he would work them out.

In celebration of the publication of *Le Messager*, the French edition of *The Go-Between*, Hartley stayed at the embassy in Paris, fêted for three days, punctuated by three interviews, two literary luncheon parties (one given by Cynthia Jebb), a reception and a broadcast, for which he agreed to read but not to *talk* in French. A disagreeable guest at one of these occasions reminded him that most British writers, including Cyril Connolly, could speak French well, but that Connolly, who he claimed had learned his French from restaurant menus, was weak in verbs. It was a relief that *A Perfect Woman* had been delivered to Hamilton, whose enthusiasm for the new novel and eagerness to have it in the shops by the autumn overrode Hartley's fears that the typescript was full of errors and loose ends. He had shaken off the book by the time he went to Assisi in June, but could not settle to anything, despite having the ever dependable Jimmie Smith as his fellow guest. Together, they motored to Venice for a few days to see some friends, but in truth Hartley had little appetite left for the place.

The demands of celebrity sent him on a lengthy lecture tour across Germany – including Hamburg, Hanover and Cologne – in November, a feat made bearable by his being accompanied by Charlie. The country, still recovering from the great conflict that had ended only eleven years before, had the opportunity to see and hear the most British of novelists, whose newly found international fame sprang largely from a book about that most peaceable of ages, Edwardian England. It depressed Hartley to see how the great cities of Germany had been so destroyed.

Less successful, Kitchin (to whom the thought of such a foreign foray was anathema) had now given up his Brighton home and was living in London at 23 Montpelier Street. He urged Hartley to abandon Avondale and settle close to him – very close, for number 25 was free. Why, Kitchin implored, did not Hartley take it? The arrangement appealed even more strongly to Kitchin because at weekends and bank holidays his new lover, George, had to report back home to his wife and family, leaving Kitchin alone. In the handful of Kitchin's letters that have survived, there is one that suddenly evokes a flavour of the friendship he and George enjoyed – the mention of a stolen afternoon at Great Yarmouth's pleasure beach. It is confirmation enough of Kitchin's links with the real world and counters any accusation of snobbery; it is also at complete odds with Hartley's condemnation of the holidaymakers that parade through the seaside town in 'The Face', proof of his absolute refusal to allow vulgarity any place in life. Both men, of course, were increasingly isolated from the world they wanted. Kitchin's sense of isolation was compounded by the changes in society he saw all around him, the encroaching threat to civilised life. Escaping for Whitsun to a long-loved, select hotel at Margate, Kitchin was horrified to find it was in the process of being taken over by Butlins;

guests were being hastily sorted into sheep and goats (Kitchin had no doubt to which he belonged). Young ladies in bathing-costumes cajoled him to join the Keep Fit class in the ballroom.

Clearly, Kitchin's lack of ease with the modern world was aggravated by his lack of security about being published; not for him Hartley's certainty of getting everything into print. Before sending it the dreary round of the publishers, Kitchin sent him the typescript of his new novel *The Secret River*.[30] Teeming with Kitchinesque characters, this was the meandering account of a young woman's eventual emancipation from an overpowering mother into that 'secret river' of life and love that had been denied her. Tilting at Hartley's penchant for titled ladies, Kitchin asked in what form he might dedicate the book to him – as 'the Countess of Hartley' perhaps?[31] Hartley's propensity may also be the model for Justin Bray, the aged bachelor novelist in Kitchin's *Ten Pollitt Place*, entertaining 'three ladies of title to tea. It gave him a very faint glow of snobbish satisfaction, such as he himself had ridiculed in one or two of his novels.'[32] Perhaps it was with some feeling that Hartley was to write, after Kitchin's death, that 'Any reader with a serious inferiority complex may have felt, despite Clifford's lambent tongue, "How is he getting at me?"'[33] But Kitchin was a true friend. At the beginning of 1956 Hartley seems to have suffered a repeat of the nervous trouble that had plagued him as a young man. He considered psychoanalysis. Kitchin tried to dissuade him from 'this tampering with the psyche [which] strikes me as a form of murder. Take care of yourself, dear child, (a Walpolism) and let me know if there is anything I can do. I can't bear to think that our sweet Leslie may be brainwashed into a hard-headed business-man, a conventional debauchee, or a Puritan.'[34]

The frustrations attending the filming of *The Go-Between* were one source of aggravation. There was a flurry towards the end of the year, with John Sutro trying to put together a deal with London Films, telling Hartley that he was considering replacing the mooted director Puffin Asquith, who was tied up with other projects, with Peter Glenville. Sutro's deal involved the American producer Israel M. Berman of Viking Films, who wanted the picture done on a low budget, preferably with Alec Guinness as the older Leo. He also intended to retain the older Leo's voice as an off-screen narration only, which would make dubbing simpler and more effective when it came to selling the film abroad. Hartley was concerned about this disembodied voice, while Sutro suggested that leaving the child out of certain scenes and writing new ones might be a good idea.

Kenneth More, 'a highly intelligent man',[35] was Sutro's first choice for Ted Burgess. John Creswell had written a script for Aubrey Baring which Berman thought almost good enough but 'rather too far below the potentiality of the book . . . For one thing it must serve the dramatic purpose of releasing from his unconscious mind, the memory of these events which have blocked his emotional development.'[36] In Creswell's script Leo seemed to be aware of it all along, which Berman considered reduced the story to nonsense or, at least, sentimentality. Creswell had also overlooked cinematically natural moments which were in the book, and Berman dismissed his effort as needing 'much more thought, better integration of camera and story, and a more sensitive touch'. Hartley apparently found little to complain of when he read the script, by which time Rank was expressing an interest in it. Creswell warned Hartley that if Rank's boss, the accountant John Davis, got hold of it, he was unlikely to treat the story as it should be treated, and would go all out to give the film more popular appeal.

An antidote to the uncertainties of the film world, *A Perfect Woman* was published on 30 September 1955, 'a strangely old-fashioned novel' according to the *Listener*, in which the author handled his story 'as a cavalry major might handle his first motor-bicycle'.[37] For the *New Statesman* there was 'an ambivalence of melodramatic occurrences grafted on to a mannered high comedy'.[38] Hartley felt cheated by a lukewarm review in *Time and Tide*, to which he was a regular contributor ('am I getting persecution mania?' he asked Hamilton)[39] but he admitted to Kay Dick that it was 'rather a bleak and uncompromising book which doesn't woo the public as (I suppose) "The Go-Between" did'.[40]

A Perfect Woman is Grand Guignol on a suburban scale, and there is always about it a sense of Hartley trying to find a way beyond *The Go-Between*. Its central imperfection is its focus on Isabel Eastwood, the wife of an accountant, Harold, in a sleepy seaside town. Through a meeting on a train between her dull husband and a best-selling, middle-aged bachelor writer, Alec Goodrich, Isabel becomes bound up in the writer's life and inspiration. The dangerous liaisons which Hartley hinted were at the centre of the story are never quite convincing as they tread over territory familiar and painful to its author. Isabel's husband becomes another go-between, working on Alec's behalf at the affections of a local barmaid, Irma. Alec, meanwhile, is in the grip of a witch-like mistress, Elspeth Elworthy (in whom Kitchin detected shades of Ottoline Morrell). In resolving the dilemmas of its characters, the novel breaks out into melodrama and death – this being the part of the book that Hartley considered the most successful – delivering martyrs in Alec and Irma that resolve the emotional problems at its heart. It is the quality of relationships that must be sorted in *A Perfect Woman*, from which Harold and Isabel emerge triumphant. After the martyrdom of those who had come into their lives with such terrible consequences,

> Each was conscious of the other as a person in his or her own right, a person who for a short time had meant to someone else as much as any human being can do – a sovereign with one adoring subject – no, that wasn't true, for Harold had meant more to Irma than she, apparently, had ever meant to Alec. Still it was nearly the same thing. Each brought to their relationship, and pooled, this gift of personal sovereignty which neither had possessed before, or recognised in the other.[41]

The dangers of attraction to, of immersion in, another being, are vanquished. *A Perfect Woman* is a book that does not readily give itself up to enjoyment, perhaps because the effort it demands of decoding its messages never lets up. And suburbia does not yield to Hartley's touch, as it might have to Kitchin's, even if Kitchin had assured him that there was 'such wisdom without any heavy moralising'.[42] August Closs, the German professor with whom Hartley enjoyed a long friendship, considered it his best work after *The Go-Between*, a difficult decision with which to agree. The novel has an almost perceptible sense of being a struggle between its author, milieu and characters.

Knopf published the American edition in March of the following year, despite having considerable reservations about it. Internal memos at Knopf spoke of 'dull passages', tempered by the realisation that they had perhaps expected more of Hartley 'than we had any right to expect in the case of a man [of his] age'.[43] Blanche Knopf wrote to Hartley – a 'not very judicious letter' according to Hamilton[44] – asking him to eliminate Janice and Jeremy, the Eastwoods' children, from the book. He was outraged: 'my public expects me to write about children. I'm supposed to understand them better than grown-ups!'[45] He had, anyway, thought them so important that he had wanted to call the book, 'Janice, go back', a title not liked by Hamilton (who, for once, had no hesitation in supporting his author over the Knopfs criticisms). 'A great many American children seem intolerable to the British', Hartley told Blanche Knopf, 'in real life as well as in fiction, but we seldom suggest their obliteration.'[46] He threatened to sell the book elsewhere. But the reviews to a degree confirmed Knopf's doubt. The *New York Times* detected a lack of commitment to the characters, and the *Saturday Review* described it as an 'urbane comedy where none of the characters is quite so real as are all their gestures and inflections'.[47]

The momentum that *The Go-Between* had accelerated had its official recognition when Hartley was named a CBE in the 1956 New Year's Honours List; his worry was that, the Queen being so short, he would cut a pretty picture having to bow almost to the ground. As it happened, their conversation at the investiture was hardly sparkling. 'And what do you do?' the Queen asked. 'I write novels', Hartley replied. 'Oh really', said the Queen, and Leslie stepped back.

He was writing a new one throughout the year; from working titles such as *Lady Franklin's Awakening* and *A Car for Hire* emerged *The Hireling*. For Hartley and Hamilton this was a crucial work, one that needed to take the success of *The Go-Between* forward in a way *A Perfect Woman* had not. The procrastination over the book's completion was part of a pattern that would be repeated many times. As a sort of accompaniment Hartley would unload his other concerns on to Hamilton. When it came to having a garden, 'I should be only too glad to give up mine, if I could find someone to take it over, or even live like a Sleeping Beauty of Bath, surrounded by impenetrable thorns and briars.'[48] The book was finished in September, but he could only tell Hamilton that he was 'rather apathetic' about it, and that he had 'hurried terrifically at the end. You'll tell the reader, won't you, that the story is more or less sub rosa?'[49]

When Hamilton shared his author's reservations, insisting that he would not publish the book as it stood, Hartley was incensed. It was one thing that he should criticise his own work, quite another that someone else should do so. He pointed out to Hamilton that there seemed to be a clash of opinions; what Hartley of course meant was a clash between the verdict of his friends and that of Hamilton. Cecil, the arbiter of good taste, was summoned to give his opinion, which proved to be directly opposed to Hamilton's. This was tactlessly relayed to Hamilton. How he must have groaned to received Hartley's full transcription of Cecil's long letter, painstakingly copied in longhand, which assured Hartley that 'The critic [presumably Hamilton or Machell or the Hamilton reader] doesn't seem a man of any perception ... dismiss him from your mind.'[50] But Hamilton was adamant, agreeing only to publish (for an advance of £750) if the novel was made up with 'the revisions I think fit'.[51]

Hartley had already invited comments about *The Hireling* from other quarters and, having invited them, again put himself in the position of having to consider the responses. Kitchin's views were as ever coloured by his close knowledge of Hartley: 'I search for Leslie in every line, confirmations of what I know of him, new angles from which to study him.'[52] His chief criticism was that Lady Franklin was 'too much of a vague, ineffectual angel'; Leadbitter was magnificent, especially in the first chapter, which was a 'masterpiece'; perhaps Leadbitter could meet Clementine by chance, and he could turn her down – '"What, a blowsy old cow like you? Keep your tits to yourself!" or whatever is said by such persons in such circumstances.' Kitchin also gently pointed out Hartley's ignorance about motorcars (an ignorance repeated in *My Sister's Keeper*): 'Really good cars can be safely run in at 50 m.p.h., except up hill . . . I speak as an ex-Bentley fan.' And finally, 'I don't think you need worry about a libel-action! But I shall be interested to hear the reception of Lady F.'s butler to the story.'

Meanwhile, there was a 700-mile, eight-day lecture tour around the north of England, with Hartley setting out from his hotel after a Yorkshire high tea to find remote libraries and schoolrooms in Rotherham, Bradford, Leeds and less well-known destinations, along the dark, slippery roads. He did not think the lectures worthwhile, and had almost fainted at one. Peering from the car, he failed to see a single bookshop to which his inspired audience might flock to buy his novels.

At Renishaw that autumn, Osbert Sitwell was in better health than Hartley had feared, with David Horner and Edith enjoying a precarious harmony, despite the fact that Horner had complained of Edith having made a deal of mischief for him. Hartley wondered if it had been mischief or fair comment, but the Sitwell ménage was a diversion from the worries of the continuing confrontation with the 'nearly dotty' Hamilton over *The Hireling*,[53] and from his efforts to write a short story for *Woman's Own* with a strong feminine interest and a happy ending. This unlikely assignment was never completed, but anyway he was feeling disinclined to work. 'It seems clear', he told Christabel, 'that my subconscious regards that little decoration I got as the climax of my career, and doesn't want to take the field again.'[54] There was little inducement to write at San Lorenzo in October either, despite the strong feminine interest of the party (Molly Berkeley, Lady Anne Fumini and her daughter, and the Belgian ambassadress from Rome) 'but where is the LOVE?' he asked Ethel Sands.[55] As always, Molly's breathless way of life impressed him: she was planning a house in Ischia, building an annexe at San Lorenzo, preparing to travel to India to see the Taj Mahal by moonlight, and making all sorts of plans for the future of her remaining two orphan boys. From Assisi Hartley went for a few days to Montegufoni where a relieved David Horner informed Christabel that Hartley was 'less nervy' than usual,[56] and then on to Venice.

The unpleasantness surrounding *The Hireling* was only a little assuaged by a letter of apology from Hamilton, which quickly moved on to reiterate Hamilton's original view. 'I admit I didn't consider "The Hireling" up to the standard of the others', he told Hartley. 'I don't think that either critics or public will like it, thereby harming the prospects of your future works.'[57] This was not a balm likely to soothe Hartley, and must have contributed to his increasing pessimism. 'How hateful (excepting for one's friends) the human race is!' he told Violet Hammersley. 'I don't distinguish much between them – I wish I could say, "I hate the Russians, but of course I *adore* the Greenlanders!"'[58]

The Hireling appeared in the summer of 1957 (despite Hartley's only having signed the contract with Hamilton in March) to a mixed reception. In the *Spectator* Francis Wyndham wrote that, though not a masterpiece, it was 'as accomplished and absorbing a novel as anyone could wish. It is really a one-man book', even if the relationship of its two main characters was 'brilliantly established and explored'. By mid July Hamilton could report the book was selling well, a much-needed compensation for the unhappy dealings the book provoked with Knopf, for Hartley's relationship with his American publisher was now on a collision course. The American sales of *The Go-Between* had been sluggish – only 6873 copies sold by the end of May 1957 – which may have coloured Knopf's reaction to the new book, 'very second-rate Hartley'.[59] It was, according to Knopf's reader, a 'mannered, indifferent novel ... his uneconomical style can become dreadfully tedious in a drama that seems so manufactured, enacted by a set of characters from whom he seems so detached that in the end you feel you have done nothing but waste your time reading this'. Recommending rejection, it continued, 'I frankly do not feel it would be much of a loss if this latest effort is any indication of the turn his talent has taken.'[60]

In an intemperate but honest letter to Hartley, Blanche Knopf advised that 'to publish this book over here would not get you anywhere at all'.[61] Hartley, still smarting from Hamilton's dissatisfaction with the novel, was furious. From Assisi he replied that

'Personally, though I'm sure it has many faults, I quite like this book.'[62] He told Hamilton, 'I am tired of being buggered about (if you will pardon the expression) by these American Jewish tycoons.'[63] By August, Knopf was in a pickle. Alfred Knopf wrote to Blanche Knopf confessing that 'we put our necks out altogether too far, and in this case we had to saw the limb off ourselves. Now we have to go ahead and try our best to make everything you said in that letter prove false.'[64]

In a panic of reversal, Hartley was informed that decisions at Knopf had been taken in too much of a hurry and that they were scheduling *The Hireling* for publication. It was too late. Bitterly, but with a sense of victory, he wrote to Blanche Knopf on 4 September, 'I feel that your decision to accept it must have gone very much against the grain ... I am very sorry if this is a disappointment to you, but I can't help feeling that in another way it may be a relief – not to be saddled with a piece of goods that you felt more than doubtful about.'[65] The book was published in America the following year by Rinehart.

For a novel that provoked such dissatisfaction from both Hamilton and Knopf, *The Hireling* has survived surprisingly well; at the moment of writing, it is the only one of Hartley's novels, apart from *Eustace and Hilda* and *The Go-Between*, in print.

The Hireling is Hartley's Canterbury Tale. Stephen Leadbitter, a self-employed chauffeur (the hireling), is handsome, proud, self-possessed, isolated by his completeness; the book's opening chapter shows perfectly Hartley's perception of this lonely yet fulfilled working man, whose greatest friend is, perhaps, the telephone. A summons to take a new customer, the widowed Lady Franklin, to Canterbury, changes everything. Her husband, fifteen years her senior, had died when she was out at a cocktail party. She unburdens her guilt to Leadbitter:

> 'I could have got over that – the shock and so on. But you see it broke off something, in the way a tune is sometimes broken off. It was the tune of our lives, I suppose. We were singing it and listening to it at the same time: I'm sure you will understand that ... I never met him on the plane of our deepest feelings, not in the shadow of eternity.'[66]

Now, Lady Franklin travels to Canterbury to commune with her husband, who loved cathedrals. She is as isolated as Leadbitter, isolated by her feeling of loss and incompleteness; her mistake is in not having made her love clear to her dying husband. 'Is there anything in life that matters – really matters – except that somebody you love should know you love them?' she asks.[67] But there is another design in her pilgrimage. She is obeying advice that she unburden herself to a complete stranger, someone from a sphere of life quite beyond her wealthy, protected own – Leadbitter. When she asks Leadbitter questions about his own happiness, he invents a wife and three young children. The wife, in his mind's eye, bears a resemblance to Lady Franklin.

Leadbitter drives her on other pilgrimages, and the 'cure' of Lady Franklin's unhappiness is achieved; Leadbitter 'had saved her from herself'.[68] In saving her, he is lost in infatuation of her. On the way back from Winchester catherdal he tries to kiss her. She gets out of the car and dismisses him. Alone, Leadbitter's frustration explodes in a celebration of vulgarity and obscenity. Hughie, an artist friend of Lady Franklin's, who has been having a sexual relationship with the long-suffering Constance, proposes to her ladyship, and is accepted. (Leadbitter only learns of this and other developments when he chauffeurs Hughie, who is unaware of his hireling's association with Lady Franklin.) Hughie means to carry on his relationship with Constance after his marriage. Leadbitter, after much anguish, warns Lady Franklin of this in an anonymous letter. She rejects Hughie. In the car, Hughie and Constance wonder who can have known about their situation; who could have written the letter? Leadbitter admits to being its author. The car, wildly out of control, crashes. Hughie dies in hospital, but Leadbitter dies instantly: 'it was found that a strut broken off the driving wheel had run into his chest, a chromium-plated spike of metal, so thin that when they pulled it out the wound was scarcely visible.'[69] Leadbitter, like so many other Hartley figures, has sacrificed himself for love and is blessed by the miracle of the stigmata.

It falls to Constance to pass on his final words, 'Tell Lady Franklin that I – '; should she convey this uncompleted sentence, or finish it on his behalf? She grasps the opportunity. 'He loved you, Lady Franklin', she tells her. 'The last thing he said was, "Tell Lady Franklin that I love her" – he died saying it.'[70] Now, Lady Franklin has the strength to open her wedding presents, tokens of yet another potential happiness lost. Among them she finds the medallion of St Christopher 'hoping it may bring you luck, my lady. From S. Leadbitter.'[71] Tears fill her eyes as she studies the present, the one present that cannot be returned, the naked St Christopher, in one hand his staff, in the other a child, striding into the water:

She couldn't help identifying him with the giver, who had escorted her through waters deep as these and who had parted with his luck to make it hers. 'Behold St Christopher, and fearless go thy way.' She felt the reassurance of his presence, a promise like the dawning of another day; he had awakened her once, though into other arms than his, and had he not awakened her again?[72]

It is only through the understanding of a disinterested party that Leadbitter does not go to his grave having committed the same sin as Lady Franklin, the sin of not having declared his love. How, this new go-between wonders, can she hope to convey the urgency of Leadbitter's last message without its meaning? In the silent understanding that both have committed that failure of the heart, the chauffeur and the rich lady are at once unified and absolved.

The troubles that surrounded the publication of *The Hireling*, the squabbles with Hamilton and Knopf, the sense of nagging discord with Cynthia over the publication of *The Go-Between*, the inability of Venice to submit to his love for it, the feeling that England had somehow done him down, the knowledge that at Avondale, even now without Bessie's distant worrying, he was not at peace, left Hartley uneasy. He had always taken liberal doses of alcohol, and was now drinking heavily. There may have been reasons in anger, in frustration, in the suspicion that his writing life and personal life both suffered from the same disability, whatever that might be. Criticism of his work could only be damning; he was enraged by it, striking as it did at his essential need for approval, his winning of the prize, the guarantee of the place at the fireside. He was to discover, in the years that lay ahead, that he could do little to prevent the corrupting influence of the outside world that threatened to destroy the idyll he expected.

But there was one impediment to his happiness that could be dealt with, easily, swiftly, without question, because it undermined the only true joy of his existence. A male swan on the river had been rushing at his boat. It was his enemy. On the morning of Good Friday in 1958, Hartley and Charlie walked down to the water's edge. The cob and its mate came up from the river to meet them. Hartley fed the cob bread pellets in which he had wrapped barbiturates. Charlie attempted to divert the pen with undoctored bread, but in her greed she too swallowed up the poisoned offering, and it was she who was the first to collapse. Hartley described to Enid how the creature folded up before his eyes.[73] The cob weakened and fell lifeless to the ground shortly afterwards. Hartley was surprised at the speed of their deaths. The two men hid the corpses, returning that night to bury the cold, white bodies. Hartley, in life as well as in art, had demanded another's sacrifice for his own.

PART III

Blackthorn Winter

Running Shadows

HARTLEY KNEW THAT in real life, as well as in fiction, the price of
love must be paid. When that love had come from friendship, his
insight was at its finest, it had the whiteness of passion in it. It was
to Ethel that he turned when Nan Hudson died on 17 September
1957. Death had come as no surprise; she was, after all, an old
woman, eighty-eight years old. But her dying had been long,
watched over by the heartbroken Ethel, herself now quite frail.
Nan's health had declined after a fall in 1954. By 1956 senility
overcame her. Devoted friends, like Hartley and Raymond Mortimer, offered what support they could, aware that Nan's mental
disintegration at least put her beyond the pain of recognition that
Ethel was forced to endure. Exhausted, Ethel had to give up the
battle of looking after her, and in early 1957 Nan was moved into a
nursing home in Kilburn. Death, so long kept waiting, was caused
by bronchopneumonia. Two days later, Hartley wrote to Ethel:

> Nan's and your beautiful life together makes a memorial to love
> which still, when it is over, warms the heart and helps one to
> believe in eternal values – just as does your devotion to her
> throughout those last years, when the partnership of a lifetime
> was so sadly breaking up ... I seem to see her always in the
> sunlight and on some intimate informal festive occasion that you
> and she had been hatching for my delight – they are among my
> happiest memories. And although I know her nature had a stern
> side, which didn't always take things lightly in the realms of
> religion or politics or people, it was those principles and prejudices
> which gave her so much character and made her affection and
> friendship so precious. One associates [her] with a definite *line*,
> both morally and aesthetically: she was always herself, with no
> blurred edge. How quick and sure her reactions to every kind of
> art were! She knew at once, and never compromised ... though
> Nan didn't 'like' people very much, and you do, the effect of your
> joint menage was to give a kind of radiance, a glowing amenity of

civilisation and joyful life, which spread far beyond the Vale and Chelsea Square and Newington – though, alas, I didn't know you there. It has already become legendary, but it lives on in you, dear, dear Ethel, even if there is now only one lamp instead of two.[1]

How thrilled Ethel must have been to receive this letter, this tribute to the memorial of love: love that had emerged from friendship, and stayed the course. Hartley's understanding of love is somehow perfected by the knowledge that he will never find it. He had not dared, he could not win. The pain is in the understanding of it.

The anger and frustration that almost threatened to consume Hartley would not die. Towards the end of April 1958, he was in Ireland for ten days with Violet Hammersley, beset by misgivings at the thought of her as his constant companion. New clouds were forming. On 11 May Philip Toynbee wrote an 'extraordinarily disagreeable article' for the *Observer*, alluding to him in a manner to which he took such exception that he consulted Cecil Binney about issuing a libel action. Under the heading 'Misgivings about Mr Hartley', Toynbee's reaction to the complete story of Eustace (the three novels, with 'Hilda's Letter', were published as one volume that spring) was very different to the fulsome praise handed out by Cecil and Walter Allen. Noting the influences of Proust, Henry James, Norman Douglas and Aldous Huxley, Toynbee felt that Hartley had not transcended them, had found no new voice of his own. This fiction, said Toynbee, was on a level with one of the better novels of Maurice Baring, a poet and scholar whose reputation did not survive his death in 1945. Damnation with faint praise was not enough. Though he thought *The Shrimp and the Anemone* by far the best novel of the three, the 'trilogy' was overlong, it was pedantic, ludicrous, perfunctory, absurd. With perception, he suggested things might have been very much better if Hilda had been the book's central character, but, he wondered, would the author have been able to cope with her if she had been? – a question to which both Toynbee and Hartley must have known the obvious answer. Meanwhile, Toynbee could detect nothing of the masterpiece about *Eustace and Hilda*, no merit as a work of art, the whole nothing more than three novels and a short story that told the reader something of the attitudes of an English novelist born at the turn of the century.

A visit from Kitchin did not help matters, for Kitchin was in a bad temper and made scenes because there was no sherry in the house.

He went on to list the several occasions that Hartley had been late for their meetings. 'I certainly mustn't be late for him again', Hartley decided, 'but shall I ask him again?'[2]

It was a relief to escape to Assisi in mid June. Cecil and Rachel had planned to accompany him to Molly Berkeley's, but cried off at the last moment, disappointing but not surprising him. San Lorenzo offered up its special comforts, though its hostess, aware of Hartley's growing fondness for alcohol, would not let him have his pre-lunch gin. There were two visits to the musical festival in Spoleto, to see Verdi's *Macbeth* and some ballet, but for much of the time Hartley was preoccupied with his income tax problems and his futuristic novel, for which he felt little enthusiasm; he was not writing much, and did not like what he *was* writing, but the book was 'finished' by mid September.

Avondale would not settle into blissful domesticity. Like some ageing actress reluctant to give a definitive farewell performance, Miss Romaine was once more introduced into the household. True to form, she gave notice, was asked to stay when the new cook walked out, but eventually retired from the scene with diabetes. Mrs Holt was enduring a double rupture, but filled the breech with her solid if unimaginative cooking; sage omelette followed by jam omelette was typical fare. A radio adaptation of *Eustace and Hilda* gave Hartley a boost, but left him wondering why he had killed off Miss Fothergill so early in the story. Kitchin went some way to redeeming his reputation when, on returning from a trip to Amsterdam, he wrote to tell him, 'Never have I had such continuously good food, and it has other aspects about which I will tell you.'[3] Almost certainly, these 'other aspects' concerned Amsterdam's homosexual attractions, about which Hartley would have been interested. A visit to Christabel at Maenan, where he slept next to the haunted room and was awoken by strange noises, and to Renishaw, where he had a frightening attack of high blood pressure, helped to fill August.

Peter Bien, researching his book about Hartley, arrived in England in the autumn and was invited to lunch at Avondale, consolidating a friendship that provided a stream of letters from Hartley revealing a good deal about his writing. Now, Hartley was coping with a demanding series of lectures (as always, he dreaded such commitments as they drew nearer) beginning in Liverpool on 24 October when he spoke on eighteenth-century novelists, first to an audience of 400 children, and then to a gathering of adults which included six nuns, the sight of whom filled him with horror. The next month there was a lecture tour of Rome, Florence, Milan and

Venice, where he was received 'almost with enthusiasm', though he faced a sticky crowd in Bologna, 'a nest of communists'.[4]

But the year ended with a blow when Hamilton rejected the futuristic novel, *Facial Justice*. He reminded Hartley that *The Hireling* had sold only 12,000 copies whereas *A Perfect Woman* had sold 18,000, and that Hartley needed to follow up with a strong book. Denying the suggestion that he wanted his author always to write about childhood and adolescence as in his best known works, Hamilton insisted that 'The man who wrote those books ... not to mention the stories, can't surely feel seriously that he is too old to write more novels of the same calibre.'[5] Hartley told Peter Bien that he did not think Hamilton knew much about books, and fired off a letter to Roger Machell telling him that if this rejection was final he would have to find another publisher. In his defence, Hartley rather tactlessly informed Machell that several of his friends had said that Hamilton must be mad. Walter Allen was on hand to assure Hartley that 'Hamilton is obviously entirely and stupidly wrong about it', but went on to recommend some re-writing, suggesting that in the final section of the novel 'a failure in story-telling occurred'.[6]

The unhappiness with Hamilton was aggravated by Charlie's illness. He had been in indifferent health for several years; ulcers and a collapsed spine had both been blamed. Towards the end of 1958 it was obvious that his condition was serious. Hartley's concern, agitated by the 'incredible' delays over doctors and consultations, was ratified when terminal cancer was diagnosed. At the beginning of the new year Charlie was discharged from the hospital, which could do nothing more for him. Hartley paid for him to be cared for at the Woodside Nursing Home in Bath, despite the fact that the fees threatened to precipitate 'the biggest plunge into the red that I have ever taken!'[7] Watching Charlie's struggle against death was a horror to Hartley. He could not live in the house, and began a pillar-to-post existence of living in hotels; by mid February he had spent only three nights at Avondale since returning from Italy in November. Effectively homeless, he took refuge in a Knightsbridge flat belonging to Freda Listowel, making regular excursions to Bath to see Charlie. Charlie was not told of his condition, but it must have become obvious to him – by the middle of January he was already being given three-hourly injections of morphine. Death did not hurry itself. Charlie died on 1 March 1959, leaving Hartley without the one person in his life on whom he had always depended. It was a loss from which he never recovered. Charlie, as Hartley was to discover, had been without equal. His death, his one dereliction of duty, left Hartley vulnerable and alone.

When Hartley returned from staying with Bertie Landsberg at Sintra in Portugal in late March (where Freda Listowel was a fellow guest), the atmosphere at Avondale had changed; Charlie had gone, and it could not be otherwise. The house was in turmoil after the arrival of the new staff, Eric Hurrell, an ex-policeman, and his wife. By mid April, after a visit to Maenan (on which Eric had accompanied him), he returned to find that much of the furniture had been rearranged and his bedroom reorganised. 'I was so angry I thought I might have some sort of attack.'[8] Victor Cunard came in early May, but the Hurrells pronounced themselves 'whacked' at entertaining Hartley's guests. 'Sometimes I think that the private house has become an anachronism', Hartley told Christabel, 'and we shall all be reduced to living in hotels (where "servants" seem so much happier) ... But my most besetting trouble is my book. I have no inclination to revise it – indeed, I have a strong disinclination ... Jamie Hamilton has been so tiresome over these last two books. No single person (I don't mean unmarried) has ever given me so much discouragement! – not what one wants in one's publisher!'[9] There is no doubt that he was genuinely concerned about the deterioration of dealings with Hamilton and 'I need the money. I'm not really rich, as you well know.'[10]

The time away from home, and the new faces around him, left Hartley feeling so strange that he could hardly recognise himself. Charlie's widow was gone, too, to live with her policeman-son at Bradford-on-Avon, leaving Hartley's welfare to the Hurrells. When Hartley took on another husband-and-wife team as daily helps, this new couple ran to him with tales of the Hurrells' misdoings, hoping that they might get taken on in their place. More problems came with floods after a mid May cloudburst, and a threat by the Gas Board to erect a 'structure' in the garden. The realisation of what Charlie had meant to him kept cutting across such incidents. 'For some reason', he wrote to Christabel on 30 May, 'I am missing Charlie today very much.'

It was a diversion to go to Molly Berkeley at Assisi in June, while at home the theatre was holding out promises of dramatised versions of his work. The impresario Harold Fielding paid £200 for the option of presenting *A Perfect Woman*, intended for an opening in Liverpool, but after both Peggy Ashcroft and Diana Wynyard declined the leading role, the production was abandoned. The writer

Mabel DeVries Tanner came to London in July to find a producer for her play of *The Go-Between* and to see Hartley, who rather dreaded meeting 'a most overpowering and volcanic woman'.[11] A proposed British musical comedy version of the novel (which would probably have been a fascinating disaster) fell by the wayside. Between the *longueurs* of waiting for theatrical events that were destined not to happen, Hartley had a spate of writing the short stories that were to make up his next collection. Reading one of these, 'The Face', Kitchin wondered if an incident that had occurred at Fletton many years before had been the inspiration for its 'doodling' theme, for while playing piquet there with Hartley, Kitchin had drawn Clive Preen's face on the scoring-block, years before he had ever set eyes on him.

In August there were visits to Renishaw, where Osbert, Edith and David Horner were in residence, 'David most assiduous and devoted, and Edith in very good form', the two getting on much better with one another than Hartley had imagined.[12] In letters, Horner kept him abreast of Edith's drinking problems, which struck a chord. 'I'm sorry to hear of Edith's lapses', Hartley wrote, 'but am ashamed to say that her progress from room to room sounds rather like mine – I can hardly answer the telephone without pouring myself out a tot.'[13] Later that month, he went to Sissinghurst to lunch with Vita Sackville-West and Harold and Nigel Nicolson. These excursions coincided with the Hurrells' holiday, and in their absence the Avondale daily woman campaigned against them constantly, denouncing Eric as 'all mouth and trousers' and saying of his wife that 'her hair is her religion'.[14] Miss Romaine had not helped by telling the Hurrells that Charlie had waited on Hartley hand and foot.

Perhaps partly to get away from the maelstrom of Avondale, but also to have a base for his London life, Hartley had been considering buying a flat, and towards the end of 1959 acquired flat 12 at 58 Rutland Gate in Knightsbridge. His occupancy of number 12 was to be brief, for number 10 – reached by a rackety lift – came up for sale and Hartley, preferring this to number 12, bought it from its owner, one Buckshot B. Lieu. In February, he told Enid that 'Clifford liked the flat very much – indeed, without his urging me on I should never have got further than thinking of taking it. I like it too, except for the low ceilings. It is right at the top and has a view both sides – the treetops of Rutland Gate and house-backs of Ennismore Gardens. It will be free on March 20th. Clifford says I shall have to have the flat done up. As you know, I have never had anything done up in my life! – and don't know how to.'[15] There was now the need to have *Facial Justice* revised and ready by 1 December, after which he felt he would be able to reform his drinking habits, for, as he told Christabel, he had taken to drink 'in quite a big way'.[16] Christmas had to be faced with the feud between the Hurrells and the rest of the staff at its height, leaving Hartley feeling flattened and dreading the festivities and the food. A provisional demand for £1500 surtax contributed to the general depression.

But it would be quite wrong to give the impression that he was totally obsessed by his domestic arrangements, or the dissatisfaction that he found all around him. It is an easy impression to accept, but untrue. When the opportunity presented itself, Hartley was always happy to encourage other writers; to have his support, to have sustaining letters from him, was of great importance to many struggling to get into print and gain recognition for their voice. In the case of the Indian writer Fredoon Kabraji, the correspondence spanned twenty-three years. In 1959, Hartley, writing to Kabraji about his novel *A Love was Born*, assured him that 'I have seldom read a novel with which I have felt a stronger temperamental affinity. I believe the whole thing is to be a trilogy.'[17] As late as 1970, Hartley was offering to write a preface to the book if Macmillan agreed to publish it, but Kabraji's work never saw the light of day. Hartley also championed Ralph Ricketts' novel *The Manikin*, trying to interest Hamilton in it (he did not take it but Faber did).

Others cherished the letters of support that dropped through their letter-boxes. In 1961, Sybil E. Bowen ('I am not a successful person')[18] was delighted when Hartley wrote to her about a letter she had written to the *Sunday Telegraph* following his review of Winifred Gerin's biography of Branwell Brontë. She promised to keep his letter as 'a very precious possession',[19] and wrote again about Branwell to him 'and am encouraged now to think, Sir, that it will interest you'. And, later, 'it is such a privilege, such a release to be able to confide these things in someone who is an authority.'[20]

The most colourful of Hartley's corresponding protégés was a Mrs Mabel Lewis who, as Emma Smith, had enjoyed a remarkable success with the autobiographical *A Cornish Waif's Story*. She first contacted Hartley in 1954 ('Dear Sir or Madam') about her dissatis-faction with A. L. Rowse, who had taken up her book and got it published. The correspondence lasted until at least 1969, Mrs Lewis regaling Hartley with tales of her mortgaged cottage and its wet walls in Redruth, Cornwall, and her husband – 'an old man of 74'.[21] A year later, she had Hartley's photograph and decided 'No – No

Malice Aforethought shows in that face.'[22] She spoke of the lack of
education of herself and her husband who had been struggling to
get through *The Pilgrim's Progress* for years: 'he has got about half
way through the second chapter I think – perhaps this will tell you
more than it would be loyal for me to say or write.'[23] Hartley's
support, the constant supply of reassuring letters, meant a great deal
to her. 'I do not know', she told him, 'how I could bear it now if
they ceased all-to-gether.'[24] She savoured the letters, fragrant with
Hartley's tobacco. 'Have you ever fallen in love with a handwriting?'
she asked. 'You have? Then you will understand.'[25] Hartley tried to
persuade Putnam to publish her, but without success. Her budgeri-
gar fluttering about her room as she wrote to him, she described her
life with 'My dear old man [who] is the dullest person on earth for a
woman with any intelligence to live alone with'.[26] Her letters were
sent off to be received in what was for her a benefaction of
friendship: 'it is your insight and your wonderful perception – that
makes you so patient with me and my letters.'[27] By 1962 she was,
she told Hartley, 'finished body soul and spirit', 'depressed and pain-
racked'.[28] By the end of the sixties, she and 'the old man' had moved
to Tarves in Aberdeenshire. Still she wrote to Hartley, still she was
determined to write as well as she could, despite having had no
further luck with publishers. It was not for the want of Hartley's
trying. He even prodded Hamilton, assuring him that 'she writes
better when her pen is dipped in gall than it's dipped in treacle',[29]
but Hamilton was not impressed. In her last surviving letter to
Hartley in January 1969, she told him she would be seventy-five
come January. 'The old man' had been out for a walk and had a
fall.[30]

The move to Rutland Gate was not a signal for an improvement at
Avondale, for after a furious row with Hartley, the Hurrells, much
to his relief, gave notice. An extraordinary document survives in
which Hartley, following a visit from them in London during which
they had obviously tried to plead their case, set out his grievances
against them:

> It is now evident [he wrote] that either you and your wife were ill-
> informed as to the duties normally undertaken by a 'married
> couple' in charge of a gentleman's establishment, or that you
> never had any intention of carrying them out. This was definitely
> brought home to me by your wife who, when I drew her attention
> to the state of my study, produced the astounding reply, 'Do you

think I'm a skivvy to get up at half-past seven?' (The reaction of the average employer to this piece of impertinence would have been to dismiss you both on the spot without character.) You yourself, when I reminded you that one of my guests – I think it was Sir Roderick Meiklejohn – would expect his clothes to be brushed and his shoes cleaned, said, 'Oh is he one of those?', incidentally showing your ignorance of the routine of a well-conducted household.[31]

Hartley had promised the Hurrells a yearly bonus commensurate with the excellence of their work, but informed them that in their case he felt £5 was generous (he had already let slip that he had sometimes given Charlie a Christmas bonus of £50). In defence of his late manservant, he told the Hurrells that 'It is typical of you that on occasion you should presume to make observations to me about Charlie's conduct and character ... Any ideas you may have formed about him can only be derived from the idle gossip of the servant's hall, and I wish to hear no more of it.'[32] After threatening to put their complaints in the hands of his solicitor, Hartley fired two parting shots:

(a) I shall be glad to have an explanation as to why my car had L-plates fixed to it when you drove up to see me in London. I have never authorised your wife to drive it, and I have a strong objection to her – or any other Learner – doing so.
(b) Your last letter to me was written on 'Avondale' note-paper. I provide this paper for my own use and that of my guests – not for that of my staff. It occurs to me to wonder if you have been foolish enough to use it for the purpose of answering advertisements of situations. If so, I am not surprised you have been unsuccessful. Such petty pilfering is soon detected by a prospective employer and cannot fail to create an unfavourable impression of the applicant.[33]

Though this typed document was addressed to the Hurrells, the heading (in a different typeface) of 'For Amusement Only' suggests Hartley may never have shown it to them, but by mid April 1960 the Hurrells had gone. Hartley was left with what he described as a curious sense of emptiness.

Cynthia Asquith's unexpected death on 31 March 1960 contributed to this, as well as Charlie's death and the upheavals of Avondale. Hartley had known that Cynthia had collapsed and been taken to a nursing home in Oxford where meningitis had been diagnosed. He had thought meningitis was something from which everybody recovered. It was a consolation that she had been unconscious for much of the time, and that her dying had lasted little more than twenty-four hours. Cynthia's last years had been a steady decline. Despite a brief tenure in 1957 as a TV personality, when she won £3200, courtesy of the quizmaster Jerry Desmonde, as a contestant on ITV's popular '$64,000 Question', there had been much unhappiness. In 1958 she underwent major surgery and the following year was left desolate when her last lover, Collin Brooks, died. Her remaining joy was the biography of Sonya Tolstoy she was writing, and which was published posthumously.

How important Hartley was to her in these last years we do not know, for his letters to her have vanished, and those that we have of Cynthia's to Hartley, which belong to an earlier period, are sketchy. Many of his letters to Cynthia perished in the warehouse fire that destroyed so many of her effects in 1973, but it is possible that after her death some were returned to him. It may be that this correspondence was put to the fire, either by Hartley or by others after his death. Ultimately, we are left with little proof of their feelings for one another, despite the assertion of such friends as Ralph Ricketts, who maintained that Hartley loved and admired her. We cannot doubt that Hartley was profoundly affected by her death; by dying she had taken from him one of the most enduring of his relationships. When he gave the address at her memorial service at St Martin-in-the-Fields on 28 April, it was all he could do not to break down. He told the congregation:

One cannot think of her apart from her physical presence and the beauty, sunshiny at one moment, shadowy the next, that was as various and unpredictable as her talk. But I won't say more of the physical and mental graces that were the vesture of her spirit and that are, for each of her friends, a treasured possession, not to be disturbed by any attempt of mine to paint the lily. You could truly say of her, in the words of Shakespeare, whose plays she knew almost by heart, that a star danced when she was born and went on dancing till she died ... It was her special gift to be ironically detached from herself and yet vitally concerned with other people. She saw herself in a mirror, often as a figure of fun. Perhaps we saw her in a mirror too, for in spite of her directness she had a mysteriousness, a moonlit, leprechaun quality that was not quite of this world. She was not called Cynthia for nothing, and she had at least as much in common with the regent of the night as with us ordinary mortals. And so, even though she has left us, she shines for us still.

Revelations of the Hurrells' regime continued after their departure from Avondale, Hartley discovering that they had got cigarettes on his account under the guise of tinned peas. Now, he depended on his daily help and the gardener (who doubled as chauffeur) to cope with the daily round and the demands of such guests as the infirm Roderick Meiklejohn, who was so overcome at the sight of parsley that it had to be rushed from the room. In the spring, the move to 10 Rutland Gate meant a busy time, for Hartley had committed himself to some television appearances. He felt under par for the first of these, blaming too much gin, and made a vague vow to let up on his drinking. In May, he was at Avondale, relieved by the reasonable reviews for *Facial Justice*, which Hamish Hamilton had at last reluctantly agreed to publish.

No novel could have been so unexpected from Hartley, this great imaginative leap from his well-rehearsed criticisms of the relationship between man and the state, to the creation of an entirely new society. At once simplistic and subtle, artless and passionate, the book apparently has Hartley turning from the highway of gentlemanly novel-writing into the side-street of science fiction. He brings all the cleanliness of a fable newly told to his account of this 'relaxed and invalidish' civilisation ruled over by a 'Darling Dictator' known only by his omnipresent voice. Again we are in the world of fairytale. Nuclear warfare has sent the world's population underground until, inspired by a little child, half of the remaining people clamber back on to the surface of the earth. In Cambridgeshire, Jael 97 (citizens, or Patients and Delinquents as their Dictator prefers to call them, are all named after famous murderers) is persuaded by her brother to report to the Ministry of Facial Justice for a new, 'Beta', face, a standardisation of features that follows the state's philosophy of a levelling-down of all individuality. Equality is everything good, envy bad, as the slogans promulgate the Dictator's thinking ('Betas are buxom', 'Be Beta and you won't have to beautify!' Another slogan, 'Excellence belongs to the Elect', is surely one that Hartley himself would heartily have endorsed). In a world where sackcloth and ashes are everyday wear, only the privileged Inspectors (each named after one of the seven Archangels) are sartorially distinctive with their high shining boots, white breeches, golden helmets and nodding plumes.

Jael's private rebellion begins when she evades being 'betafied', but it is the last vestige of aesthetic beauty, the western tower of Ely cathedral, still standing erect in the desolate country, that liberates her individuality. Confined to hospital after an accident arranged by the Dictator for those insisting on going on motor excursions, Jael does not realise that she has been 'betafied', and is consoled by a sweet old lady who does the rounds of the beds. The anger Jael feels on learning the operation has been done is only eased by the loveliness of a rare real flower, a cineraria, which she takes with her to face the world. Throughout, there is the growing love between Jael and the Inspector Michael, tall, handsome, smiling, who bears her through the air as if on wings; if this romance verges on the syrupy, this is the stuff of fairy-tales. Revolution threatens to ruin the structure of life when the Dictator, identified by Jael as having a birthmark just below the heart, is revealed as the sweet old hospital visitor. She is about to die at Jael's hands when Michael appears, begging her to show herself to the crowds who are crying out for their Dictator.

'I can't,' she said. 'I'm dying, didn't you know? But you can go to them – only don't let them see you.'

'We can go?' said Jael and Michael, in the same breath.

'Yes, you can go, for all they want's a Voice – a Voice to tell them what I didn't tell them. You have learned by my mistakes.'

'What shall we tell them?'

The dying woman made a great effort.

'Say what I tried to say … And then … And then … You must think out a new play for them – a better one than mine. Together you can do it … I had to do it alone …' She smiled, an open, child-like smile. Then a line appeared between her brows and her hand fidgeted. 'God bless you both,' she said mechanically. 'Michael knows … he knows where everything … he was the Announcer … He knows how to … Take me away from here, because I shouldn't like to stay here … and the birthmark …'

'I'll see to it,' said Michael.

'But it's the play, the play that matters. Some sort of play, with a happier ending … Jael, do you forgive me?'

'If you will forgive me.'[34]

Now, Jael feels 'the fullness' of Michael's lips as he confesses that he has wanted to love her, come to her, before, but had no excuse for doing so; 'we all need an excuse', he tells her.[35] Beyond them, the world is in flames, flames that will at least consume the old lady, flames that will keep the secret of her birthmark. Rescuing the scorched cineraria, Jael is plucked up in Michael's arms.

Mounting, she held it in her arms, as he held her; mounting, she saw, through a drifting curtain of prismatic raindrops, lines of fire running along the roofs, a blue-print of the township drawn in red: the world that Jael knew was being destroyed. Mounting, she felt power flowing into her, she knew not whence. The place they came to was unknown to her, as were the faces that surrounded her. She was clothed in authority, a ritual began of which she seemed to be the centre; Michael bent his knee. Wordless they watched her but she recognised her mission in their eyes and knew what she must say.
    'Every valley . . . every valley . . .'
    It was a triple summons.
    'Ladies and Gentlemen,' the Voice said. 'God bless you all.'
    But Jael did not speak with her own voice, she spoke with Michael's.[36]

'In "Facial Justice",' Hartley told Peter Bien, 'my sympathies were really with the Dictator, who did her best with her intractable material and suffered for it, as so many reformers and idealists have. Hers was the tragedy, and whether Jael was going to do any better, I doubt . . . I tried to create, in a very sketchy way, a world in which it was possible for the kind of human being we know to live a kind of life still recognisable to us.'[37] And in an earlier letter: 'The end of "Facial Justice" was a "get-out" – I hoped I could bounce the reader into believing it . . . I wanted to end on "a note of hope," and also Jael had learned something from her experiences.'[38]
    Lightly as Hartley spoke of it, the vision of *Facial Justice* is strongly individual, without the conviction of Orwell's *1984* or Huxley's *Brave New World*. To what extent the Dictator's ideals reflect Hartley's longings would alone provide material enough for a thesis. Sometimes the attitude is skittish. One of the severest penalties for not taking the obligatory daily dose of bromide is two rounds of golf; Joab, Jael's chauvinistic brother, tells her that the state rightly imposes fines on bachelors; the Dictator thinks that indecency is an aid to relaxation (easy to accept when we believe the Dictator is a strong-minded male, another matter when we learn he is a frail lady pensioner). The Fenland is the book's setting, and Ely cathedral the symbol powerful enough to awake Jael's awareness of beauty, its remaining tower contrasted with the 'sort of toadstool architecture . . . in which circles and curves predominated' which has sprung up.

The effect of masonry is as overpowering for Jael as it is for Eustace, confronted by the glories of Frontisham church; for Lady Franklin, intent on her pilgrimage to Canterbury cathedral in *The Hireling*; for Richard Mardick's mother in *The Brickfield*, shielding her son's eyes from the ugliness of the 'M'; for Timothy Casson, bewitched by the architecture of his watery cathedral in *The Boat*.

If Jael's triumph is to assert the individuality of the will, the final irony is that she becomes what she has abhorred, a typically puzzling resolution in a book that is sometimes almost juvenile in its enthusiasm. There are curious passages. What are we to make of the saga of the five-year-old boy who emerges from the underworld and is apparently the mouthpiece of another? The only explanation of the child is that 'the pretty gentleman' told him. And what of the unmasking of the Dictator, stripped bare, her weak arms across her breast in a last effort to hide the stigmata that identifies her, a mother-figure, blessing her children and waiting for the anonymity that death can offer? We cannot help but notice that this sweet little Dictator has been the most well-meaning of rulers who has killed with kindness. In *Facial Justice* motherhood has much to answer for.

One of the wonders of *Facial Justice* is that a writer who so consistently looked to the past for inspiration and consolation here manages to look beyond the present into so distant, unlikely and imagined a future. The safety of that future ultimately rests in the love between Jael and Michael, he who came to Jael as a kindly knight in shining armour, the fabled figure that Hartley would again use in his very last published story, 'The Ugly Picture'. For Hartley, as for Jael, knights in armour, bearing away sadness and pain, have a faultless potency that eradicates doubt.

Facial Justice was published in the US by Doubleday in the spring to a generally sympathetic response. The *New York Herald Tribune* thought it would remain a minor fluke in the Hartley canon, while the *San Francisco Examiner* pronounced it 'a signal achievement. Hartley's ideas are superb, his insights penetrating, his satire often devastating. But he has too frequently forgotten the novelist's cardinal rule – when in doubt, the story is supreme.'

Hamilton's praise was less fulsome, a view that seemed to be confirmed by the poor sales, but the relationship picked up when, returning from his June holiday with Molly Berkeley at San Lorenzo, Hartley heard how much Hamilton had liked the new collection of stories (to be published as *Two for the River*). Roger Machell's less ready enthusiasm was kept from Hartley. 'One learns much of Leslie while reading', he told Hamilton after reading the stories – 'he sees himself clearly as a hypochondriac fuss-pot; incapable of decision, terrified of servants, and quite ready to give anyone his house in a moment of panic!'[39] Hartley was also urging Hamilton to re-launch *The Boat*, which had long been out of print. Machell was 'bogged down hopelessly' in it by July 1960: 'All the stuff about the maids seemed to me too idiotic for words. Also the endless letters.'[40] Ten months later, Machell was complaining that Hartley was going 'on and on' about its reprint having an introduction.[41] It appeared, without one, in 1961.

A link with Charlie was kept when his nephew, who could cook and was in the army, came to Avondale for a few days' work in late July, and then accompanied Hartley to Maenan in August, where the time spent with Christabel was one of the happiest Hartley had ever had. Christabel's special talent lay in bringing to his life elements of mystery, uncertainty and danger that he treasured, though most of the things they did were unattended by any risk 'except of me getting sozzled'.[42] News from Renishaw was discouraging. In July Osbert Sitwell had met Violet Hammersley, who had spoken of her intention of visiting Montegufoni with Hartley, prompting Horner to tell Hartley he could not imagine a worse travelling companion. By September, Edith had broken her wrist in a fall and was in Sheffield hospital awaiting her transfer to the Sesame Club. 'I dread to think what the future will be when she gets control of the bottle again', Horner told Hartley, 'thereby losing control of herself ... Moreover he [Osbert] and even more I are in deep disgrace – the old persecution mania coming out.'[43]

Hartley, dubious about taking on Charlie's nephew as a permanent henchman, was thinking of selling Avondale. The property was valued at between £5000 and £6000, but Hartley could not bring himself to give the house up (he never did). With so much on his mind, writing was slow work. On 29 August he sat for an hour in front of a blank page, decorating it only with a 'huge thunder-drop of gin'.[44]

A new servant, Martin, was left in charge of the Rutland Gate flat when Hartley went to stay with Eddy Sackville-West in Ireland in late September, but the homecoming, as so often before, brought unhappy news, for Henry Lamb, so old and valued a friend, died on 8 October. Lamb had been part of that small circle who had always appreciated the benefits of Hartley's companionship; after a visit to Avondale in 1949, he had written of his time there as 'a wondrous haven of warmth, beauty, every kind of comfort, and the bliss of sacred friendship'.[45] Lamb's son Valentine replied to Hartley's letter of condolence in eloquent acknowledgement of the friendship between his father and godfather, for Henry Lamb 'realised in you he had the kindest and most considerate of friends ... I feel that I wish I could in some way repay your supreme kindness which you have shown to all of us over the years. But I do know that you have shown me how one should model their lives ... Your letter has also made me realise what a wonderful man my father was; because you have seen him in a true light.'[46]

In November Hartley was in his element when a brief correspondence about the Brontës began with Daphne du Maurier.[47] They were delighted to be throwing their knowledge and enthusiasm at each other, while resisting some of each other's theories. Hartley clung to a belief that there must have been a close feeling between Branwell and Emily. Du Maurier disagreed, insisting that the legendary status of Emily had gone too far and that if they had met her they would probably have found her spotty, sallow and tongue-tied. She jokingly suggested that she and Hartley should tell the world that Emily had written *Villette*. Hartley never met du Maurier, who was loath to leave Menabilly, and no longer knew where to have her hair done in London.

Christmas 1960 passed with the Cecils, and with Hartley writing to ask Terence Rattigan if he would turn *The Go-Between* into a play. Rattigan had re-read the novel when in the London Clinic with pneumonia the previous spring. He made it clear that he loved the book, and would happily do the job if the jungle of the book's rights was ever cleared. Such delays and disappointments might have been compensated for by a steady domestic life, but here, too, Martin, who at first had seemed kind, willing and pleasant, let Hartley down by getting into trouble with the police. Martin's personal life spilled over into the flat. When Hartley returned unannounced one day, Martin was out, but had prepared a party for a female guest; a twin bed had been made up, ladies' underwear was strewn about. Martin appeared in court in late March on a charge of bankruptcy, and was sentenced to three months' imprisonment. The police had asked Hartley to keep him on so that they could be sure of his whereabouts. Hartley knew that, ultimately, Martin must go, for watching him all the time had become wearing.

Hartley began to realise that with the passing of Charlie, and even Miss Romaine, the sun had set on a Golden Age of domestics. For Martin, at least, the business had a reasonably happy end when, following an appeal, he was acquitted and given three days to find the money he owed to his debtors (Hartley helped him to do so). It was a relief to have a cleaning lady at the flat who amused him with her malapropisms; he rejoiced when she spoke disgustedly of a man who had 'laxative' morals. Meanwhile, the Cornells, the couple now looking after Avondale, told Hartley they would only continue in his service if they could live in, and reluctantly he agreed.

It may be that 1961 was the last of the good years at Avondale, for afterwards the number of guests that were welcomed there declined significantly, partly because Hartley was spending so much time in London, but also because he increasingly felt unable or unwilling to extend his special brand of hospitality. But this year they still came to stay for this Indian summer of Avondale's 'comfortedness' (to use Elizabeth Bowen's expression): August Closs and Rex Littleboy in January; Jimmie Smith in March; Pansy and Valentine Lamb, and Enid, in April; Rex Littleboy (again) in May; Clifford Kitchin, Mary Wellesley, Jimmie Smith (again), and David Horner, during the summer; David Cecil in September; J. B. and Jacquetta Priestley in October.

The publication, that spring, of *Two for the River*, Hartley's last substantial collection of stories, was a diversion, despite its mixed reception; the reviews left him 'bloodied but unbowed'.[48] The *Times Literary Supplement* praised Hartley as 'one of our most professional writers, but in *Two for the River* there is not a great deal that shows him at anything near his best'. Among the more successful stories are those that have Hartley, his life and preoccupations, at their centre. The title story is one example, where a middle-aged, bachelor author living in a riverside house (called 'Paradise Paddock', in case there should be any doubt about it being Avondale) is pestered when out boating by two swans, and then welcomes into his house a white-clad man and wife who have rowed up to his garden to see if he will sell the property. Here, the line between reality and those forces that lie outside it is skilfully blurred. The isolation of the writer, separated from the world by water, the vitality of water, the luxuriance that water brings to the river-banks, the ability of water to bring to and carry away from life, is immaculately suggested. So threatening is his experience that, returning to the house, 'A moment's doubt remained: would the switch work? It did, and showed me what was still my own.'[49]

In 'Per Far L'Amore', set in Venice, a hostess decides to stage the party of a mosquito-ridden season by decking out her rooms in a sea of mosquito nets of various dimensions and intended for various purposes. On the morning after the party a father finds his strangled daughter in a tent reserved '*per far l'amore*' (another of Hartley's characters sacrificed by merely trying to love). Equally claustrophobic is 'The Corner Cupboard', where a 'helpless' hypochondriac bachelor takes on a cook whose influence extends, it seems, into rearranging his medicaments into martial ranks, ready for battle, and 'A Very Present Help' in which an equally hypochondriac bachelor is impressed by the solicitations of his daily help against the callous disregard of his socialite girlfriend.

Something else to emerge strongly from this collection is Hartley's censorious attitude to the working class, expressed with almost savage strength, as in 'The Face', where the bachelor reluctantly takes himself to a seaside town to investigate the suitability of a female for a friend who has always been fascinated in only one 'face'. The unfortunate girl, a waitress, is rather unsympathetically drawn; tired of waitressing, she goes on the game. One character berates another for suggesting that the working class are another type of human being, but it is for the holidaying mass that Hartley reserves his contempt:

> The appalling vulgarity of that town! Nowhere has the proletarianization of the English race gone so fast, or so far, as it has at Restbourne. It is the apotheosis of the synthetic ... an exhibition of what was, to my middle-class mind, a substitute for every form of pleasure. Not that it was not expensive, for it was; everyone seemed to have money to burn. But how joyless that sometimes gay proceeding made them! How they trailed about on the seafront, well fed, well dressed (so far as they were dressed), well tanned, well oiled (sometimes in both senses of the word), but among the lot not one whom a photographer, still less a biographer, would ever want to make his subject.[50]

Evidence enough, of course, of Hartley's belief that there was 'the *Elect*, a body to which [he told Peter Bien] you and I and our friends belong – and I think that most people really have the same belief'.[51]

But it is 'The Pylon', the book's final story, perhaps the most tellingly autobiographical he ever wrote, that astounds. We are in familiar territory. Eleven-year-old Laurie, one of three children, is the Hartley-figure, the inheritance of Eustace and Leo – short, plump, sensitive, too eager to please, always ready to conform. The pylon that stands, elemental, indestructibly rigid, just beyond his garden, is the 'standard by which he has measured himself';[52] he needs to attain its strength, its straightness, needs to become 'Laurie-the-pylon'.[53] When the pylon is demolished, Laurie longs for its return and – in dreams – it reappears. In dreams, he climbs to its zenith, wearing no clothes because that would be 'a kind of cheating'.[54] But the pylon cannot be overcome. He bleeds. He crashes to the ground and is violently sick.

Laurie's father, the main inhabitant of his dreams, provides comfort. There is an ageing handsomeness about him, and an overpowering sense of strength. 'I'm often frightened of you, but still I want to sleep with you', his wife tells him.[55] Facing Laurie, the father pulls at his moustache, but 'was such an adult, masculine gesture quite suitable in front of a small boy?'[56] He moves into Laurie's bed, and in the morning light the boy watches his father's body 'through the thin stuff of his pyjamas ... [his] hairy, muscular chest.'[57] In the presence of the man, Laurie cannot escape 'a feeling of helplessness';[58] he confesses that 'you make me think I've been doing something wrong.'[59] When the other children excitedly break the news that the pylon is indeed returning, Laurie is overcome.

> 'Oh, Daddy!' he exclaimed. 'Oh, Daddy!' But what he meant by it he could not have told, so violent and discordant were the emotions that surged up in him. Indeed, they seemed to sound inside his head, drowning another voice that punctuated but did not break the silence: the hammerstrokes from which would rise a bigger and better pylon.[60]

In choosing to write of so blatant a phallic object as a pylon, it may be that Hartley imagined the meaning of the story would be cancelled out because of its very obviousness. He appears to have had no concerns about how the story would be received. We can only guess now at the quality of innocence with which he wrote it. But it is a telling and dreadful piece, in which the leading parts seem cast from life itself – father and son. As an almost classic example of a child writing out his experiences of sexual abuse, we may read the story in a very different way from how it was read even thirty-five years ago. We know that Hartley made use of short stories to carry the disguised fundamentals of his life into the world beyond. And we are reminded of Richard Mardick's insistence that his biography should show him as the product of the experience that must not be described: 'If they want to know about me, I'd rather they knew the truth. They mustn't know it, that's the difficulty.'[61] If Hartley's emotional honesty, the autobiographical honesty of fact, ever breaks through into his fiction, we can only respond to what we suspect, or believe, to be his own truth, the substance of the 'running shadow'. The trauma that makes the running shadow of his life may be the trauma of *Eustace and Hilda*, of *The Go-Between*, of *The Brickfield*, of 'The Pylon'. If the last, the story provides a glimpse into the darkest of secrets. Whatever the shadow, it runs and runs.

Hartley's evident distrust of the 'W.C.', worked up in *Two for the River*, continued to spill over into his dealings with staff. Now, he was so suspicious that he locked everything, including himself, up at night, sometimes forgetting where he had put the keys. Domestic mishaps followed in succession. Immediately before leaving for Assisi in June (where the one highlight seems to have been a much anticipated visit to Siena to see the famous horse-race, the Palio), the daily help at Rutland Gate let the sink overflow, drawing the anger of Hartley's neighbours who said it was the third flood he had caused. Back at Avondale, Kitchin's three-day visit in July went off well, though Hartley had difficulty in persuading him that Avondale's tap-water was drinkable. Kitchin insisted that at home he always drank from a separate tap not, Hartley supposed, connected to the mains. A new man, John, had departed by the end of July. Hartley had thought him slightly mad, and the disappearance of Bessie's travelling-clock had been a last straw. After reporting the loss to the police, he wondered if someone other than John might have taken it.

With his usual lack of confidence in his character-reading abilities, Hartley interviewed new applicants, and appointed David Foster, from Bangor. This young man was to play a significant part in Hartley's life for the next few years, providing him not only with companionship but, so far as Hartley was concerned, high drama. He was also a stimulus for the two pivotal, linked novels of Hartley's old age, *The Brickfield* and *The Betrayal*, where he is transmuted into the much less sympathetic character of Denys Aspin. Hartley professed himself delighted with David, who was gentle and biddable, but only took him on as a stopgap, for he had already appointed a Manxman aged twenty-four, also called Foster, to begin duties on 31 August, and would not cancel the arrangement. Hartley said an unwilling goodbye to David Foster when the Manxman Foster arrived, but, for once, fate seemed to deal Hartley a kind hand when, at the end of October, the Manxman vanished and David returned.

David (whom Hartley came to call his 'Forza del Destino') had a wife in Bangor from whom he was legally separated. Dissatisfied, David would often leave Hartley a note to say he had gone back to her. He told Hartley that when he had come out of the army, he had wanted to become a monk, though the frequent trips to Bangor suggests this would have been unwise. His disappearances became so usual that in April 1962, when David had once again vanished, Hartley took on a new man (and his wife, whom he had not bargained for). They lasted a mere four days, after which David returned, he said, for good. Hartley ruefully confided to Christabel that it was no wonder such domestic troubles led to an addiction to the bottle.

Bearing the loss of friends had become familiar to Hartley, as illness or old age made some losses inevitable and expected, as was that of Ethel Sands, who died on 19 March 1962 at the age of eighty-nine. She had first appeared to Hartley simply as a brilliant hostess, and become a dependable and much-loved soulmate, who understood and extended that sense of comfort that was so essential to his emotional well-being. After Nan's death in 1957, Ethel had tried to take up the threads of her old life, finding consolation in the good fortune of friends. She had last stayed at Avondale in May 1958; two years later Hartley described her as 'petrified', but in some ways more like herself than she had been through the years of Nan's illness. She had even made one last visit to Auppegard, where she and Nan had created their life together, and a salon that could be enjoyed by kindred spirits. David Horner once described their retreat to Hartley as 'a beautiful but dead house – and I feel that they take more than they give, which is rather pathetic, only I hope they don't realise it, which would be tragic'.[62] Hartley remembered Ethel surrounded with an aura of wonder, seeing her walking through the rooms not like a muse or a goddess, but with a gentleness almost in spite of her air of elegance. Ethel's skill had been in creating a special glow in which her guests felt they could say anything without running the gauntlet of being criticised or ridiculed. Someone had once said of Edith Wharton, a much less sympathetic hostess, that she despised the rich for not being writers, and writers for not being rich, a criticism that could never have been levelled at Ethel, who never passed judgements on her coterie. The most damning comment ever made about her was Ottoline Morrell's insistence that 'Ethel doesn't like scallywags.'

In her unknowing way, Ethel had represented for Hartley the climate of Henry James' novels, embodying the intuition, the understanding, the understatement, at their core. Like Maisie, Ethel had known more, much more, than she had ever admitted to; unlike Maisie she never got caught up in the unhappy dramatic situations that lay in wait for so many of James' heroines. Hartley understood the driving forces of Ethel's personality, forces that made his response to her ideal. She had been the most discreet of friends, able to feel his troubles as keenly as she did her own, strengthened by an unfailing spirit in which feelings, like the works of art she so loved, were ranked in relation to their importance. Her delicately adjusted and balanced character appealed directly to Hartley's sensibility. Perhaps above all he admired the way in which she had lived out her love for Nan. Ethel's successful marriage of aesthetic and personal passion seemed to him, unable or unwilling to hazard such an adventure, the rarest of accomplishments. Her life had been under-pinned by a truthfulness and faultlessness that Hartley knew was quite beyond him.

The 'M'

By May 1962 Hartley was halfway through his new novel, 'but it sticks, and also it seems to me a good deal the same old stuff served up again. I often wish I *could* write a novel without moral pre-occupations, but what I write about individuals is a reflection, an anagram of what I feel about people in general – a microcosm of the macrocosm. For instance, I am almost obsessed by the way that the working-class, in England, only keep a promise if immediate financial gain results from doing so.'[1] The air of dishonesty that seemed to surround him in London and Bath irritated him, as did new teeth which made speaking and eating difficult, and his increasing weight. In June, Molly Berkeley offered the sanctuary of San Lorenzo where Hartley, spurred on by a threatening letter from the Inland Revenue, worked at his novel, but felt he had got almost out of the habit of writing, and that what he did was more remarkable for quantity than quality. There was a summer escape to Eddy Sackville-West at Eigg, after which Hartley came back to prepare for a writers' conference in Edinburgh where on 20 August he addressed 2000 delegates on 'Commitment and the Novel', a lecture described by the *Scotsman* as 'terribly urbane'.

His travelling done, Hartley was faced with his reluctance to return to Avondale, where the troubles were now so bad that, as he told Violet Hammersley, he dared not write of them without risking the law of libel. His self-confessed obsession with the working class fed on itself. David Foster was still coming and going. When severe eczema forced him to have his leg in plaster, Hartley hoped his movements might be prescribed. By October, the leg was poisoned, but any hope that David might stay had vanished by the end of the month when he departed, this time apparently for good. Hartley heard rumours that Foster had left Bangor and his wife without a penny; she did not know where her husband was; Hartley knew, or thought he knew, but was not supposed to tell her. When a friend of Foster's asked Hartley for his help in retrieving some money he had loaned to David, Hartley replied that the man's only option was to report the matter to the police. Foster's wife wrote to Hartley, imploring him not to pursue her husband. The bank informed Foster that Hartley had no recollection of ever having given him two cheques to help him out of his difficulties, but Mrs Foster assured Hartley she would see that any money owing to him was repaid: David was trying to pull himself up, doing manual work and earning good money. Before long he was back at Rutland Gate and making less frequent excursions to Bangor, possibly because Christabel had put a spell on him, that he should be more faithful to her beloved Hartley. Eventually, despite Christabel's sorcery, he simply slipped out of Hartley's life. He was replaced by a deaf pensioner called Hal, who almost fell over backwards if spoken to suddenly. Hal's culinary specialities were pastry and rice pudding, which he forever served up as he talked to himself ('Now the plate, now the dish').[2] As a chauffeur, he lacked any sense of direction and was so cautious that 'we are overtaken by almost every vehicle and quite a number of pedestrians'. He also drank. His struggles to cope with his employer's needs were fortified by gin charged, without permission, to Hartley's account.

Despite such domestic upheaval, by 14 March 1963 Hartley had completed *The M*, the first of two parts of what was to be one novel. The second part was yet to be written; meanwhile, could not Hamilton publish the first instalment? Bracing themselves for another round of difficulties with their author, Hamilton and Machell agreed that it would be 'a grievous mistake' to separate the two linked parts of the book.[3] Springing to the assault, Hartley's response was untypically straightforward. He wrote accusing Hamilton of 'losing interest in my books', pointing out that 'you were so discouraging about *The Hireling* and *Facial Justice* that my pen has lagged and sagged during these last years ... So I think it would be better for both of us if you released me from my contract for *The M*.'[4] A month later he reported to Christabel his 'startling triumph' over Hamilton:[5] Hamilton would publish the first part of the book separately and with an advance (£1500) twice as large as that he had been given for his previous book. Hamilton was happy enough to seem to be the defeated party for, whatever doubts he had about the quality of the new work, it was clear that this was Hartley's finest novel for a decade, and its theme truly Hartleyesque. It was also his first novel in four years, after *Facial Justice*, which hardly seemed to be part of the Hartley *oeuvre*. Between had come the muted stories of *Two for the River*, but *The M*, published as *The Brickfield*, was his first major novel since *The Hireling* six years before. Unlike that book, so disliked by Hamilton, the new work was in direct line of succession to the *Eustace and Hilda* novels and *The Go-Between* – a return to the foreign country of childhood.

Hartley's sense of victory over Hamilton did not, of course, extend to his being able to make a quick delivery of a final version of the manuscript. Revising the text proved as troublesome as ever, aggravated because 'One of my difficulties has been that a lot of the book is autobiographical, and I don't know if my family will like it!'[6] For his part, Kitchin thought the manuscript showed 'a highly Balzacian technique – five hundred pages of build-up and fifty of plot!'[7] In October, Hartley was still considering alternative titles, among them *The Clay Pit* and *Love among the Ruins*, but it was as *The Brickfield* that the laboriously reworked typescript went to the printers.

The reviews, when the book appeared in the spring of 1964, were as mixed as Hamilton must have expected, and almost certainly better than he feared. Even the most subtle hint of criticism was as always irksome to Hartley, who dismissed the reservations of the *Sunday Times* review as the work of 'a second-rate Jewish hack'.[8] A few days after Francis King's notice had appeared in the *Sunday Telegraph*, Hartley met him 'and found it quite hard to be polite . . . He said "I enjoyed your book so much." I longed to reply, "Then why didn't you say so?"'[9] Writing several years later, Paul Bloomfield felt that 'by the time we have got a little way into *The Brickfield* we know . . . that Richard Mardick is Eustace, is Leo, is Timothy, is Simonetta too, perhaps? – well the only person he could be. Or the only *persona*; and it is something to inspire awe that Hartley should so regularly have an air of giving himself away with both hands and not have disqualified himself for high honours.'[10]

This 'giving himself away' reaches its apogee in *The Brickfield*, Hartley's only 'Fenland' novel, his one book that centres on the fen landscape (barring *Facial Justice*, where the landscape has been made unrecognisable) and the novel in which Hartley gives the most accurate picture of his own family life; he knew that the deaths of Bessie, of Harry and of Kathleen had made this possible. Now, Richard Mardick is the Hartley-figure, a bachelor writer like Timothy Casson and the bachelor writer of 'Two for the River', aged, unwell and hypochondriac. Within the framework of conversations between Richard and his young male factotum, Denys Aspin, we listen to Richard's confession of the 'running shadow' that has followed him through life. It is a secret told on the understanding that Denys will keep it (immediately betraying what an incompetent judge of his fellow man Richard is). And Richard's family is Hartley's family: Bessie and Harry play the parts of Mr and Mrs Mardick; Aunt Carrie is a poignant portrait of Aunt Kathleen; the aunts and uncles that make up the supporting cast are still-life reproductions of specific relatives of Hartley's, or an amalgam of traits distributed among them; the Mardick's Dr Butcher has the philosophy, the time, the knowledge, that the Thompsons' or Hartleys' doctor would have made available to them. We know Hartley's childhood the better for having *The Brickfield*, realising what has been denied us in *The Shrimp and the Anemone* and *The Go-Between*; here, the element of truth is so much more powerful. The sense of place, too, is overpowering as, from half a century away, the strength of Hartley's feeling for the surroundings of his childhood permeates the book.

> I remember best the landscape frost-bound, with the tussocks of coarse grass that lined the dyke-sides, mop-heads white and stiff and bowed with their coating of rime, and the roads which normally had a muddy surface, brittle and crackling and striking sparks from horses' hoofs. Or under snow, or in a thaw, with pools of blue-black water cupped in the whiteness.[11]

If not named, the great Fens are evoked – Morris, Farcet, Flag, Tydd St Giles, Whaplode – and, turning from *The Brickfield* to a map, the place names come alive – Thorney, Cowbit, Gedney Hill, Pondersbridge. The places of Hartley's boyhood are disguised, but transparently. Fosdyke, the site of the bank where Richard's father is manager, is Whittelsey; Medehamstead is Peterborough; St Botolph's Lodge is St James' Lodge. Rookland, of course, is Crowland, whose great abbey gave the novel its original title, for the 'M' is the shape made by the three buttresses built on to the north side of the tower. Though it had the practical role of stopping the tower from collapsing. Richard's mother (or is it Hartley's mother?) thought the buttresses an abomination, and always shielded Richard's (or is it Hartley's?) eyes from them. Ugliness is something that must be kept away in *The Brickfield*, but the mere fact of human knowledge opens up the possibilities of ugliness, and knowledge (or the lack of it, specifically sexual knowledge) leads to the eighteen-year-old Richard's downfall. The pampered but lonely boy begins a friendship with the younger Lucy Soames, the daughter of a reclusive couple, and together they make the abandoned brickfield their trysting-place.

Some of the pools were very deep; rumour gave out that they were bottomless. We approached them warily and hand in hand, peering over the edge until we could see our united reflections looking back at us. Or we would lie side by side under a bush, or scramble up a bank and down again, rejoicing in the differences of level that were as strange to her as they were to me, for neither of us had been about much, we were Fenlanders, as accustomed to the horizontal view as clothes-moths on a billiard table.[12]

Here, the affection between Richard and Lucy grows, out of loneliness. 'And so we clung together [the elderly Richard tells Denys], as all lovers have, and I thought what happened had to happen, though it doesn't seem so inevitable now as it did then.'[13] It is in one of the pools that Lucy is discovered, drowned, whether by accident or her own hand we cannot be sure. It is her governess, the chilling Miss Froxfield (how like and unlike dear Miss Fothergill) who had made her think she might be pregnant; she had, in fact, missed a period. The sensational Miss Froxfield reveals that Mrs Soames is not Lucy's mother, but Mr Soames' deceased wife's sister (at the time of the story it was illegal for an Englishman to marry such a relation). Though a few loose ends are thus cleared up, the blame cannot be tidied away: that is for Richard to agonise over for the rest of his life. In *The Brickfield* it is, unusually for Hartley, the heroine of the story who is sacrificed to love – who is, to be more exact, the first sacrifice, for Richard's is lived out throughout his remaining years.

But in his 'giving away himself' does Hartley offer us a plot from life as well as characters, situations, feelings? Book in hand, it is possible to tread the path that the young Richard Mardick would have taken to reach St Botolph's Lodge, the great long roads stretching ahead of him. The brickfield is still there, pretty well inaccessible in summer when weeds hide it from view, but reachable in the spring or winter. Crowland abbey, the 'M' gone, is still there. Wild bees nest in its walls during the summer months. Standing in the ruins of its arches one can appreciate Hartley's love for it. And there is a house, standing alone, that Hartley must have passed on his journey, where Lucy Soames, in fiction, must have lived.

The Brickfield, although launched on its own career, was intended as the preparation for its sequel. In June, Hartley was at Molly Berkeley's villa on Ischia, with its stunning views across the island towards Naples, bathing and working at the Richard Mardick story.

Progress was halting: he was unhappy with his writing, and coping with his hostess's policy of limiting his drinking, alcohol not being served as early in the day as at home. There, 'Sergeant' Roger Radford was his new factotum. He had only been in the job a few days when he wrote to Hartley (on Avondale notepaper, a lapse for which the Hurrells had been slapped down):

> Your absence has shown me that you are part of Avondale, perhaps the reverse is also true. I could well understand it being so. In the few days I have been here it has a strange effect on me. Not by any means frightening but little uncanny. I find myself in constant conflict with my 'alter ego', the stronger of the two always wins, but which one that is a mystery because I do not know which is the true 'me'. . . . Thank you for your remarks with reference to my testimonials, for that, I will not charge to your account the money I bribed my referees with. Very costly you know?[14]

After asking if he might sometimes bring in a friend to keep him company, Roger, in his neat copperplate, concluded: 'I am sitting at your desk now and have exceeded my normal letters by about four pages. I wonder. Big ha-ha.'

Roger's usefulness was increased when he passed his driving test, but Hartley was already looking out for another man who could tend to him in London. In mid November, Roger accompanied him on a lecture tour of France, when Hartley delivered five performances of 'The Novelist's Responsibility', in Paris, Bordeaux, Nantes, Tours and Caen. Roger's place in Hartley's life appeared to be settled, so much so that Hartley, aware of Roger's 'mutually devoted family', invited his parents to come to live at Avondale. By this time the master–servant relationship between the two men had shifted perceptibly. Roger no longer addressed Hartley as 'sir'. On Roger's thirty-second birthday, Hartley took him out to lunch, and listened as the distressed young man protested that he thought himself already old and ugly. Hartley, no doubt, was happy to contradict him, content to be in the company of this attractive and personable creature, interested to listen to the doubts and passions that nagged at him. Roger seems to have spent much of his time in a highly charged state. On one occasion, when Anthony and Violet Powell arrived at Avondale, Hartley greeted them by saying he did not know if they would get any dinner because Roger was crying on the stairs. If, as it seems, Hartley had a fondness for Roger, such affection did not stand in the way of his exploiting aspects of their relationship. The friendship with Roger gave him material. Just as *The Boat* had been made possible by the unwitting participation of much of the population of Lower Woodford, so Hartley's festering dissatisfaction with life was encouraging him to a fictionalisation of the uneasy relationships with those he employed. Such men can hardly have been expected to know what Hartley ultimately needed from them. The boundaries of their relationship, if the Richard Mardick books provide the evidence, were almost, so far as Hartley was concerned, undefined. It was in the fine blurring of the line between employer and employed, master and servant, that hope and, in every case, disappointment lay. Richard Mardick, teasing at the edge of his business arrangement with Denys Aspin, treads the dangerous tightrope of flirtation across which Hartley longed to stride. In fiction, Hartley could at least show the possibilities of joy that existed in the master–servant affection, and could go on to show how the unfaithfulness of the servant was the one destructive element, the snake in a potential Eden.

Such vituperativeness is only glimpsed in *The Brickfield*, but Hartley was not done. The sequel, with its possible titles of *Beyond the Brickfield* and *The Imperfect Witness*, was bluntly renamed *The Betrayal*. A first draft was done by 24 April 1964, but this clearly needed the revision that was a trial to its author, who seemed bewildered and lost in it. By the end of July he had got 'into a hypercritical state (if that is possible) about the book and seem[s] to want to re-write every sentence.'[15] Hamilton and Machell were reading the manuscript in September, but for Machell, long out of sympathy with Hartley, it proved a depressing experience. Hamilton was, perhaps charitably, inclined to think this second instalment was superior to *The Brickfield*, though he now regretted having published that volume separately; he had, after all, done it to keep Hartley happy and with Hamish Hamilton.

However, an internal memorandum from Machell to Hamilton makes Machell's despair over *The Imperfect Witness* (as it was then known) quite clear. 'I think it's a sad mess', he wrote, 'and that poor Hartley will get yet another lambasting from the reviewers.'[16] Machell objected, too, to the book's snobbishness which he thought 'dreadfully pronounced. I started to squirm on the very first page.' In one 'quite appalling' passage, Hartley had not only referred to the working class as the 'W.C.', but had gone on to describe them as 'the Toilet', leaving Machell wanting to 'upchuck'. Besides this, he was irritated by the book's Hartley-figure (as he was by Hartley), an 'exhaustingly distressing central character'. With as much tact as could be mustered in the circumstances, some of these difficulties were pointed out to Hartley, who at once shrugged off any accusation of snobbery on his part. He told Hamilton, 'Anyone who thinks that *I approve* of this sort of conversation is making a big mistake!'[17] He agreed to drop the 'Toilet' sequence but spelled out the message of the novel. 'In a way the book is a denunciation of working-class dishonesty – from which I have suffered for many years ... Surely it is time that the working-class came in for their time of abuse!'[18] Hamilton could only sit back and wait for a final version of the book.

Much of Hartley's time for the first five months of the year was taken up with preparing for a major public appearance. When the invitation to deliver the Clark Lectures at Trinity College, Cambridge, had arrived in January 1962, he readily agreed, deciding he would speak on Nathaniel Hawthorne. The lectures, subsequently published in *The Novelist's Responsibility*, were given in June 1964, but, Hartley told Peter Bien, 'I didn't do them well ... Nathaniel Hawthorne for Beginners would have been a suitable title for my lectures.'[19] As always, he had reached so far back into his own history, seemingly having no suspicion that students in the mid 1960s were less *au fait* with, and probably less interested in, Hawthorne than the literary-minded of his own generation had been. When confronted with academia Hartley forgot, or chose to ignore, the fact that new vitalities were surging through literature; if he insisted on bringing out old lamps, it needed bold and original thought to make them seem new, and this was not a talent that he possessed. No doubt if his hosts had wanted vibrancy, modernity and controversy, they would have looked elsewhere. For the Clark Lectures, Hartley was cast as the grand old man of letters, a distinction that did not always sit easily on him. Playing the part offered him an irresistible opportunity to extol the literature of the past, in what he saw as the desert of the present.

The Clark Lectures over, there was one less excuse not to get back to work on *The Betrayal*. Despite having submitted it to Hamilton in September 1964, Hartley continued to struggle with the revision throughout the whole of the next year, only sending the final typescript to Hamilton on 15 December 1965. Otherwise, the months trundled by. There were lectures to the Brontë Society at Haworth in May, where Hartley's well-practised reticence was needed, since 'apparently the members would not accept my unconventional view of Emily, and would walk out in a body if I expressed it';[20] then it was time to worry until, eight weeks later, he delivered a lecture to the Jane Austen Society. An even more nerve-racking experience was a book talk from the BBC at Manchester, at which Hartley 'didn't imagine the BBC would serve drinks at teatime – but they *did*. A large cabinet was wheeled in, which seemed to contain *everything*. The result was to make me argumentative and pugnacious, but not very coherent.'[21] Drink was also blamed for how he looked in the portrait Derek Hill painted when Hartley stayed with him in Ireland in April: 'every martini I have ever drunk shows in my face!'[22] Hartley thought the picture should be called 'Cheek by Jowl'. It was hated by Christabel, who presented Hartley with a *cache-portrait* so that it might be covered over whenever she visited him; when Joan Hall saw the green baize curtain drawn over the painting she knew that Christabel had called. When Molly Berkeley saw Hill's effort she told Hartley that if he looked as he did in the painting she would never have let him into her house.

Now, when Hartley was using his remembrance of childhood among the Peterborough brickfields as the setting for his great Fenland novel, his lifelong association with the clay that burns was coming to an end. On 3 March 1966 he travelled to Peterborough for the last board meeting of the brickworks of which he had been a director for over forty years. The fortunes of the brickmakers had always been unpredictable, a good year followed by a bad, and only the previous September the bottom had dropped out of the building industry, a victim of the credit squeeze. Before this decline, the National Coal Board had made an offer to purchase the works, which the directors decided to accept. Enid and Norah had mixed feelings about severing the link, regretting that the cause for which their father had worked so long and hard was being abandoned. Hartley, while welcoming the sudden access to a great deal of money (the National Coal Board had paid some £2 million), cannot have sighed too deeply to relinquish the duties he had inherited from Harry. Hartley had never derived any pleasure from such participation; the whole thing had been an irritation to him. Harry had handed on the prize but not the commitment. Bricks had made Hartley's life possible (perhaps he might have said impossible), just as servants, the Rogers, the Charlies, the Miss Romaines, had made it possible; Harry's determination and courage, the work of the 'W.C.', the fathers and sons clocking in at the factory gate, the immigrant families toiling at the bricks, had made it possible. If the bonds were about to be cut, the debt to the bricks could not be paid off so simply. *The Brickfield* is in part the expression of Hartley's unhappiness at Harry's bequest, a bequest that Hartley describes there as emotionally crippling as well as materially essential. He understood that in the richness of the brickfields were forces of good and evil. The life-enhancing clay was, for Hartley, irresistible territory through which he might follow the pattern his own life had formed. The very success of Harry had given his son an inheritance as rich in anguish as in comfort.

So it was with a perfect sense of timing that *The Betrayal* was published in September to a reception that did not altogether live up to Machell's discouraging prediction. There was criticism, but an awareness, too, that Hartley's voice was still worth listening to, that something worthwhile was being said or at least attempted. Irving Wardle in the *Observer*, while describing the division between *The Betrayal* and *The Brickfield* as artificial, praised the new novel as a modern retelling of the Orestes legend;[23] in the *Sunday Telegraph* Rivers Scott, although recognising Hartley's comical attack on his own *bêtes noires*, thought the book one of his most trenchant and profound.[24] To Hartley, the novel now seemed 'very unpleasant, but perhaps not unpleasant enough – no mention of the Moors Murders, or the shooting of the 3 policemen. But they are *there*, if not referred to.'[25]

The central unpleasantness in the book is Denys Aspin, the traitor who betrays Richard's secret. Had Roger, one wonders, read *The Brickfield*? It seems unlikely that he had not. And perhaps the manuscript of *The Betrayal*. He could not but be aware of Hartley's obsessions with the shortcomings of the working man, of the sense of abuse that runs through these pages. How much of himself, or of his potential, did Roger recognise in the writing? If Roger (like others before him) was not the specific subject of Hartley's pen, his breed was; he was an embodiment of Hartley's most time-consuming grievance, he was art come to life. And while he (like others before him) lived with Hartley, Hartley benefited from the particular brand of emotional security without which Richard Mardick could not exist. There could be no doubt that Hartley could never make the disclaimer that his characters bore no resemblance to the living or dead.

Despite this passion on which the book is built, *The Betrayal* is an inferior work to *The Brickfield*. Its anger is transparent. Denys' perfidy launches Richard into emotional seas through which he has no ability to navigate, but there is an uneasiness in the writing, a suspicion that the writer is not in control of his sprawling material. There is, too, the sometimes desperate railing against the ills of modern life and the working class that rages through the book, the consciousness of the ugliness that Richard's mother (or is it Hartley's mother?) so strenuously tried to keep from him. Along the way, the qualities that illuminate much of *The Brickfield* fall away. The letters that fill so many of its pages tell us as much about Hartley's need for correspondence as of the characters by whom they are supposedly written. A now elderly Aunt Carrie makes a brief return in the final pages, leaving no doubt about Hartley's lack of interest in what had happened to the carefully delineated character who plays so prominent a part in the first novel. Reduced to a sweet, harmless old biddy, Carrie can only remind Richard of how his mother hated the 'M' of Rookland Abbey:

> But do you think she was right? [she asks] – right to look the other way, I mean? Those buttresses were a warning – a warning against evil, and you can't escape evil by not looking at it.[26]

The wretched and devious Denys is violently attacked after being suspected of making homosexual advances to a stranger – allowing Hartley to demonstrate with vicious force that sex must be kept to oneself – but it is Richard (Leo, Eustace, Leadbitter, Simonetta, Hartley) who must pay with his life, his secret no longer intact. If Denys is any sort of martyr, he is a martyr to his sexuality, helping his author to prove that, yet again, the expression of sexual feeling is a very dangerous affair – better to subdue it, to leave it vanquished. Richard already knows this to be a fact of life, for his whole life has been sacrificed on the memory of such an experience. It is not for such truths to be told. He confesses to Denys, discussing his best-known novel (Richard's first), 'that there was an emotional experience – a trauma, if you like – that made it possible for me to write the book. I wrote several more, as you know, and they seemed all right to me, but they didn't come off because everything I had went into the first one.'[27]

Is this Richard's truth, or Hartley's? To whomever it belongs, we cannot overlook its importance, the fact that it was an emotional experience, a trauma, that *made the writing of the book possible*. It is the scarring event that inspires Richard to write this one successful novel, *The Imperfect Witness*, as surely as *The Go-Between* and *The Brickfield* are born of trauma. Richard is certainly as dried up by life as the elderly Leo and neither can be saved by returning to what he has known. *The Brickfield* cannot begin to compare with the greatness of *The Go-Between*, but it is Hartley's last book to have considerable greatness in it, and it is the power of the trauma that makes this possible. By the time of *The Betrayal*, the Hartley-figure has turned to the friendship of old acquaintances, the potential love of new admirers, and the salaried affections of his staff. When these are exhausted, there can only be comfort in the past. The quietude in *The Betrayal* only comes when Richard, tired after the complexities of his relationship with the dead Lucy's sister and his cheating helps, returns to Rookland. And it is, of course, Rookland abbey that offers the salvation, Rookland abbey from which the buttresses have been torn down, revealing the beauty of a traceried window which had for years been obscured by the hideous 'M' (a revelation of beauty behind ugliness that is reiterated in 'The Ugly Picture'):

> Richard felt a lightening of the spirit. All my life, he thought, I have been turning away from something ugly, and now it isn't there! . . . did it mean that evil had vanished from the world?[28]

Of course, the 'M' itself, in Hartley's hands, is an obfuscation of the one ugliness he could not bring himself to confess, offered in bewildering translation both in *The Brickfield* and *The Betrayal*. The coy playfulness between Richard and Denys is one of the most perplexing, embarrassing and destructive features of the books; it is the most refined form of cock-teasing imaginable. The relationship between the elderly employer and his young factotum provides the framework for the story, presenting a gauze through which the secrets of Richard's past are disclosed. But there is something painful in Hartley's portrait of the couple, in Richard's almost desperate attempt to draw affection out of Denys. In a letter to Jocelyn Brooke Hartley confessed that:

> As for Richard's relation with Denys, I agree that it would have been more convincing if I had made it declaredly homosexual. But reading between the lines I think one can see that it was; to have made the relationship plainer would have turned the book into a 'homosexual novel', which I didn't want to do. Denys' blackmail took another form than the ordinary one, with which we are familiar, – but of course he couldn't have tried it on, without his conviction of Richard's affection . . . Also, I do think it is quite possible for men, as for men and women, to have a Platonic relationship in which sex, though always present, is suppressed and kept in the background.[29]

So we have Hartley's assurance that 'reading between the lines' is essential to the Richard Mardick novels, as, of course, it is essential to the great bulk of his work. Thus, we can better appreciate the power of *Simonetta Perkins* as a story of an unspoken love between two men transmuted into a heterosexual infatuation. Here, indeed, there is so much potential reading between the lines that the lines themselves sometimes seem only to act as a prop to their imagined companions. Later, Hartley had reined in *My Fellow Devils* in the same way, casting homosexuality at the centre of the story in a thick fog of his own making, fearing to turn it into a 'homosexual' novel. The result is to render the novel pretty well meaningless. It is a trick from which *My Fellow Devils* does not recover, and a trick played out again and again in much of Hartley's work. He is restricted, on one hand by the urge to please, and on the other by the fear of offending; the central truth of his life, meanwhile, cannot be disclosed. We are not granted the explanation for what we read; we can only guess at the truth about Eustace, about the elderly Leo, about Colum and Nick, about Richard Mardick.

Jocelyn Brooke was not a close friend of Hartley's; the two or three letters from Hartley to him seem to represent the sum of their relationship, but it was to Brooke, who had reviewed *The Betrayal* in the *Scotsman*, that Hartley vouchsafed what must have been the truth of the relationship between himself and David Cecil, his belief that two men may 'have a Platonic relationship in which sex, though always present, is suppressed and kept in the background'. Richard and Denys, of course, provide perfect examples of this truth. Brooke cannot have realised that here was a succinct description of the life Hartley and Cecil had lived together. The quality of their friendship, in which sex was present but never used, was for Hartley the perfect arrangement.

A Responsibility of Morals

As HARTLEY REACHED his seventies, he had no reason to regret the importance he had always attached to friendship. Above love, above anything else that human life could offer, friendship was sacrosanct, but the quality of most of his relationships did not extend to anything approaching a comfortable familiarity. Even with those whom he had known for years, an air of formality, the keeping of a distance, prevailed. It was not only that, with so many of his grand friends, he was a minnow swimming behind a whale; the Grand Tour of houses, acquaintances, weekend parties – although now pretty well a thing of the past – allowed him so often to escape the threat of any intimate confrontation. If he was now not such a social gadfly as he had been in former years, it was in this ever changing environment, each guest or host supplying some new sensation, that he had been most at ease. Among those who made up his circle, a title, or reputation, or wealth, was almost a prerequisite. The 'Social Offensive' he had engineered over forty years before had paid lasting dividends; the exclusivity of his world seemed almost impossible to breach.

Early in 1964, from beyond the social boundaries that hedged him, a stranger who was to play a leading role in his last years came into Hartley's life. Joan Hall was a housewife living with her husband Lindsay, a chartered accountant, in Bramhall. Their daughter, Margaret, lived away from home. Interested in literature, Joan belonged to the Literary Guild at Wilmslow, and had already read *The Go-Between* and *A Perfect Woman*, with whose heroine, accountant's wife, she could not help but identify. Lindsay told her that the author was speaking at the Library Theatre in Manchester, and suggested they went to the lecture. They were late in arriving, but Joan was soon enchanted and amused by the man on the platform. As the audience sat, shuffling or eating sandwiches, she was carried away by the beguiling, drawling charm of which Hartley was such a master. A day or two later, she wrote to him at 'the House beside the River, Bath'. A letter came back inviting her to lunch at

Avondale. At this first meeting, from which Joan came away clutch-
ing a signed copy of *The Brickfield*, 'it was as if he'd known me all my
life.'[1] One of Hartley's last friendships, with his most devoted
admirer, had begun. For the first year or so that friendship remained
almost business-like, with Joan going for lunch every few weeks,
until Christian names began to be used and, during one Christmas
visit, Hartley kissed her on the cheek, in the way of 'that friendly
sort of family friendship'.[2]

Intelligent, well-read, and with a lively sense of fun, Joan proved
not only a solid ally but of practical use. Hartley had never typed,
and Joan was a capable typist. She was delighted to transcribe his
work, he was pleased to have found such a capable technician, but it
was soon clear that her part in the proceedings was not so prescribed.
Hartley had total confidence in Joan, trusting her not merely to
decipher his work, but organise passages from which, in manuscript,
all sense of organisation had fled. Where there were alternatives, she
was often asked to exercise her preference. Having crossed the line
that separated him from the real world, Joan was in a country whose
emotional boundaries were rigid. Her real affection for Hartley, her
concern for his well-being, was something he had never experienced
so strongly. Increasingly, as Joan's life itself underwent devastating
changes, she wanted happiness for Hartley, longing for such happiness to transform him. His difficulty, throughout much of their
relationship, was in being unable to grasp the opportunity of
outstanding friendship that Joan offered. With his distrust of love,
of any of Emily's 'hundred kinds of love', he was ultimately incapable
of responding naturally to the demands of a deeply felt attachment.

His association with life below stairs might not run such deep
emotional risks, but it was about to move into a darker phase. What
had begun as the light comedy of Charlie and Miss Romaine was
accelerating into farce, the farce into Gothic drama, the drama into
tragedy. The 'W.C.' was out to confirm Hartley's worst suspicions,
though there was still one shining exception to the treachery of the
breed. Spending a weekend at Montegufoni in the summer of 1966,
Hartley was heartened to see how Osbert, now in a sad physical
decline, was tended by his servant Frank Magro. Magro's devotion
was thoroughly resented by David Horner, who denounced him to
Georgia Sitwell as 'that frightful Maltese ... the Maltese dwarf goes
from bad to worse and the whole household here detest him – quite
rightly and, indeed, he is detested by everyone – except Osbert.'[3]
Through Christabel, Hartley offered to send out Roger to give
Magro a break from his duties, which included having to take the

helpless Osbert to the bathroom eight or ten times a day. Magro thanked Hartley for his kindness, but 'Everything is done in a most natural way, as if we were born to do just that. My relationship with Sir Osbert is on a higher level than that which exists between father and son. So I just cannot make him suffer by getting a new person.'[4] Commitment of this order from any servant would surely have answered Hartley's prayers.

In fact, Frank Magro had probably done Osbert Sitwell a good turn in declining Hartley's offer: only a few days later, Hartley was complaining that 'Roger is being rather difficult ... and sometimes I quite detest him.'[5] In late 1966, three more members of the Radford family arrived to live at Avondale, but this did not improve Roger's temper, especially when the house filled with guests. On occasions, these gatherings also exercised Hartley's tact, as when the combination of Lennox and Freda Berkeley, Christabel and Joan proved to be an unhappy one, with some friends complaining to their host about the unsuitability of others. Christabel provided drama by falling headlong down the stairs (she was, according to Freda Berkeley, 'absolutely plastered')[6] and breaking her wrist. Everybody knew the reason for her stumble, but Hartley blamed Avondale itself: 'I do wonder if the house has a slight hoodoo on it ... All the same, I feel quite happy in this Wuthering Heights – or House of Usher, would perhaps be a more appropriate term for it.'[7] The tension between Roger and Hartley lasted until June 1967, when Roger gave notice:

> We had a violent row, but parted, I thought, on the best of terms ... he has offered to find me a successor ... he can't be a worse chooser than I am. I shall miss him very much for he had been with me nearly four years, and was good in most ways, except in temper; his temper grew progressively worse. He said he only stayed 'in subjection' to me so that he could provide for his parents ... What will happen to the five other Radfords at Avondale?[8]

'The Commander', ex-Royal Navy, was appointed as Roger's replacement. Amiable, and with every breath addressing Hartley as 'sir', he was a good cook and driver, and settled in on good terms with the Radfords. The commander dropped hints that he had once known better days: 'I only met King George VI twice', he told Hartley;[9] before the war, he had twice played Chopin at the old Queen's Hall. Disappointingly, the commander proved so fond of Hartley's drink that Hartley began locking up the bottles last thing at night. After a dinner-party at Avondale, he was on his way to secure them when he found the commander at the foot of the staircase in an alcoholic stupor, 'with blood and coffee all round him (he had been carrying down a tray) and seemingly unable to move. Mrs Radford who – by doctor's orders, is not allowed to *bend*, her sister-in-law who *can* bend, and I, who because of a rupture don't *want* to bend, tried to haul [him] upstairs ... He looks very ill but I don't feel a bit sorry for him.'[10] Only a few weeks later, the commander was heard on the telephone ordering cigarettes and wine on Hartley's account. It was inevitable that he would have to be dismissed, but as always Hartley lacked the will.

Rutland Gate was as much a bolthole as a home, for Hartley simply did not want to go to Avondale. Roger's parents sickened and died there. These deaths 'coming soon after each other, have given me a painful feeling about the place'. Avondale was now known by the Bathford locals as 'The House of Death'. The commander was replaced by Hartley's cleaner in London, but by December 1968 Fred too had become the victim of a whispering campaign in the village, being talked about as a con-man. Fred neither spoke nor smiled, and loaned Hartley's car to 'unauthorised persons'. When the car was involved in an accident, Patrick Woodcock, Hartley's doctor, wrote to the court pleading clemency, for if Fred lost his licence Hartley would be housebound. When Fred gave in his notice, Hartley offered him inducements to stay, to no avail. An advertisement in *The Times* brought in many applications. 'Some of them were so funny – one man said he was tired of having his good nature imposed upon ... and another said that although he was a boxer his features had not been disfigured!'[11] Hartley appointed the first man he interviewed, Tony, a forty-four year-old and an ex-Navy bachelor. According to Joan, he 'could speak several languages and be rude in all of them'.[12]

Tony was barely installed at Avondale when his apparently psychic powers were given full play: he felt a hand on his shoulder and a voice saying, 'Get up, get up, get up!' Whilst reading in bed, he heard a female voice asking, 'What are *you* doing here?', and a man instructing him to 'Fall in at the double, fall in at the double!', a manifestation worked up into the story of the same name in *Mrs Carteret Receives*. Hartley wanted to exorcise the house but was persuaded against doing so by the fear that news of such sensational goings-on might affect its value. Before long, disenchantment had set in with Tony. The daily help called him a liar. Eventually, he was revealed as a married man with three children. When he had his girlfriend to sleep at the flat, Christabel discreetly suggested to Hartley that he might be given a 'further-away' bedroom. Tony's suitability for his post seemed in doubt, but Hartley could not act decisively. 'I know now', he told Joan, 'that when I was a child, all my decisions were taken for me by my parents (especially my mother) and I had no say in them: which is the chief reason why I can't make up my mind.'[13]

Hamilton had accepted the idea of bringing out a book of Hartley's essays – eventually published as *The Novelist's Responsibility* – but 'not with a good grace'.[14] There was originally the possibility that it would include some of the fiction reviews written between 1929 and 1940, an idea abandoned as the essays proved substantial enough to make the collection publishable. The Clark Lectures on Hawthorne are the backbone of the book, almost a hundred pages of Hartley's most considered (and sometimes pedantic) argument, in which he readdresses and redresses his boyhood passion. The territory covered by the remaining pieces is never surprising: his lectures on Jane Austen and Emily Brontë, salutes to Osbert and Edith Sitwell, Henry James, Leo Myers and Clifford Kitchin. The Kitchin piece had been published some years before in the *London Magazine*; now, Hartley simply tacked on a brief paragraph listing the four books Kitchin had subsequently produced. Such lack of interest in the modern literary world permeates *The Novelist's Responsibility*, where Hartley expects the past to offer up its old magic. He is persuaded by recollections of pleasure. What else can explain his readiness to include 'Some Aspects of Gregariousness', a piece lifted from almost fifty years before? It had been, he told Hamilton, written 'in a more emotional and flamboyant style'[15] than he could manage now – delivered *con amore* – but four months later he was regretting its inclusion, for 'the style seems so inflated that it embarrasses me.' There is nothing embarrassing about 'Remembering Venice', grudgingly written for the *National Geographic Magazine*; here, it is only Hartley's love for the city that he gives away.

Of the three brief essays that deal with the craft of writing, 'In Defence of the Short Story' is a no-nonsense plea that the art form be properly and popularly recognised, while 'The Novelist and his Material' succinctly defines much of Hartley's attitude towards the decline of individualism, the fact that he sees the symbol of modern civilisation as the orderly queue, taking away the need for any coherent or aggressive moral responsibility. Recalling the very different world in which the 'Golden Age' of the novel flourished,

Hartley nevertheless declared his own passionate reaction to the conditions modernity had forced on the writer:

> Today the middle class is being squeezed out of existence, and it is indeed difficult for anyone observing the political or social scene to believe there is such a thing as a really disinterested action. Yet art demands altrusim as no other activity does; the artist *must* believe that his work is more important than he is; he must be prepared to sacrifice himself to it in order to be reborn in it.[16]

It was one thing that Hartley believed that the writer had to give his life up to writing, another that Hartley believed the moral responsibility of the novelist was of paramount importance. Like so many obligations, this was as much a hindrance as a touchstone. But it is in the essay that bears the book's title that Hartley's stance comes over most clearly. It has all his charm, his irritable recourse to private exasperation, his delicate appreciation of words, his persistent theory that morality affects the writer – it is the responsibility of, if not writers in general, the novelist in particular. In 1951, Kitchin had told Hartley, 'I have never had any instinctive veneration for the moral law as such, and have regarded its existence – if it exists – as a necessary evil – no more an end in itself than lavatories or bathrooms which make one fitter to enjoy gold music-boxes in the boudoir.'[17] Hartley could hardly be expected to sign up to so libertine a philosophy, and neither did his disgust with so many aspects of the modern world extend to Kitchin's declaration that 'My antinomianism increases day by day. I can hardly write "He was a policeman", without adding, "and therefore a thief," – or "He was a judge", without adding, "and therefore a hypocrite"'.[18] Hartley, whose stern acceptance of justice and the rightness of morality could not be doubted, treads more warily, though he is as full of doubt as Kitchin.

> Something must matter, either as an object of attainment or avoidance, and what is it to be? If the question 'Whither Fiction?' is raised, the novelist will have to make up his mind which side he is on. Is he to write: 'She was a beautiful woman, witty, clever, cultivated, sympathetic, charming, *but*, alas, she was a murderess'? Or is he to write: 'She was a beautiful woman, witty, clever, etc., *and* to crown it all, she was a murderess'?[19]

Kitchin died in Brighton on 4 April 1967, mourned by the few close friends whose existence had been so important to him. Nevill Coghill confessed to Francis King that 'I loved Clifford, as much as he allowed himself to be loved, by me at least.'[20] Kitchin's beloved

George, who almost suffered a nervous breakdown under the pressure of his double life, shared between Kitchin and his wife and children, had left Kitchin in December 1964. Before long, it was clear that George was terribly ill; ringing his home to ask how he was filled Kitchin with nightmarish apprehensions. On 12 December 1965 he told Hartley, 'My dear George died yesterday afternoon . . . It seems very cruel that twice in my life my dearest companion has been taken from me. How many times have I prayed that George would see me out.' Soon, Kitchin himself was in the grip of the cardiac asthma from which he never recovered. Ken Ritchie, David Cecil and Nevill Coghill were among close friends who made the last journey to see him, while Francis King paid regular calls in the final months. Hartley, despite Kitchin's wish that he might do so, did not make the journey to see his old friend. He admitted to Christabel:

> I reproach myself that I didn't see more of him when he was there (in London I used to see him at least twice a week) but it wasn't altogether easy to go there, and make one's visits fit in with his routine of life, about which he was adamant . . . he was such a strange and gifted person, who always went his own way, – not altogether an easy one, for he did not hesitate to say where you exceeded, or fell short, he was nothing if not critical.[21]

Four years after his death, Hartley paid tribute in his foreword to Kitchin's last novel, *A Short Walk in Williams Park*, which Kitchin had made no effort to have published. As always when looking back over a long and treasured friendship suddenly cut off, Hartley was at his most generous and perceptive. Kitchin, he explained, had more talents than any one else he knew. Kitchin would almost certainly have protested (as did Hartley on his behalf) that it was as a novelist he had wished to succeed. There had been success, but he had never won favour with the public. Both men had led 'privileged' lives, cushioned against so many of life's knocks; both had inherited wealth, though Kitchin's was the most natural, and assured, inheritance. But while both watched the world they had known slipping away from them, it was Hartley who was outraged by it – Kitchin was content to mourn its passing with a sigh. He felt that the middle-class territory his work inhabited was anathema to critics. 'They lap up proletarian studies of delinquency and they tolerate a plunge into high life, but they can't abide the stratum between these extremes, though to me it seems the basis of our civilisation.'[22]

The Book of Life, the last of Kitchin's novels to be published in his lifetime, appeared in 1960.[23] It must have occurred to Hartley that this joyful celebration of a happy childhood was in some ways strikingly reminiscent of *The Go-Between*. In 1909, nine-year-old Francis Froxwell comes to terms with life and an awareness of sexual dimension in the adult world that surrounds him in the Kentish seaside town of Whitgate. Like Leo, Francis is transplanted into social environments that are foreign to him, with hopes (unlike Leo) of inheriting family money, the money recorded in Grandfather Froxwell's Book of Life. Kitchin's novel is charming and inconsequential (Francis has to face none of the *Sturm-und-Drang* tolerated by Leo), with its characterful list of aunts, the worldly Uncle Demetrius, and the ex-boys' schoolteacher, the swarthy, attractive Mr Jimmy, who tells Francis that they must ignore one another if they meet in the street. A homosexual ostracised by an unfeeling society, Mr Jimmy is a telling portrait of an outsider with whom Francis (and Kitchin) feels such an affinity. Here, as elsewhere in *The Book of Life*, darkness is avoided, as it should be in what is essentially a valentine to the past; it is the work of an old, but satisfied, man.

Living up to Kitchin's expectations, the novel did not sell well, despite several ecstatic reviews, and was quickly forgotten. In the literary climate of the new decade, it was of little interest that Francis' prospects of financial security and his hopes of becoming 'Sir' Francis are delightfully squashed in the book's last pages. In such a way, Kitchin seems to throw into the air the concerns that had consumed both Hartley and himself over so many years. It was Kitchin's misfortune that by 1960 his reputation had so dwindled that *The Book of Life* was not recognised as the very considerable achievement it was. After it, he turned away from writing. If his work could not survive by itself alone, he could do nothing for it; he insisted that he would not do the things necessary to make a bestseller, 'going to the right parties, cultivating influential literary ladies, chumming up with the BBC and cutting, in some fantastic way, a public figure'.[24] Like Hartley, he had washed his hands of the modern world, to which *The Book of Life* is a perfect antidote; unlike Hartley, he had never fallen prey to the grudges that offered themselves up, he had never lost the dimension of sympathy.

Kitchin retained an energy and vividness in his last works that is lacking in Hartley's final novels. *Poor Clare*, despite having been 'finished' by August 1966, was still in a sadly muddled state, promised but undelivered. 12,000 words of it had vanished between Assisi and England; its pages were 'a kind of jungle'.[25] Written in

haste, the book filled Hartley with doubt: 'I wished I liked it better.'
Hamilton was understandably exasperated when Hartley took on a
new diversion. 'As expected', he wrote in an internal memo, 'the
Presidency of the PEN will provide ample excuses for non-work.'[26]
Hartley's reluctance to say no when invited to take on such
responsibilities always led to him regretting the easy decisiveness of
saying yes, and the Presidency of the English Centre of PEN was
no exception. The offer of the position demonstrated that he was
still a man of literary reputation, perhaps considered by many to be
almost non-participating, his fiction belonging to the past. The
various duties, including public appearances, that devolved on him
in his new role were wearying. 'Their activities', he told Joan,
'though useful, bore me inexpressibly – I get so tired of hearing what
the Russians and the Czecho-Slovaks have done to writers who are
"out of step".'[27] Hartley's compassion had never been particularly
cosmopolitan.

His dealings with Hamilton continued uneasily. There were plans
to bring out an omnibus of the short stories, excluding *Night Fears*
and *The Killing Bottle* but including the novella *Simonetta Perkins*.
Hamilton firmly informed Hartley that the collection would not be
appearing until after *Poor Clare* was in the shops, thus annoying
Hartley, who felt the omnibus was being dangled on the condition
that the new novel be completed. By the end of the year there
seemed little hope of that: the messy text still had three different
endings and two alternative beginnings and no shortage of confusion
and contradiction between. By the start of the new year it was
obvious that something would have to be done to rescue the book.
He informed Joan that 'I told [Hamilton] I thought of asking Francis
King to vet it ... it was just an idea, but he immediately wrote to
Francis, or rather rang him up, who has accepted this horrible
assignment! – and I shall have to stick by what he says.'[28] In King's
hands the manuscript was soon tidied up, and shortened by at least a
quarter, so that Hartley, on 20 February, could at last send off the
results of King's work ('I haven't read his version myself').[29]

It may have been with mixed emotions that Hamilton learned, by
this same letter, that Hartley had written yet another novel, begun
on 27 December 1967, *The Love-Adept*, 'vaguely founded on the
relationship of Turgenev with Pauline Viardot'.[30] An advance of
£750 was agreed on, and by 9 April Hartley was able to send off a
'final' typescript. Only a month before he had written to ask Joan if
she would type the manuscript for him; she accepted, beginning her
working relationship with Hartley that went far beyond her being

his typist. 'I can't be grateful enough to you for making *The Love-Adept publisher-worthy*', he told her.[31] Hartley was fast growing dependent on Joan, not only for her considerable secretarial skills, but for advice and her ability to interpret and (within the bounds he tolerated) criticise his writing.

Joan must already have been aware of Hartley's drinking, but kept her counsel. Christabel, who had discussed it with Molly Berkeley and Patrick Woodcock, wrote to Hartley (the letter has apparently not survived) expressing their concern. 'It is quite true', he replied, 'that I drink too much, but I hoped it wasn't noticeable, in any way . . . After 70, it seems to me, there is no further need for self-discipline (e.g. avoiding the gin-bottle), or *any* form of self-improvement.'[32] He was suffering from periods of acute deafness. Sleeplessness plagued him, not least on the rare occasions he went to Fletton, always calculated to bring on his nervous agitation: when it was necessary to go there, he would usually arrive a day later than expected and leave a day earlier than planned.

Enid's precarious health had drawn him back on several occasions over the last months, but she had always recovered from the heart attacks that had taken her away from her busy public life in Peterborough. On 17 June she suffered a seizure from which it soon became clear she would not rally. After paying her a visit, Hartley left Fletton knowing that in all probability he would never see her again. She died nine days later, at the age of seventy-five. 'I shall miss my sister very much', Hartley told Joan, ' – she was a dear and most constant friend, but latterly she had been only a shadow of the Enid I used to know.'[33] Many years before, after reading *The Shrimp and the Anemone*, Kitchin had written to him begging him to 'Tell Enid from me, that I never, in the slightest way, visualised her as Hilda. I must emphasise this, even at the risk of being thought undiscerning.'[34] Ill-health had made her the shadow of herself, but the shadows had been so many. The plump, Edward Ardizonne-like figure of later life standing outside Fletton beside Osbert Sitwell seems to bear no resemblance to the Enid we see in the photographs of the young woman; surely, this can only be Hilda staring out at us, beautiful, strong, assertive. The high brow, the full, defined curve of the lips, the receptivity of the eyes, the cascade of hair – all this is Hilda. And again, on the brink of womanhood, in collar and pinned tie, self-possessed, ready, her hair coiled to the back of her neck, hands restful in her lap. A few years later, the figure filling out, the hair now organised, parted, kept in place, the practical look of a young woman looking after her parents, seeing to the staff, checking

menus, blankets, provisions, interviewing servants, encouraging gardeners; Enid, who loved children, and would have loved children of
her own, whose only child had been her baby brother, who would
have found happiness in marriage.

Even now, with Enid's death, Hartley could not reveal the truths
of Eustace and Hilda; the past must be obscured. All he would admit
to Christabel was what he was ready to confess to the world at large:
'We were very close to each other when we were children . . . she
was sweet and gentle.'[35] Perhaps his continuing reluctance to declare
himself was to some extent caused by the bad press Hilda had
received over the years: Edith Sitwell and Kitchin had both loathed
her; she had been perceived as a terrible, manipulative woman, a
judgement that Hartley must have felt to be harsh. He recognised
that whatever influence Enid had once had over him had been the
result of a natural ascendancy of spirit: there had never been
anything cruel in Enid, nothing to justify the hatred poured on
Hilda. If there had been a fault, it was perhaps in her loving Hartley,
one of Emily Brontë's 'hundred kinds of love'. It is Hilda's love of
Eustace, after all, that leads her on, makes her what she is: love,
Bessie's inheritance, until time, school, Oxford, Venice, the welcome
of friends, broke childhood's bonds. Now Enid, like Hilda, receded
into Hartley's past.

It seemed sometimes as if Hartley was one of the last guardians of
that past, the only soldier left at a deserted fort. In this guise, he was
approached by Ottoline Morrell's daughter, Julian Vinogradoff,
about Michael Holroyd's treatment of her mother in the second
volume of his biography of Lytton Strachey. 'It's absolutely unfair
to her, from the first patronising pages to the end of the book', she
told Hartley.[36] And, asked Vinogradoff, had not Holroyd's verdict
on Ethel Sands been 'very unpleasant'?

On all sides, attempts were being made to topple the idols of
Hartley's past from their pedestals, a situation highlighted by the
publication of Cynthia's diaries of 1915–18, for which Hartley wrote
the eulogistic foreword. A mild controversy began when Leonard
Woolf reviewed the book (which he thought appalling) in the
Listener in April 1968. Woolf's dissatisfaction with Cynthia, as a
person or writer, could hardly have been more obvious: her work,
said Woolf, was lacking in any vestige of talent or intelligence, and
she and her generation of aristocrats (the very set with which
Hartley had been intimately associated) had spent the war years in
frivolous denial of the horrors that were taking place. All around

her, Woolf identified the slow death of English élitism. Uncomplimentary as it was, the tone of Woolf's notice can have been no
surprise to the *Listener*'s editor, Karl Miller, whose choice of Woolf
had of course been mischievous. But Woolf was not alone in
condemning the book; the *Times Literary Supplement* suggested that
'Admirers of Lady Cynthia will greatly regret that what was light-
hearted and high-spirited should have now been launched, giving
pain to others and (much more to the point) a false impression of
herself.'

Hartley was incensed by Woolf's review, which he saw not only
as an attack on a dear, dead friend and a condemnation of the class
to which she had belonged (and he had aspired to), but as a slur on
his own integrity. It was perhaps unfortunate that Hartley's was the
only name associated with the book; the editors, incredibly, preferred to remain unknown. The lone soldier once more manned the
fort, firing, it must be said, in a great many directions. Hartley wrote
to the *Listener*, damning Woolf's words as 'a model of what a review
ought not to be. It is "engaged", "committed", and we all know what
that means. It means that the critic has a left-wing prejudice which
blinds him to whatever merits the book may have.'[37] Having accused
his opponent of a political motif Woolf would not have denied,
Hartley set about displaying his own right-wing prejudices. After
much word play, toying with Woolf's description of himself as
'plebeian', he refuted the accusation that the diaries showed a lack
of concern with the misery of war, excusing the careless lifestyle of
Cynthia's set as their doing 'what they could to keep their spirits up
and to keep up the spirits of the soldiers from the war returning.
Did they, the soldiers, want to find their friends and relations and
the general public shrouded in grief? No, they wanted something
comic, something to take their minds off, like George Robey in *The
Bing Boys are Here*,[38] or Vesta Tilley strutting up and down the stage
in soldier's garb, singing "I joined the Army yesterday, so the Army
of today's all right."'

The suggestion that Tilley's encouragement of young men to
enlist for the Front was an acceptable entertainment for war-weary
soldiers seems unfortunate. There is something too easy in Hartley's
argument, a suggestion that popular songs (and how important those
of the Boer War had seemed to him) explain and excuse. But he was
not done. He must defend the society he had known in the war, the
Oxfords, the Asquiths, the imputation that they had somehow got
away without doing their 'bit'. He explained that 'Man for man, and
woman, the aristocracy suffered more in the First World War than

any other stratum of society.' Did he mean to say here that the upper reaches of society had put more effort into the war, had given more lives? Did he mean that the deaths in the upper classes were of more significance than the loss of the butcher's assistant, the apprentice engineer, the out-of-work hopeful? However it is read, it seems an extraordinary assertion. To this ill-considered brew Hartley then adds a dash of vindictiveness about Woolf's wife: Virginia had been 'a colossal snob ... who had neither wit nor humour, but a certain effective cruelty in conversation'. Lady Violet Bonham Carter wrote to Woolf, reassuring him that his comments about her sister-in-law, Cynthia, and the book were fair. It seemed to Woolf extraordinary that the book had seen the light of day, and

> I can't understand Leslie Hartley's performance. I simply cannot believe that he did not read the book. Is it conceivable that, if you were suddenly given the MS of the most intimate diaries of your most intimate friend and read five pages of Lady Cynthia's, you would not have sat down and read every word of it before committing yourself to write an introduction to it? I have never known him well, but I have known him for a terrible long time ... He always seemed to me a rather gentle and sensible person.[39]

That Violet Bonham Carter should have implicitly criticised Hartley's association with the publication was a smarting blow: he told Christabel, 'I will never willingly speak to her again!'[40] It was no relief in July to turn to the proofs of *Poor Clare*: 'Oh the mistakes, the inconsistencies and the repetitions.'[41] He confessed to Joan (who herself found some of his female characters wooden) that he did not find it easy making his inventions talk:

> I wish I had my sister Norah's ear for dialogue. She can report a conversation, with any sort of person, and make it all sound exactly right. I have to translate it into Hartley-ese! – which is not so stylised as it would be with Henry James or Miss Compton Burnett, but may well miss the mark of realism (or reality).[42]

Recent events might have warned him that he was now seriously out of step with modern literary trends, a fact that the publication of the troubled *Poor Clare* in October 1968 confirmed. Its reviews show the prevailing critical attitudes to Hartley's work as the sixties drew to a close. Dennis Potter in *The Times* described his 'instinctive desire to pay tribute to the superiority of his talent, and yet also a distaste for the tradition or, more particularly, for the prejudices which so clearly inform it. Yet *The Go-Between* remains, in my opinion, one of the three or four genuinely outstanding novels to have been written in England since the war.'[43] When it came to *Poor Clare*, however, Potter felt that 'The nearer he approaches to our own times the less solid and convincingly "placed" are his characters, the more petulant their asides and the less credible their behaviour.' For the *Observer*, Angus Wilson resisted any attempt at a synopsis, arguing that the story was the shape of *Poor Clare* as much as the shape was the story.[44] Wilson complained that Hartley's social standpoint (which Wilson detested) threatened to negate his ability to translate his obsessions with morality, or the lack of it, into art. In *Poor Clare*, Wilson thought evil had been reduced to an outpouring of venom against modern life, reducing Hartley's sense of moral discrimination to nothing more than a self-pitying moan.

If none of this was music to Hartley's ears, Cuthbert Worsley (writing in the *London Evening Standard* as Richard Lister) delivered the *coup de grâce*.[45] Under the headline 'The most flavourless, colourless, characterless, featureless, passionless, bloodless woman in modern fiction', Worsley complained that 'no jeans are unzipped or mini-skirts slipped off, not only because his characters do not inhabit the jeans and mini-skirt world – far from it! – but because if the equivalent of such indelicate operations were performed it would reveal precisely nothing. His characters are . . . "dead from the waist down".' As for the book's Hartley-figure, he was 'a wet, feeble, sloppy, flaccid, flabby, degutted, invertebrate, prissy, precious, aesthetic nincompoop, tame as a neutered tabby'. With an exasperation that Machell himself might have applauded, Worsley insisted, 'I should prefer even the straight hint of a healthy vulgarity, especially of that most vulgar of all things – life.'

Worsley's journalistic spree so infuriated Hartley that he began proceedings against him, a process that dragged on for months, despite the solicitor's hint to Hartley that he was pursuing a 'borderline' case. *Poor Clare* hardly deserved Worsley's outpouring (there is the distinct feeling that it is an attack on Hartley's work in general rather than this particular novel) but Hartley, always ready to accept praise, could not tolerate a brand of criticism that teetered into abuse. Francis King, hoping Hartley would abandon the libel action, told him that Worsley was a very sick man, but Hartley would not be deflected. When his solicitor asked if he wanted to spoil Worsley's Christmas, Hartley replied 'Yes!'

In fact, *Poor Clare* is the most delicate of the last novels. When Gilbert, a composer of 'difficult' modern music, inherits the estate of his Aunt Clare, he sets about disposing of some of her most treasured paintings – works by Girtin, Vuillard and Munnings – by presenting them as gifts to his friends. With the presentation of each gift comes an obvious (though undeclared) cessation of friendship – in the act of giving, valued associations are consigned to Gilbert's past. Edward, a painter friend of Gilbert's, and the novel's narrator, shares Gilbert's longing for Myra who, alone of Gilbert's close friends, has received no gift. Edward persuades her that Gilbert had only given him the Girtin to hold in trust for Myra, and makes her a present of it. Edward escapes with Myra to Assisi (Hartley's descriptions of which are among the finest pages of the book) and can do nothing but try to keep the truth of Gilbert's feelings from her.

In the Church of the Poor Clares, at the Chapel of Perpetual Adoration, Edward thinks he sees Gilbert, 'his head towards the altar, and its extraordinary pallor, as of parchment, lit by a candle from within'.[46] Returning, Edward sees the figure again, and 'fancied I saw a faint gleam between his fingers, such as sometimes shows between the fingers of a man who strikes a match on a windy night to light his cigarette; but that is a rosy gleam, and this gleam, unless I imagined it, had the luminous pallor of a glow-worm'.[47] News arrives from England that Gilbert has killed himself. Told that Gilbert wanted to give Myra a gift, but had been unable to, Edward asks what the gift was. 'His love, just his love. You see, he always adored her, and he proved it by dying. Dying was the form his adoration took.'[48] Thus, in its last pages, is Gilbert revealed as the book's Hartley-figure, dying, like Eustace, like Leadbitter, like Fergus in *The Harness Room*, not for want of love but for the realisation of it.

All of Gilbert's acts of generosity are a preparation for death, preceded by the deaths of the relationships his gifts automatically confer. And Edward is fascinated by the death, 600 years before, of the Poor Clare's patron, Santa Chiari: he stands at the grille behind which her body lies, its face turned slightly towards his. At the end of the book, it is his own death to which he must reconcile himself. But this is a book that has in it many fine things. Above all, it is the exigencies of the moral dimension that give the novel its solid qualities, and the depth of human feeling, though lacking definition, is refined. The line between life and death, territory that so often brings fine writing from Hartley, is walked. Friendship, death and the importance of material objects may be obsessional subjects to Hartley (just as Aunt Kathleen, in her last years, had been obsessed with how her possessions would be disposed of after her death), but there is a calmness in the writing of *Poor Clare* that prevents the argument of Hartley's obsession from being obscured; the obvious disappointment of the author does not degenerate into hysteria.

As Christmas 1968 approached, there was little to cheer Hartley. He recalled to Christabel how he could not remember Cecil ever having sent him a Christmas card. 'He *receives* a great many ... He may send one to the Queen Mother (this is a catty, in the bad sense, remark), but I feel annoyed with him, for, having proposed himself about seven times to come and see me, he has about seven times chucked me, at the last moment.'[49] Of course, Hartley's indecisiveness could easily match Cecil's. Telephoning the estate agent to make an offer for Lynch Farm at Alwalton, Hartley decided to drop the plan when the telephone went unanswered. By mid March, he was in the process of becoming a landowner, and by the end of the month had acquired some farmland in the Fens from his cousins (a purchase that would mean a substantial reduction in death duties). 'I feel I have become a different person', he told Christabel. 'How this will express itself, I don't know. Shall I walk about the Fens, saying "Put this tractor here, or I don't like this haystack here, or I should like this field of potatoes changed to beetroot?" It would be rather nice to throw one's weight about, in whatever direction!'[50]

In fact, Hartley's world was getting smaller. Osbert Sitwell died on 4 May 1969. The previous autumn he had been struck down in Venice with double pneumonia, from which he had recovered, but his speech was almost unintelligible (Frank Magro translated everything he said) and his memory feeble. On 2 May, after a heart attack, Sitwell lapsed into a coma, dying two days later. It was an ending of physical misery and deep personal unhappiness, not least with Sachie Sitwell and his abrasive wife. 'Surely', Hartley wrote, 'there never was a greater triumph of the spirit over the flesh than his.' With Edith (who had died in 1964) and Osbert gone, Renishaw and Montegufoni, retreats that had offered Hartley essential escapes from himself, had gone for ever. He had lost touch with David Horner, making no effort to see him in the last years, and had never been one of Sacheverell's set (Sachie's wife had years before christened him 'Bore' Hartley). Reflecting on the long decline of energy, inspiration, and life that had been endured by so many of his old friends was a discouraging thing.

Such consolation as might be found in writing was not straightforward. *My Sister's Keeper* (originally titled *The Road to Hell*) had been accepted by Hamilton. Hartley referred to it as 'my indecent novel'[51] and told Joan, 'I feel ashamed at asking you to type out the "cottage" chapter. If by then you are too disgusted to go on, I shall quite understand!'[52] In subsequent letters to Joan, his concern over the tastefulness of his material was reiterated: surely the 'cottage' chapter could be reduced to decency, although it might help to sell the novel if it was left as it was. Perhaps it might be condensed into a couple of paragraphs that could only give offence to a few prudes? Perhaps it might be wise to publish under a pseudonym? A sense of muddle and indecisiveness was threatening to swamp him, surrounded as he was by the piles of manuscripts in various states of incompleteness. In February he had begun a new novel, *The Grievance*, 'but can't think what the grievance should be. I suppose we all have one?'[53]

Hartley was at Assisi, where Molly had built a special arbour in which he might write, trying to work and surrounded by papers, when *The Love-Adept* was published in the summer. He was disappointed by its reception: 'there is a movement on the part of some of the younger reviewers to down-grade me. They are nearly all left-wing.'[54] Hartley wrote to the *Listener* 'complaining that the fiction-reviewers of today were upstarts no one had ever heard of, or would hear of, whereas I was a writer of international reputation' (he wisely withdrew the letter).[55] The book had 'flowed so easily when I wrote it, more easily than any of my books'.[56]

The *Times Literary Supplement* thought it had 'the air of an entertainment written more for himself and his friends than for the general reader – who can nevertheless pick up a bit of pleasure from it ... Unfortunately, *The Love-Adept* by James Golightly, is a far worse book than *The Love-Adept* by L. P. Hartley.'[57] Stephen Wall in the *Observer* thought the book reflected not so much the real world as the novelist grappling with it. If *The Love-Adept* is a long way from Hartley's best work, it is nevertheless a fascinating document from which the reader who knew nothing of Hartley might glimpse some essentials of his character. James Golightly is a novelist, writing a novel (*The Love-Adept*) about whose ending he is uncertain, and wonders what each of his four friends, all of them called Elizabeth, would recommend. He sends the novel, dedicated 'to Elizabeth', to each. Each assumes she is the dedicatee. Letters follow. The first two Elizabeths make attempts at intelligent criticism without convincing us (or James) that their words should be taken to heart. Elizabeth III, an astute reviewer of fiction, rejects the novel and its author as being out of touch with modern life, and sloppily written. A happy ending arrives when Elizabeth IV, breaking a long silence, proves to be the only one to have enjoyed and appreciated the book, the only one who asks the questions the author might have asked himself. Of course, what even Elizabeth IV cannot manage is a perfect understanding of James' book. Through substantial passages taken from James' novel, we are able to follow the story that so tests the four Elizabeths, a story of the devotion of the middle-aged Alexey for an actress who prefers the charms of her admirer's chauffeur. How, Elizabeth IV asks James, does the book end? 'Well', says James, '*this* is how it ends', and kisses her.

The children in James' novel watch the performances of the adults without understanding their underlying sexual dimension. Their innocence, or inexact information about people, throws a veil over events. The veil is not necessarily lifted for readers of Hartley's novel. The technique in *The Love-Adept* is often heavy-handed, and there are too many dull pages. It is, of course, the knowledge of Hartley that makes the book as fascinating as it is. The elements so essential to him cannot be resisted, the need for reassurance, the ability to take on the advice of friends, the ability of the author to see his work as sterile, the relevance of giving, and – certainly in James' novel, if not in Hartley's – the harm that love will do. *The Love-Adept* may be little more than a plaything, but James (and Hartley) at last, ignoring all advice, gives it the ending he most desires, an ending from a fairy-tale.

By August, another book, *The Harness Room*, 'my homosexual novel', was 'more or less finished' and despatched to Joan. Begun as a short story and expanded into a novella, the manuscript went through half a dozen versions before Hamilton was presented with a final typescript. Hartley told Joan, 'What I want the book to convey is the genuine love the boy feels for the man – you put it together and see what you can make of it.'[58] As Joan sat in her garden sifting through the pages, trying to make sense of Hartley's confusion, her daughter Margaret warned her that she might be about to ruin a masterpiece. When Joan sent Hartley the result of her work he, true to form, sent it straight off to Hamilton without bothering to read it.

Meanwhile, Hamilton was struggling to get *My Sister's Keeper* into a publishable state, but it was uphill work. The frustration that must often have ruled at Hamilton's office whenever one of Hartley's novels was being got ready was sometimes relieved by a sense of the ridiculous. Referring to a passage in which one of the characters describes a sporty car, Machell told Hamilton, 'This originally read "It's a dream. Its minimum speed is 100 m.p.h.", and when I pointed out the absurdity of this to Leslie, he *of course* missed what I was getting at and merely changed 100 to 70 m.p.h. Nothing short of a lecture on the internal combustion engine would make him understand the absurdity of a minimum speed of 70!'[59] After reading this memo, Hamilton wrote alongside it, 'Oh *how* I have laughed!'

The comings and goings of staff at Rutland Gate and Avondale showed no sign of letting up. When Tony, denounced as 'a tremendous mischief-maker',[60] abruptly left in August, Hartley was looked after by Colin Radford (Roger's brother) and his wife Muriel. Despite their kind ministrations, all around Hartley the hideous century seemed to be tightening its grip. The bank to which he had given his business for fifty years became difficult about the overdraft he had built up. 'I get rather irascible in the evenings! . . . The world seems to me a depressing place', he wrote to Christabel. 'Present company excepted, I don't like the human race as a whole, do you? Perhaps it will be nicer (the H.R. I mean) on the Moon?'[61] Christabel replied that he had never, since Charlie, had kind people to look after him, 'And you deserve, and need, cherishing . . . I *love* the Human Race – and loathe the pox marked Moon.'[62]

But what effort had Hartley made to get the people he deserved? The men were never recruited through a reputable agency such as Bessie had used in her regular searches for nurses and companions. In the main, Hartley trusted to responses from advertisements he placed in *The Times*. He seems to have attached little importance to references. So many of the men that drifted into his life in these last years were on the rebound of some financial, criminal or sexual crisis. The last thing he looked for in them was a faultless existence or a particularly virtuous disposition. Once, when Hartley was badly in need of a couple to look after him, Francis King suggested an exemplary husband and wife who had 'done' for Kitchin. Their reputation could hardly have been more spotless but, as King's description of their perfection proceeded, so all interest drained from Hartley's face.[63] There could be no hope that they might bring into his life the sense of danger, of sexual incongruity, that he longed for in those who shared his home. At the very least, if we are to be guided by the friendship of Richard Mardick and Denys Aspin in *The Brickfield*, Hartley wanted a dimension to the master–servant relationship that allowed a gingerly step across the edge of propriety – exercising his theory that two men might enjoy a relationship 'in which sex, though always present, is suppressed and kept in the background'. Was the line ever crossed? The question has no answer.

An advertisement in *The Times* produced Roy, 'mild, meek, polite and totally un-self-assertive',[64] but Hartley was disappointed because he understood the new man could only stay with him as a stopgap. Three weeks later, Roy was pronounced 'the nicest I ever had; even in a company of *angels* he would still shine out. Why does Fate torment one so?'[65] After appointing Roy's replacement, Douglas, a 'be-whiskered guardsman',[66] Hartley discovered that Roy would have been prepared to stay. Roy's brief tenure, during which 'I have had to revise my whole opinion of the working-class, which, after 10 years of suffering from them, I had come to regard as utterly selfish and untrustworthy',[67] was over, and Hartley was once more in uncharted waters. The autumn was not improved when rumours that he was about to be awarded the Nobel Prize for Literature proved untrue; he smarted from this disappointment, just as he had after failing to get a First at Oxford.

In November, Hartley sent Hamilton the final typescript of *The Harness Room*, still concerned that the book would 'injure my private image'.[68] 'I actually took more trouble over *The Harness Room* than over any of my novels.'[69] Hartley sent a copy to Cecil asking for his comments. Cecil remained silent. His discomfort may have been aggravated by the feeling that the book might encourage private or even public debate not only about the author's sexual preferences, but, more alarmingly, their friendship. But even when it became obvious that Cecil's coolness was a lack of endorsement Hartley was not deterred. His letters of this period to old friends are filled with a concern that the book might upset them, a concern that Hartley was inclined to assure them had emanated from Hamilton. Among such old friends, Cecil was surely the one to be the most considered, a fact that Cecil may have hoped might help sway Hartley's resolve to have the novel published. There is the feeling that, whatever uncomplimentary advice Hartley might have received, he would not let it stand in the way of his new work, just as James Golightly, having received the opinions of the four Elizabeths in *The Love-Adept*, eventually imposes his own.

Hartley wrote to Joan:

> I think the question of sex, and the sexes, is very obscure. Homosexuals of both sexes, there have always been: Sappho was, by tradition, a Lesbian, Achilles was bi-sexual, and so was Julius Caesar ... Even Oscar Wilde managed to produce a child or two. And now it seems as though the sexes, by their dress and general demeanour, were approximating more and more to each other, so

that in the end they may become indistinguishable! The cessation of the urge to procreation might be a good thing, since we are threatened with a surplus of population – and less harmful, and less unnatural, than the pill![70]

Meanwhile, Hamilton was inflicted with Hartley's constant worries. Should he publish under a different name? (Hamilton felt that his style would be recognised and that readers would think he had been ashamed to have it appear under his own name.) Should the book only be published in America? (Hamilton suggested Hartley might send the book to his agent there.) Should he regard *The Harness Room* as Forster had regarded *Maurice* – for posthumous publication only? '*That*', Hamilton replied, 'is a matter on which I can hardly advise you!'

It was unlikely that Hartley would ever shake off the fear of public exposure that his one honestly homosexual novel threatened. What would Christabel say, what would Molly say? Yet it was only in the disguise of fiction that an attempt could be made at the truth, the truth that was carefully hidden from even the most sympathetic of his circle. It was only after Clifford Kitchin's death that Francis King noted Hartley's new willingness to speak freely about his sexuality:

There was one manservant, very handsome, but tough-looking and dangerous, as if he'd just come out of prison. Leslie gave me the impression he might have had sex with him. When he left the room, Leslie said, 'Hasn't he got a wonderful figure?' Leslie liked to hear about my exploits, but I could never be totally frank with him as I could with Clifford. I always thought Leslie slightly effeminate – he was given to giggling a lot – but not enough to be sent up in the streets. One day he told me that David Cecil had been the love of his life. He said no more. I was too stunned to ask him to elaborate.[71]

❧ 13 ❧

'What are we going to do?'

WITH THE TURN of the new decade, Hartley's health was declining to such an extent that it could only further aggravate the increasingly uneven quality of his writing. There was so much worry. Hamilton, his letters to Hartley as measured and tactful as ever, was expected to placate any anxiety, but his author's procrastination now sometimes extended over two or more books at once. Hartley could not resist defending any suggestion – which had certainly never been made by Hamilton – that *The Harness Room*'s theme was unsavoury, insisting that the book treated homosexuality 'in a more discreet manner than it is in many modern novels, in which the words "fuck" and "bugger" appear on every page. I am now trying to write another novel, but have rather lost my way in it.'[1] As for *My Sister's Keeper*, he was having 'cold feet' about the 'cottage' sequence. 'What would Molly Berkeley say?' he asked Hamilton. 'I feel I should keep *My Sister's Keeper* out of her reach, but how?'[2] Like so many of the questions he now put to Hamilton, these were almost impossible to answer. If Hamilton's responses were always temperate, Machell's view of Hartley, confided to Hamilton, made no attempt to hide his weariness. He told Hamilton that 'Leslie goes on and on about how after all he would like us to publish his *The Harness Room* as he has shown it to two friends who were not shocked.'[3] Three months later the novel had been expanded to novel length, but was still in need of revision. 'Personally', Hartley told Joan, 'I think "The Harness Room" has less dead wood in it than most of my books, and now that "My Sister's Keeper" hasn't, *so far*, been greeted with howls of execration on account of its obscenity, I feel bolder about "The Harness Room".'[4]

Hamish Hamilton's willingness to publish the final novels seems no less than an act of charity. If he had followed up his (and Machell's) disenchantment by rejecting them, Hartley's life would have been shorter and unhappier. But now, as he pulled each new book from the jumble of papers that surrounded him, he seemed almost to be trying to make up for the writing time he had lost over the years. Suddenly, he was prolific, but as the quantity increased the quality declined. By May 1970 he had 'completed' *The Will and the Way* (originally called *The Grievance*). 'The *doctors* might enjoy it', he wrote to Joan, ' – the *dockers* certainly won't.'[5] Hamilton, in a long letter of criticism, informed Hartley that 'it seems to us to fall sadly below your usual excellent form ... Wouldn't it be better to put it aside and let us publish the revised *Harness Room*?'[6] That, for the moment, seemed out of Hartley's hands. Nothing could be done with the book until Cecil had given his verdict, but he 'won't say anything, except that he has misgivings ... It is really annoying.'[7] There was also a collection of short stories, *Mrs Carteret Receives*, which Hamilton had agreed to publish but was holding up, partly as an inducement to Hartley to submit an absolutely final vision of *The Harness Room*. 'Hamish Hamilton is really a mean-minded man, he could quite well publish the stories', Hartley complained.[8] Amid all this writing activity (or lack of it), he was able to write to Joan from Assisi at the beginning of July that 'My new novel "The Collections" is so improbable that even I can hardly believe in it!'[9]

He had been reluctant to visit Molly this summer, unhappy as he was in England, dissatisfied with the amount of money in Enid's estate, and with the domineering Douglas, to whom he gave notice. By the time he set off for Assisi in June, a new man, another Roy, had arrived – '*very* nice (at least I think so now), and Douglas was not nice at all and went away with my wireless set, saying he would return it, but I wonder'.[10] The theft of a rug was also discovered, and 'My blood-pressure has taken an almost sensational plunge downwards, which I believe leads to depression.'[11] Once arrived at San Lorenzo, Hartley's health did not improve. He was suffering badly from insomnia, and his legs would only just carry him downhill. At night, he had got into the habit of taking a teaspoonful of 'Cosylan' to prevent him 'wheezing like a grampus'.[12] Molly was now almost always in a wheelchair, much assisted by her servants summoned by one of the many bells that festooned her garden. Hartley told Christabel, 'Since she left her flat in Rome she seems to be still more affluent, and in spite of her criticism of my drinking habits the vodka flows and I even get it for tea!'[13] Molly informed him that 'she thought "my system" might *need* vodka, which was a great concession. One of my systems certainly does.'[14]

Returning home, Hartley asked Douglas to Rutland Gate to discuss the fate of the wireless and the missing rug, and arranged that the police should call during the interview. Meanwhile, Hartley confessed to Norah that 'Roy is not quite the paragon he seemed to be, and wants to be bought out of his present job. He may be well worth the price of a rug, but who knows?'[15] Hartley was also harbouring suspicions that the rug might have been removed by Fred the cleaner, and would not have involved the police at all but for the requirements of his insurance company. Later, Hartley found the rug.

It was the summer of the filming of *The Go-Between*. 'A friend tells me,' Hartley wrote to Norah, 'that "The Go-Between" is [to] be "shot" near East Dereham, though not at the house where it happened.'[16] *Where it happened* – a slip of the pen or a careless confession that the book had its foundation in truth? What can the 'it' that Hartley refers to be? If not the central plot of the novel, perhaps the trauma that so affected both Leo and Hartley? The unwanted learning about physical love, the dangers of adoration? For Hartley to have been so imprecise in his meaning as to have written of the place 'where it happened' is perhaps unthinkable; this is at once the flimsiest, and most suggestible, evidence that may tell us that the running shadow that followed Hartley through his life had its true origins here.

Thoughts of the filming, of course, pulled him back not only to the book but to the experiences that had gone into it. 'The idea that one's life is all of a piece from the cradle to the grave is true, I think', he told Joan. 'I wish I had reminded them that it was Leo's natural function to be a Go-Between.'[17] In one of his first letters to her, he said that the writing of the novel had given him more pain than any other – presumably, not the pain that came from the Cynthia–Huntington–Hamilton triangle around its difficult publication. If there was pain in the composition of *The Go-Between*, it must surely have stemmed from having to recall the malevolence that had struck him down in childhood, the trauma that made the writing possible. With whatever imagination or invention, whatever veneer or pretence, Hartley overlays the truth, the trauma is always the base of its strength, its strength unquestionable. Whatever fiction supports the trauma that is at the heart of *Eustace and Hilda*, *The Go-Between* and *The Brickfield* cannot hide the essential distress of their author. Can it have been at Bradenham Hall that Hartley's life was forever altered? Could it have been the house 'where it happened'?

Now, Losey's gift of a film offered the possibility of basking in an Indian Summer of recognition and recollection, but Hartley resisted invitations to travel to Norfolk to see the filming. He, James Lees-Milne and Wilhelmine Harrod had suggested suitable replacements for Bradenham Hall, though none suggested the house that was ultimately chosen, Melton Constable Hall. The picture was made entirely on location. Carmen Dillon, its designer, used the Norfolk landscape to splendid effect, sometimes extending Hartley's recollection of the county, as with the introduction of a horse-fair on Tombland (this was Losey's idea). The harvest scene and cricket match were enacted at Thornage Green; Ted's home was found at Park Farm, Hanworth, his cornfield at the nearby Meadow Farm; the swimming sequence took place at Hickling Broad; the church service at Heydon; in Norwich, the scene shifted from Leo and Marian's lunch at the Maid's Head Hotel to Leo's arrival at Thorpe station and his visit to the cathedral (a visit that the older Hartley would certainly have made). The evocation of this foreign country of Hartley's could not have been more lovingly created. Everywhere, the people of Norfolk contributed to the authenticity of the film. Villagers made up the spectators at the cricket match, with a master from Gresham's School at Holt, Oliver Barnes, playing a handsome cricketer. The butler from the Ketton-Cremer estate at Felbrigg, Mr Ritchie, buttled. A florist from Holt, Charles Winn, appeared in the greenhouse scene, trowel in hand.

Wilhelmine Harrod organised a charity première in Norwich in October, for which a 'rather shaky' Hartley travelled down, staying with Lady Harrod at the Old Rectory, Holt.[18] The day after the London première, he lunched with Joan at the Dorchester, but he was deeply agitated and unhappy, 'he kept crying and kissing my hands.'[19] The enjoyment that the tremendous success of the film might have given him was muted by his uneasiness and ill health, though he fully appreciated the achievements both of Joseph Losey and Harold Pinter. He would not, he told Richard Roud in a *Guardian* interview, have minded if the film had ruined the book, but of course he knew it had not; if anything, he considered that Pinter had made his dialogue seem rather more up-to-date. Losey's struggle to make the picture had been, in Pinter's words, 'a year's work and eight years conviction', and had only come off by persuading the actors to work initially for 'no cash at all'. When Hartley complained about the lack of money he had received from the film, Losey wrote, more in sorrow than anger, that he was 'somewhat shocked and disturbed' by his comments.[20]

My Sister's Keeper, Hartley's last attempt at a substantial novel, can have won him few converts. Janice Elliott in the *Sunday Telegraph* wrote that the book 'seems deep frozen in floes of disenchantment.

Does [Basil] harbour a homosexual passion for his brother-in-law? Probably. Is his attitude to his sisters based on hidden incestuous yearnings? Most likely. Is he a bore? Yes ... It's the transfiguring imagination which is missing – the sympathetic sensibility and artistry which for so long have been Mr Hartley's essential gifts.' Basil Hancock, the Hartley-figure of the novel, is brother to three sisters, Gwendolen, Amabel and Evelyn, and suffers, like Eustace, from what his doctor diagnoses as 'sisteritis'; his life is scarred by their misadventures, for which he shoulders an overwhelming guilt. Each of the sisters presents him with a crisis, for which the inadequate Basil is ill-equipped. He is an all too typical Hartley-figure of the later books, brought up by Victorian-minded parents to believe 'that it was dangerous and improper to do what one liked'.[21] His mother hopes that he will remain single 'for he must not be the prey of any designing female – he was hers'.[22] When Gwendolen becomes engaged to Terry, Basil feels he should warn her of Terry's sexual feelings for men. Basil and he had been schoolboys together. Basil, though not a 'cock-teaser', had been Terry's 'steady' in what Basil regarded as 'a muted emotional relationship'. But Basil does not warn Gwendolen who marries Terry. Married life brings them happiness, until Terry is caught in a public lavatory with a youth (the beginning of the 'cottage' sequence of which Hartley was so fearful). Basil, with highly improbable pluck, proves Terry innocent by himself going into the lavatory and entrapping the boy. Evelyn's life is ruined when Basil supports her husband's lust for a nifty sports car (the same vehicle that had achieved the remarkable 100 m.p.h. minimum). Driving in the car, Evelyn is almost killed. Then, Amabel is made pregnant by a scoundrel introduced into her life by Basil. Abandoned, she considers an abortion but marries the father and has the child. Some months later, she dies. Meg, a social worker friend of Basil's, wants to adopt her child, and Basil obligingly proposes marriage to her.

Basil's motto, 'Agree with thine adversary quickly, whiles thou art in the way with him', is clearly one to which Hartley himself might have subscribed, but of course Hartley is everywhere in this book. At the coming together of Basil and Meg, for example, 'Basil looked round the room, so comfortable and so apparently secure, and his thoughts roved from the cradle to the grave. They were not so much unalike – a small compartment for an angry, self-exhausted, life-exhausted body. He had little sense of what life could be, compared to what life might be.'[23] When Basil proposes to Meg, she can only cross-examine his motives. 'It isn't something you are saying in spite of yourself? It's your desire, your *inclination* – not some form of self-sacrifice?'[24] Tellingly, Meg receives no answer, or perhaps two answers. '"No, *no*," cried Basil, hearing the steps at the door, the world's intrusion. Trying to remember what Meg had said he was confused and could hardly distinguish between yes and no. "Yes, yes," he cried.'[25]

Indecision could want no finer definition. In his last years Hartley told J. W. Lambert that each night at Avondale he was racked by an agony of deciding which of his twin beds he should sleep in. The decision that all around him was unhappiness seems, by 1970, to have been one of the few of which he was capable. 'I think, without going as far as the Buddhists, – that all existence is suffering', he informed Joan.[26] The spirit of evil had long ago worked itself into the fabric of his life. 'I have long felt that there was a bad spirit abroad in the world, perhaps the Devil.'[27] Modernity, and youth, and the rights of franchise, he held in contempt. 'I think the "students" are the worst aspects of a democracy-mad society. They should all be slain, or sent to some Devil's Island, of which we must still have some.'[28] That summer, some boys got into Fletton Tower, an incident used for 'The Silver Clock' in *Mrs Carteret Receives*; at Avondale, youths threw egg-sized stones at Hartley when he was out on the river. A fishing friend of his apprehended them on the bank and gave them over to a stern policeman who reduced them to tears. To Hartley, 'One of them looked as wicked as the boy in "The Turn of the Screw"';[29] and a few days later, 'I wish we could be ruled by Mr Enoch Powell, who wouldn't stand this nonsense. The Welfare State (or the Farewell State) and the permissive society have much to answer for.'[30] As if all this was not enough to bear, his one remaining idyll, the joy of the river, was again threatened by his oldest and most natural enemies, swans, and a pair of cygnets: 'I shall have to see what their behaviour is before I take more serious steps!' But his obsession with the hideousness of his century went far beyond the door of Avondale or the water-bank of Avondale. Joan was with him one day when he walked to his balcony and breathed deeply. 'I can smell the evil in the air', he said.[31]

The moral responsibility of making a riposte to the permissiveness all around him did not confine itself to his fiction; by the late sixties, he had already established almost another career as a writer of letters to the national press. If, in 'Too Much Compassion?', he had suggested that he favoured a less sympathetic attitude to the wrongdoer, in his outpouring of letters to the *Daily Telegraph* and other journals he left all shred of doubt behind. From the Athenaeum or from Rutland Gate he fired his salvoes: he equated the restoration of capital punishment with the restoration of morality; its restitution would stimulate recruitment to the police. He expressed horror at the juvenile delinquents who had thrown stones at him, and at the boys playing with pistols in the churchyard of Holy Trinity, Brompton. He told of a south London lavatory attendant with a wooden leg who had been set on after trying to stop two youths smashing "a lavatory bowl" (if that is the correct expression)'. He resisted any attempt to pass off criminality as a mental disorder; 'there are other ways of dealing with a mad dog than by psychiatry.' Criminals should be sent to Coventry, and bear the mark of Cain; they should be 'literally branded' by a mark on their cheek: M for the murderer, F for the forger, V for the perpetrator of violence. Francis King, when confronted by Hartley's branding theory, asked if Leslie was to be branded with a Q for queer. Hartley, after all, thought there was 'nothing cruel in branding: half of the men in the Services eagerly get themselves tattoed, to enhance their sex appeal.' The unconscious humour of this sad little archive is stopped only by the knowledge that there is left in the man who wrote it no compassion; the heart is hardened against forgiveness. Better to forget the flimsy wisps of newsprint that represent the collected letters of L. P. Hartley to the press. After reading them, one feels that, faced with such austerity of spirit, there can be no going back on one's judgement.

Financially, too, Hartley felt threatened. His excursion into libel against Cuthbert Worsley had cost him £900, which he was loath to part with, but 'Jews are so crafty, I expect I shall have to pay. I don't suppose you know of any anti-Semitic lawyer who could put a spoke in their wheel?'[32] He was also nursing his hatred for the Inland Revenue, against which his impotence could only devise an idea for demolishing this despicable organisation in a novel 'about an innocent character who has no accountant, but takes these [tax] demands as accurate, and having been made bankrupt commits suicide'[33] – another book that promised to be as much vendetta as fiction. Hartley felt persecuted by such attentions: 'It seems to me that the Income Tax writes me *every* day a threatening letter, written in red, saying prosecution, distraint of goods, and prison.'[34]

All this against the background of dealings with the 'W.C.' that were moving into a final, dark phase. Early in 1971, a new man, Robert, was appointed, a young ex-bomber pilot 'responsible for many deaths' who nevertheless seemed 'very nice'.[35] Hartley's lack of talent for choosing the right person had never been so pronounced. When she first met Robert, Joan was alarmed to see him so unshaven and unkempt, as if he had been living on the streets. At the end of her visit to Rutland Gate she went down to the garage where the Mercedes was kept and Robert drove her to Euston. 'I felt as if I was in the presence of something quite unknown to me; there was something evil there.'[36] During the journey she asked Robert to stop the car so that she could buy some flowers for Hartley. She thrust them into Robert's hands. 'I thought they would somehow change him, but they only made him worse.'[37] By the time of her next visit, Robert had smartened up, but Joan felt he wanted to draw her to him and against Hartley. In Robert's company, Hartley's drinking seemed to increase alarmingly, 'from morning to night. His glass was never empty. Robert was always replenishing it.'[38] Joan was aware, too, that Robert was trying to keep Hartley's friends away from him. Telephone calls were deflected, messages seemed not to be passed on, Hartley was increasingly unavailable. Robert had told him, 'I'm going to get a dog for this flat, a very fierce German dog. Even Miss Hartley doesn't know about this breed.'[39] At the end of March, Robert found Hartley unconscious in the bathroom, but 'Even my doctor doesn't think it was due to drunkenness.'[40] In May, he fell downstairs at Avondale and lay unconscious for some time before Robert summoned help; his hand, hurt in the fall, was X-rayed and put in a sling.

Robert was also insinuating himself into Hartley's business affairs, a sure sign that things were beginning to go seriously awry. Hartley explained to Hamilton that 'my latest factotum has constituted himself my secretary or "personal assistant"', regularly discussing financial matters.[41] It was Robert who telephoned Hamilton to inform him that Hartley had no intention of subsidising publication of Anne Mulkeen's book on his work by £350: there had earlier been talk about Hartley contributing to the cost of her study of 'the symbolic novels of L. P. Hartley', *Wild Thyme, Winter Lightning*; when it appeared in 1974, Kay Dick pronounced it 'unreadable'.

With so much domestic upheaval, there was little to enjoy in the publication of the final volume of short stories, *Mrs Carteret Receives*, in June, despite its generally kindly critical welcome. Janice Elliott in the *Sunday Telegraph* recognised 'The L. P. Hartley Person [who] is not unlike Mole without Ratty or Toad', but detected an increased constriction of the Hartley world: 'If anything, the vision of a moral and ultimately pitiless universe is darkening further, the victim growing more vulnerable and defenceless before the invading shadows.'[42] Of shadows there are plenty in *Mrs Carteret Receives*, the pages of which are peppered with the relationship between master and servant, and of course the habits of the 'W.C.' One of the most substantial pieces is the title story, a portrait of the long-dead Mrs Johnstone. Here, her mission to keep out the profane vulgar is lost against Death, the only guest ever able to force himself upon her. This, and 'Fall in at the Double', are the only supernatural stories. 'Paradise Paddock' is inevitably a portrait of poor beleaguered Avondale, with its gardener's daughter killed by a lorry (dying as Charlie's daughter had died), and its guest crashing down the stairs (just as Christabel had). A scarab is blamed, and causes the death of the daily help who light-fingeredly helps herself to it. Yet the Hartley-figure is consoled, although accused by a friend of having the Evil Eye, that Paradise Paddock is locally known (just like Avondale) as the House of Death: 'the association between Death and Paradise is rather encouraging and beautiful, I think. Out of one, into the other.'[43]

'The Silver Clock' has Norah appearing as Nerina Willoughby, a dog-breeding spinster whose philosophy, 'Better be by oneself, if sometimes lonely, than attached to another human being', seems borrowed from Hartley.[44] It is the love of the working man for the motor car that inspires 'The Prayer', in which a chauffeur, Copperthwaite, leaves his employer for another who has a more inspiring model, the Roland-Rex. 'The God in the car!' is Copperthwaite's fixation, but on finding he can make no difference to the perfection of the Roland-Rex he returns to his original job. 'Pains and Pleasures' extends the discussion between employer and servant to include a troublesome, much loved, cat, whose death (the factotum's doing?) removes a problem between the two men. In 'Please do not Touch' Vivian Vosper, the Hartley-figure, leaves a poisoned bottle of sherry marked 'Please do not Touch' on display; a thief, taking a swig from it during a burglary, dies. Far from regretting his action, Vivian prepares some Amontillado laced with cyanide for any future uninvited guests.

In many of these stories there is much that is disquieting if (to those who knew Hartley) unsurprising, but it is 'Roman Charity' that, alone in the collection, has the ability to shock. Set 'In some day and age which I won't try to identify',[45] this has the quality of a fairy tale, is almost Ruritanian in its atmosphere, with a hero called Rudy Campion, and has a Gothick bitterness. When he is imprisoned as an international spy, Rudy's wife and daughter desert him. Fettered and starved, his body weakens. His daughter comes to the prison. 'Her head bent forward; her smile grew more inviting as if it was the very messenger of love' until 'The beautiful hand drew down her black velvet bodice, and exposed her breasts. "I have a wet nurse," she said, "should I need one, but I have plenty of this to spare." '[46] On subsequent visits, her invitation in eyes and lips is overwhelming, and Rudy again drinks from her breasts. She engineers his escape, taking him to the home she shares with her husband and child, where she waves him towards a sideboard

> where the bottles gleamed, whisky, gin, vodka, each with its special appeal, its message of encouragement to the weary human race. 'Or would you like something else, another sort of cocktail?'
> 'I would like you,' he said, and before she had time to assent or dissent he had clapsed her in his arms. Gently she released herself, and bared her bosom to him for the last time.[47]

It would be simple to dismiss 'Roman Charity' as about the potency of incestuous love; as it happens, the daughter's offer of her milk has as much malevolence as lust or Cordelia-like devotion; there is a design in her bounty that is not made clear. Is her father drinking a mother's milk, or tasting gall? The savagery of that final offer, 'another sort of cocktail', is dreadful. Physical repulsion and attraction are married in a story that is at once unsavoury, repugnant and dimly understood. But it gave Hartley, apparently, no doubts, none of the concern with which he invested *My Sister's Keeper* or *The Harness Room*.

The master–servant relationship that Hartley had nurtured for so long now erupted in violence. At 5 o'clock one morning, Robert broke into Hartley's bedroom at Rutland Gate, punched him on the shoulder and shouted, 'Your sister hates you.' A new man, Brian, had been appointed as Robert's successor and was already living in, as was Robert. Then, on 17 September, Hartley wrote a muddled, erratically punctuated letter to Christabel from Avondale:

> I have just arrived here after a series of misfortunes – murder is one of the least, but I will tell you about it.
> Happily for me, I was in bed, or half asleep, when the two men, who I mistakenly thought would get on with each other, fell out, and late at night, they tried to murder each other, at least he (Rupert) [sic] tried to murder him) Brian.'
> David Cecil rang up the Bath Police, and though they didn't pay much attention at the time, they came the next morning, and took the miscreant away, who meanwhile had been locked up in

his bedroom by a device worthy of the Scarlet Pimpernel. I was not a witness to any of this, but when I heard the lock beginning to grate on its hinges (for Robert is a very strong man) I was most thankful when the sergeant and his assistant arrived. I tried to console myself by thinking how much braver Diana Cooper would have been in difficult circumstances.

Now Robert has gone, escorted by police, where I know not, and Brian, his successor remains, lucky to be alive – such is life in Bathford. He has a lump on his foot as big as a football and as red as the sun, where the dumb-bell hit him.

As well as the dumb-bell, Robert had attacked his replacement with a broken dinner-plate and an 18-inch carving knife. The shock of these events contributed to Hartley's decline. Christopher Hudson, then a young journalist working as literary editor at the *Spectator*, had long been an admirer of Hartley's work, and first met him when they sat together on a panel of judges for a short story competition run by the periodical. The encounter was not as Hudson had imagined it:

> He was slovenly to a degree, bulky, his clothes hung badly on him. We had lunch. He had been drinking quite a lot and continued drinking through the afternoon. He had great red jowls, and dribbled – he couldn't stop dribbling from his lower lip. For someone who'd read *The Shrimp and the Anemone* it was a coming of age. He was a man who had let himself go, a disgusting spectacle. It had a considerable effect on me. One believes there should be a connection between the work and the man. I hadn't expected to meet an old queen.[48]

Rumours circulated in the *Spectator* office that Hartley had been attacked by his chauffeur with an axe. To some, it seemed a natural outcome of Hartley's fondness for rough trade. The publication in the autumn of *The Harness Room*, about which Hartley had suffered such anxiety, might have added fuel to such gossip. Unhappy as Joan had been about the quality of its writing (and he confessed to being 'devastated' by her comments about the book's ending), she had never flinched from its subject-matter, doing her best in rearranging the text to achieve what Hartley wanted – the strength of feeling between the two men.

In an unspecified time – presumably contemporary, though both manners and dialogue belong indisputably to an earlier age – Fergus, the seventeen-year-old-son of staid Colonel Macready, is attracted to his father's chauffeur, Fred Carrington, aged twenty-eight. To harden up his bookish son for Sandhurst and a soldierly career, the colonel (who is about to marry a younger woman, Sonia) asks Fred to give Fergus some physical training. In Fred's harness room, its walls hanging with old bridles, bits, stirrups, cruppers, the smell of leather everywhere, Fergus is initiated not only into the bodily exertions that his father has instigated, but into sex. Fred shows him a photograph of himself. It fascinates the virginal Fergus:

> He had never seen the original or even the picture of a man where the emphasis was laid on his nakedness, where the lights and the darks, the cavities and hillocks, bone-wise or muscle-wise, in the physical structure, got their pictorial effect from contrasting and contending each other, as a hill contrasts with a valley. Especially as they did here, where the triangle of the body, reaching down to its narrow inverted climax, where the darkness of the loins took possession of it, seemed a strange miracle of the skeleton enclothed in flesh – the architectonic breadth of the shoulders, for which scapular and deltoid seemed inadequate words, the ribs expanding and clutching each other, and below them, what? The dark, hidden secrets which the painter, for whatever reason, had concealed under a casual but ample swathe of material, colourless in the photograph.[49]

It is Fergus who finally seduces Fred, who has promised to show Fergus his 'whole bag of tricks'. Fred warns him of the machinations of women as, under the influence of Sonia (herself sexually attracted to her stepson) the house begins to take on a more feminine aspect, from which only the harness room, with its sadomasochistic trappings, is exempt. Fergus, we are told, is 'perhaps' the only person the bisexual Fred has ever really loved. The price of love must, of course, be paid. At a boxing-match between Fred and Fergus, staged to impress the colonel and Sonia, Fergus trips in the ring and dies. Sonia leaves the colonel, as does a heartbroken Fred. In one of the book's most devastating sentences the colonel's emotional predicament is neatly described: 'He had lost his wife, his son and his chauffeur.'[50]

The *Listener* compared the book to 'a late Lawrence short story – bare, casual, yet sketching its persons as if in steel ... it's Mr Hartley's economy of art that finally impresses.'[51] What Cecil's final opinion of the book had been we do not know. Another friend, Rex Littleboy, recalled after reading the novel that 'all art came from the "gathered secret treasure of the heart!" (I thought at once of "The

Harness Room").'[52] What singles out *The Harness Room* is the fact
that it deals with sexuality with something approaching passion, even
if the sexual act between Fred and Fergus actually happens off-stage.
And on deciding to write more openly about the feelings of sexuality,
it is homosexuality that Hartley turns to, writing with a direct and
sensual sureness. To Hartley, the male physique is revealed as a
temple of mystery. There is no guilt in either Fred and Fergus that
they have made love to one another. It is the gentlemanliness of
homosexuality that is stressed, the handshake on parting, the feeling
of trust between two men who have explored one another to the
full. Fergus, more fortunate, or at least more worldly, than so many
of the Hartley-figures that have gone before him, is allowed full
sexual knowledge, a knowledge that is experienced and not inherited.
Eustace and Leo might have envied him. Richard Mardick might
have warned him that sexual experience can lead only to unhappiness, that the one experience is in effect a cutting off of any
subsequent emotional or sexual life. So it is with Fergus, transplanted
into a knowing world of which he is innocent, crossing the barrier
that separates his class from the working class. In his fascination for
the working man, and his sexual enjoyment of him, Fergus finds a
fulfilment that would otherwise have been denied him. It is the
master–servant relationship (begun by Eustace and Minney in *The
Shrimp and the Anemone*) that has been the only relationship of real
value in his life. With Fergus gone, however, the positions of the
others are rethought. The colonel persuades Fred to return as his
chauffeur, but Sonia, though hoping the colonel may ask her to
return to his side, is excluded. 'We are not the masters of our fate',
she tells her husband.[53]

Hamilton was now faced with another novel, but Machell's
patience was almost exhausted. His first reaction was to reject *The
Collections*, but on second thoughts he recommended a reluctant
acceptance. Machell thought the new book was 'pointless and idiotic
if intended realistically ... the only moral drawn by [the hero] is
that he doesn't want the Inland Revenue to get much in the way of
estate duty when he dies.'[54] The manuscript, one-third of it crossed
out or pasted over, presented an almost impossible challenge and
Machell felt Hartley was incapable of giving clear instructions for its
revision. 'Its publication will do him no good', he concluded.
However, if they decided to turn down *The Collections* Hartley would
anyway only come up with another novel 'just as bad. After all, if he
could get away with *Poor Clare*, *The Love-Adept* and *My Sister's
Keeper*, he can with this.'[55] Once more, Joan's skill was to prove

essential in making sense of the muddle. 'My impulse', Hartley told her, 'is to leave the whole book to you and we could describe it as a "collaboration"? But is that fair? . . . Alas, I have so many books to read, as well as to write. Why are we not given more time?'[56] A few weeks later he was assuring her, 'It won't matter if your words are my words! . . . Please do *whatever you like* with the MSS. Your English is *at least* as good as mine.'[57]

Brian (himself an alcoholic) had now been replaced by another young man, but he seemed as unreliable as others that had gone before. When he lent out Hartley's car to a friend to spend the night in, the friend stole it (it was later found dumped). Whatever confidence Hartley had ever had in these men had evaporated, but he simply could not exist without their presence. Whatever privilege and the brickworks had given him, they had not given him the strength to live with himself, by himself. Behind him, until the end, were the men from whom he had once sought so much, but now they often seemed only half-real, imagined. Derek Parker, who went to Rutland Gate to interview Hartley during the summer for the 'Myself When Young' radio series, remembers him 'more or less drunk' throughout the recording, and 'some tall, dark young man in attendance, sliding through the shadows'.[58]

The forces of evil would never be vanquished now. To Hartley the state of the world was '(especially here) too depressing for literary effort. What are we going to do? . . . Murders have increased, and will increase all the more in the black-out. I can imagine the criminals sharpening their knives and fixing their sawn-off shot-guns – under cover of darkness.'[59] Nothing now but mayhem. 'You or I might be blown up by a petrol bomb at any time', he told Joan. There could be no sympathy for dissension. 'I wish Ireland could be sunk in the depths of the sea.'[60] The past had slipped almost completely away, the hideousness of the century had done its utmost. And there seemed consolation in nothing.

It is saddening to see Hartley's letters of these last months, the writing jagged, ugly, thoughts unfinished, phrases repeated, words missed. He worked, painfully, at a new novel. It would have given Machell no hesitation, for it was clearly unpublishable. Hartley's obsession with money, fuelled by the abhorred Inland Revenue, had taken over.

> He had begun to hate the idea of money; he had really only wanted to share it with Lydia – what was going to happen to it (if any) now?

He had left it to Lydia for her lifetime, after which it was to go to her niece, Cornelia, if Cornelia had any heirs or assigns. If she hadn't, it must go *somewhere*, provided always it didn't go to the *State*. Long before Lydia died, and long before he knew he might have any considerable sum to dispose of, (if any) he had been trying to work out with his Accountant how the money could be disposed of without increasing too much (or if needs be, at all) the revenue of the National Exchequer.

But now that Lydia was dead, what was the position? He had left his money (whatever it might be) to her, for her lifetime; he had also left her his aunt's money, though he did not know what it would be, Capital Gains Tax deducted.[61]

And so pointlessly on and on.

Joan could no longer turn away from the fact that Hartley was constantly drinking. 'I did the most awful thing – I interfered with his life. I telephoned Patrick Woodcock and told him what was happening.'[62] She knew her action could mean the end of their friendship. A few days later he asked her out to lunch. 'He was white with rage. He said our friendship was over. It was terrible.' But when they said goodbye at the entrance to Rutland Gate, Hartley suddenly took hold of her hand and said, 'I don't think we shall ever stop being friends, shall we?'

In May, he received radium treatment at Westminster hospital for a skin cancer on his face. In a life that had for so long been plagued by hypochondria, it was one of the very few times he underwent hospital treatment, for serious illness had always been kept at bay. At Rutland Gate, he was being looked after by Anthony: 'his manner, and his manners, are both very bad', Hartley reported;[63] Anthony was 'a little M., you know'.[64] He had higher hopes of his replacement, Michael, but 'I don't like him very much. He has pleasant manners, but he is drunk and more than a little mad.'[65] Madness, it seemed to Hartley, surrounded him. At least when he collapsed in his bath, as he sometimes did, Michael was on hand to rescue him: 'I suppose I owe my life to him.'[66]

A final honour was conferred on Hartley in June 1972 by the Royal Society of Literature, when along with David Cecil, Angus Wilson and Cyril Connolly, he was named a Companion of Literature. The morning after the date fixed for the ceremony, he remembered with horror his obligation to attend. He telephoned the Royal Society and profusely apologised for having forgotten to turn up. A puzzled official explained that he had not missed it but had in fact spent a considerable time there after the presentation, chatting to this and that person. Hartley could remember nothing of it. He had spoken to Cecil but failed to recognise him. The impossibility of his condition was becoming increasingly obvious. Francis King, so long a recipient of Hartley's hospitality, invited him out to lunch in Knightsbridge. When he collected him, Hartley had already been drinking heavily. At the restaurant Hartley wanted nothing to eat, but ordered more drinks. King toyed with his food. When the time came to leave, Hartley fell off his chair on to the floor. With the help of the waiter, King bundled Hartley into a taxi. He never saw him again. Enduring such indignities was made worse by the knowledge that the power to write had almost completely deserted him. He let slip to Hamilton a rare glimpse of the regret he felt about his career: 'I wish now I had been bolder about creative writing, and taken more trouble about "The Shrimp and the Anemone" which took me 20 years.'[67]

The decline accelerated as the autumn came on. On 20 September he was complaining to the novelist Anne Wignall of '"the flu" or whatever it is I am having. I haven't had it for nearly 40 years, but the symptoms are unmistakeable – feeling quite well one moment, and ghastly the next. How I wish you were in London. I seem to be fated to be separated from my dearest friends. But I can't blame them.'[68] He was running a high temperature, and shivering uncontrollably. Writing was an agony of effort. So much was slipping away. In November, Teresa Berwick, eighty-one, was killed outside the gates of Attingham Park, just as her sister had been. With her death, one of the last, slender threads with his old Venetian life was broken off.

The last of the queue of unsuitable young men, sliding through the shadows, had gone. It was clear now that only a professional nurse would suffice. By the middle of November Hartley was still blaming his condition on a 'nasty virus'. 'I am a little better, I think', he told Joan, 'but not much. The swellings don't go down.'[69] Avondale was forgotten; he would never see it again. Venice, a dream long lost, could still be remembered with affection, as one recalls the charms of an old lover whose face is half-forgotten. When he had first known it 'you could hire a gondola for under a pound a day. Now £10 would be nearer the mark and Venice isn't Venice without a gondola.'[70] In these final memories of the one place on earth where happiness offered itself to him, he seemed to have come to terms with the parting. He attached no blame to Venice now, defining it as really a state of mind – not always a very happy one – Elizabeth Bowen once told me she leaned over a bridge and tears poured from her eyes, she knew not why! I think it is the sight of so much perfection, I think, to which one can add nothing, or take anything away. I used to have an acute nostalgia when I left it, but that wore off, and the last time I left I was thankful to get away, with the heat pouring down like a great wet blanket. But I was much older then, and what I could get out of Venice I had had.[71]

Venice, like life, had failed him at the last. 'I seem', he told Cecil, 'to have become part of my past.'[72] If there had been any joy in his life, it had been with Cecil. His mind went back to the days – 'our lovely times' – they had spent together as young men, days that Hartley hoped might turn into a lifetime. Forty years before, he had written to Cecil from San Sebastiano: 'I rejoiced to see your writing on the green baize table on which we have both spilt so much tea. But though it makes such a brilliant letter your life doesn't sound very happy. How I wish you were here.'[73] Now, he remembered their long, passionate talks at Beaumont Street, 'but they gave more to me than they gave to you'.[74] It was too late to hope that any happiness might lie ahead. He recalled Mrs Johnstone telling him that at her age all that mattered was that one should make a good death.

The blackthorn winter was outside the door. By the second week in December, it was clear that the end was near. Cecil and Ralph Ricketts came, sitting on either side of him and holding his hands. Norah came. Joan, alerted by Patrick Woodcock, travelled down from Bramhall. Woodcock told her he had always imagined Hartley would be terrified of facing death, but that he had calmly accepted its arrival. It was lunch time when Joan arrived at the flat. Hartley was sitting at his desk, a pen in his hand. 'He couldn't stop writing. I felt if he stopped it would be the end of him.'[75] His ankles were so swollen that Joan wanted to lift his feet, 'but I couldn't overstep the mark, it would have been too intimate a thing.' They had lunch, but 'what could we say? We both knew it was going to be the last time.' Afterwards, when Joan was putting on her hat and coat, he asked his nurse to play the record of Schubert's Trout Quintet, which Joan had given to Hartley. She walked to his chair, and, standing behind him, rested her hands on his shoulders. Her tears ran on to her hands and he kissed them. 'I think now', she remembers, 'he must have been thinking of Emily Brontë.'

On the morning of 13 December Hartley's nurse sat down in the Rutland Gate flat and wrote to Joan:

> It will comfort you to know that I was with Mr Hartley, and he closed his eyes in sleep after I attended to him in the early morning hours, in complete comfort and without pain peacefully passed from us, his face having an expression of absolute and permanent peace ... A major novelist in our time has passed away, a great loss to many who loved him.[76]

It is somehow apt that at the last Hartley was in the company of a pleasant stranger.

Epilogue

THE OBITUARY COLUMNS acknowledged Hartley's place in the life
of literature to which he had devoted himself. David Cecil, writing
in tribute in *The Times*, described him as 'aware in himself of
unearthly immortal longings, not to be, as he realised, satisfied in
this world'. David Holloway wrote of the loss of 'one of the most
singular and most English voices among those writing today . . . he
knew a great deal about human relationships of many different kinds,
and within the limits that he set himself he wrote about them with a
skill that at moments touched on genuis.' Walter Allen spoke of
Eustace and Hilda as one of the finest and most accurate evocations
of boyhood and young manhood in English fiction, and of Hartley
as, within his limits, a consummate artist.

Seven people attended the Harrods' cremation at Golders Green
– Norah, Joan, Mary Wellesley, Ralph Ricketts' wife Margaret,
Patrick Woodcock, Hartley's male nurse and his cleaning lady from
Rutland Gate. Cecil told Norah he was too upset to attend. Joan sat
between Patrick Woodcock and Norah. It was the first time the two
women had met, and was the beginning of an enduring friendship.
Joan remained composed throughout the service, until the moment
came when the coffin slid away: 'All I could see was this dark, dark
tunnel.'[1] The ashes were not scattered. On 3 January, a memorial
service was held at Holy Trinity, Brompton. After the congregation
had sung 'Let saints on earth in concert sing', Jonathan Cecil read
from the Apocrypha, the Wisdom of Solomon, chapter 3. The
address, as Hartley would have wished, was given by David Cecil,
followed by the hymn 'God moves in a mysterious way'.

Hartley left no definitive will ('I haven't the will to make one', he
had told Joan). He had been preparing a new document, in which
Francis King was named as literary executor, but the matter had
never been resolved. In a will that dated from some years before,
Walter Allen had been appointed literary executor. The mass of
Hartley's manuscripts was given to Allen, who subsequently sold
them to the John Rylands University Library in Manchester. A claim

was made by a Mrs Sybil Dreda-Owen, who produced two wills said to have been made by Hartley in 1972 in which she and her daughter, Mrs Barbara Gordon-Hatje (whom she alleged Hartley had fathered), were left the entire estate. Mrs Dreda-Owen, who had an address in Garsington, said she had known Hartley for over thirty years, after their meeting in a tea-shop, and that their friendship was well known and documented. Their supposed child was known to him as Babette. But in a letter to Cecil, written in June 1971, Hartley said he had promised to dine with Mrs Dreda-Owen, 'a very, very strange woman . . . who lives at Garsington. She has a daughter, and they cling together, and to me, (literally, I mean), which must cause surprise at Claridge's.'[2]

The two women visited Norah at Fletton atttended by a priest. When Mrs Dreda-Owen and Norah talked, the priest walked in the garden; on his return he said he had 'lost' the will in some bushes. Norah was quite prepared to support any child of Hartley's – Joan had the feeling that she would have enjoyed doing so – but she demanded proof. Detectives were called in. Much depended on Hartley's whereabouts on the dates on which the new wills were supposed to have been written. The witnesses to the document had both died. Later it transpired that in 1970 Mrs Dreda-Owen had contested the will of the Revd Thomas Wilfred Liddle Caspersz. In 1983 she was to make a claim on the estate of no less a character than Dr John Bodkin Adams, who in 1957 had been cleared of murder. She was awarded £53,000.

Only in February 1979, seven years after Hartley's death, did Mrs Dreda-Owen withdraw her claim, leaving the way clear for the validity of the will submitted by Norah to be proved. Everything passed into her hands. She was faced with the difficulty of deciding what bequests should be made to which of Hartley's expectant circle. A cheque was sent to David Cecil.

There was difficulty in removing Hartley's male nurse and his wife from the flat at Rutland Gate. Hartley had been powerless to stop them from moving in. For Joan, the loss of Hartley was followed by another tragedy, the loss of her only child, Margaret. She was left with no other family. Hamilton's commitment to Hartley did not stop with his death. A final novel, *The Will and the Way*, its punctuation, according to Machell, of the sort that would make Eric Partridge think he had lived in vain, was published in April 1973. The *Times Literary Supplement* saw it as 'the work of an old man beginning to see the things of this world from a great distance'. A 'complete' edition of the stories (still missing those not included in the 'collected' edition) followed.

A final short story, 'The Ugly Picture', appeared in the Christmas edition of the *Spectator* a few days after Hartley's death. The tribute that accompanied it spoke of him as possessing 'the stoic and Olympian melancholy of a man who has faced and come to terms with worse things than death ... His life, he knew, was, in its way, tragic: and this his novels reflect. Their autobiographical content was high; he chose Venice, knowing marriage to be impossible. . . . His reputation seems certain to rise.'[3]

Is it too easy to see 'The Ugly Picture' as Hartley's epitaph? It rings in the mind as the perfect *envoi*, bringing together many of his obsessions. Here they are, the relationship between a brother and his older sister, the potency of water, the need to be the hero, the transfiguration of hideousness into beauty. It is the simplest of pieces. Rupert is a shy, sensitive boy of eight, with a domineering sister, Celia, aged ten. Rupert's friend, Matthew, whom he looks up to, has inherited an ugly painting depicting an angry crowd at the time of the French Revolution. Rupert is fearful of the picture, but Celia insists that he visits Matthew. On arrival, Rupert finds the house ransacked, the picture stolen and Matthew trussed up by the robbers. Running from the house to get Matthew a 'creamy' cake which he thinks will cheer him up, Rupert spots the thieves making off to sea in a boat. He jumps into another boat and pursues them. The thieves' vessel is smashed up by the waves, and Rupert's boat also overturns. He is saved by clinging on to the picture, which is itself dashed against the rocks. When he comes to, in Matthew's house, Rupert finds himself the hero of the hour. He is told that the 'ugly' picture was an overpainting of an earlier work. Speechless, Rupert stares on.

> He just stood, looking. All he knew was that the ugly picture had vanished and now, coming towards him out of the frame, was a glorious knight in armour, riding through a wood. Proudly his spear flashed in the sun. His white horse arched its neck; his armour glittered; while ahead of him through the trees a path wound up to a fairy castle, standing defiantly on the top of a hill.[4]

It is naïve, improbable stuff, creamy cakes and adventures and happy ending, the stuff of fairy tales. But the vision persists: a saviour in shining armour, riding on and upwards to a foreign country that promises only delight.

After Hartley's death, squatters moved into Avondale and lived there for four years. Meanwhile, the property was bought by an architect, Graham Bell, and his wife Maddie, who had plans to turn it into a nursing home. When the authorities decided the property was unsuitable for such use, the Bells transformed it into the Avondale Riverside Hotel. In September 1994 Maddie Bell appeared in the *Bath Chronicle*, complaining that work on the Batheaston bypass had ruined her business. The idyllic driveway had been purchased by the Department of Transport. Raw sewage was pouring out of a new sewer and man hole on to the lawns. The bank had collapsed into the river because of sheet piling work. Mrs Bell campaigned vociferously against the onslaught, bombarding the Department of Transport with letters that filled five files. Her plight was a classic example of the individual against the state. Hartley would have been proud of her. I wrote to Maddie Bell, asking to book a room at the hotel. The week after my visit to Bath, I was leaving for Venice. It was time to place some giant pieces of the jigsaw puzzle of Hartley's life.

As this book was nearing completion, I wondered how Norah would react to what I had written. I knew that since Hartley's death she had fiercely protected his life from prospective biographers. Many well-known writers had approached her; all were turned away or discouraged. Ursula Codrington, incensed at revelations about Hartley's sexuality that began to filter into print, made efforts to compile a collection of purely complimentary essays, at the same time as persuading Norah that another, more eminent, claimant to the biography should be spurned. She hoped that David Cecil might undertake it, but he did not. Had he done so, the result would probably have been enveloped in the mist he had successfully thrown over Hartley's work for a lifetime. His determination was that the biography should not fall into unsuitable hands. Even the most distinguished applicants he dismissed as 'dull' or 'lacking in perception'. Of course, in shielding Hartley's life he was also shielding his own.

After his father's death in 1986, Jonathan Cecil inherited the need to keep a biography at bay. On the second visit I paid to him, he disowned everything he had said at the first, of which I had made a careful transcript. In an effort to throw doubt on this book, he used the opportunity of speaking to a reporter from the *Evening Standard* to describe me as a 'chorus-boy', which caused hilarity to my friends and family. Francis King sent a riposte to the *Evening Standard* in which he explained that 'Adrian Wright neither looks nor behaves like a chorus-boy – unless it were in *Oklahoma*.' I might, he said, 'well be taken for a rugger player'. More hilarity. In the absence of fact, press reports began to appear in which Hartley was labelled a 'notorious homosexual'. He had once, apparently, been found at Renishaw in bed with the butler, who was reading the Bible to him. The sound of Norah turning in her grave was faintly audible.

When I wrote to Norah in 1992 asking if she would agree to my writing a biography of her brother, I was invited to lunch at Fletton Tower. Knowing her to be elderly and, from everything I had heard, of formidable character, I imagined our meeting would be brief and the answer (as it had been to so many before me) in the negative. We talked for six hours. 'What sort of book do you want to write?' she asked. I surprised myself by throwing all caution to the wind. 'I want to write a truthful book about Leslie', I replied. There followed one of those long pauses I came to know so well. Before we parted, she agreed that I might go ahead with such a book, but she was still uncertain about anybody having access to the mass of Hartley's papers in her possession. Weeks passed, until a letter arrived giving me her permission. 'I think that, on the whole', she wrote, 'you are a suitable person to write the book.' On my next visit to Fletton, I came away with carrier bags full of Hartley's letters and manuscripts.

It was early in October 1994 when I finally travelled to Bath to meet Derek Hayes and Robert Waller, two of the survivors of Hartley's life. At Bathford, Derek gave me the friendliest of welcomes – 'I was expecting an old man', he told me – and lunch at the Crown Inn. It pleased me to think that the teenager Derek had probably been one of the very few people to have seen Hartley at his happiest – alone and sculling across the Avon. Afterwards, Derek pointed out Hartley's favourite walk, and the seat on which he rested, overlooking the valley. As he drove me to Avondale, I wondered why Maddie Bell had not answered my letter. She came down from the house, thinking we might be enemies from the Department of Transport, and prepared to shoo us away. Derek introduced us. She told me she had written to me weeks before I had written to her. Our letters to one another had never arrived.

The following morning I returned to Avondale, and Maddie showed me over the house. We walked to the terrace across the lawn, spongy under our feet. After I had left the previous day waterpipes had burst and flooded the garden. 'There is a trauma every day', Maddie said. 'The house has a jinx on it, no doubt about it. I leave a gap in the diary every day for a disaster.'[5] The Quaker burial ground had been dug up, the remains removed to another site.

Maddie and the locals were determined that none of the stone would leave Avondale. Graham Bell's younger son made furniture with it, tables for the terrace, even an armchair hidden beneath a great tree in the furthermost corner of the garden. A local builder, Fred Bundey, stored the rest.

Maddie told me of the ghost she sees, perhaps two or three times a year, of a young man with sandy hair, wearing the uniform of a soldier in the Great War. She has seen him in the window of the breakfast room when she looks up from the garden, or standing on the terrace. Sometimes he sits at a table in the room, turning his head when she enters, but never looking directly at her. One guest suggested exorcism, but there is nothing malevolent about the young man; he belongs to Avondale. 'I couldn't imagine being anywhere else', said Maddie. 'The house gets hold of you. But you have to have had pain in your life to be able to cope with Avondale.'[6]

On my way back to East Anglia through an England at its loveliest in the October sun, I heard that Norah had died on 27 September at the age of ninety-one. I think what I felt most keenly was the passing of a great strength. I knew that never again would I go to Fletton Tower, helping her to carry through the lunches that Olive Gausden, who worked at the house for more than fifty-seven years, prepared for us, cheese dishes with whole eggs in them, wonderful nursery puddings the making of which remained a mystery to Norah to the end of her days. A few months before, on a spring day, we put her frame into the back of my car and drove to Alwalton. She stomped across the perilously uneven graveyard as we searched for Hartleys laid to rest there. 'There's one missing', she said, 'but I don't intend it to be there for a little time yet.'[7] Only now did I realise how she had entrusted me with Hartley's life. 'People *will* say Leslie was a *Fenland* writer', she said, 'but he was just as much a *Venetian* writer.' She smiled, dropping her head and lifting her eyes, a characteristic attitude. 'I hope you won't let me down.'[8]

I knew suddenly that with Norah's death the story, the book, the truth, was complete. It was, for me, a profoundly moving moment. I knew that the dead could not be hurt. 'They'll pull this house down when I'm gone', she told me.[9] Norah left her affairs in perfect order. She had made arrangements for her remaining dogs – 'these are my last' – to be cared for. According to her instruction, the family papers, including the great archive of Leslie Poles Hartley's life, were burned.

WORKS BY L. P. HARTLEY

(Dates of first British publication)

Night Fears and Other Stories (Putnam 1924)
Simonetta Perkins (Putnam 1925)
The Killing Bottle (Putnam 1932)
The Shrimp and the Anemone (Putnam 1944)
The Sixth Heaven (Putnam 1946)
Eustace and Hilda (Putnam 1947)
The Boat (Putnam 1949)
The Travelling Grave (Barrie 1951)
My Fellow Devils (Barrie 1951)
The Go-Between (Hamish Hamilton 1953)
The White Wand and Other Stories (Hamish Hamilton 1954)
A Perfect Woman (Hamish Hamilton 1955)
The Hireling (Hamish Hamilton 1957)
Facial Justice (Hamish Hamilton 1960)
Two for the River (Hamish Hamilton 1961)
The Brickfield (Hamish Hamilton 1964)
The Betrayal (Hamish Hamilton 1966)
The Novelist's Responsibility: Lectures and Essays (Hamish Hamilton 1967)
The Collected Short Stories of L. P. Hartley (Hamish Hamilton 1968)
Poor Clare (Hamish Hamilton 1968)
The Love-Adept (Hamish Hamilton 1969)
My Sister's Keeper (Hamish Hamilton 1970)
The Harness Room (Hamish Hamilton 1971)
Mrs Carteret Receives and Other Stories (Hamish Hamilton 1971)
The Collections (Hamish Hamilton 1972)
The Will and the Way (Hamish Hamilton 1973)
The Complete Short Stories of L. P. Hartley (Hamish Hamilton 1973)

NOTES

Introduction

1. Despite the absence of any biography, three substantial books have been written on Hartley's work: Peter Bien's *L. P. Hartley* (Chatto and Windus 1963), Anne Mulkeen's *Wild Thyme, Winter Lightning* (Hamish Hamilton 1974) and E. T. Jones' *L. P. Hartley* (Boston 1978). Jones gives a potted and frequently inaccurate account of Hartley's life in his opening chapter.
2. LPH to Kay Dick 11 January 1953.
3. Told to Peter Burton, mentioned in Burton's letter to author 26 February 1993.
4. The novelist Ralph Ricketts.
5. The writer concerned is identified in David Cecil's letters (in the possession of the author).
6. Jonathan Cecil in conversation with author.
7. The destruction of much of the Hartley archive is confirmed by Joan Hall.
8. Jonathan Cecil in conversation with author.
9. Joan Hall in conversation with author.
10. *The Brickfield* p. 193.

Chapter 1: LITTLE SAUSAGES, REALLY

1. Typescript at Fletton, undated.
2. *The Brickfield* p. 10.
3. Interview with LPH by Joan Hurford in *Peterborough Standard* 25 March 1966.
4. Ibid.
5. MS at Fletton, undated.
6. Norah Hartley in conversation with author.
7. 'Three Wars' MS at Fletton, undated.
8. Ragtime song by American composers Lewis F. Muir and Maurice Abrahams. Written in 1912, it was made popular in Britain in 'Hullo Ragtime' at the London Hippodrome, sung by Lew Hearn and Bonita.
9. John Bark to Earl Fitzwilliam 29 May 1824.
10. Earl Fitzwilliam to John Bark 4 June 1824.
11. MS of lecture by Harry Hartley at Fletton 1938.
12. Ibid.
13. Ibid.
14. *The Brickfield* p. 13.

15. Norah Hartley in conversation with author.
16. Ibid.
17. The family portraits were hung on the great staircase at Fletton Tower. In her will, Norah made bequests of them to members of her family.
18. *The Brickfield* p. 48.
19. Norah Hartley in conversation with author.
20. The information relating to the Peterborough brickmaking is largely taken from Richard Hillier, *Clay that Burns: a history of the Fletton Brick Industry* (London Brick Co. Ltd 1981).
21. Harry Hartley MS at Fletton, undated.
22. *The Betrayal* p. 22.
23. Elizabeth Bowen to LPH 21 October 1952.
24. *The Betrayal* p. 69.
25. Norah Hartley in conversation with author.
26. Ibid. p. 15.
27. 'Three Wars' MS.
28. Ibid.
29. Ibid.
30. LPH to Peter Bien 16 October 1957.
31. 'The novelist L. P. Hartley talks about his childhood to Derek Parker', *Listener* 31 August 1972.
32. *The Brickfield* p. 90.

Chapter 2: TO BE THE HERO

1. MS at Fletton, undated.
2. Ibid.
3. Ibid.
4. Norah remembered the existence of this play, but nothing of it has survived.
5. Organist at Peterborough cathedral.
6. Norah Hartley in conversation with author.
7. Bessie Hartley to LPH 9 October 1908.
8. LPH to Bessie Hartley 10 October 1908.
9. LPH to Bessie Hartley 17 November 1908.
10. LPH to Bessie Hartley 7 November 1908.
11. LPH to Bessie Hartley 16 August 1909.
12. Frank Delaney, *Betjeman Country* (Paladin 1985) p. 194.
13. *The Brickfield* p. 10.
14. J. D. Holt to Harry Hartley 13 May 1909.
15. LPH to Bessie Hartley 6 June 1909.
16. MS at Fletton, undated, probably 1910.
17. 'The novelist L. P. Hartley talks about his childhood to Derek Parker', *Listener* 31 August 1972.
18. C. H. B. Kitchin to LPH 9 January 1942.
19. LPH to Bessie Hartley (unspecified) August 1910.

20. LPH to Bessie Hartley 8 October 1911.
21. 'The novelist L. P. Hartley talks about his childhood to Derek Parker', *Listener* 31 August 1972.
22. LPH to Bessie Hartley 2 February 1913.
23. LPH to Bessie Hartley 14 December 1913.
24. MS at Fletton, undated.
25. LPH to Bessie Hartley 26 November 1911.
26. Jonathan Cecil in conversation with author.
27. Published by Heath, Cranton and Ouseley.
28. *The Novelist's Responsibility* p. 134.
29. Ibid. p. 55.
30. Ibid. p. 70.
31. LPH to Peter Bien 20 November 1956.
32. *The Novelist's Responsibility* p. 113.
33. Ibid. p. 181.
34. Ibid. p. 182.
35. 'The Conformer' by LPH in *The Old School: essays by divers hands*, edited by Graham Greene (Oxford University Press 1984) p. 66.
36. *The Shrimp and the Anemone* p. 40.
37. LPH to Bessie Hartley (unspecified) 1912.
38. After Norah's death, her executors filled six bin-liners with Hartley's letters to Bessie. All were destroyed.
39. LPH to Bessie Hartley (unspecified) 1914.
40. 'Three Wars' MS at Fletton, undated.
41. LPH to Bessie Hartley 17 October 1915.
42. MS at Fletton, undated.
43. LPH to Bessie Hartley, undated, probably 1915.
44. Ibid.
45. Unknown to Kathleen Lund 10 October 1915.
46. Kathleen Lund to LPH 10 November 1915.
47. Kathleen Lund to LPH 19 December 1915.
48. 'Three Wars' MS.
49. LPH to Bessie Hartley 5 February 1916.
50. 'Three Wars' MS.
51. Harry Clifford Pilsbury's portrait of Leslie in khaki is in the author's possession.
52. 'Three Wars' MS.
53. Ibid.
54. LPH to Harry Hartley 21 December 1917.
55. Treves' association with the 'Elephant Man' has made his name familiar to a more recent generation.
56. LPH to Harry Hartley 21 December 1917.
57. Kathleen Lund to LPH 19 December 1915.
58. Both books were published by Heath, Cranton and Ouseley.
59. Kathleen Lund to LPH 10 November 1915.

Chapter 3: A PLACE AT THE FIRESIDE

1. LPH to Bessie Hartley 25 July 1919.
2. Kathleen Lund to Bessie Hartley (unspecified) 1919.
3. LPH to Bessie Hartley 15 June 1920. A pastiche on the satirist Thomas Brown:

> I do not love you, Dr Fell;
> But why I cannot tell;
> But this I know full well,
> I do not love you Dr Fell.

Dr John Fell (1625–86) was Dean of Christ Church, Oxford, and Bishop of Oxford.
4. LPH to Bessie Hartley 21 March 1921.
5. Cyril Bailey, *Francis Fortescue Urquhart* (1936).
6. LPH to Bessie Hartley 21 October 1919.
7. *The Sixth Heaven* p. 239.
8. Ibid.
9. LPH to Bessie Hartley 28 November 1919.
10. Ibid.
11. 'Some Aspects of Gregariousness', *The Novelist's Responsibility* p. 193.
12. LPH to Bessie Hartley, undated.
13. 'David's Closest Friend', *David Cecil: a portrait by his friends* (Dovecote Press 1990) p. 72.
14. Ibid. p. 73.
15. Ibid. p. 75.
16. LPH to Bessie Hartley, undated.
17. LPH to Bessie Hartley 26 January 1920.
18. 'Talent', *Night Fears and Other Stories* p. 35.
19. Ibid.
20. LPH to Bessie Hartley 22 February 1920.
21. No records of this society can be traced at Balliol College, Oxford.
22. LPH to Bessie Hartley 25 October 1920.
23. LPH to Bessie Hartley 6 June 1920.
24. Ibid.
25. LPH to Bessie Hartley 20 July 1920.
26. Ibid.
27. LPH to Bessie Hartley 25 July 1920.
28. Ibid.
29. LPH to Bessie Hartley 27 July 1920.
30. LPH to Bessie Hartley 28 July 1920.
31. Ibid. Bessie had a passion for mountainous country, and delighted in visits (when health permitted) to the Lake District.
32. LPH to Bessie Hartley Easter Sunday 1922.
33. MBL to Elizabeth Haldane 29 February 1916.
34. C. H. B. Kitchin to LPH 7 October 1921.
35. Kathleen Lund to LPH (unspecified) 1921.

36. Kathleen Lund to LPH 26 December 1921.
37. LPH to Bessie Hartley 29 July 1922.
38. HBH to Bessie Hartley, undated.
39. C. H. B. Kitchin, *Mr Balcony* (Hogarth Press 1927) p. 16.
40. Ibid. p. 34.
41. Ibid. p. 60.
42. Ibid. p. 162.
43. Ibid. p. 62.
44. LPH to Bessie Hartley 27 August 1922.
45. LPH to Bessie Hartley 14 September 1922.
46. LPH to Bessie Hartley 17 September 1922.
47. Ibid.
48. *Mrs Carteret Receives and Other Stories* p. 4.
49. Marie Belloc Lowndes to LPH 10 June 1947.
50. LPH to Bessie Hartley 2 January 1923.
51. Elizabeth Bibesco to Bessie Hartley 16 October 1923.
52. Virginia Woolf, *Diary of Virginia Woolf*, vol. 2, *1920–24* (Hogarth Press 1978) p. 243.
53. Ibid.
54. MS at Fletton, undated.
55. LPH to Ottoline Morrell 15 March 1923.
56. 'Disparity in Despair', *Oxford Poetry* (Basil Blackwell 1922) p. 10.
57. LPH to Ottoline Morrell 26 March 1923.
58. LPH to Bessie Hartley 23 June 1923.
59. Norah Hartley, letter to author 1 November 1993.
60. Norah Hartley in conversation with author.
61. Ibid.
62. Evelyn John Strachey 1901–63, writer and Labour MP.
63. *Sketch* 6 November 1929.
64. LPH to David Cecil 7 June 1931.
65. L. A. G. Strong to LPH 30 September 1929.
66. J. B. Priestley to LPH August 1929.
67. Hugh Walpole to LPH 1 July 1927.
68. Hugh Walpole to LPH 2 September 1931.
69. C. H. B. Kitchin to LPH 26 June 1925.
70. Pamela Hansford Johnson to LPH 2 February 1944.
71. Louis Golding to LPH 6 December 1950.
72. LPH to Bessie Hartley 23 September 1923.
73. LPH to Ottoline Morrell 19 June 1923.
74. LPH to Bessie Hartley 13 December 1923.
75. 'The Island', *Night Fears and Other Stories* p. 24.
76. 'The Telephone Call', *Night Fears and Other Stories* p. 53.
77. Ibid. p. 50.
78. 'The Last Time', *Night Fears and Other Stories*, p. 214.
79. Ibid. p. 217.

80. 'A Tonic', *Night Fears and Other Stories* p. 174.
81. 'St George and the Dragon', *Night Fears and Other Stories* p. 80.
82. LPH to Bessie Hartley, undated.
83. LPH to Ethel Sands 19 October 1925.
84. *Saturday Review* 7 November 1925.
85. *Calendar of Modern Letters* December 1925.
86. MS at Fletton.
87. Ibid.
88. *Simonetta Perkins* p. 46.
89. Ibid. p. 24.
90. Ibid. p. 54.
91. C. H. B. Kitchin to LPH 2 November 1925.

Chapter 4: THE VENETIAN YEARS

1. LPH to Hugh Walpole 27 September 1927.
2. 'The White Wand', *The White Wand and Other Stories* p. 297.
3. *The Novelist's Responsibility* p. 216.
4. Ibid. p. 211.
5. LPH to David Cecil (unspecified) 1927.
6. LPH to Bessie Hartley 12 May 1928.
7. LPH to David Cecil 31 October 1927.
8. LPH to Bessie Hartley 12 October 1927.
9. LPH to Ethel Sands 7 November 1927.
10. LPH to David Cecil 18 November 1931.
11. Ibid.
12. The Bakers' and Hartley's visits to Casa Baker feature frequently in Hartley's correspondence, but I have been unable to identify the family.
13. LPH to Ethel Sands 7 November 1927.
14. LPH to Ethel Sands 2 July 1928.
15. LPH to Elizabeth Bowen 12 April 1929.
16. LPH to Ethel Sands 12 May 1930.
17. Ibid.
18. Ibid.
19. LPH to Elizabeth Iddesleigh 18 November 1947.
20. The nomenclature of Myers' tetralogy is confusing. *The Root and the Flower* comprises three novels: *The Near and the Far*, *Prince Jali* and *Rajah Amar*. A fourth novel, *The Pool of Vishnu*, was added to the original trilogy, all four novels then known as *The Near and the Far*.
21. David Cecil to LPH (unspecified) 1932.
22. LPH to Ethel Sands 25 August 1932.
23. LPH to L. A. G. Strong 23 October 1932.
24. LPH to Ethel Sands 25 August 1932.
25. LPH to Ottoline Morrell 21 December 1932.

26. 'Mr Blandfoot's Picture', originally in *The Killing Bottle*, reprinted in *The White Wand and Other Stories* p. 351.
27. Ibid. p. 356.
28. 'A Visitor from Down Under', originally in *The Killing Bottle*, reprinted in *The Travelling Grave*, reprinted in *The Collected Short Stories of L. P. Hartley* p. 73.
29. Ibid.
30. 'A Change of Ownership', originally in *The Killing Bottle*, reprinted in *The Travelling Grave*, reprinted in *The Collected Short Stories of L. P. Hartley* p. 167.
31. Ibid. p. 174.
32. Ibid. p. 173.
33. 'Conrad and the Dragon', originally in *The Killing Bottle*, reprinted in *The Travelling Grave*, reprinted in *The Collected Short Stories of L. P. Hartley* p. 195.
34. Ibid. p. 200.
35. Ibid. p. 208.
36. Ibid. p. 204.
37. Ibid. p. 208.
38. LPH to Bessie Hartley 1 April 1933.
39. LPH to Bessie Hartley 7 April 1933.
40. LPH to Marie Belloc Lowndes 20 April 1933.
41. LPH to David Horner 31 March 1940.
42. Ibid.
43. LPH to Ethel Sands 27 April 1933.
44. LPH to Marie Belloc Lowndes 20 April 1933.
45. LPH to Ottoline Morrell 18 October 1934.
46. LPH to Ottoline Morrell 30 April 1933.
47. Ibid.
48. LPH to Marie Belloc Lowndes 20 April 1933.
49. LPH to Bessie Hartley 30 May 1933.
50. LPH to Bessie Hartley 10 June 1933.
51. LPH to Ethel Sands 4 April 1934.
52. LPH to Ottoline Morrell 28 November 1934.
53. LPH to Bessie Hartley 13 May 1934.
54. LPH to Ethel Sands 3 August 1934.
55. LPH to Ottoline Morrell 28 May 1934.
56. LPH to Ottoline Morrell 11 June 1934.
57. Ibid.
58. LPH to Ottoline Morrell 10 September 1934.
59. Ibid.
60. LPH to Ottoline Morrell 28 November 1934.
61. Cynthia Asquith to LPH 12 April 1935.
62. LPH to Elizabeth Bowen 12 August 1935.
63. LPH to Marie Belloc Lowndes 26 June 1935.

64. LPH to Marie Belloc Lowndes 21 June 1935.
65. LPH to Ethel Sands 9 June 1935.
66. Ibid.
67. LPH to Bessie Hartley 1 August 1935.
68. Ernest Saltmarshe to LPH 29 August 1935.
69. LPH to Marie Belloc Lowndes 3 November 1936.
70. MS at Fletton, undated.
71. Ibid.
72. LPH to Marie Belloc Lowndes 6 May 1937.
73. LPH to Ottoline Morrell 16 August 1937.
74. Ibid.
75. LPH to Ethel Sands 21 November 1936.
76. LPH to Ottoline Morrell 16 October 1936.
77. LPH to Ottoline Morrell 16 August 1937.
78. MS tribute to Ottoline Morrell at Fletton.
79. LPH to Ottoline Morrell 28 June 1934.
80. MS tribute to Ottoline Morrell at Fletton.
81. LPH to Marie Belloc Lowndes 5 May 1938.
82. LPH to Marie Belloc Lowndes 1 November 1938.
83. LPH to Bessie Hartley 10 November 1938.
84. LPH to Ethel Sands 14 November 1938.
85. LPH to Bessie Hartley 27 November 1938.
86. LPH to Bessie Hartley 15 November 1938.
87. LPH to Bessie Hartley 11 June 1939.
88. LPH to David Horner 27 June 1939.

Chapter 5: WHY DO WE HAVE TO HAVE A WAR?

1. MS of lecture at Fletton, undated.
2. LPH to Kathleen Lund 5 September 1939.
3. Walter Allen *As I Walked Down New Grub Street* (Heinemann 1981) p. 161.
4. LPH to Bessie Hartley (unspecified) 1939.
5. Charlie Holt to LPH, undated.
6. LPH to Bessie Hartley 9 May 1940.
7. LPH to Bessie Hartley 14 May 1940.
8. LPH to Bessie Hartley 23 June 1940. Hartley spoke admiringly of Mussolini, and told Joan Hall that he considered Hitler a very clever man.
9. LPH to Bessie Hartley 23 June 1940.
10. LPH to Kathleen Lund 12 November 1939.
11. LPH to Bessie Hartley 5 July 1940.
12. LPH to Bessie Hartley 11 April 1940.
13. Ibid.
14. LPH to Bessie Hartley 14 October 1940.
15. LPH to Bessie Hartley 3 September 1941.

16. LPH to Harry Hartley (unspecified) 1941.
17. LPH to Bessie Hartley 30 July 1941.
18. LPH to Bessie Hartley 22 March 1941.
19. LPH to Ethel Sands 15 September 1941.
20. LPH to Bessie Hartley 27 April 1941.
21. LPH to Bessie Hartley 18 February 1941.
22. LPH to Bessie Hartley 26 June 1941.
23. LPH to Bessie Hartley 30 July 1941.
24. LPH to Bessie Hartley 21 October 1941.
25. Ibid.
26. Jonathan Cecil in conversation with author.
27. LPH to Bessie Hartley 9 October 1942.
28. Ibid.
29. Ibid.
30. In 1903 a Mr Wall of Stratford-upon-Avon published a postcard depicting the successful novelist in her gondola, propelled by her private gondolier.
31. LPH to Bessie Hartley 23 May 1942.
32. LPH to Ottoline Morrell 10 August 1934.
33. LPH to Bessie Hartley Whit Monday 1942.
34. Constant Huntington to LPH 17 April 1942.
35. Ibid.
36. Ibid.
37. LPH to Bessie Hartley 22 October 1942.
38. LPH to Bessie Hartley 22 August 1943.
39. Ibid.
40. Margaret Kennedy to LPH 28 February 1944.
41. LPH to Bessie Hartley (unspecified) 1943.
42. LPH to Bessie Hartley 10 August 1943.
43. Constant Huntington to LPH 12 October 1943.
44. LPH to Bessie Hartley 21 November 1943.
45. Nancy Mitford to Violet Hammersley 14 January 1958.
46. LPH to Bessie Hartley 18 November 1943.
47. *The Shrimp and the Anemone* p. 35.
48. Paul Bloomfield, *L. P. Hartley* (British Council 1962) p. 11.
49. *The Shrimp and the Anemone* p. 68.
50. Ibid. p. 85.
51. Ibid. p. 102.
52. Ibid. p. 198.
53. Ibid. pp. 151–2.
54. LPH to Bessie Hartley 4 July 1942.
55. Kathleen Lund to LPH 29 March 1925.
56. Constant Huntington to LPH 22 March 1944.
57. Constant Huntington to LPH 30 May 1944.
58. LPH to Christabel Aberconway 10 September 1944.

59. Ibid.
60. LPH to Ethel Sands 26 May 1944.
61. LPH to Bessie Hartley 16 January 1944.
62. LPH to Ethel Sands 24 October 1944.
63. Constant Huntington to LPH 17 April 1944.
64. *The Novelist's Responsibility* p. 145.
65. Kay Dick, 'Dancing with Death', *Books and Bookmen* February 1974.
66. C. H. B. Kitchin to LPH 18 July 1941.
67. Ibid.
68. *Olive E* was published by Constable, and *Death of my Aunt* by the Hogarth Press.
69. C. H. B. Kitchin, *Birthday Party* (Constable 1938) p. 125.
70. Ibid. p. 126.
71. C. H. B. Kitchin to LPH 21 December 1941.
72. C. H. B. Kitchin to LPH 18 July 1945.
73. C. H. B. Kitchin to LPH 15 May 1944.
74. C. H. B. Kitchin to LPH 17 July 1944.
75. C. H. B. Kitchin to LPH 17 July 1944.
76. C. H. B. Kitchin, *The Auction Sale* (1949; reprinted Chatto and Windus 1971) p. 190.
77. C. H. B. Kitchin to LPH 18 July 1945.

Chapter 6: ENDINGS AND BEGINNINGS

1. LPH to Bessie Hartley 14 March 1945.
2. LPH to David Horner 12 March 1945.
3. LPH to Ethel Sands 6 June 1945.
4. LPH to Bessie Hartley 2 June 1945.
5. LPH to Christabel Aberconway 12 December 1944.
6. LPH to Elizabeth Bowen 6 December 1944.
7. Constant Huntington to LPH 19 September 1944.
8. Constant Huntington to LPH 23 January 1945.
9. Constant Huntington to LPH 19 April 1945.
10. LPH to David Horner 15 April 1945.
11. LPH to Bessie Hartley 28 July 1945.
12. LPH to Bessie Hartley 13 October 1945.
13. LPH to David Horner 14 December 1945.
14. Ibid.
15. Ibid. A copy of *The Go-Between* is in Britten's library. Despite its supreme suitability as the material for a Britten opera, there is no record of him ever having considered its adaptation.
16. LPH to David Horner 14 December 1945.
17. LPH to Bessie Hartley 21 May 1946.
18. LPH to Ethel Sands 15 May 1946.
19. LPH to David Horner 31 March 1946.
20. *The Sixth Heaven* p. 250.

21. Ibid. p. 273.
22. Ibid. p. 389.
23. Ibid. p. 405.
24. Ibid. p. 394.
25. LPH to Bessie Hartley 11 October 1946.
26. Ibid.
27. LPH to Bessie Hartley 30 January 1947.
28. LPH to Bessie Hartley 27 February 1947.
29. LPH to David Horner 21 January 1948.
30. Ibid.
31. Derek Hayes, letter to author 18 August 1994.
32. Ibid.
33. Robert Waller in conversation with author.
34. Ibid.
35. Ibid.
36. Ibid.
37. LPH to Ethel Sands 8 January 1947.
38. LPH to C. H. B. Kitchin 27 August 1947.
39. LPH to Ethel Sands 10 June 1947.
40. LPH to Ethel Sands 22 June 1947.
41. LPH to Ethel Sands 10 June 1947.
42. LPH to Bessie Hartley 8 June 1947.
43. LPH to Bessie Hartley 28 May 1947.
44. Donald Elder to LPH 23 January 1947.
45. Walter Allen *As I Walked Down New Grub Street* (Heinemann 1981) p. 163.
46. P. H. Newby, *The Novel: 1945–50* (British Council 1951) p. 36.
47. Edith Sitwell to LPH 9 August 1947.
48. C. H. B. Kitchin to LPH 27 December 1946.
49. C. H. B. Kitchin to LPH 24 August 1947.
50. *Eustace and Hilda* p. 672.
51. Ibid. p. 690.
52. Ibid. p. 724.
53. Ibid. p. 736.
54. Ibid. p. 657.
55. Ibid. p. 661.
56. *A Perfect Woman* p. 10.
57. In conversation, Norah Hartley told Joan Hall that Enid had once been in love. The identity of the loved one is unknown, as are any other details. According to Norah, Enid longed to have a family.
58. *Eustace and Hilda* p. 655.

Chapter 7: THE DISSATISFACTION WITH TRUTH

1. LPH to Bessie Hartley 7 August 1947.
2. LPH to Bessie Hartley 9 March 1948.

3. Constant Huntington to LPH 22 June 1948.
4. Constant Huntington to LPH 10 June 1948.
5. LPH to David Horner 29 April 1948.
6. LPH to David Horner 18 May 1948.
7. LPH to David Horner 28 May 1948.
8. C. H. B. Kitchin to LPH 27 December 1946.
9. LPH to Ethel Sands 19 February 1948.
10. LPH to Bessie Hartley 17 February 1948.
11. Ibid.
12. LPH to Bessie Hartley 18 February 1948.
13. LPH to Bessie Hartley 4 April 1948.
14. LPH to Bessie Hartley 9 June 1948.
15. LPH to Christabel Aberconway 23 September 1948.
16. Christabel Aberconway *A Wiser Woman?* (Hutchinson 1966) p. 33.
17. Ibid.
18. Ibid. p. 42.
19. Ibid. p. 157.
20. LPH to Ethel Sands 30 September 1948.
21. LPH to David Horner 14 April 1949.
22. Constant Huntington to LPH 4 April 1949.
23. Constant Huntington to LPH 5 April 1949.
24. LPH to Ethel Sands 10 May 1949.
25. Millicent, Duchess of Sutherland to LPH 16 May 1949.
26. LPH to Ethel Sands 10 May 1949.
27. LPH to Enid Hartley 9 June 1949.
28. Ibid.
29. LPH to David Horner 29 September 1949.
30. Constant Huntington to LPH 25 September 1949.
31. Edith Sitwell to LPH 8 February 1950.
32. Walter Allen, *As I Walked Down New Grub Street* (Heinemann 1981) p. 164.
33. Constant Huntington to LPH 5 February 1950.
34. *The Boat* p. 105.
35. Paul Bloomfield, *L. P. Hartley* (British Council 1962) p. 19.

Chapter 8: The Go-Between

1. LPH to Ethel Sands 23 September 1950.
2. LPH to Ethel Sands 27 August 1950.
3. LPH to Ethel Sands 23 September 1950.
4. LPH to Roderick Meiklejohn 23 June 1951.
5. LPH to Harry Hartley 17 April 1951.
6. *My Fellow Devils* p. 366.
7. Ibid. p. 391.
8. Ibid. p. 392.
9. Ibid. p. 402.

10. Ibid. p. 412.
11. Ibid. p. 413.
12. Ibid. p. 242.
13. DH to Christabel Aberconway 30 October 1951.
14. *The Go-Between* p. 9.
15. Ibid. p. 10.
16. LPH to Enid Hartley 17 June 1952.
17. MS at Fletton, undated.
18. Ibid.
19. Ibid.
20. 'Too Much Compassion?' (*National Book League*, no. 288, October 1954) pp. 197–9.
21. LPH to Hamish Hamilton 12 December 1954.
22. Norah Hartley in conversation with author.
23. MS at Fletton, undated.
24. *The Go-Between* p. 296.
25. Ibid.
26. *The Brickfield* p. 61.
27. *The Hireling* p. 27.
28. Ibid.
29. LPH to Peter Bien 15 February 1959.
30. LPH to Hamish Hamilton 5 May 1953.
31. LPH to Hamish Hamilton 6 July 1953.
32. David Cecil, *Sunday Times* 20 December 1953.
33. David Cecil, *Times Literary Supplement* 6 November 1953.
34. Reader's report for Knopf (unspecified) 1953.
35. Hamish Hamilton to Blanche Knopf 16 September 1953.
36. LPH to Blanche Knopf 2 July 1954.
37. Alfred Knopf to Hamish Hamilton 8 December 1953.
38. LPH to Blanche Knopf 17 December 1953.
39. *New York Times* 18 August 1954.
40. *New York Times* 25 July 1954.
41. *New York Herald* 25 July 1954.
42. LPH to David Horner 29 June 1948.

Chapter 9: THE SLEEPING BEAUTY OF BATH

1. LPH to Christabel Aberconway 24 September 1953.
2. 'The Sleeping Sewer', *Time and Tide* 3 December 1955.
3. LPH to Enid Hartley 21 July 1953.
4. C. H. B. Kitchin to LPH 26 May 1953.
5. C. H. B. Kitchin to LPH 14 March 1954.
6. C. H. B. Kitchin to LPH 6 August 1954.
7. 'The White Wand', *The White Wand*, p. 272.
8. Ibid. p. 283.
9. Ibid. p. 288.

10. Ibid. p. 293.
11. Ibid. p. 285.
12. Ibid. p. 293.
13. Ibid. p. 302.
14. 'W. S.', *The White Wand* p. 385.
15. Ibid. p. 386.
16. 'A Rewarding Experience', *The White Wand* p. 381.
17. John Calmann *The Letters of John Calmann 1951–1980* (John Murray 1986) entry of 15 June 1954.
18. LPH to Ethel Sands 18 July 1954.
19. LPH to Ethel Sands 12 August 1954.
20. LPH to Hamish Hamilton 24 October 1953.
21. LPH to Hamish Hamilton 20 February 1955.
22. LPH to Roderick Meiklejohn Good Friday 1955.
23. LPH to Christabel Aberconway 4 December 1954.
24. Ibid.
25. LPH to David Cecil 21 December 1971.
26. *The Brickfield* p. 71.
27. Ibid. p. 79.
28. *The Betrayal* p. 176.
29. Ibid. p. 158.
30. Published by Secker and Warburg in 1956.
31. C. H. B. Kitchin to LPH 9 August 1955.
32. C. H. B. Kitchin, *Ten Pollitt Place* (Secker and Warburg 1957) p. 30.
33. LPH's foreword to Kitchin's *A Short Walk in Williams Park* (Chatto and Windus 1971) pp. xi–xiii
34. C. H. B. Kitchin to LPH 18 January 1956.
35. John Sutro to LPH 3 November 1955.
36. Israel M. Berman to John Sutro 6 December 1955.
37. *Listener* 13 October 1955.
38. *New Statesman* 1 October 1955.
39. LPH to Hamish Hamilton 3 October 1955.
40. LPH to Kay Dick 24 October 1955.
41. *A Perfect Woman* pp. 314–15.
42. C. H. B. Kitchin to LPH 25 September 1955.
43. Memo to Blanche Knopf 13 June 1955.
44. Hamish Hamilton to Blanche Knopf 22 June 1955.
45. LPH to Blanche Knopf 22 June 1955.
46. Ibid.
47. *Saturday Review* 17 March 1956.
48. LPH to Hamish Hamilton (unspecified) April 1956.
49. LPH to Hamish Hamilton 18 September 1956.
50. LPH to Hamish Hamilton 12 October 1956, quoting letter from David Cecil to LPH of 10 October 1956.
51. Hamish Hamilton to LPH 10 November 1956.

52. C. H. B. Kitchin to LPH 23 August 1956.

53. LPH to Christabel Aberconway 17 September 1956.

54. LPH to Christabel Aberconway 16 October 1956.

55. LPH to Ethel Sands 18 October 1956.

56. David Horner to Christabel Aberconway 28 November 1956.

57. Hamish Hamilton to LPH 19 December 1956.

58. LPH to Violet Hammersley 14 December 1956.

59. Knopf internal memo 28 May 1957.

60. Ibid.

61. Blanche Knopf to LPH 29 May 1957.

62. LPH to Blanche Knopf 8 June 1957.

63. LPH to Hamish Hamilton 1 August 1957.

64. Alfred Knopf to Blanche Knopf 19 August 1957.

65. LPH to Blanche Knopf 4 September 1957.

66. *The Hireling* pp. 24, 25. A film version of the novel, directed by Alan Bridges and featuring Robert Shaw and Sarah Miles, appeared in 1973. Hartley had read a draft of its screenplay and was anxious as to what his 'staid readers' would make of its explicitness.

67. *The Hireling* p. 26.

68. Ibid. p. 102.

69. Ibid. p. 220.

70. Ibid. p. 237.

71. Ibid. p. 238.

72. Ibid. p. 239.

73. Hartley's elimination of the swans is detailed in a letter to Enid Hartley (Easter Monday 1958). In 'Sin and Swans', *Time and Tide* 6 December 1958, he gives an account of his various battles against the birds. He tried squirting paraffin at them. An RSPCA officer told him 'I suppose you realise that it is my duty to protect the swan against you, not you against the swan.' The article does not include any mention of Hartley's final solution.

Chapter 10: RUNNING SHADOWS

1. LPH to Ethel Sands 19 September 1957.

2. LPH to Enid Hartley 10 June 1958.

3. C. H. B. Kitchin to LPH 14 August 1958.

4. LPH to Peter Bien 10 December 1958.

5. Hamish Hamilton to LPH 3 January 1959.

6. Walter Allen to LPH 18 January 1959.

7. LPH to David Horner 18 January 1959.

8. LPH to Christabel Aberconway 16 April 1959.

9. Ibid.

10. LPH to David Horner 18 January 1959.

11. LP to Enid Hartley 14 July 1959.

12. LP to Christabel Aberconway 19 August 1959.

13. LPH to David Horner 1 February 1960.
14. LPH to Christabel Aberconway 19 August 1959.
15. LPH to Enid Hartley 5 February 1960.
16. LPH to Christabel Aberconway 24 November 1959.
17. LPH to Fredoon Kabraji (unspecified) 1959.
18. Sybil E. Bowen to LPH 23 August 1961.
19. Ibid.
20. Sybil E. Bowen to LPH 16 September 1961.
21. Mabel Lewis to LPH 1 December 1954.
22. Mabel Lewis to LPH 27 January 1956.
23. Mabel Lewis to LPH 14 February 1956.
24. Ibid.
25. Mabel Lewis to LPH 19 April 1956.
26. Mabel Lewis to LPH 11 October 1956.
27. Mabel Lewis to LPH 4 May 1957.
28. Mabel Lewis to LPH (unspecified) 1962.
29. LPH to Hamish Hamilton 11 February 1956.
30. Mabel Lewis to LPH 3 January 1969.
31. Typescript of 'For Amusement Only' at Fletton.
32. Ibid.
33. Ibid.
34. *Facial Justice* p. 254.
35. Ibid. p. 255.
36. Ibid. p. 256.
37. LPH to Peter Bien 5 May 1962.
38. LPH to Peter Bien 28 July 1960.
39. Memo from Roger Machell to Hamish Hamilton 13 June 1960.
40. Memo from Roger Machell to Hamish Hamilton 25 July 1960.
41. Memo from Roger Machell to Hamish Hamilton 23 May 1961.
42. LPH to Christabel Aberconway 14 August 1960.
43. David Horner to LPH 14 September 1960.
44. LPH to Christabel Aberconway 29 August 1960.
45. Henry Lamb to LPH 1 January 1949.
46. Valentine Lamb to LPH 17 October 1960.
47. In 1960 Gollancz published Daphne du Maurier's *The Infernal World of Branwell Brontë*.
48. LPH to Hamish Hamilton 23 May 1961.
49. 'Two for the River', *Two for the River* p. 26.
50. 'The Face', *Two for the River* pp. 45–6.
51. LPH to Peter Bien 31 May 1962.
52. 'The Pylon', *Two for the River* p. 204.
53. Ibid. p. 205.
54. Ibid. p. 210.
55. Ibid. p. 213.
56. Ibid. p. 206.

57. Ibid. p. 216.
58. Ibid. p. 219.
59. Ibid. p. 221.
60. Ibid. p. 223.
61. *The Brickfield* p. 10.
62. David Horner to LPH, undated.

Chapter 11: THE 'M'

1. LPH to Peter Bien 5 May 1962.
2. LPH to Christabel Aberconway 13 January 1963.
3. LPH to Hamish Hamilton 13 June 1963.
4. LPH to Hamish Hamilton 4 August 1963.
5. LPH to Christabel Aberconway 6 September 1963.
6. LPH to Hamish Hamilton 24 October 1963.
7. C. H. B. Kitchin to LPH 11 June 1963.
8. LPH to Hamish Hamilton 19 May 1964.
9. LPH to Hamish Hamilton 21 May 1964.
10. Paul Bloomfield, *L. P. Hartley* (British Council 1962, revised 1970). p. 25.
11. *The Brickfield* p. 25.
12. Ibid. p. 146.
13. Ibid. p. 156.
14. Roger Radford to LPH 7 September 1963.
15. LPH to Hamish Hamilton 23 July 1964.
16. Memo from Roger Machell to Hamish Hamilton 10 September 1964.
17. LPH to Hamish Hamilton 5 November 1964.
18. Ibid.
19. LPH to Peter Bien 17 July 1964.
20. LPH to Christabel Aberconway 28 April 1965.
21. LPH to Christabel Aberconway 14 August 1965.
22. LPH to Christabel Aberconway 28 April 1965.
23. Irving Wardle, *Observer* 4 September 1966.
24. Rivers Scott, *Sunday Telegraph* 4 September 1966.
25. LPH to Christabel Aberconway 18 August 1966.
26. *The Betrayal* p. 234.
27. Ibid. p. 142.
28. Ibid. p. 203.
29. LPH to Jocelyn Brooke 31 September 1966.

Chapter 12: A RESPONSIBILITY OF MORALS

1. Joan Hall in conversation with author.
2. Ibid.
3. David Horner to Georgia Sitwell 8 August 1964.
4. Frank Magro to Christabel Aberconway 2 August 1966.
5. LPH to Christabel Aberconway 31 July 1966.

6. Lady Berkeley in conversation with author.
7. LPH to Christabel Aberconway 22 October 1966.
8. LPH to Christabel Aberconway 5 June 1967.
9. LPH to Joan Hall 20 September 1967.
10. LPH to Christabel Aberconway 7 August 1968.
11. LPH to Norah Hartley 2 February 1969.
12. Joan Hall in conversation with author.
13. LPH to Joan Hall 30 April 1969.
14. LPH to Joan Hall 19 February 1967.
15. LPH to Hamish Hamilton 15 February 1967.
16. *The Novelist's Responsibility* p. 190.
17. C. H. B. Kitchin to LPH 2 December 1951.
18. C. H. B. Kitchin to LPH 15 September 1953.
19. *The Novelist's Responsibility* p. 17.
20. Nevill Coghill to Francis King 4 April 1967. Coghill, like the present author, longed to write a biography of Kitchin; like the present author, he decided there would be little public interest.
21. LPH to Christabel Aberconway 6 April 1967.
22. C. H. B. Kitchin to Jocelyn Brooke 4 June 1961.
23. Published by Peter Davis.
24. C. H. B. Kitchin to Francis King 22 April 1960.
25. LPH to Hamish Hamilton 24 May 1967.
26. Memo from Hamish Hamilton to Roger Machell 24 May 1967.
27. LPH to Joan Hall 18 October 1967.
28. LPH to Joan Hall 13 January 1968.
29. LPH to Hamish Hamilton 20 February 1968.
30. Ibid.
31. LPH to Joan Hall 21 May 1968.
32. LPH to Christabel Aberconway 23 January 1968.
33. LPH to Joan Hall 1 July 1968.
34. C. H. B. Kitchin to LPH 26 January 1945.
35. LPH to Christabel Aberconway 30 June 1968.
36. Julian Vinogradoff to LPH 8 March 1968.
37. LPH to *Listener* 30 May 1968.
38. A hugely popular revue that played in London during the Great War, making famous the song 'If you were the only girl in the world'.
39. Leonard Woolf to Violet Bonham Carter 3 July 1968.
40. LPH to Christabel Aberconway 13 May 1968.
41. LPH to Christabel Aberconway 14 July 1968.
42. LPH to Joan Hall 29 April 1968.
43. Dennis Potter, *The Times* 26 October 1968.
44. Angus Wilson, *Observer* 27 October 1968.
45. Cuthbert Worsley, *Evening Standard* 29 October 1968.
46. *Poor Clare* p. 136.
47. Ibid. p. 144.

48. Ibid. p. 154.
49. LPH to Christabel Aberconway 20 December 1968.
50. LPH to Christabel Aberconway 31 March 1969.
51. LPH to Hamish Hamilton 14 December 1968.
52. LPH to Joan Hall 18 December 1968.
53. LPH to Hamish Hamilton 1 February 1969.
54. LPH to Hamish Hamilton 24 July 1969.
55. LPH to Joan Hall 9 July 1969.
56. Ibid.
57. *Times Literary Supplement* 3 July 1969.
58. Joan Hall in conversation with author.
59. Memo from Roger Machell to Hamish Hamilton 14 August 1969.
60. LPH to Christabel Aberconway 28 August 1969.
61. Ibid.
62. Christabel Aberconway to LPH 2 September 1969.
63. Francis King in conversation with the author.
64. LPH to Christabel Aberconway 9 September 1969.
65. LPH to Christabel Aberconway 29 September 1969.
66. LPH to Christabel Aberconway 1 October 1969.
67. LPH to Joan Hall 12 September 1969.
68. LPH to Hamish Hamilton 25 November 1969.
69. LPH to Hamish Hamilton 12 December 1969.
70. LPH to Joan Hall 14 November 1969.
71. Francis King in conversation with author.

Chapter 13: WHAT ARE WE GOING TO DO?

1. LPH to Hamish Hamilton 31 January 1970.
2. Ibid.
3. Memo from Roger Machell to Hamish Hamilton 9 February 1970.
4. LPH to Joan Hall Good Friday 1970.
5. LPH to Joan Hall 28 May 1970.
6. Hamish Hamilton to LPH 9 June 1970.
7. LPH to Joan Hall 10 November 1970.
8. LPH to Joan Hall 6 November 1970.
9. LPH to Joan Hall 5 July 1970.
10. LPH to Christabel Aberconway 1 July 1970.
11. LPH to Hamish Hamilton 13 April 1970.
12. LPH to Christabel Aberconway 26 January 1970.
13. LPH to Christabel Aberconway 1 July 1970.
14. LPH to Christabel Aberconway 25 July 1970.
15. LPH to Norah Hartley 24 July 1970.
16. LPH to Norah Hartley 10 July 1970.
17. LPH to Joan Hall 6 September 1970.
18. Lady Harrod in conversation with author.

19. Joan Hall in conversation with the author.
20. Joseph Losey to LPH 11 October 1971. In Losey's film, Alan Bates played Ted Burgess, Julie Christie was Marian, Margaret Leighton Mrs Maudsley, and the young and older Leo were played respectively by Dominic Guard and Michael Redgrave.
21. *My Sister's Keeper* p. 17.
22. Ibid. p. 25.
23. Ibid. p. 239.
24. Ibid. p. 241.
25. Ibid. p. 242.
26. LPH to Joan Hall 29 October 1970.
27. LPH to Joan Hall 29 November 1970.
28. LPH to Joan Hall 23 November 1970.
29. LPH to Norah Hartley 5 August 1970.
30. LPH to Norah Hartley 13 August 1970.
31. Joan Hall in conversation with the author.
32. LPH to Hamish Hamilton 25 September 1970.
33. LPH to Joan Hall 23 November 1970.
34. LPH to Joan Hall 7 May 1971.
35. LPH to Christabel Aberconway 14 April 1971.
36. Joan Hall in conversation with author.
37. Ibid.
38. Ibid.
39. Ibid.
40. LPH to Christabel Aberconway 29 March 1971.
41. LPH to Hamish Hamilton 5 June 1971.
42. 'The L. P. Hartley Person': Janice Elliott, *Sunday Telegraph* 20 June 1971.
43. 'Paradise Paddock', *Mrs Carteret Receives and Other Stories* p. 87.
44. 'The Silver Clock', *Mrs Carteret Receives and Other Stories* p. 31.
45. 'Roman Charity', *Mrs Carteret Receives and Other Stories* p. 91.
46. Ibid. p. 104.
47. Ibid. p. 115.
48. Christopher Hudson in conversation with author.
49. *The Harness Room* p. 71.
50. Ibid. p. 127.
51. *Listener* 4 November 1971.
52. Rex Littleboy to LPH 4 December 1971.
53. *The Harness Room* p. 131.
54. Memo from Roger Machell to Hamish Hamilton, undated.
55. Memo from Roger Machell to Hamish Hamilton, undated.
56. LPH to Joan Hall 5 December 1971.
57. LPH to Joan Hall 24 January 1972.
58. Derek Parker, letter to author.
59. LPH to Joan Hall, undated. By 'black-out', Hartley is referring to power cuts.

60. LPH to Joan Hall 10 March 1972.
61. Typescript of unfinished (and untitled) novel at Fetton, unpublished.
62. Joan Hall in conversation with author.
63. LPH to Joan Hall 17 July 1972.
64. LPH to Joan Hall 23 August 1972.
65. LPH to Joan Hall 15 September 1972.
66. Ibid.
67. LPH to Hamish Hamilton 20 July 1972.
68. LPH to Anne Wignall 20 September 1972.
69. LPH to Joan Hall 17 November 1972.
70. Ibid.
71. Ibid.
72. LPH to David Cecil 10 March 1972.
73. LPH to David Cecil 12 October 1931.
74. LPH to David Cecil 10 March 1972.
75. Joan Hall in conversation with author.
76. LPH's nurse (unidentified) to Joan Hall 13 December 1972.

Epilogue

1. Joan Hall in conversation with author.
2. LPH to David Cecil 13 June 1971.
3. *Spectator* 23 December 1972.
4. 'The Ugly Picture', *Spectator* 23 December 1972.
5. Maddie Bell in conversation with author.
6. Ibid.
7. Norah Hartley in conversation with author.
8. Ibid.
9. Ibid.

INDEX

The strands of Hartley's life were so interwoven that only the broadest of headings have been used as sub-divisions for his entry in this Index. References to his relationships with the individuals in his life are noted under the individual concord.